FEAR
AND
LOATHING
IN
LA LIGA

FEAR AND LOATHING IN LA LIGA

Barcelona vs Real Madrid

SID LOWE

YELLOW JERSEY PRESS

LONDON

Published by Yellow Jersey Press 2013

2 4 6 8 10 9 7 5 3 1

First published in Great Britain in 2013 by
Yellow Jersey Press
Random House, 20 Vauxhall Bridge Road,
London SW1V 2SA

www.vintage-books.co.uk

Addresses for companies within The Random House Group Limited
can be found at: www.randomhouse.co.uk/offices.htm

The Random House Group Limited Reg. No. 954009

A CIP catalogue record for this book
is available from the British Library

ISBN 9780224091787 (Hardback)
ISBN 9780224091794 (Trade paperback)

The Random House Group Limited supports the Forest Stewardship
Council (FSC®), the leading international forest-certification organisation.
Our books carrying the FSC® label are printed on FSC®-certified paper. FSC®
is the only forest-certification scheme supported by the leading environmental
organisations, including Greenpeace. Our paper procurement
policy can be found at www.randomhouse.co.uk/environment

Typeset in ITC Galliard by Palimpsest Book Production Limited,
Falkirk, Stirlingshire

Printed and bound in Great Britain by
CPI Group (UK) Ltd, Croydon, CR0 4YY

'A book!'
For Claire and for Charlie

Españolito que vienes
al mundo te guarde Dios
Una de las dos Españas
Ha de helarte el corazón.

Little Spaniard coming into the world
May God protect you
One of the two Spains
Will freeze your heart.

– Antonio Machado

Madrid or Barcelona? Oviedo

– Michu

contents

AUTHOR'S NOTE

Hundreds of pieces of paper and thousands of words strewn about. My office floor has become a cutting-room floor. This book has evolved and changed since I began writing it. It has also dramatically shortened from first draft to last. It is primarily based on archive material, some of which casts significant new light on the rivalry, and a large series of interviews conducted over the last couple of years with players, coaches, directors and presidents from Real Madrid and FC Barcelona. In the process, it has become a kind of oral history and I'd like to thank those who have generously given their time to tell their stories, relive experiences and/or respond to questions and clarify doubts, including Alfredo Di Stéfano, Amancio Amaro, Andoni Zubizarreta, Andrés Iniesta, Ángel Cappa, Ángel Mur, Antoni Ramallets, Carlos Villarrubí, Charly Rexach, Dani García Lara, Darcy Silveira dos Santos 'Canário', Emilio Butragueño, Evaristo de Macedo, Fernando Argila, Fernando Hierro, Fernando Sanz, Henrik Larsson, Hristo Stoichkov, Ignacio Zoco, Iván Campo, Joan Gaspart, Joan Laporta, Johan Cruyff, Jordi Cruyff, Jorge Valdano, José Antonio Camacho, José Emilio Amavisca, José Luis San Martín, José Martínez 'Pirri', Josep Fusté, Josep María Minguella, Josep Seguer, Juan Manuel Asensi, Juan Santisteban, Louis Van Gaal, Luis Figo, Luis Milla, Luis Suárez, Marcos Alonso, Michael Laudrup, Míchel, Míchel Salgado, Miguel-Ángel Portugal, Pedja Mijatovic, Pichi Alonso,

Radi Antić, Rafa García Cortés, Ramón Calderón, Santi Solari, Silvio Elías, Steve Archibald, Steve McManaman, Txiki Beguiristain, Vicente del Bosque, Víctor Muñoz, Xavi Hernández, Zinedine Zidane and a number of others.

Thanks are also due to the protagonists who spoke to me for this book but preferred not to be named and the many others who have enriched the story. Other interviews conducted over the years with players like Oleguer Presas, Raúl, Paco Pavón, Paco Gento and David Beckham have also been drawn upon. As well as material from state archives, private papers and the clubs, I've naturally leant on the expertise and the work of reporters, writers, broadcasters and historians, and drawn on the accounts of protagonists. Part of me wanted to include footnotes throughout. That was impractical but a select bibliography has been included. My debt to those authors is evident.

This book does not claim to be the definitive history of the two clubs – the definitive history of just one of them would require countless volumes and, despite substantial editing, this is a long book already. Some of the chapters I most enjoyed writing have been cut because they weren't truly central to the narrative while others have been shortened significantly. Diego Maradona, for example, may be the best player of all time, but in this story he appears only fleetingly, while Laurie Cunningham's spell at Madrid and Quini's kidnap also failed to make the cut and the pre-civil war origins have been substantially reduced and restructured. Instead, this book is about the episodes that have shaped the rivalry and made Real Madrid and FC Barcelona what they are and about the human stories behind them. This is *their* story.

Sid Lowe, Cantabria, June 2013

A NOTE ON CURRENCY AND LANGUAGE

Money appears in its original currency, usually pesetas or euros. Although in a handful of cases some sterling or dollar alternatives have been included for clarity, that has not been done as a matter of course. Fluctuating exchange rates, changes to standards of living and inflation volatility make any accurate modern-day sterling equivalent difficult to calculate and occasionally meaningless. However, as a rough guide, between 1948 and 1999 the Spanish currency ranged between 110 and 200 pesetas to the pound with a mean exchange rate for the period of 164 pesetas to the pound. In 1999 the euro was introduced to Spain at an exchange rate of 1.42 euros to the pound.

Place names are given in Spanish except where there is a clearly accepted English equivalent, such as Castile or Catalonia. The names of buildings, streets, etc. in Catalonia are written in Catalan; elsewhere in Spain, they are given in Castilian Spanish.

People's names are given, wherever possible, in the local language. Some Catalans' names were Castilianised in the media and official correspondence during the Franco dictatorship but are left in Catalan.

Under the Franco regime, club names were forcibly changed. For instance, Athletic Bilbao became Atlético Bilbao and that is reflected in the text. In 1998 Español changed their name to Espanyol. Their name appears throughout as it would have done at the time.

1

THE MORNING AFTER

Life and death. And between the two, football.

On one side, the maternity hospital; on the other, the cemetery. In the middle, the Camp Nou, Europe's largest stadium. In the cemetery of Les Corts, there are rows upon rows of crypts, blocks of them stacked seven-high like lockers. A ladder leans against a wall of them as if waiting for a librarian to reach a book from the top shelf. There are 28,399 graves in all, spread across 34,417 square metres and among them lie some of Football Club Barcelona's greatest players. Paulino Alcántara, the club's all-time top scorer who retired to become a doctor in the rough streets of the *barri xino* off the Ramblas. César Rodríguez, the man who follows Alcántara and Lionel Messi in the goalscoring charts. Josep Samitier, the Magician, player and technical secretary at Barcelona – and at Real Madrid. And Javier Urruticoechea, the goalkeeper whose save clinched the league title for Terry Venables's side after an eleven-year drought, Barcelona's first under a democracy, prompting that famous line, screamed out on the radio: 'Urruti, I love you!'

From the grave of László Kubala, the player they say built the Camp Nou and whose statue stands at its entrance, all rippling muscles and bulging thighs, you can see the north end of the stadium poking up above the cemetery wall. Julio César Benítez is here too. He died of food poisoning in 1968, just three days before Barcelona faced Madrid. Today is the morning after Barcelona faced Madrid, forty-four years later. It is quiet now, empty, and the sun is shining.

'You should have seen it yesterday,' says the woman who works here, helping to guide people through the labyrinth, past the roses on the Kubala family plot and the pennants, pictures and ribbons in Catalan red and yellow and Barcelona blue and claret dotted around the cemetery.

Why, what happened yesterday?

'What happens every time they play Real Madrid,' she replies, nodding in the direction of the stadium. 'It was packed with people visiting family and friends, visiting players' graves too. Asking for help in the game, asking for a victory.'

2

THE NIGHT BEFORE

Sunday 7 October 2012. Football Club Barcelona versus Real Madrid, week seven in the Spanish league. It is the first meeting of the season between the two greatest rivals in the sport, in any sport, and it is huge – for what it symbolises off the pitch as well as what it means on it. On the morning of the game, the headline in the Catalan newspaper *La Vanguardia* asks: 'Only football?' They know the answer: Barcelona versus Real Madrid is never just football and today less than ever. This clash is billed as the most political match of them all, certainly since the death of General Francisco Franco in 1975.

The game comes against a backdrop of economic crisis, failed fiscal negotiations between Barcelona and Madrid, the calling of Catalan elections and talk of a referendum on independence. It is three weeks since Catalonia's 'national' day, the 11 September *diada*, brought the city to a standstill, with some estimates putting numbers on the streets at one and a half million. Among them was the Barcelona president Sandro Rosell. He insists that he was there in a personal capacity, but today the club's traditional pre-match mosaic will be a *senyera*, the Catalan flag, and it seems to hold greater meaning than normal. Almost 100,000 people will hold up yellow and red cards, covering the entire stadium. Some call for fans to carry the Catalan independence flag, adorned with a star, and those who say they will include Joan Laporta, the former Barcelona president.

It has been building in the media for weeks, months, and the divide is a familiar one. The right-wing newspaper *La Razón*, a vociferous campaigner in defence of Spanish unity, dedicates twenty-seven pages to politics to decry the fact that the match has been politicised. *El Mundo*, also opposed to secession, solves a two millennia-old mystery to reveal that Jesus Christ was in fact killed by Catalans.

Before the game, Barcelona's hymn is sung a cappella. Two gigantic red and yellow striped Catalan flags are unfurled at either end, independence flags are dotted around the stadium and there is a banner written in English that declares Catalonia Europe's next state. But the Catalan 'national' anthem, *Els Segadors*, which marks the beginning of the Reapers' War in 1640 when Catalonia defeated Philip IV and declared independence under French protection for twelve years, isn't sung as expected. And the protest is not unanimous, nor as hostile, as many anticipated.

Everyone is waiting for the moment that Toni Strubell describes as a prophecy. Strubell is a member of the Catalan parliament whose father, an exile in England during the Franco dictatorship, always told him that the day the Camp Nou chanted for independence would be the day independence arrived. Barcelona fans had started the chant during a league game against Granada, but today is bigger; today they play Real Madrid. And when the stadium clock ticks up to seventeen minutes and fourteen seconds, the chant begins: 'Independence! Independence!'

11 September 1714 marked the end of the siege of Barcelona, when the city fell to Philip V. The Catalans had chosen the wrong side in a war of royal succession, but the battle has since become projected as a central moment for the 'nation', the point at which 'independence' was lost. The *diada* 'celebrates' defeat – a fact that is not lost on many both inside and outside Catalonia, seen as somehow symbolic of the Catalan mindset – and reinforces the idea of Madrid as the natural

enemy. Philip V abolished Catalonia's political institutions and banned Catalan in schools, virtually ending Catalan aspirations until the *Renaixença*, or cultural renaissance, of the mid-1800s. A Catalan parliament, the mancomunitat, was set up in 1914 but abolished by the dictatorship of General Miguel Primo de Rivera in 1925. With Primo de Rivera's fall and the arrival of the Second Republic, Spain's first real democracy, Catalonia was granted autonomous government but the outbreak of the Spanish Civil War and dictatorship under General Francisco Franco brought those ambitions to an end. Following his death, Catalonia now has significant autonomous powers but polls suggest that over 50 per cent of Catalans want independence.

Today, some at the Camp Nou certainly do and in many minds, that political battle is played out on the football pitch. Only this morning, Barcelona defender Gerard Piqué has been forced to distance himself from a statement in which he said that Barcelona versus Madrid is Catalonia versus Spain. But Laporta has no doubts: 'At one level, that's true,' he says. 'It's a sporting confrontation with political connotations. Madrid has always represented Spain and we have always represented Catalonia.'

Yet the chant is not the only thing that sticks in the mind from the first *clásico* of the 2012–13 season. This game is Barça versus Madrid in a nutshell: symbolism, identity, politics, rivalry . . . and the best football on the planet. The homage to Catalonia turns into a homage to Real Madrid and Football Club Barcelona. The match finishes level: ten shots each, one post each and two goals each. As the final whistle goes, there is satisfaction. Just as importantly, the promise of more hangs in the air. With a real rivalry it always does; it is self-perpetuating. As one Barcelona player puts it: 'It is the *game of the century* every time, even though there are eight of them a year.' 'We're here and they're here,' says the Madrid coach Jose Mourinho afterwards, stretching his arms and holding his hands at roughly the same height.

It is some height.

Above all, the homage to Catalonia becomes a homage to Lionel

Messi and Cristiano Ronaldo. Ronaldo scores, then Messi scores; Messi scores, then Ronaldo scores. If Madrid versus Barcelona is the greatest sporting rivalry on earth, it has come to be personified in two of the finest footballers there has been, men who dominate the game and define their clubs – in personality and play, style and substance. You cannot mention one without the other. Type 'Ronaldo has scored a hat-trick' into twitter and watch the responses. A rubbish hat-trick, says the *culé* or Barcelona fan; better than Messi, says the *Madridista*. Rival fans have discovered the best possible way of winding Ronaldo up – to chant 'Messi' at him.

With Messi and Ronaldo, records seem to fall weekly. Their four goals mean that they move on to exactly one hundred club goals between them in 2012. 'Talking about who is the best player in the world should be banned because these two are just so good,' says Mourinho. When Ronaldo strikes after twenty-two minutes, it marks the sixth successive *clásico* in which he has scored, the first player in history to do so. Messi moves to within one goal of Alfredo Di Stéfano's all-time record for *clásico* goals, at the age of just twenty-five. 'From another planet,' says the cover of the country's best-selling newspaper.

Three months after the *clásico*, Messi won the Ballon d'Or. Ronaldo was second. Natural, said the Barcelona fans; a scandal, said the Madrid ones. What the ceremony in Zurich really showed was just how brilliant they both are; how dominant Madrid and Barcelona had become in terms of the sport and the spotlight. Messi has won it four times in a row, taking him past anyone else in history; Ronaldo was runner-up for the fourth time and has won it once. Between them, Madrid and Barcelona boast the last eight winners of the Ballon d'Or and when the 2012 FIFPro team of the year was announced, ten of the eleven players were from Madrid or Barcelona. There was something convenient about the fact that they had five each, parity restored. No two teams had dominated like this before, still less two rivals.

These are the men, the teams, who eclipse all else, and when the *clásico* clock ticks up to 17.14 in the second half, time for another burst of 'Independence!', some Barcelona fans almost miss it. They're busy celebrating Messi's goal.

There have been 225 *clásicos* in all, with Real Madrid winning ninety and Barcelona eighty-seven. The numbers rack up quickly: October 2012 was the thirteenth *clásico* in less than two years, such is the dominance of these two sides, and by the end of the season there would be three more of them. It all began at the Madrid Hippodrome on 13 May 1902, just a few hundred yards south of the Santiago Bernabéu. *Foot-ball* was far from the mass sport it is now. Barcelona began with a sixty-three-word classified advert in *Los Deportes* inviting those who wanted to arrange games to turn up at the newspaper's offices. Twelve people did so. Madrid began with informal games in the Retiro park that were fortunate to attract six- or seven-a-side. 'We wasted a lot of time smoking and drinking,' one participant recalled. Some saw the sport as immoral, played by 'shameless youths daring to run through the streets in their underwear and probably mentally diseased'.

Around two thousand people attended that first game between Madrid and Barcelona, sitting on chairs rented from a trader in the Rastro market; 98,000 spectators attended the match at the Camp Nou in the autumn of 2012. Two million watched on subscription television in Spain, a number dwarfed by the last free-to-air *clásico* in December 2011, which had been watched by twelve million. TV companies claimed a global audience of four hundred million and, although that was an exaggeration, it was shown live in over thirty countries. Deloitte's latest figures showed that in 2012 Madrid and Barcelona generated more money than any other clubs on the planet for the fourth consecutive year.

Former Barcelona coach Bobby Robson described the *clásico* as the biggest game in the world and it is hard to argue. FIFA named Madrid the best team of the twentieth century; the International Federation of Football History and Statistics ranks Barcelona the best of the twenty-first. Although 2013 ended with semi-final exits for both teams for the second successive year, since 1998 only two clubs have won the Champions League three times: Madrid and Barcelona. Madrid have won nine European Cups, more than any other club; Barcelona have won four, three in seven years, and more international trophies than anyone else.

They are two of only three Spanish teams to have spent their entire history in the top flight – the other is Athletic Club de Bilbao – and between them they have won fifty-four league titles, thirty-two for Madrid, twenty-two for Barcelona. The nearest challenger is Atlético Madrid, on nine. And just look at those who have played for them: Kubala, Di Stéfano, Maradona, Cruyff, Stoichkov, Czibor, Puskás, Sánchez, Butragueño, Netzer, Schuster, Iniesta, Romário, Ronaldo, Raúl, Guardiola, Laudrup, Luis Suárez, Kopa, Figo, Rivaldo, Zidane, Ronaldinho, Casillas, Xavi, Messi, Cristiano Ronaldo. Every single winner of the FIFA World Player Award for seventeen years has played for Madrid or Barcelona at some stage of their career.

They are two footballing behemoths, eponymous representatives of the two biggest cities in Spain – different cities with different identities, seemingly locked in permanent confrontation, cities whose political and cultural contexts are different. Barcelona stands on the Mediterranean, looking out towards France and Italy, the city where the maxim has it that fashions and political -isms hit Spain first. Madrid sits on the central plateau of Castile, the *meseta*, over six hundred metres above sea level. Freezing in winter and boiling in summer, Madrid is located on a river along which no boats pass. Philip II made it the capital in 1561 simply because it stood in the geographical centre of Spain: a plaque in the Puerta del Sol marks kilometre zero, the theoretical starting point of every road in the country, a mark of centralism that most *Madrileños* barely notice.

Spain is a two-team country. 'Everyone supports Madrid or Barcelona,' says Spain manager Vicente del Bosque. According to statistics from the Centro de Investigaciones Sociológicas, Madrid have 13.2 million fans while Barcelona have 10.4 million. An Opinea study in May 2013 showed that 28 per cent of those match-going supporters questioned considered themselves Madrid fans, 26 per cent Barcelona fans, but the national tallies are even higher, with over 60 per cent of Spaniards supporting one of the big two. On top of that, one of the most striking features of Spanish football is that virtually every fan, from Almería to Zaragoza, has an inbuilt, permanent preference and really cares who wins the *clásico*; these two matter even when they don't matter. 'Half of Spain is Madrid, half is Barcelona, even if they support Oviedo or Ponferradina,' says Luis Milla, who spent six years at Barcelona and seven at Madrid. When Opinea asked 'Madrid or Barcelona?' only 11 per cent said 'neither'.

More than just football clubs, these are powerful and democratic institutions. Two of only four Spanish clubs owned by their members, they carry a colossal social weight that is often brought to bear on the protagonists. Four national newspapers a day are essentially dedicated to them, two in Madrid, two in Barcelona, and the pressure can be as brutal as the power is seductive. Radi Antić coached both clubs, one of only two men to do so. 'Being a director of Barcelona or Madrid is more important than being a minister in any country,' he says. When the former Madrid president Ramón Mendoza expressed a similar sentiment, he got a letter from the US ambassador telling him he was absolutely right. Ramón Calderón was forced out of the Madrid presidency in January 2009. 'I should have stayed,' Calderón admits, 'but I would have paid for it with my life. The strain is so great that I would have had a heart attack in the directors' box one day. If I hadn't left then, I'd have left in a box.'

Madrid and Barcelona can't be taken in isolation from society, nor from Spain's history. You won't catch many in Catalonia insisting, as others in Spain do, that sport and politics should not mix. Like it or not, sport and politics *do* mix, especially here. The symbolism is inescapable and no match is so infused with politics as the *clásico*, even if that can feel one-sided at times.

Marcos Alonso's father played in Real Madrid's European Cup-winning team in the 1950s and his son played for them too. As a child he played in the garden with Alfredo Di Stéfano and Ferenç Puskás, two of the club's greatest ever players, but as a professional he played for Barcelona. 'They are the two biggest teams in the world,' Alonso says. 'But Barcelona have a social significance I didn't see at Madrid; in Barcelona, you have a sense of *complete* identification with the club. It means a massive amount for Catalan society.' Madrid's meaning is, from their own point of view, simpler. 'Madrid represented an identification with success,' says Ramón Calderón. Jorge Valdano, a former player, coach and director at Madrid, defines the *clásico* as 'a club versus more than a club'.

'Every time Madrid and Barcelona meet, it becomes a rebellion against the Establishment,' says the former Barcelona striker Hristo Stoichkov. When Barcelona face Madrid it is, according to many *culés*, the nation against the state, freedom fighters against General Franco's fascists, the Spanish Civil War's vanquished against its victors – a confrontation represented by the assassination of Barcelona's president at the start of the war. Bobby Robson once claimed: 'Catalonia is a country and Barcelona is its army.' The message is delivered early: a children's history of Barcelona, complete with a prologue from president Rosell, has an explicitly political narrative. Cartoon illustrations depict armed Spanish civil guards closing the club's stadium, scenes from the civil war, and Franco's police running on to the Camp Nou pitch, truncheons in hand.

Asked the central question at the heart of the *clásico* – can the rivalry be understood in purely footballing terms, without a social or political element? – Joan Gaspart responds simply: 'Impossible.' The former Barcelona president continues: 'History has transformed us into something more than just a football club: Barcelona is the defence of a country, a language, a culture. Barcelona felt persecuted.' Joan Laporta followed Gaspart into the presidency. Another direct question, another eloquently short answer. Is Barcelona the unofficial Catalan national team? He smiles: 'Yes, exactly.' The slogan *més que un club* is famous now and it is everywhere: *more than a club*. 'It is not just a slogan, it is a declaration of principles,' says Laporta. Barcelona's identity is explicitly about something other than the football alone and in their version of history, so is Madrid's – Barcelona fans project on to their rivals an identity that Madrid fans largely dismiss.

And this is where the familiar accusation comes in: Real Madrid as Franco's team.

The former Barcelona coach Louis Van Gaal tells the story the way it was told to him: 'The people of Catalonia are a proud people and they want to be better than Madrid. Franco was the boss and he was in Madrid; central government was always in favour of Madrid, European champions because of Franco. One of the big aspects of society there is the desire to show that Catalonia can compete with Madrid.' This allegation lies at the heart of narratives of the *clásico* – on one side of the divide at least. It has become widely held: even Alex Ferguson famously referred to Madrid as Franco's club. '*Mès que un club* starts because of that: the phrase would have no *raison d'être* but for the dictatorship,' says Pichi Alonso, a Barcelona player who later became the Catalan 'national' team coach. 'People identified being a Barcelona fan with fighting the regime.' Francoism was transposed on to Madrid, the Catalan sociologist Luis Flaquer noting: 'You couldn't shout "Franco you murderer" on the streets so people shouted at Real Madrid's players instead. It's a psychological phenomenon.'

'It was almost impossible to beat Madrid because they were Franco's team,' said Salvador Sadurní, a Barcelona player between 1961 and 1976, while the former Catalan minister of culture Jordi Vilajoana claimed: 'The regime used sport to assert its power: that's why Real Madrid won.' Eighty-five per cent of Barcelona fans, according to a poll conducted during the club's centenary, believe that the Franco regime systematically handicapped them. Never more so, they say, than when Barcelona lost out on the signing of Alfredo Di Stéfano and he joined Madrid instead, the turning point in the history of the game.

Even now, almost forty years after Franco's death, with Catalonia enjoying significant autonomy, there's deep mistrust. Some of it is conscious, some subliminal, but it is there. A political rift runs through the footballing feud, and the hatred can be genuinely shocking. Two politicians who helped usher in democracy after Franco's death, Felipe González and Miquel Roca, wrote a book together about the relationship between Catalonia and the rest of Spain. Its title translates as *Can We Still Understand Each Other?* It is tempting to answer: could you ever?

'All that comes together in the football' says Míchel, who played for Madrid for over a decade having come through the club's youth system. It comes together in a kind of Spain versus Catalonia and all that supposedly entails, reduced to a simple narrative and a basic dichotomy: *Barça democrats, Madrid fascists; Barça civil war losers, Madrid civil war victors and repressors; Barça left, Madrid right; Barça good, Madrid bad.*

That at least is the theory. The reality, of course, is rather different and there are countless questions. Like: where do those identities become forged and how have they survived? Is an identity founded on opposition still valid in a democratic regime when Catalonia is one of the wealthiest, most vibrant parts of Spain? Where do the football teams fit into all this? And, anyway, *who*, or *what*, are the clubs?

Things are not always as they seem. Symbolism is central, the construction of a narrative plays a key role and myths matter, but there are caveats everywhere, important flaws in the popularly held identities of the two clubs. Like the *other* presidential victim of the civil war, *Barcelona's* success during the darkest days of the regime, or the fact that Madrid and Barcelona's great figures are Argentinian and Dutch respectively. It is Barcelona, not Madrid, who have provided more players for the *Spanish* national team than anyone else, including seven of the men who started the World Cup final in 2010. It runs right to the very foundation of the two clubs, the day it all began. Barcelona, the Catalan national flagship, was founded by a foreigner who was only supposed to be passing through, while Real Madrid, the greatest embassy Spain ever had, was founded by two brothers who were Catalan.

With Barça and Madrid, it is so often about each other; they are defined by what they are and by what they are *not*. Being a Barcelona fan *necessarily* means being an *anti-Madridista* and vice versa – even if those identities, like any identity, are built at least partly on myths. In a recent poll carried out by *AS* newspaper, 97 per cent of Madrid fans considered Barcelona the team they hated the most; the only surprise was that there were 3 per cent who did not. There is a mutual dependency that is a mutual fear and loathing. It wasn't only a pig's head thrown at Luis Figo when he crossed the divide from Barcelona to Madrid in 2000 – there were bike chains, golf balls, bottles, mobile phones, rocks and screws too.

'It has become a dialogue of the deaf and we have reached a ridiculous point where you're obliged to talk badly of the opposition,' Valdano says. 'That latent violence is always there and if we are not careful it will overflow with great ease. Sometimes the spark is called Gaspart, Figo or Mourinho, but any flammable element sets it off again.'

The clubs are embarked on a constant search for supremacy and have a burning need to outdo each other – and the rest of the world. Witness their centenaries: Barça visited the Pope, making him a *soci* or member; Madrid visited the King, the UN *and* the Pope. The very fact that they *can* is significant. Barça celebrated by playing Brazil; three years later Madrid celebrated by playing the whole wide world. They requested that all football everywhere on the planet be halted that day so that the Bernabéu was the focus of everyone's attention. Joan Gaspart, Barcelona president at the time, having spent two decades as vice-president, feigned an apology: 'Oh,' he said mischievously, 'I think San Andreu may have a game that day.' San Andreu is a Catalan side that play in the regional Third Division, of whom Gaspart just happened to be president.

A poll in 1999 showed over half of Barcelona fans preferred Madrid losing to Barça winning. It is all about them, even when it is not about them. Barcelona won the 1997 Copa del Rey against Real Betis, a victory that remains special to them as much because of *where* it was as because of *what* it was: the Santiago Bernabéu was packed with Barcelona fans and the players did a lap of honour while supporters sang: 'Madrid is burning down!' Sergi Barjuan, a Catalan brought through the club's youth system, was beaming: 'To win at the Bernabéu and see the ground full of Catalan flags is as good as it gets.' 'That was a double victory,' recalls Gaspart, grinning. 'And after the game, I did something I wouldn't have done if the final had been at any other ground: I made them play the Barcelona hymn over the loudspeakers . . .

'. . . five times.'

Even as Barcelona celebrated the greatest season in their history, winning the treble in 2009, there were digs at Madrid; the Madrid press feigned offence when Gerard Piqué got the Camp Nou rocking by chanting 'whoever doesn't bounce is a *Madridista*'. '¡*Madrid, cabrón, saluda al campeón!*' is a staple chant when Barcelona win. *Madrid, you bastards, salute the champions!* Madrid like to insist they couldn't care less about Barcelona, that they're above that, but it is a lie. 'They are very much focused on each other,' says Milla. 'If Madrid are third that's fine, so long as Barcelona are fourth. They have built a story based, in part, on each other and that mirrors Spanish society.' Barcelona's hymn is sung at Madrid's stadium, the final line adapted to '¡*Barça, Barça, mierda!*' *Mierda* means shit.

For years, Madrid fans laughed that Barcelona were obsessed with them: they said they suffered *madriditis*, a chronic persecution complex, an inability to live their own lives, always focused instead on their rivals. José Martínez 'Pirri' played for Real Madrid for sixteen years. His remark sums it up: 'They hung on our every move; we didn't care about them. Why would we?' That may have been partly true then; it is not now. There has been an outbreak of *barcelonitis*. Pichi

Alonso played for Barcelona during a period when he says that the club was 'quite clearly' obsessed with Madrid, to the point of 'trying to copy them'. 'Now the roles have been inverted,' he claims.

Success lies at its heart, shifting the parameters of a rivalry that is cyclical. Identities are not always permanent, even when they appear utterly entrenched – and trenches often seem the natural habit of Madrid and Barcelona fans. Apparently irreconcilable footballing models have been inverted, while some of their experiences have been shared, right down to both clubs suffering kidnappings – Alfredo Di Stéfano was abducted in Venezuela in 1963, Enrique 'Quini' Castro was dragged off in a van in 1981. These days, Barcelona are proud of their academy but it was Madrid who reached a Copa del Rey final against their own youth team that same season and who soon after swept all before them with a side defined by a generation of home-grown players. Nineteen eighty-one was also the year in which Madrid lost a traumatic European Cup final; five years later, Barcelona did the same.

Some of their attitudes and characteristics are shared too. 'Both clubs were born in the same place, with the same ideas. They are different in terms of the outward symbols but, in their souls, I don't know if they are so different really,' says Míchel. To fans of other teams in Spain, they feel much the same: two superpowers obliterating all opposition. They are, the stats show, not only the best-loved clubs in Spain but also the most hated: Madrid are singled out as the team most despised by 51 per cent of match-going fans across the country, Barcelona by 41 per cent. And that is despite the fact that Madrid make much of their *señorío* and Barcelona do the same with their *valors* – gentlemanliness and values, respectively. Both seek a moral dimension that differentiates them and, in both cases, such talk can appear flawed. Perhaps inevitably, those most obsessed with talking about Madrid's *señorío*, or the lack of it, are Barcelona fans while those quickest to highlight Barcelona's *valors*, or the lack of them, are Madrid fans.

Ultimately, their complaints are similar too. Barcelona fans remember the name of Emilio Guruceta, the referee who gave the most famous penalty ever against them, and that of José María Ortiz de Mendíbil – the official who added eight minutes of stoppage time to a *derbi* in 1966, allowing Madrid to win 1-0 and afterwards shrugged, 'my watch stopped'. That has not gone unnoticed by Madrid fans. A banner in the Bernabéu early this century pointed the finger at Barcelona, declaring refereeing conspiracies to be the refuge of losers and cry-babies. Yet now it is they who claim they are robbed and it is the Madrid media that invented the 'Villarato' – the 'theory' that the president of the Federation, Ángel María Villar, is out to get them and the country's referees are his executioners.

If the rivalry is partly explained by their success, their success is partly explained by the rivalry. *Anything you can do I can do better.* The relationship is symbiotic: they are necessary enemies, feeding off each other, trying to outdo each other. 'Like cathedrals in the Middle Ages,' as Valdano puts it. 'If Barcelona didn't exist, we'd have to invent them,' Madrid president Florentino Pérez once claimed. 'I think he's right,' Laporta smiles. Ignacio Zoco captained Madrid and played for the club for twelve years: 'Real Madrid wouldn't be so great if Barcelona didn't exist and vice versa. It is competition that makes you,' he insists. Victory over a weakened rival leaves doubts. 'The rivalry lost a bit of edge, a touch of magic, with Barcelona struggling so badly,' admitted Raúl of the Catalans' crisis in 2002.

'Madrid and Barcelona are like two sides of a scale,' says the Catalan midfielder Xavi Hernández. It is impossible for both to be up at the same time, even when they're both successful. Few recall that while Madrid won the first five European Cups, Barcelona won two league titles and the Copa del Generalísimo, a better domestic record than their rivals over the same period. Madrid's triumph was Barça's failure and, for all their disputes at home, European competition has marked them and continues to do so, acting as the ultimate arbiter.

When Florentino Pérez returned to the Real Madrid presidency in 2009, he had to respond to Madrid's institutional crisis but also to

Barcelona's unique league, cup and European Cup treble. Miguel Pardeza, the new sporting director, insisted: 'We must put Madrid back where they belong; we have to try to remove Barcelona from their dominant position.' Ronaldo, Kaká and Karim Benzema all arrived for a fraction short of €200 million. There was a historic precedence: when Madrid completed the signing of Di Stéfano in 1953, Barcelona had just won successive doubles. The signing decisively shifted the balance of power. Michael Laudrup and Luis Figo crossed the divide and tipped the scales too. And the arrival of Jose Mourinho in 2010 was even more clearly driven by the desire – the *need* – to overhaul Barcelona. The parallels with *Barcelona's* signing of Helenio Herrera as manager in 1958 are startling.

Laporta claimed in 2009 that Madrid's spending did not worry him, insisting: 'I'm trebly tranquil.' But still he complained that Madrid's signings policy was 'imperialist' and 'arrogant'. The Catalan media splashed the words 'scandal', 'disgrace' and 'shameful' across their front covers and even the Catalan Church expressed its distaste. How dare they throw away such colossal quantities of money in times of crisis? The key word was 'they'. Madrid. Few in Catalonia complained when Barcelona made Diego Maradona the most expensive player in history, signing him for £3 million in 1982. Or when they made Johan Cruyff the first million-dollar player nine years earlier. Or when they signed Romário, Ronaldo and Ronaldinho. When that had happened, it had been the national press – and for 'national' read 'Madrid' – that complained.

Confrontation can be traced right back to 1916, when Madrid and Barcelona faced each other in the cup and a first replay finished 6-6. The second replay ended with Barcelona walking off when Madrid were winning 4-2, the Catalans' star player Paulino Alcántara later writing: 'That defeat produced in me tremendous sadness . . . it was the first time that I cried like a child, such was the terrible and unexpected humiliation, that atrocious conviction that the tournament legitimately belonged to us.' Real Madrid's official history instead maintained that everything was entirely fair. Well, almost everything. 'The [Catalan press] campaign was tremendous, implacable, and clumsy,' it recalled, 'they even claimed that Barcelona could beat Madrid any time they wanted – in the middle of the Puerta del Sol . . .' Some things never change.

Some things do, though. The rivalry has not been a constant and nor has its intensity – even calling it the *clásico* is a relatively new phenomenon, borrowed from the name given to River versus Boca clashes in Argentina. For years it was the *derbi*. Some of the ingredients have always been in place; some have not. It is mostly a rivalry forged after the civil war and just how good the two teams are is a key factor, of course. Madrid and Barcelona have not always been the best two teams in Spain: their current domination is unprecedented. Only once before could they have laid claim to being the finest two teams in the world at the same time: that was in the mid- and late-1950s and even then they were not so powerful as now. When Madrid were finally knocked out of the European Cup for the very first time, having won the opening five editions of the tournament, it was inevitably Barcelona that defeated them. The previous month, England had met Spain at Wembley and the official match-day programme told its British reader-ship: 'Since [1955] the entire domestic scene has changed in the Peninsula. Up to that time, League or Cup honours could go to six or seven clubs – now two colossi dominate all, Royal Madrid and Barcelona.' Yet speak to Madrid players of a certain generation and some will tell you that Atlético Madrid are the club's real adversaries, even if the *Real Madrid Book of Football*, published in 1961, describes Barcelona as 'the eternal rival'.

During the 1960s and early 1970s, hit by financial crisis, forced to sell their best players, Barcelona slipped well behind – but that too contributes to the rivalry. Cup success salvaged their seasons and so did victory in the *derbi*. Barcelona came out of a fourteen-year period without winning the league upon the arrival of Johan Cruyff. At the start of the 1980s, meanwhile, Barcelona and Madrid went four years without winning the league, the longest run since the 1950s, when the Basque sides Real Sociedad and Athletic Bilbao won it twice each. For a brief period, crystallising in the 1984 cup final, Barcelona's most intense and aggressive rivalry was with Athletic. Diego Maradona even went so far as to publicly declare that he wanted Madrid to win when playing the Basques.

'There are those who use football to create an enmity that doesn't really exist in sport,' says Míchel. 'I see an opponent, not an enemy. Rivalry is also admiration.' That may be a bit optimistic but it is true that this is also not a story built purely on conflict. During the 1950s, players appeared in exhibition games for their opponents. Barcelona's star László Kubala never forgot the fact that it was Real Madrid president Santiago Bernabéu who intervened with Hungary's Communist government to allow him to see his estranged mother. Juan Manuel Asensi and José Martínez 'Pirri' recall how players from both sides used to go out for drinks together after matches in the late 1970s. On the night that Barcelona played the Cup Winners' Cup final in Basel in May 1979 – one of the most emotive, emblematic games in the club's history, their first final after Franco's death, and a match attended by thousands of fans carrying Catalan flags – a visitor came to the dressing room to wish them luck. That visitor was Madrid's president, Luis de Carlos. When Roberto Carlos was pelted by missiles during a *derbi* in 1997 it was Pep Guardiola who escorted him to take corners, acting as a human shield. And in 2010 Barcelona and Real Madrid's players won the World Cup together, even if the media in each city tried to make it more *their* success than *theirs*.

Some of the moments that helped to create the current rivalry can be located exactly, staging posts on route to their current domination and the relationship as it stands. Others are less tangible, less obvious, even with hindsight. And some of those that are assumed to exist do not, or at least not as they are often presented. The rivalry appeared to reach a zenith – at least until they meet in a European Cup final

– when Barcelona and Madrid faced each other four times in eighteen days in 2011, in the league, the Copa del Rey final and the Champions League semi-final, a kind of World Series of *clásicos* that reinforced the dominance of the big two, the utter eclipse of the rest of Spain. At times, it was nasty and suffocating; there appeared to be no escape.

There also appears to be no way now of the rivalry returning to a time when it was anything other than the driving force behind Spanish football – to the cost of the rest of the country, rich in history and sentiment. There is little chance of the other clubs closing the gap: the big two have won the last nine league titles, twenty-five of the last twenty-nine, twelve for Madrid, thirteen for Barcelona. 'The duopoly is a historic fact, now,' says Fernando Hierro, the former Real Madrid captain and, more recently, sporting director of the Spanish Football Federation. 'They are two clubs used to success so when they do not win it has a real impact.'

Madrid and Barcelona are powerful and their strength self-perpetuating. Their television deals dwarf others clubs': they take over €140 million a year in TV rights, plus the money they make from the Champions League; the next highest, Valencia, take €42 million, less than the relegated teams in the English Premier League. Multiply that over five years and Valencia make over €415 million less than Barcelona or Madrid. Real Madrid's operating budget in 2012–13 was €517 million, Barcelona's €470 million; Atlético and Valencia were the only other clubs over €100 million and next year they will dip below three figures. Valencia finished third for three consecutive years from 2009–10: each time they were closer in points to relegation than they were to winning the league. In 2012–13, third-placed Atlético finished twenty-four points behind Barcelona. It is not that the rest of the league is necessarily bad, although the trend is to their debilitation, but that Madrid and Barcelona are just too good.

That economic muscle reflects a social reality seen in those supporter statistics. Television companies pay Madrid and Barcelona what they pay them because they have to. The editor of one newspaper admits that every Madrid win is 10,000 more in sales and the director of a TV channel insists it would be a 'disaster' if anyone else won the league. Officially, statistics for pay-per-view hits remained unknown but industry insiders reveal figures from four years ago in which Madrid and Barcelona generated twice as much as anyone else. According to a source at the Spanish Football Federation, a First Division game not involving either of the big two was bought by forty-seven viewers. Yes, *forty-seven*. When a new football channel launched in PPV's place in 2010, it was proud to offer the league but prouder to offer Madrid and/or Barcelona every week. In 2011–12, fifteen league games involving Madrid or Barcelona were shown free-to-air in Spain; they were the fifteen most watched of the year.

Barcelona–Madrid in October 2012 boasted an audience six times the size of Málaga–Atlético on the same day. Many teams fill their stadiums only twice a season, when the big two come to town. Internationally, only two Spanish clubs count – another shift in the rivalry. Fans want to see the best players in the world and they are at the big two: when new talents emerge at other Spanish clubs their career paths now inexorably lead to Madrid, Barcelona or abroad. 'The rivalry has grown because of television, radio, social media and so on. Now people talk about it abroad even more than in Spain: you see Madrid and Barcelona shirts in England,' says Marcos Alonso. 'Go to the moon . . . Madrid, Barcelona,' laughs Hristo Stoichkov.

Within Spain, the media are cause and consequence, digging the trenches deeper. The sports newspapers claim varying degrees of objectivity when none should claim any at all. *El Mundo Deportivo* and *Sport* are openly pro-Barcelona; *Marca* and *AS* are pro-Madrid. Sometimes as much propaganda outlets as papers, they tend to see themselves as an arm of their clubs, increasing the pressure at institutions where winning is no longer an objective but an obligation. The director of a Catalan radio station publicly applauded the decision to cheer Madrid's European opponents as an 'ingenious' way of getting closer to supporters. Never mind getting closer to the truth. Together, the two clubs, their fans and the media have created, or tapped into, a kind of footballing fundamentalism. Those who do not side entirely with them, occupying the same trenches, are dismissed as *obviously* anti-Madrid or anti-Barcelona. Bias, like beauty, lies in the eye of the beholder.

Andoni Zubizarreta is the Barcelona sporting director and former goalkeeper. He was also a columnist with the broadsheet *El País*. Few have expressed this kind of fundamentalism better than him: 'We demand accuracy, precision and objectivity,' he wrote, 'but with one condition: that it is in our favour.' The phrase could be directed at much of the milieu – media, fans and presidents – but was in fact about the inevitable protagonist of the rivalry, the support role elevated to the status of lead actor: the referee. Men whose mistakes are rarely judged simply as mistakes but are manipulated to fit a partisan agenda.

There may be years when other clubs challenge, but unless there are significant changes they will probably be isolated outbreaks. It is hard to see another team winning the league again, still less a return to the period between 1980 and 1984 when neither team won the title in four years, or a decade like the 1970s during which Barcelona claimed a solitary championship. In 2008, Real Madrid broke a La Liga points record; the following year, Barcelona broke it back and then bettered that total the year after, racking up ninety-nine points. Madrid reached one hundred points in 2011–12; Barcelona matched that total the following season. No one had reached ninety points before: between 2009 and 2012, Barcelona and Madrid *both* achieved that feat three seasons running. The ten highest points totals of all time have come in the last six years. The figures, to use Pep Guardiola's words, are 'fucking barbaric'.

Barcelona reached the halfway point of the 2012–13 season with eighteen victories and a draw in their first nineteen games. The solitary draw was the 2-2 with Madrid in October 2012, that homage to football. The following morning the sports newspaper *AS* splashed a huge 'MEMORABLE!' across its cover. 'It is a pity to get into the controversy when the football is so good,' Valdano says. But it is never about just the football, there is always more. Barcelona versus Madrid, Madrid versus Barcelona. It is a political story, a social one, a cultural one. Above all, it is a human story.

They say that Barcelona is more than a club. They're right, it is.

So is Real Madrid.

3

THE MARTYR PRESIDENT

Warning shots were fired but the driver took no notice. The black Ford, number plate ARM 2929, sped past and up the mountain, a Catalan flag on its wing. Sitting in the back were a militia lieutenant, the journalist Pere Ventura i Virgili and Josep Sunyol i Garriga, the president of Football Club Barcelona. A kilometre further up the road was another armed checkpoint. This time the car did stop. And there, at kilometre 52 of the NVI road to the north-west of Madrid, Barcelona's president and his companions were assassinated by fascist troops. Shot in the back of the head and left, their bodies were never recovered. The date was 6 August 1936.

Today, the La Coruña motorway heads out of the Spanish capital towards the Guadarrama mountain range, past the Valley of the Fallen, General Francisco Franco's giant mausoleum with its five-hundred-foot cross. The NVI, the old road, breaks off from the motorway and snakes up the mountain, climbing steeply through the forest. At the top, four kilometres further on, is the Alto del León, the pass that controls much of the *sierra*. A point of huge strategic significance, 1,511 metres above sea level, it was to here that troops raced when an unsuccessful military *coup d'état* became the Spanish Civil War in July 1936. And it was here that some of the bitterest, most insistent fighting took place in the early stages of a conflict that cost almost half a million lives.

On a clear afternoon the views are stunning but in winter this point lies above the clouds, grey and gloomy. There is little here: a car park, a roadside restaurant, a military pillbox and a solitary stone cross, shrouded in an eerie cold mist. Back down at what is now kilometre 51.3, below the cloud, is a bend in the road. Madrid spreads out in the distance below: far away on the horizon, four gigantic skyscrapers now tower over the city, built on Real Madrid's former training ground. At the side of the road is a sanatorium. Constructed soon after the civil war and named, like so much else, after the Generalísimo, it was not there in August 1936. What was there, directly opposite, was a small stone house-turned-staging-post known as the *Casilla de la Muerte*. The house of death. Now, there is no sign of it; just an overgrown bank of weeds and moss at the side of the road.

The Spanish Civil War lasted three years between 1936 and 1939. The conflict was caused by a variety of political tensions between right and left, religion and secularism, centre and the periphery, rich and poor. It started with a military coup launched on 17 and 18 July 1936 by army officers and right-wing civilian collaborators seeking to overthrow the Republic's left-wing Popular Front government, which had been in power since the February general elections. The build-up became known as the Ominous Spring; political tension increased and plotting accelerated. General Franco, who had been posted to Gran Canaria, prevaricated at first, his coyness earning him the nickname Miss Canary Islands 1936. But he eventually joined the conspiracy, became the *Caudillo*, a Spanish equivalent of *Duce* or *Führer*, led Fascist forces and established a military dictatorship that ruled Spain until 1975.

The coup was successful in the right's heartlands of Galicia and Castile and unsuccessful in the strongholds of the left. The city of Madrid, like Barcelona, stayed loyal to the Republic. In Barcelona the coup was defeated by socialists and anarchists who joined forces with Assault Guards during three days of street-fighting; in Madrid, members of left-wing parties and trades unions were armed by the Republican government as its best means of protection and, alongside loyal forces, stormed conspirators in the Montaña barracks. In doing so, power shifted forever. Revolution broke out in Barcelona; workers' groups took control in Madrid.

By 22 July 1936, the battle lines were drawn. On one side, the Nationalists: the rebelling military, supported by fascist and conservative civilians and the Church hierarchy, aided by Hitler and Mussolini. On the other, the Republic: those defending democracy and the political left, aided by the International Brigades and the Soviet Union. Meanwhile, the West hid behind the Non-Intervention Agreement, described by the first Indian prime minister Jawaharlal Nehru as 'the supreme farce of our time'. With Nazi and Fascist help, troops were airlifted to the mainland from Africa to fight on the Nationalist side and, from north and south, soldiers marched towards Republican Madrid, which was soon surrounded on three sides. Republican troops left the city to meet them, starting a sprint to control those mountain passes. In August 1936, Guadarrama was the front line; what Sunyol and his driver did not know was exactly where that line lay. It was a tragic mistake that cost them their lives.

Josep Sunyol came from a rich family that originally made its money importing sugar. Unlike most of those who had run FC Barcelona until then – many from the textile industry with ties to the conservative Lliga Catalana – his concerns didn't lie with the Catalan bourgeoisie. Instead Sunyol, who had become Barcelona president in the summer of 1935, was a parliamentary deputy for the Esquerra Republicana Catalana, the Catalan Republican Left.

The most voted-for parliamentarian in Catalonia's history, he founded a newspaper called *La Rambla* in which he wrote on a range of subjects, including a regular column on sport and citizenship. 'When we say sport,' he explained, 'we mean our race, enthusiasm, optimism, the noble struggle of youth. And when we say citizenship, we mean civility, *Catalanism*, liberalism, democracy, generosity.' In practical terms that meant support for the democratisation of sport; the opening of municipal facilities and sport's extension to all, beyond the elitism of gentlemen's clubs. The newspaper also placed a chalkboard outside its offices by the Canaletes fountain on the Ramblas on which they kept supporters informed of the score when Barcelona played away. To this day, the fountain remains the meeting point for fans celebrating Barça's triumphs. A plaque on the pavement, trodden by millions, noticed by few, marks the spot.

Sunyol's columns were a manifesto of what he believed FC Barcelona had come to represent, and what, many years later, it would seek to recover. As Joan Laporta, the former president, puts it: 'Josep Sunyol, our martyr president, was someone whose concern was to improve society through sport and through Barça. He is an example for all of those of us who have had the honour of presiding over the club. The phrase 'sport and citizenship' embodies a Catalanist, progressive view of life.' After the war, Franco's new state would process Sunyol under the law of political responsibility. *La Rambla* stood accused of having led an 'active' campaign that was 'separatist and Marxist', while Sunyol was a 'Communist and a separatist', responsible for 'the markedly anti-Spanish direction taken by FC Barcelona'.

Sunyol spent 6 August 1936 in Madrid and was due to travel to Valencia on the overnight train that evening. He was ferrying messages between representatives of the Republican government in Madrid, Barcelona and Valencia. According to some accounts, he was also planning to make new signings, including the star of the era: Real Oviedo striker Isidro Lángara. Like many key Republican figures, he wanted to see the front for himself.

At around 6 p.m., Sunyol's car went past the last Republican checkpoint, oblivious to the shots fired by troops warning the driver that he was about to cross the front line. A little further up, at kilometre 52, the car pulled up alongside the *Casilla de la Muerte*. In total, the position was held by about twenty-five infantry soldiers, seven or eight artillerymen, four sergeants, fifteen troops from Galicia and a handful of members of the Falange, the fascist movement that would ultimately become the single party of the Franco state. When they reached the checkpoint and saw troops outside, Sunyol and his companions got out of the car, holding their pistols, and gave the obligatory greeting: '*¡Viva la República!*' The Catalan flag on the wing of the car had already identified them as the enemy but now there was no doubt. They were greeted in the same manner and invited into the *casilla*. They had no idea that they had been intercepted by Nationalist troops.

Once inside, Sunyol and his companions were made to put their hands up, their pistols were taken from them and they were searched. Sunyol had a significant amount of money on him – Barcelona secretary Rossend Calvet claimed 25,000 pesetas; other versions suggest twice that. According to the account of one of the sergeants present, the driver was shot trying to escape, while Virgili pleaded with his captors saying that he could be useful to them. 'Naturally,' the sergeant recalled, 'he got an adequate response.' Virgili and Sunyol were shot on the spot, their dead bodies were searched and dumped somewhere outside. 'It was then that we realised that one of them was some guy called [Sunyol] Garriga.' In 2009, at a time when mass unmarked graves were being exhumed across Spain, it for their bodies began, led by the Catalan history magazine *Sàpiens*. So far, it has proven unsuccessful.

When Sunyol failed to show up in Valencia or return to Barcelona, concern grew and so did the rumours. Had he been taken prisoner? Or crossed the lines? Gone into exile? The first unconfirmed reports of his death reached Barcelona within the week. In his honour, a Josep Sunyol centurion was founded and a Sunyol Sporting Battalion, made up of footballers and other sportsmen, was created in Madrid to fight against fascism and with the promise to arrange a benefit match against the Soviet Union. The battalion's HQ was established at Madrid's offices and its members were trained at Chamartín, the club's stadium, by Madrid's physical coach Heliodoro Ruíz. Madrid's Felix Queseda, José Luis Espinosa and Simón Lecue were among those who played in a game held that month against Atlético Madrid, the proceeds of which were handed to anti-fascist militias raised in the working-class neighbourhood of Vallecas. Barcelona's assassinated president was being honoured, supported and promoted as an anti-fascist symbol by Madrid.

For years, that was as much as Sunyol's own club did to honour their president. In the aftermath of the civil war, with Francoist officials and state fascists handpicking Barcelona's presidents, there was little interest in remembering him. Sunyol had been killed; now he was 'tried' as an enemy of the Franco regime, his assets seized. Even the fiftieth anniversary of Sunyol's death passed virtually without comment and when a group called The Friends of Josep Sunyol tried to have his memory marked on the sixtieth anniversary in 1996, they encountered initial resistance from the then Barça president Josep Lluis Nuñez – more 'evidence', according to opposition groups, that Nuñez did not faithfully reflect Barcelona's 'true' character. A memorial stone was eventually placed, but Sunyol's son insisted that the name be spelled with a Spanish 'ñ' rather than a Catalan 'ny'.

Further down the mountainside, three and a half kilometres from where Sunyol was shot and just to the north of the town of Guadarrama, is a small park filled with pines, gently sloping southwards. The park is largely forgotten and empty but for the very occasional dog-walker. There is no sign, no announcement. It is quiet and still, but for the light swoosh of cars passing alongside on the main road. The early evening sun streams through the trees and across a small, grey stone:

Josep Suñol i Garriga
Barcelona 21-VII-1898
Guadarrama 6-VIII-1936

Toni Strubell sits in the restaurant at the Catalan parliament, a beautiful former Bourbon palace and arsenal alongside the Barcelona city zoo. Strubell, an MP for Solidaritat Catalana per la Independència, fought to recuperate Sunyol's historic memory and exhaustively investigated and reconstructed the most complete and convincing account of the killing, based in part upon the report of the artillery sergeant.

Strubell recalls the time that he brought the stone to Guadarrama in 1996. He was heading down the motorway with it in the boot of his car, while Real Madrid fans were busy spraying anti-Barça graffiti round the town. But they did not know where the stone would be placed – and, once it had been, it was left alone. The Friends of Sunyol had not been given permission to place it at kilometre 52 so they approached the mayor of Guadarrama, a representative of the right-wing Partido Popular but also the son of a Republican gunner, and on 4 June the stone was unveiled. The president of the Catalan parliament, Joan Raventós, attended, as did Jaume Sobrequés – historian, politician and board member of FC Barcelona. Nuñez did not.

Things are different now. In 2011, under Sandro Rosell's presidency, Sunyol was honoured at a ceremony at the Camp Nou prior to a league game against Levante. Barcelona's website refers to him as the 'martyr president' and he is given pride of place in the club's museum. He has come to represent Barcelona and its conscious combination of sport and society – football and Catalonia. Democratic, liberal, left-wing, a victim of the Franco regime and a symbol of resistance, Sunyol has become a key component in Barcelona's identification, the first step towards that famous definition, *mès que un club*.

The Catalan Marxist writer Manuel Vázquez Montalbán arguably did more than anyone to construct Barça's narrative and articulate their sense of identity, defining the club as the 'symbolic unarmed army of Catalonia'. Importantly, it is a defeated army; theirs is a history of suffering. Never more so than when they lost their president, shot dead without trial in 1936. Vázquez Montalbán's list of historic griev-ances, the building blocks of an identity, invariably includes the line: 'in the first days of the war, up on a mountain pass in the *sierra* de Guadarrama, the president of Barcelona, señor Sunyol, was shot by a Francoist squadron.'

Nine days after Sunyol's death Ángel Mur was working at Les Corts, preparing the ground for the new season, when he saw a car pull up with CNT-FAI painted on the side in huge letters. A handful of armed militiamen in blue overalls got out, made their way to the main gate and put up a notice announcing that the anarchist trade union was requisitioning the stadium in the name of the revolution and the fight against fascism. It was a familiar scene in Barcelona in the opening weeks of the war – a city where the anarchist movement was stronger than anywhere else in Spain and where, in George Orwell's famous words, the 'working class was in the saddle'. Orwell describes Barcelona in the summer of 1936 as a city where 'every wall was scrawled with the hammer and sickle', churches had been sacked and burnt and notices declared businesses to have been collectivised: 'practically every building of any size had been seized by the workers and was draped with red flags or the red and black flag of the anarchists.'

Although Les Corts' dressing room had been used to hide priests from the anti-clerical fury of the early days of the war, football clubs were not immune to this process. The city's other big club Español was collectivised; now Barcelona was going to be. Mur dashed up to the small flat that Manel Torres, the caretaker, had in the stadium and from there Torres called his father-in-law, the Barça secretary Rossend Calvet, at the club's offices. Then he ran down to speak to the militiamen, convincing them to give Barcelona time to help process the collectivisation of the club. As their car pulled away, Mur and Torres tore down the posters.

An emergency meeting was called. Barcelona had no president but some of the pre-war board remained. They had to find a way of maintaining control and preventing Barça from slipping into anarchist hands. That was when they came up with the idea of collectivising the club themselves in the name of the revolution; they would conduct an *auto-incautación*, a self-confiscation. Sixteen employees formed a workers' committee affiliated to the Socialist union UGT, which included Torres, Calvet and Mur, the caretaker at the stadium and at the club's offices, the accountant, office staff and the kit man. The committee then publicly announced the confiscation of the club by the UGT, i.e. themselves, thus effectively short-circuiting the CNT-FAI. If the club had already been taken over by the workers, it could not be taken over by the workers again.

The notice that was now stuck on the doors read: 'These offices, the Les Corts stadium and Barcelona's training ground have been confiscated by the UGT, the organisation to which its workers belong.' Meanwhile, a formal announcement explained the move: 'The confiscation and collectivisation [of this club] is due to the imperatives of the present time, which is profoundly revolutionary. We are looking into the best way of ensuring that Barcelona fulfils its duty to popularise and democratise sport within the laws of this new situation, provoked by the deplorable seditious, fascist and military movement.'

It needed more than just a declaration, though. When the CNT returned and pulled down the UGT posters at the club's offices, they were warned off by a militiaman who ran a garage across the road and just happened to be a Barcelona fan and friend of the caretaker, Josep Cubells. Calvet also managed to strike a deal with the police to ensure that the stadium was only used by Barcelona, the Catalan Football Federation and the police force. Manel Torres later told the journalist Enric Bañeres: 'not one of the employees at the club actually belonged to any workers' association, but the trick worked.' Barcelona had been saved.

Saved but not safe. The financial situation was desperate – 'terrifying' in the words of one committee member. The number of Barcelona *socis*, or members, had already declined during the Republican years, a period when Madrid had emerged as the stronger side, winning the league in 1932 and 1933 and the cup in 1934 and 1936. Now they dwindled further, dropping from 7,719 to 2,500 between the start of the civil war and its close in 1939. Football was no longer a priority as food shortages continued and the climate of fear and suspicion worsened.

In May 1937, the 'civil war within the civil war' concluded with three days of fighting within the Republican ranks in Barcelona and the definitive ascension of the previously minuscule Communist Party, backed by the Soviet Union. And when aerial attacks started in Barcelona, with 670 dead and 1,200 injured on the first day alone, Barcelona's club offices on Consell de Cent were hit by a bomb dropped by Mussolini's pilots on behalf of Franco. Cubells was at the back of the building when the bomb struck the front, almost entirely destroying the façade. Battered and bruised, he crawled through the rubble and rescued 2,500 pesetas hidden inside a water pipe. With the help of other club employees who raced to the scene, some trophies were salvaged but more than three hundred were lost for ever. Those that were saved were later smelted together to make a Cup of Cups.

But the war had not brought an end to Barcelona's activity. They played in the Catalan Championship, the Mediterranean League and in friendlies, travelling to games by train at night, the lights off to avoid bombardment from the Nationalist warships out at sea. Some players travelled back and forth to the front to play matches, Irish coach Patrick O'Connell – who had arrived from Betis in 1935 – returned from a trip home and Ángel Mur ended up training members of the International Brigades. In 1936–7, Barcelona played nine friendlies, ten in the Catalan Championship, and fourteen in the Mediterranean League, winning the competition held between January and May 1937 with a solitary defeat in fourteen games. Their city rivals Español came second. The two teams had faced each other in the first game held in Catalonia during the war in August 1936, just ten days after Sunyol's killing and during another game fighting broke out between opposition supporters accusing each other of being 'fascists'; fortunately, announcements had already been made asking fans not to take arms to games.

In early 1937, an offer reached the Barcelona player Josep Iborra from a businessman by the name of Manuel Mas Serrano. He proposed that Barcelona travel to play a series of exhibition matches in Mexico, one of only two countries to openly support the Republic. According to the offer, Barcelona would be paid $15,000 with all costs covered. Despite their initial reluctance, Barcelona agreed and embarked upon the fourteen-day crossing to Mexico with twenty men on board – sixteen players plus O'Connell, Mur, Calvet and the doctor Modest Amorós.

Mur was taken as the club's physio, even though he protested that he did not know anything about medicine or even massages. O'Connell was adamant. 'Don't worry,' the Irishman told him, 'I'll teach you on the way.' In so doing, O'Connell started a spiritual dynasty at the club. Ángel Mur senior bought all the anatomy textbooks he could get his hands on and was eventually succeeded by Ángel Mur junior in 1973 – between them they gave over sixty years' service as caretakers, kit men, physiotherapists, psychologists, confessors and defenders of the Barcelona faith. As Mur senior put it: 'Stay in Barcelona and risk getting blown up or go on a football tour of America. It wasn't much of a choice, was it?'

It was better than that. The Mexican tour initially comprised seven games but Mas offered them the chance to extend it in exchange for $5,000. From Veracruz, they took a four-day boat trip to the US. 'I've travelled a bit since then but that is still the most memorable journey of my life,' Mur told the British writer Jeff King. 'God knows why but there were several hundred women on the ship. Let's just say those women kept us busy. You had to be careful where you stepped when you went on deck because there were couples on the floor everywhere. We'd had a great time in Mexico but that boat trip was a four-day carnival. A few of the guys thought it was too much but we were young and I had a great time.'

The schedule included four games in New York, against Hispano, a New York selection, an American Soccer League XI and, finally, an evening match against a Jewish XI – the first time Barcelona had ever played under floodlights. The honorary kick-off against Hispano was taken by Fernando de los Ríos, the Spanish Republic's ambassador to the US. Calvet later recalled that he tried to make the tour apolitical but inevitably Barcelona were greeted as a kind of Republican embassy and fêted everywhere they went, elevated to the status of representatives of democracy in its battle against fascism, cheered on as if they were the home team. The Franco regime reached the same view, judging Barcelona's tour to have been a political expedition, and at the end of the civil war every player who had taken part was banned from football for two years. Calvet was banned for eight, later reduced to two.

Barcelona eventually set sail for home in late September 1937. They had played fourteen games and won ten of them. More importantly, they made an overall profit of just under $12,900, clearing their debts. The money was deposited in a French bank account to protect it from confiscation: the American tour had saved them. They returned to win the Catalan Championship in 1938.

Some of them did, anyway. At the end of the tour, Calvet offered everyone on the trip four choices: return to Barcelona and the Republican zone, stay in exile in Mexico, go into exile in France, or return to Spain and cross into the Nationalist zone. Although some subsequently left for Spain or France after the civil war was over, initially nine players opted to stay in Mexico, among them Martí Ventolrà and Josep Iborra. Ventolrà married the Mexican president Lázaro Cárdenas's niece and their son Martín played at the 1970 World Cup for Mexico. Meanwhile, in a bizarre historical footnote, Iborra befriended a fellow Catalan exile, Ramón Mercader. One day during lunch together, Mercader abruptly announced that he had to dash off to do something. When the police turned up the next afternoon and took Iborra to see a bloody body, the penny dropped: Mercader had killed Leon Trotsky with an ice pick.

Of the twenty who set sail for Mexico, nine returned to Spain: Calvet, Mur, Amorós, O'Connell and five players. None of the twenty-man expedition crossed into the Nationalist zone.

The Nationalist army reached Barcelona at the end of January 1939. The eastern front had collapsed and the troops encountered no resistance from an exhausted and terrified city. 'The people were tired of the war and long before the enemy's arrival had only hoped for a sudden end to it,' as one contemporary account succinctly put it. As the Nationalists marched in, others marched out: in total, 10,000 wounded, 170,000 women and children, 60,000 male civilians and 220,000 Republican soldiers escaped by crossing into France from Catalonia. The few people who did come on to the streets did so to welcome Franco's troops with fascist salutes, some out of political conviction, others out of political expediency: survival was all that mattered.

For the Nationalists, who shared an iron centralism, this had double significance. They had reached the east coast and conquered Catalonia for Spain – a notion that would come to take on ever-greater significance, for both sides. The sports newspaper *Marca*, founded in Nationalist-controlled San Sebastián in December 1938, later declared: 'Liberation! A magical word, so desired over two and a half years. On that unforgettable afternoon of 26 January the brave and invincible soldiers of the Generalísimo arrived in the central avenues of the city, marching with astonishingly calm, serene steps, rifles in their shoulder bags, singing songs, every balcony draped with the vivid colours of our holy flag.' Franco's troops, 'the army of liberation', marched along the Avenida Diagonal – later renamed the Avenida of the Generalísimo – and took the city. Among their ranks was a forty-three-year-old volunteer corporal by the name of Santiago Bernabéu.

Bernabéu was a bruising centre-forward who had played for Real Madrid and would become the living embodiment of the club. The historian Josep Solé i Sabaté insists: 'Sunyol was Barcelona's standard-bearer, its alter ego – the embodiment of liberty, plurality and democracy. In other words, of Barcelona. Meanwhile, that other president, Real Madrid's Santiago Bernabéu, is the alter ego of Francoism.'

When the Spanish Civil War is looked at through the prism of Real Madrid and FC Barcelona – and it often is – and when the two clubs are looked at through the prism of the Spanish Civil War – and they often are – their stories tend to be reduced to the figures of two presidents: Sunyol and Bernabéu. One, the Barcelona president and democrat assassinated by Franco's troops in Madrid; the other, the future Madrid president and right-winger who escaped the Republican zone, signed up to fight for Franco's forces and boasted of having conquered Catalonia.

And yet the story is not that simple, right down to the fact that when Bernabéu marched along the Diagonal he was not the president of Madrid and he wouldn't be for another four years. When Bernabéu marched along the Diagonal, Madrid's rightful president was six hundred kilometres away and on the other side, still fighting fascism.

4

THE FORGOTTEN PRESIDENT

Spain's Second Republic was born in April 1931 and died in April 1939, a dictatorship installed in its place. Rafael Sánchez Guerra was there at the start and he was there at the end, accompanying the Republic from its first day until its last. Few were so broken by the experience: 'there is,' he wrote bitterly in 1946, 'nothing left that can hurt me now.' On 14 April 1931, from the balcony of the *Ayuntamiento*, or city hall, Republican tricolour in hand, he watched excited crowds enter Madrid's Puerta del Sol central square to celebrate the proclamation of the country's first democracy. Eight years later, on 28 March 1939, from the basement of the Treasury a couple of hundred yards away, he watched General Franco's troops finally enter the city after a brutal, thirty-six-month siege.

Others had gone; some fled to the east coast, some into exile, desperate to escape the inevitable. Sánchez Guerra sat and awaited his arrest, defending democracy to the last and paying the penalty for it. Loaded into a van, he was taken to the Porlier prison with twenty-one others. The Spanish Civil War officially ended on 1 April 1939, with the capture of Madrid. By 3 April, the 'trial' against Sánchez Guerra was underway, processed for military rebellion, Franco's new state prosecutor demanding the death penalty. Sánchez Guerra had been the Secretary-General to the Republic's president Niceto Alcalá-Zamora. He had also been the president of Real Madrid.

Sánchez Guerra was not a left-wing man. His father had been a monarchist politician and in the 1920s Sánchez Guerra himself had fought in North Africa with Franco, getting shot in combat: he was even included in Franco's published diary of the war. He was a practising Catholic and a columnist on the monarchist conservative daily *ABC*. But his political journey took him away from the monarchy after its dalliance with the Primo de Rivera dictatorship, and he founded the Republican Liberal Right, defining himself as 'centrist: equidistant from the extremists of left and right'. He was a democrat, a liberal, and he was committed to the Republic.

Imprisoned by the Primo de Rivera dictatorship – he missed the 1929 Spanish Cup final between Español and Real Madrid because he was in jail – Sánchez Guerra was on the victorious Republican–Socialist slate at the municipal elections in 1931 that forced Alfonso XIII into exile and ushered in the Republic. In fact, like Sunyol in Barcelona, he received the most votes. He was the under-secretary of the provisional Republican government and became secretary-general of the presidency, in charge of military affairs upon the Republic's formal establishment. In 1935, General Franco visited Sánchez Guerra and assured him that he had no intention of rising against the democratic regime. In 1936, Franco did just that. 'Words, words, words,' Sánchez Guerra later remarked sadly.

When the coup was launched and the Spanish Civil War started, Sánchez Guerra stayed at home for four days before making his way to the Madrid council. He served there during the first two years of the war and became secretary to Colonel Segismundo Casado, in charge of the Defence Council of the Republican Army of the Centre, fighting against fascism. By 1939, the situation had become desperate. Most had given up on the Republic. The western democracies had definitively turned their back and, led by France and Britain, formally recognised Franco as the head of the Spanish state. Dr Juan Negrín, the president of the Republic, preached resistance but others believed it to be futile and costly. Casado overthrew Negrín in the spring of 1939 and sought a negotiated surrender with Franco in a bid to end further bloodshed. It was Sánchez Guerra who made the approach but the Generalísimo, whose regime had also been formally recognised by FIFA in 1938, refused. Franco wanted total victory: not just unconditional surrender, but annihilation.

The Madrid front was getting weaker and the Republic was crumbling. Negotiations for peace had failed. Casado's 'council' held its last meeting on 27 March 1939. Just before seven the following morning, Casado called Sánchez Guerra to his office and told him that he was departing on a flight to Valencia. There was a seat reserved for Sánchez Guerra and his wife on board but he decided instead to stay, telling Casado: 'I will not abandon Madrid, no matter what.'

'That's a bad decision,' Casado replied, 'the Nationalists will be here any moment and they hate you: it wouldn't be prudent [to stay].'

Sánchez Guerra went home, put on his uniform, picked up his 'prison bag' and returned to the Treasury. There, he and the Socialist parliamentarian Julián Besteiro broadcast a radio message informing listeners that the war was lost: Franco's troops would be in Madrid imminently. Only half the broadcast went out: fascist forces had arrived at the radio transmitter and pulled the plug.

At the end of the war, the Franco regime began the Causa General – the General Trial – brought against all those who opposed the Nationalists in any way, 'actively' or 'passively'. Some who had were tried, in an act of devastating cynicism, with 'military rebellion'. At least they got a trial of sorts; others were simply killed. Sánchez Guerra's 'identification with the reds' was, the military court heard, 'complete and absolute'; a man of 'great influence' within the Republic, he was declared 'dangerous'. It made no difference that he had denounced the worst atrocities of the left nor saved the lives of men on the other side. In the summer of 1939, 'Year 1 of Victory', he was handed life imprisonment: thirty years in jail, with release due on 25 May 1969. Moved from prison to prison, Sánchez Guerra calculated there to be 50,000 political prisoners in Madrid alone in the years immediately after the war. Night after night, he witnessed inmates being taken unannounced from their cells, never to return.

Eventually, as part of a 1944 'amnesty', Sánchez Guerra was conditionally released, only to be re-arrested. He escaped at the very moment the military police arrived at his house to take him back into custody, went into hiding and left Spain for France in early summer 1946. There, he became minister without portfolio in the Republican government in exile, a position he held for just over a year. He tried to build relations with the British in the vain hope that the democratic nations would intervene against Franco, delivered to power by the same fascist regimes the Allies had just defeated in the Second World War.

'The only thing that should concern the enemies of Spanish fascism is the fall of Franco and those who have helped him to stay in power,' he wrote. 'Franco is a poor devil favoured by chance, who believes he is God, pedantic, fatuous, stupid and cruel; cruel like all tyrants. He brought the Moors to Andalucía's coast so that they could sack and burn the houses of the Spanish people, turned his *Caudillo*'s sword into a pirate's cutlass, invited Mussolini and Hitler to raze the earth of Spain, pursues the humble, imprisons the worker, consents to hired assassins sowing terror and hatred, invokes the name of God to commit crimes, fans the flame of hate [and fills] prisons with honourable workers, thousands of peaceful citizens shot or condemned to the garrotte.'

Rafael Sánchez Guerra once claimed 'rebellion is sacred'. But when his wife died in October 1959, he withdrew entirely. He had given up, a broken and beaten man. Aged sixty-two, he contacted the ambassador in Paris and requested permission to return to Spain, telling him: 'I am a profoundly Catholic man and I want to end my days in the land where my parents' mortal remains lie. I do not think it is even necessary to reiterate that I am not contemplating taking part in any political activity. I seek in Spain the spiritual tranquillity I so badly need.' He joined a seminary and took up his habit at the monastery of Santo Domingo de Pamplona in November 1960, where he refereed football matches between the monks on the courtyard. On 2 April 1964, twenty-five years and one day since the end of the civil war, he died. Sánchez Guerra had lived a solitary life, largely forgotten. He has been largely forgotten by Real Madrid too, his story untold. But among the last people to visit him were Ferenç Puskás, Paco Gento, Amancio Amaro and Santiago Bernabéu on the day their team were due to face Osasuna. And when he died, a wreath of flowers arrived from Real Madrid.

Sánchez Guerra won Madrid's presidential elections in 1935, thanks largely to the gratitude felt after he successfully intervened with the Madrid city council to prevent the extension of the Paseo de la Castellana from forcing the closure and demolition of Chamartín stadium. Although he and many on his board were considered conservatives and distrusted by some on the left, his arrival still signalled a shift at the club and was met with a certain degree of resistance from more traditional right-wing elites who had run it until then and rejected what they saw as its politicisation. Sánchez Guerra introduced a policy of one-member-one-vote for the first time and dropped ticket prices to a single peseta. His election accelerated the evolving identity of Madrid's membership in an age of growing popularity for the sport and the arrival, at last, of mass politics as well as an increased identification with the city.

In 1902, Madrid's founders, the Catalan Padrós brothers, had organised a tournament to celebrate the coming of age of King Alfonso XIII, which included the first ever Madrid versus Barcelona. Matches were held in the presence of Alfonso and the mayor of Madrid, Alberto Aguilera, who had donated a trophy for the occasion. The newspaper *Heraldo* described the scene: 'little ladies in wasp-waist dresses and enormous can-can dancers hats, with pointed gaiters. Pastel colours and flower patterns, rice flour on pretty faces. Grave, solemn gentlemen, dark colours brightened by a carnation through the buttonhole. Dandies. Sparkling uniforms. Military men, corseted into tight waist-coats and trousers like bullfighters. Playboys who have sneaked in. In the official section, grey button-up frock coats and top hats, walking sticks with marble handles.' By 1936 crowds looked rather different and society was changing. Football too had become popular, no longer the preserve of a few well-to-do gentlemen.

The historian Ángel Bahamonde traces four groups among Madrid's six thousand members on the eve of the war: the almost aristocratic groups that ran the club from its early days; moderate, middle- to working-class members; left-wing members who had joined in the years of the Republic; and of course the apolitical. But some still saw Madrid, who had become Real (Royal) under patronage from Alfonso XIII in 1921 and then had the title forcibly withdrawn during the Republic, as representatives of the bourgeoisie. Politics and football inevitably came together. And, with the outbreak of war, remaining genuinely apolitical was made impossible – both for individual *socios* and for the club.

On the morning of 21 June 1936, a Popular Front meeting was held at Valencia's Mestalla stadium. A few hours later, they had made way for the cup final between Madrid and Barcelona. Some of them had anyway. The annual of the Spanish Football Federation written in 1950, looked back on events and recalled, 'The Communists turned up *en masse* to release all their revolutionary hate against Real Madrid, who they considered a symbol of what they were fighting against. All of their attacks centred on Ricardo Zamora; he was even nearly hit by a bottle.'

Zamora's name still adorns the award given out to the best goalkeeper at the end of each season. Nicknamed *El Divino*, the divine one, he was considered little short of unbeatable and was Spanish football's first great media star, 'as famous as Greta Garbo and better looking' as one contemporary put it. There were songs penned in his honour, drinks named after him and a film in which he starred, called *Zamora Weds At Last*. A friend of the tango singer Carlos Gardel, consumer of three packets of cigarettes a day and countless cognacs, Zamora was a famous night bird during the 1920s when Barcelona became the most fashionable city in Spain. When Niceto Alcalá-Zamora became president of the Republic, Stalin apparently asked: 'This Zamora, is he the goalkeeper?' Zamora signed for Madrid in 1930 for 150,000 pesetas from Español – the most expensive player in history at the time – on a salary of 3,000 pesetas a month plus a yearly bonus of 50,000 pesetas. He had previously played for Barcelona, the first really big name to play for both clubs.

The 1936 final is famous for a last-minute save from Zamora, immortalised in print and endlessly recalled since. The photograph of his save is perhaps the most recognisable in Spanish football history: Zamora, diving down to his left on the dry pitch, a cloud of dust rising around him. The shot seemed unstoppable, 'impossible' in Zamora's own words, but when the dust settled, the goalkeeper was standing there holding the ball. In the banquet that followed the win, Sánchez Guerra finished with a toast of '*¡Viva la República!*'. Few responded but when the team arrived back at Atocha station they were greeted by the Republic's anthem. Madrid were cup winners, the last there would be for four years.

At the start of the war, Zamora was imprisoned by left-wing militiamen in the Republican zone who suspected him of being a fascist sympathiser but, recognised by camp guards and given protective status, he eventually escaped to France where he played for Nice before returning to Spain after the war. Among his team-mates was Josep Samitier, the former Barcelona and Madrid player who had been smuggled out of Spain on a French warship. Meanwhile, a Basque 'national team' toured Czechoslovakia, Poland, Norway, Finland and the USSR. Back in Spain, clubs' experiences and activities necessarily differed depending on where they found themselves during the war and particularly at its outbreak.

Of the twelve First Division teams, eight began the war in the Republican zone, Barcelona and Madrid among them. As in Barcelona, workers' groups took control in Madrid, collectivising buildings, businesses, institutions . . . and football clubs. Madrid CF, like FC Barcelona, were a target and, like Barça, they took pre-emptive action. Pablo Hernández Coronado, a former goalkeeper and the secretary, brought together a group of employees who carried out a self-confiscation, reflecting Madrid's status as a 'democratic club with a roll-call of *socios* who are clearly Republicans and left-wingers' and whose duty was 'to fight against fascism'. 'In order to take the club in a popular direction', Madrid also extended the use of its facilities – apart from the pitch – 'to all those who are heroically defending the democratic Republic against fascism'. That, at least, is how Hernández Coronado put it at the time. After the war, he framed it rather differently, justifying his actions to the Francoist authorities by insisting that Madrid had carried out the *auto-incautación* 'in order to protect it from the red hordes'.

The original declaration was signed on 5 August 1936 and was followed a few days later by a match against Atlético Madrid to raise money for popular militias based in Vallecas. A further collection of 5,000 pesetas was handed over to the Republic's president and each member of staff gave a day's wages to the war effort. Madrid were now run by a workers' committee made up of two representatives from the Socialist-affiliated Federación Deportiva Obrera, led by Juan José Vallejo; Hernández Coronado, who, as 'technical adviser' became *de facto* president; and two *socios* and employees. According to the terms of the *incautación*, only members of Madrid who were also members of Popular Front parties could use the facilities during the war.

The sincerity of those measures is of course questionable. When the Nationalists entered the capital, Madrid's physical trainer Heliodoro Ruíz, a friend of the fascist leader José Antonio Primo de Rivera, revealed himself as a fifth columnist and Falangist sympathiser. When he later wrote his memoirs they were eloquently entitled *Thirty-two Months with the Reds* and dedicated to his brother and the rest of Spain's 'martyrs', killed by the 'Marxist hoards'. Juan Carlos Alonso, who had worked at Madrid since 1919 and would continue to do so for decades, insisted that he was 'apolitical' and had been obliged to join the 'most moderate union I could find' simply as a means of self-defence and of protecting the club. The *auto-incautación* was a way of keeping Madrid from revolutionary, left-wing hands – just as Barcelona's *auto-incautación* had been.

The city's proximity to the war and the shift in the balance of power soon brought the club into the orbit of the Communist Party. That in turn necessarily and forcibly changed its character. An October 1936 call for *socios* who had not been seen since the start of the war to turn up and pay their membership dues 'so as not to be looked upon as suspicious' has a sinister ring to it and Coronado's decision to hide membership files in order to protect right-wingers from reprisals was probably necessary. Chamartín was used for the training of the Sporting Battalion and the holding of parades and gymnastics events. The photograph from one sporting festival shows the event being presided over by Republican figures such as General José Miaja, the hero of the defence of Madrid; the Communist Santiago Carrillo, widely believed to be responsible for mass killings of suspected right-wingers at Paracuellos de Jarama; the Communist military commander Valentín González, 'El Campesino'; and Colonel Antonio Ortega, the man who, propelled by the *incautación* and promoted by the Communist Party through the Federación Deportiva Obrera, became the club's president.

Ortega was a Communist political commissar in charge of the secret police during the war. Involved in the falsification of documents and the creation of a trumped-up charge to justify the pursuit, torture and assassination of the 'Trotskyite' leader Andreu Nín, he was later sacked when it became clear that he was working for the NKVD spy Aleksandr Orlov. The story gives Real Madrid a left-wing narrative largely absent from its history, not least because Ortega has never been recognised by the club, even though the newspaper *Blanco y Negro* carries a wartime interview with him as president in which he defended Madrid's right to construct the best stadium in Spain, not least because the city was the home of the workers' resistance. 'Madrid,' he argued, 'has earned its status as the capital and should enjoy all that other cities enjoy – cities whose commitment to the war has been more frivolous.'

Ortega was driven by self-interest but this last line contained a fundamental truth. It is also one that has often been ignored, especially when it comes to Spain's greatest sporting rivalry.

The popular perception of the war, especially internationally, as projected on to and via Spain's two biggest football clubs, is one in which Barcelona is the home of revolution and resistance to fascism. The Catalan capital is assumed to be the battlefield of the civil war, the scene of suffering and tragedy; Madrid is assumed to be the home of Franco's government and thus the war becomes a kind of anti-Catalan crusade, a battle between Castile and Catalonia – as if Barcelona was the victim and Madrid the aggressor, as if the aim of the war was the occupation of the Catalan nation by the Spanish state. Taken to the football clubs, Real Madrid becomes Franco's team, Barcelona its victims. The narrative is served. It is also flawed; at times the way it is presented is simply false.

An Australian-produced documentary on the Madrid–Barça rivalry that was also broadcast in Spain in 2001 is typical. It makes the bizarre assertion that 'during the civil war, especially in Barcelona, the stadium [Les Corts] was the only place where freedom of speech could be exercised without fear'. In his autobiography, the former Barcelona manager Terry Venables notes: 'to defeat Real Madrid is like winning another battle in the civil war for [Barcelona] . . . when we won the league it was as if the Republican army was returning in triumph.' Who told Venables that? His president at Barcelona. And one recent British book on footballing rivalries sums up: 'In the 1936–1939 Spanish Civil War, Barcelona was a Republican stronghold, Madrid the base for Franco's eventually victorious Falangist rebels.'

Black and white certainties should often be painted in shades of grey but this is a step again – black as white and white as black.

To present Madrid as Franco's team and Barcelona as victims on the basis of the civil war is to stretch the boundaries of time and project on to the period between 1936 and 1939 events which actually occurred later, in different years and under different circumstances. It is to oversimplify complex occurrences and misrepresent simple ones; it is a gross misrepresentation of the Spanish Civil War and of the two cities' experience of it; it is to ignore the fact that Madrid's last democratically elected president was a Republican denounced as a 'red' and sentenced to life imprisonment by the Franco regime or the fact that when Barcelona's employees were forced to act fast to secure the club's survival it was the anarchist CNT-FAI, fighting for the Republic, that endangered them first, not the Franco régime. It also overlooks the fact that a similar, but ultimately more profound, takeover occurred at Madrid and the fact that Sunyol was not killed because he represented Barça but because he accidentally crossed the front line and represented the Republic, just as Sánchez Guerra represented the Republic.

There is a reason why Sunyol was killed on the Madrid front and it is not because he was a victim of Madrid. It was because that was where the war was fought, not in Barcelona. There is a reason why the Republican government eventually left Madrid – because that was the best way to escape the war. *Homage to Catalonia*, Orwell's evocative portrait of Barcelona at war, has helped construct an image of the city as the stage upon which the civil war was played, the book's very title cementing Catalonia in the collective consciousness as a centre of resistance. But Orwell himself wrote that in Barcelona the front came to be seen as a 'mythical far-off place to which young men disappeared' and expressed his disgust at the indifference towards the war in Barcelona, a disgust shared by those who came from Madrid where the danger was more present. 'Partly,' he wrote, '[that] was due to the remoteness of Barcelona from the actual fighting . . . partly it was a result of the safety of life in Barcelona, where there was little to remind one of the war except an occasional air raid. In Madrid, it was completely different.'

In 1999, Ernest Lluch, the Catalan former Socialist spokesman in parliament, told a TV programme celebrating Barça's centenary: '[Catalonia] lost the war.' That may well be true, but so too did Madrid. On the same programme the former Barcelona player Josep Valle insisted: 'Catalonia was the last region to fall.' Others have even referred to Barcelona as the last *Republic* to fall, even though there was only one Republic. Nicolau Causas, Vice-President from 1977 to 1989, claimed: 'Barcelona held out longest against General Franco and then suffered under his yoke until 1975.'

There is something a little macabre about comparing the suffering of cities, or peoples, especially in a civil war, and making moral judgements from that; about comparing a city's capacity for resistance with that of another and drawing sweeping conclusions. Yet that is the way in which the debate has often been posed – and inaccurately so. And that in turn forces a similarly framed corrective to be applied.

Catalonia suffered desperately. One chronicler described it as a 'city of the dead', a place the Catalan cellist Pau Casals likened to Dante's Inferno. But it was not the last place to fall. Madrid was. To suggest that Madrid gained from the civil war defies belief; to imply that Madrid was Franco's base during the war is wrong; to insinuate that Madrid did not fight Franco is absurd and offensive. Orwell wrote of revolution in Barcelona, but that does not make it more anti-fascist. Barcelona lived miles behind the lines; Madrid had the war on its doorstep. In Madrid, terrified civilians dug holes in the roads for tanks to fall into and built barricades across their streets.

The Nationalist General Emilio Mola boasted in the autumn of 1936 that he would soon be sipping coffee in Madrid's Puerta del Sol. A table was set up in defiance, in the middle of the square, with a cup and a coffee pot on it. 'For Mola', it said. He died in a plane crash soon after and Nationalist troops did not get there until after the war, three long years later. They did, though, swiftly reach the Casa del Camp and the University City – *inside* Madrid, less than ten kilometres from the Puerta del Sol. There, the Republicans, hurriedly mobilised and 'trained', fought faculty by faculty. And there they resisted for three terrible years, starving and scared, under siege. Someone had put up a sign by the statue of Neptune, god of the sea, saying: 'If you're not going to give me anything to eat, at least take this fork off me.' Madrid held Franco, Mussolini and Hitler's troops at bay; by comparison Barcelona barely saw them.

Think of those icons of the anti-fascist struggle and they were born in Madrid: *¡No pasarán!*; the famous battle cry of the Communist firebrand, La Pasionaria, 'it is better to die on your feet than live on your knees'; even the concept of fifth columnists. Asked which of the four columns advancing on Madrid was going to take the capital in the early months of the war, Mola replied: 'none of them; it will be the fifth column that is inside it.' He was wrong but once the war was lost Sánchez Guerra recalled looking out of the window to see a group of young men parade past in the blue shirts of the fascist Falange singing their *Cara al Sol* anthem. 'I was sure,' he noted, 'that I'd seen the same people singing the *Internationale* just weeks before.'

There was a fifth column in Barcelona too, of course, and Catalans who would profit from the regime. Some at Barcelona are aware of this. Although the suggestion from the current Barça director Silvio Elías that 'in 1939 or 1940, ninety per cent of the population of Catalonia was in favour of Franco' is a huge exaggeration, he is right to add: 'The civil war was a war between right and left . . . the Catalan factor was a small part of that, not decisive.' Meanwhile, even the fact that none of Barcelona's players returned to the Nationalist zone needs to be contextualised: in part, none of them did so simply because their homes were in the Republican zone: why would they return anywhere else? Others stayed away entirely, returning to Spain once the war was over – returning, that is, to what was by then Nationalist Spain.

The Spanish Civil War was a class war, an ideological war, a religious war and a nationalist war. Franco's troops harboured a bitter hatred towards Catalan and Basque separatism and that hatred would be brutally manifest when they gained control; there was a political glee in destroying and reconquering those territories, while rising up against the Republic had been provoked too by the fear of the break-up of Spain. But peripheral nationalism does not explain the outbreak of war and Madrid was certainly not the city of Franco until he set up his government there afterwards, just as every Spanish state had done since 1561.

In fact, after the war the new regime contemplated moving the Spanish capital to a more 'deserving' city like Valladolid, Burgos or Salamanca, cities where the Nationalists had always been welcomed and where they had not even had to fight. Ramón Serrano Súñer, Franco's brother-in-law, a Nazi sympathiser and simultaneously foreign and interior minister, insisted on the need to construct a 'new Madrid, more fitting for an historic Spain'. He described the *Ayuntamiento* building where Sánchez Guerra had unfurled the Republican flag in 1931 as 'the breeding ground for the worst of political germs'. It later became the home of Franco's secret police. Madrid remained the capital and would later become symbolic of centralism as it had always been, but it was a different Madrid – purged and 'purified'. Madrid and Barcelona both lost.

And that is the point. Above all, there is an inescapable fact which has too often eluded football fans: fifth columnists in both cities aside, Madrid and Barcelona were on the same side in the war, fighting against Franco's troops, even if their relationship was not always an easy one. Ultimately, the *Spanish* Republican government was based in Catalonia. In Barcelona, propaganda posters went up all over the city. One of them declared: *Defensar Madrid és defensar Catalunya.* To defend Madrid is to defend Catalonia.

Throughout the war, the Nationalists' sights were primarily fixed on Madrid. Troops only diverted away from the city in the autumn of 1936 when Franco ordered them to relieve the siege of the Alcázar in Toledo where General Moscardó was holed up with around one thousand soldiers and civilians, an emotive propaganda victory that did not change their ultimate aim. After the war, Moscardó was entrusted with the running of Spanish sport. Barcelona and Madrid would encounter him again and again.

Once Madrid fell, everything fell.

Franco's communiqué formally brought the war to a close on 1 April 1939. 'With the Red Army captured and disarmed, the Nationalist troops have reached their final military objectives,' it ran. 'The war is over.' That objective, as it had been throughout, was Madrid; Barcelona had fallen six weeks earlier. When Madrid did fall, exhausted and destroyed, Sánchez Guerra awaiting arrest, it could fight no more. The repression was vicious, with hundreds of killings daily in Madrid and Barcelona. Across Spain 200,000 were shot, 400,000 imprisoned.

One of the criticisms that is often levelled at Real Madrid is that it has washed over its civil war history. Compared to Barcelona, this is true. Much is made of the fact that the official history of Madrid published for their centenary, *100 Years of Legend*, deals with the war in a solitary paragraph: 'Barely a month later, civil conflict bloodies the country,' it runs. 'Three years (1936–1939) in which the clamour of the stadiums was silenced and hatred among all Spaniards was sparked. The life of the club was paralysed. The "old" ground of Chamartín suffered the consequences of the war. In the late spring of 1939 with the desolate panorama of the conflict, Real Madrid rose up from the ashes thanks to a group of fervent and enthusiastic *Madridistas*.' The book that celebrated the club's fiftieth anniversary, written in 1952 in the midst of the Franco régime, is similar. A single, short paragraph begins: 'Soon after, the civil war brings bloodshed to the country. The life of the club is paralysed.'

In this parsimony, critics see guilt. *Quien calla, otorga* as they say in Spain. He who opts to say nothing, reveals something; silence is a tacit confession. It may have taken a long time for Barcelona to tell Sunyol's story but Sánchez Guerra has not been rehabilitated at all, nor celebrated by the club he presided over, and much the same is true of their Catalan founders, the Padrós brothers, who are rarely lauded by the official narrative. Madrid had little interest in recovering or revising their wartime story during the dictatorship or indeed since; in fact, they have at times opposed it aggressively, even when it might benefit them to recover it. Why not undermine the accusation that they are Franco's team? Why not rehabilitate the memory of their Republican president or seek a democratic, anti-Franco heritage?

Madrid insist that their discourse is only about the football – the war and what came next is not so much an inconvenience as an irrelevance. And, at one level at least, there is not really a story of Real Madrid during the civil war waiting to be published, still less a guilty secret to hide. The accusations levelled at the book *100 Years of Legend* miss two key points: one, that it is an abridged, football-centric accompaniment to a far bigger institutional chronicle entrusted to a team of professional historians which *does* cover the war and two, that the lack of a wartime narrative also reflects something far more simple: the lack of a wartime story. 'Paralysed' is the right word. During the war Madrid barely played. And when they tried they were knocked back – by Barcelona.

It happened in October 1937. Madrid's coach Paco Bru was a former Barcelona player who had won the Spanish Cup with them in 1910 and had coached Spain to Olympic silver in Antwerp in 1920, as well as writing for *El Mundo Deportivo*. Given the impossibility of playing in Madrid after the outbreak of war, he approached the Catalan Football Federation about Madrid joining the Catalan Championship, due to start that autumn. At first, he received a warm reception in Catalonia, where smaller clubs like Badalona, Girona, Sabadell, Terrassa and Jupiter saw the potential economic benefits and where the Players' Union recalled Madrid's 'commitment to and affection for our beloved Catalonia' in honouring Sunyol. Declaring it their social duty to let Madrid play at a time of 'tragic abnormality', an act of generosity between *compañeros*, the union insisted that it would unite with Madrid and defend the club with all its 'moral and material power', adding: 'let it never be said that the gates of Catalan generosity were closed to Madrid's sportsmen.'

The agreement appeared close and Madrid even began to organise for players to move to a rented house in Masnou in Catalonia – an escape from the war in preparation for competition. There was just one condition: if Madrid won they still could not call themselves champions of Catalonia. But then at the last minute Barcelona blocked the move, the only Catalan club to do so. 'Those [other] clubs, for whom Madrid will always have the greatest of respect, voted without hesitation in Madrid's favour,' complained one newspaper in the capital, *Informaciones*. 'But Barcelona have played Madrid once again. All the declarations of friendship were a myth. The first chance they had, they forgot the fraternal ties that bond us and broke a friendship that should never have been broken.'

With that decision, Madrid virtually ceased to exist as a football club; Chamartín still had a function but not a functioning team. By the end of the war, Barcelona had played over one hundred games. Madrid hadn't played an official match, though they did compete in the Trofeo del Ejército del Centro, a competition run to honour the Republican army, and in a handful of friendlies. Three years of war had largely been three years of footballing inactivity.

The benefit was that, in the post-war period, Madrid were not so exposed to repression. Not only did Madrid, as a club and a concept, not automatically provoke Francoist suspicions like Barcelona did with its Catalan identity, there was also less to explain away. There were still reprisals, though. Ortega was killed by the regime in Alicante in 1940; Sánchez Guerra was tried and sentenced; those who carried out the *auto-incautación* under the guise of the anti-fascist fight had to explain themselves; a new board was vetted by the regime and some players were forced into exile. Madrid's president from 1943 until his death in 1978, Santiago Bernabéu moaned that 'at the end of the war they put half our team in prison'. That was not true; what was true was that of the twenty-man squad that Madrid had in June 1936, only four remained when the league restarted in 1939. At the end of the war, thanks to the money made on tour and deposited in a Paris bank account, Barcelona were perhaps the richest club in Spain. Madrid were among the poorest.

When Nationalist troops arrived at Barcelona's Les Corts stadium upon taking the city in February 1939, the caretaker Manel Torres pleaded with them not to damage the stadium. According to surviving accounts, he told the officer: 'This is a temple dedicated to sport and physical exercise. We have respected that throughout the war. Now, you decide.' The officer replied: 'We will not be responsible for damaging what you have preserved.' Over in Madrid, the club's social centre had been hit in the bombings while Chamartín, occasionally used for sporting festivals and military parades and as a dumping ground for war *materiel*, was all but destroyed. In April 1939, it began to be used as a processing centre for political prisoners, prior to them being taken to concentration camps and jails. Brickwork and masonry had been broken up, stands scavenged for firewood. 'The ground is unusable, the wooden seats and barriers have been ripped out and the pitch is in a deplorable state,' one employee wrote. 'We calculate that it would need around 300,000 pesetas to fix – and that's just a fantasy.' Juan Carlos Alonso, whose home had been bombed in the early months of the war, was living in the dressing room. In a corner of the pitch, he had grown a vegetable patch.

5

EXORCISM

Les Corts reopened its gates on 29 June 1939 for FC Barcelona versus Athletic Bilbao. More than a football match, it was an exorcism. Tickets had been sold at two pesetas for the terraces, three for the main stand, and the stadium was packed. At five o'clock, the referee led the two teams on to the pitch where they lined up in formation in the afternoon sun, facing the directors' box – Barcelona in blue and claret, Athletic in red and white. Among the authorities in attendance were the Barcelona president Joan Solé Juliá, General Álvarez Arenas, the Civil Guard captain Manuel Bravo Montero, the Catholic fascist intellectual Ernesto Giménez Caballero and representatives from the Italian navy, which had a ship docked in the port. The teams stood as the new Spanish flag – red and gold, embossed with the black imperial eagle of the Franco regime – was hoisted up the central pole. Alongside it, the flags of Fascist Italy and Nazi Germany, described in the media as 'friendly nations' with whom 'we have fought to save civilisation'.

As the flag was raised, the national anthem was played and fascist salutes were performed. According to one newspaper, 'a great patriotic sporting festival' had just begun and the anthem was greeted with 'the purest of emotions' by a 'fervent multitude, cleansed of rancour and the absurd localism of recent years'.

The players remained there for almost half an hour as a series of

speeches were made. Solé Juliá started his discourse with a shout of
'*¡Viva Franco! ¡Arriba España!*', Up Spain!, and ended with an appeal
for the members of FC Barcelona to again raise their arms in fascist
salute in honour of those who had fallen 'for God and the Fatherland'.
The new Barcelona president declared the club's 'faithful obedience
to the nation's hierarchy' and its sporting authorities, now led by
General José Moscardó, the 'glorious defender of Toledo's Alcázar'.
Solé Juliá also promised that the war wounded – from the Nationalist
side – would always have a place reserved for them at Les Corts. July
the twenty-ninth, he said, 'must forever be engraved upon our minds
as the day of liberation'.

During his speech, Giménez Caballero spoke of Barcelona's 'rancid
heritage', in which 'evil spirits' had sullied on-field glory with
'turbid and separatist politics'. Now Giménez Caballero declared that
to have been replaced by the 'smell of flowers and empire'. For the
sports newspaper *Marca*, this was an act of great solemnity carried out
with 'heightened patriotism': 'Barcelona, bathed in the River Jordan,
purified in its waters of patriotic feeling, have entered into footballing
normality.' The national anthem was played again and General Álvarez's
daughter took the honorary kick-off. Then a Barcelona team hastily
made up of players from a number of clubs and featuring only four
members of their own squad defeated Athletic 9-1.

FC Barcelona's connection to political Catalanism was long-standing.
Although the club's founder had been Swiss, Hans Gamper had
integrated into Catalan society and quickly adopted the Catalan version
of Hans to become Joan Gamper. He spoke in Catalan, minutes were
written up in Catalan and the club adopted *¡Visca Catalunya!* as a
celebratory cry. In 1919 Barça publicly backed proposals for a Catalan
statute – one of the very few Catalan institutions that did not was
Español – and on their silver anniversary in 1924, a prominent figure
from the Lliga Catalana described the club as the political and patriotic
representative of Catalonia, 'the living spirit of our land'.

In 1925, with Spain under the centralist military dictatorship of

General Miguel Primo de Rivera, that identity came to a head in a confrontation with the state when Barcelona played a friendly in honour of the choral society the Orfeó Catalá. A British ship had docked in the port and its band was invited along to play before the game but when they started the Spanish national anthem, the *Marcha Real*, it was met by whistles from the crowd. Unsure what to do, the band stopped and switched instead to 'God Save the King'. Immediately, the stadium erupted in applause.

The authorities were furious at 'an act of unclassifiable disaffection to the Fatherland made worse by the fact that it happened in front of foreigners'. Barcelona were suspended from all activity for six months and Gamper was 'invited' to leave the country. The military governor of Catalonia, Joaquín Milans del Bosch, issued a long communiqué laying down the sentence that left little doubt as to how the Primo de Rivera regime saw Barcelona, a club where 'there are many individuals who hold ideas contrary to the good of the Fatherland' and have 'a marked [anti-Spanish] tendency'. From the far right's point of view, worse was to follow when from 1935 Barcelona were presided over by Sunyol, who one Franco regime newspaper later insisted 'served the bastard aims of separatism and marxism', and the club was then 'sent to Mexico as a propagandist of the red cause'.

The civil war had been the 'iron surgery' the far right called for but violence continued afterwards too. Although physical repression was not significantly greater in Catalonia than in other parts of Spain, Franco embarked upon what one historian has described as a 'cultural genocide'. Anti-separatism had been present in the discourse of the right prior to the war and anti-Catalanism was implicit in the Spanish nationalism to which the victors subscribed. The first post-war civil governor of Barcelona claimed that Spain had 'risen with as much ferocity, or more, against the divisive Statutes of Autonomy as it did against Communism'. The regime had come, one official said, 'to Castilianise and Christianise'.

That policy may ultimately have proved counter-productive. 'If the regime had allowed Catalan as a cultural manifestation it would probably have encountered a more relaxed evolution and might well have been accepted by a greater part of [Catalan] society,' admits one current Barça director. In his view, the regime became a focal point, something against which sections of Barcelona and Catalan society could construct an identity. This argument only partly explains the phenomenon – Catalan nationalism existed before Franco and would continue after his death – but it is true that the regime gave many Catalans and Barcelona fans a tangible repressive 'other' against which to identify itself.

Catalan language was banned, books confiscated and burnt. Signs reminded Catalans to speak 'Christian' – as if Jesus had been born in Burgos rather than Bethlehem. Others declared: 'Don't bark, speak the language of Empire'. Even as late as 1966, the Catalan singer Joan Manuel Serrat pulled out of the Eurovision Song Contest after he was banned from singing part of the song 'La, la, la' in Catalan. His replacement, Massiel, sang the same song in Castilian Spanish and won the competition, beating Cliff Richard's 'Congratulations' into second place. Franco had bought off the judges. By the time the dictator died in 1975, less than 5 per cent of books were published in Catalan; forty years earlier, almost a quarter had been.

The repression of manifestations of Catalanism necessarily required attention to be focused upon FC Barcelona. Here, the comparison with Español was telling. *Marca* wrote immediately after the war of 'one club, Español, run by people well known for their patriotism', and another, Barcelona, that 'always sought to bring a Catalan tone to the heart of the club', using 'sport as a mouthpiece and means of propaganda for an insufferable region'. Such crimes could only be cured in blood: 'In Catalonia the battle was never noble and sincere; it was anger let loose, a struggle to control the Federation and sink a club that in Catalan lands had the "nerve" to call itself Deportivo Español,' the paper insisted. 'One day, the noble and victorious sword of Franco, held in his strong, secure arm, was raised up – and brought down with all the weight of reason and justice.'

Few doubted what 'justice' meant. The dictatorship used the language of purification and redemption to describe and justify a violent repression that was systematic and overwhelming. Nationalist troops shot more in the rearguard than at the front and fear had been a conscious policy from the start, Franco famously telling the American journalist Jay Allen that he would achieve total victory, even if it meant killing 'half of Spain'. After April 1939, the desire to shape society through imposition remained with the construction of a state machinery that aspired to totalitarian control. According to the figures gathered by Judge Baltasar Garzón in 2009 as he built a case against the dictatorship for crimes against humanity, 114,266 people were assassinated away from the battlefields between July 1936 and December 1951 and most experts consider the figure conservative. Closer to 200,000 were in fact killed in political repression and thousands more fled into exile.

Of the 114,266 identified by Garzón, 2,400 were killed in Catalonia, 2,995 in Madrid. No sooner had Nationalist troops entered Barcelona than killings began on Montjuic and among those shot was the president of the Catalan Generalitat Lluis Companys: arrested by German military police in Brittany and taken back to Barcelona, he was killed in October 1940. Nicolau Causas, Barcelona's vice-president from 1978 until 1999, was arrested after the war and spent seventy-two days in prison. He heard cellmates being taken out and shot nightly.

Between 1938 and the mid-1940s, a case was effectively brought against the entire population; the Law of Political Responsibilities demanded that everyone prove loyalty and usefulness to 'Spain', purging those who could not. The first edition of *Marca* was published in Nationalist-held San Sebastián on 21 December 1938, its front page offering 'a raised arm to all Spain's sportsmen'. Inside, General Moscardó explained his plans for sport. Moscardó had commanded advances on Madrid and Catalonia, and was now the head of the Spanish Olympic Committee and the National Sports Council, the DND, effectively the sports minister. The phrase that summed up his approach was simple: *todo en función del estado*, everything depending on the state – reminiscent of Benito Mussolini's famous definition of Fascism: 'everything within the state, nothing outside the state, nothing against the state'. Not even football.

Especially not football. Exorcism was just the start. Moscardó spoke of the need to 'know the names . . . and know what everyone did and what they failed to do'. He wrote: 'We will name the presidents and when there is a fundamental mistake that person will become *non grata* and his replacement will be implacable.' Military men occupied key positions throughout the state machinery and in all the major sporting institutions. The designs of the regime were totalitarian and organisationally football was turned on its head: from bottom up, it was now top down. Clubs, represented by their presidents, did not come together to create a Federation; the Federation, a representative of the regime, effectively created clubs – not just vetting presidents but naming them.

A good illustration of those aims is found in a previously undiscovered letter that Sancho Dávila sent to Moscardó upon giving up the presidency of the Federation in 1954, a position he had held since the end of the war. In the letter, which he signs off with the *de rigueur* salute 'For God, for Spain and the National Syndicalist Revolution', he looks back on his time occupying a post in which it was his duty to 'impose Falangist [fascist] postulates in all we do', 'eliminating all those who had acted against our Movement', 'putting Falangist comrades into positions at the Federation [and] not just in the directive committee', and 'impregnating the Spanish national team get-togethers with our beliefs'.

'I have always tried,' he noted, 'to ensure that presidents and members of clubs, even when elected, were those with a genuine affection for our movement.'

The change in the nature and identity of Spain's football clubs was hugely significant. All of Spain's clubs were, by definition, Francoist – at least to start with. Barcelona's interim president was later replaced, in March 1940, by Enrique Piñeyro de Queralt, the Marqués de Vega de Asta. A military man, auxiliary to Moscardó, police reports called him an 'excellent person' but he was not representative of pre-war Barça and he had had nothing to do with the club before. 'Our job,' he said upon assuming the presidency, 'is to show just how deep into our hearts the glorious exploits of the invincible *Caudillo* have penetrated – the hearts of good Spaniards born in Catalonia who feel only love and admiration for the immortal destiny of our [Spanish] Fatherland.'

Piñeyro's entire board was made up of people formally defined by the authorities as 'loyal to the regime'. A former *socio* at Español, Manuel Bravo Montero was one of those on the board. Chief of a secret police force set up in the city to oversee the 'normalisation' process, Montero expressed his pleasure at seeing a new Barcelona – 'clean, renewed, polished', at last 'ready to fulfil its true mission'. By 1948 Barcelona had almost 25,000 members and even celebrated semi-democratic presidential elections, the first club to do so, but no matter how emasculated they became, however effectively domesticated and purged, the suspicion and mistrust never entirely went away. Barcelona's different status, their 'opposition' to Spain and the dictatorship, was not just projected *by* the club at various times and with varying degrees of intensity, but projected *on to* the club.

Surveillance continued for years. In 1948 police files described Agustí Montal senior, the first post-war president hand-picked by the regime, as a man of 'good morality'. Having escaped the Republican zone and crossed into the Nationalist zone where he took part in military espionage, Narcís de Carreras, the director who would become president in 1968, was described as 'a supporter of the *Glorioso Movimiento Nacional*'. And Martí Carretó, the director who became president in 1952, was defined as 'indifferent', but his family too had been victims of the 'reds' during the civil war. All of which poses questions that prove problematic when it comes to defining Barcelona and Madrid, or indeed any club under any dictatorship: what is a football club? *Who* is it? What does it really represent? And what is voluntary and what is enforced?

Purification was profound, the purge widespread. In July 1939 maximum wages were stipulated to ensure that no player could earn more than a colonel and they required a licence to play. In order to apply, a player had to make a declaration of loyalty to the regime, with references from members of the new fascist state party, the Falange. The president of the Federation during the civil war, General Julián Troncoso, had already warned: 'the first player to break the rules will be wiped from the sporting map' and Moscardó announced 'a vigorous purge of all sporting elements.' No one could hold any kind of post if they were under investigation by the 'courts'. That was a broad category. According to the Law of Political Responsibilities, you could be tried with military rebellion for opposing the regime 'actively' or 'passively' – and that could be defined by a series of nebulous, intentionally vague and broad-ranging 'crimes' such as having belonged to any of the parties of the Popular Front, a trade union, or having displayed 'grave inactivity' during the war. Travelling to Mexico on a football tour certainly counted. Josep Raich, Domènec Balmanya and Josep Escolá were banned and not cleared to play until 1941. Hundreds of players were processed and handed bans from six months to six years – or worse.

One newspaper suggested that Barcelona should be renamed España and, although that did not happen, in January 1940 they were obliged to Castilianise their name, from Football Club Barcelona to Barcelona Club de Fútbol, while the four bars of the Catalan flag on their badge were reduced to two. They adjusted without complaint: there was no one to complain, no one to complain to and a state that punished dissent. The latter point is reinforced by the fact that Moscardó even laid down strict rules for sports media. Among the key instructions was that reporters could not question the referee because of his status as a figure of authority – effectively an extension of the state. A monument was later erected at Les Corts to honour the Nationalist war dead, Barcelona set up radio broadcasts to the División Azul so that supporters fighting 'heroically' alongside Hitler's troops could be kept informed of results back home and Moscardó was made an honorary member in 1943.

Barcelona were not alone here: most clubs erected similar monuments and all non-Castilian names were changed – Athletic Club Bilbao became Atlético, for example – and even the language of football, which had been adapted from English, was nationalised: *árbitro* was to be used rather than *referí*, *fuera de juego* rather than *offside* or *orsay*, *saque de esquina* rather than *córner*.

Despite the absence of a monarchy, Madrid recovered their 'Real' title but were also forced to Castilianise their name by placing 'Club de Fútbol' *after* Real Madrid and they were not exactly victors. The Falangist Jacinto Miquelarena wrote in 1938 of football during the Republic being 'a red orgy of the most petty and vile regional passions' in which even Madrid fans were 'regionalists, mental retards when it came to the nation'. At the civil war's close there had been fears that Madrid CF would disappear altogether. There was little money, the stadium was ruined, membership had dwindled and the club still had to undergo a purge. Twenty members of staff, from secretaries to accountants, caretakers to cleaners, were made to fill in a questionnaire saying where they were on 18 July and what they had done during the war – they were asked what political parties they had belonged to and whether they had joined any trade unions. Coronado prepared certificates of good conduct for all of them. He and Carlos Alonso, the two men who had overseen the *auto-incautación*, were ratified as members of a new board named in May 1940 yet, in October of the same year, the secretary of the Castilla Football Federation requested a formal report on Coronado himself to be carried out by the regime, which ultimately cleared him.

A group that built up around General Adolfo Meléndez, Pedro

Parages, Antonio Santos Peralba, Luis Urquijo, Santiago Bernabéu and Pablo Hernández Coronado actively sought *socios* and financial support from among the elites that had helped to develop the club in the 1920s and 1930s. Members were brought together in a general assembly in late April 1939, while discussions with the air force about a fusion were scrapped because of demands that Madrid change their name and their colours. Instead, the air force merged with Atlético Madrid to become Atlético Aviación, an agreement that brought them the pick of the best players, access to military vehicles and facilities, plus discounts on fuel at a time of desperate shortage. In early 1943, an opportunistic representative of the navy would approach Madrid, telling them: 'as Atlético are the air force team, you should be the navy team.' Madrid give them use of the club's training pitch at Chamartín, which was also lent out to infantry battalions three times a week in 1944.

Slowly, Madrid rebuilt a team. Jacinto Quincoces, José Ramón Sauto, Simón Lecue, and José Mardones, all members of their pre-war squad, were joined by ex-Atlético player Juan Antonio Ipiña, while there were other signings too – like José Luis Espinosa, Enrique Esquiva, Jesús Alonso and Sabino Barinaga. Politically and geographically, Madrid now had a significant advantage over Barcelona: being based in the capital helped remove at a stroke the suspicion of separatism and ultimately brought Madrid both physically and symbolically closer to the heart of power, facilitating the construction of relationships, some of which had already been both formally and informally forged prior to the war.

At the same time, Madrid's history was reinterpreted to fit the new era, adapted according to political expedience. While Barcelona's wartime self-requisitioning made it an enemy of the regime, Madrid's made it a victim – essentially the same act interpreted in entirely contrasting ways. Madrid's pre-1935 heritage and the political predilections of those running the club now, men who *had* been there before, meant that doing that was straightforward. An article soon appeared lauding the club's resurgence and the sentiment behind it. 'Because [Madrid] was, in the noble sense of the word, a gentleman and an aristocrat of a club, it was condemned to disappear,' it ran. 'The implacable red tide pursued it but the attempt failed thanks to the skilful manoeuvres [i.e. the *auto-incautación*] of a handful of enthusiastic *Madridistas* . . . [now,] true sportsmen have been up to the task of reorganising the club, bringing together an impressive committee made up of some of the most prestigious members of the Madrid footballing world which, having first carried out the job of purifying the club, eliminating disobedient and suspicious supporters' groups and fans, crystallised in a meeting of true lovers of the traditions of Madrid and of good sport.'

The article concluded: 'let us remember the former directors, *señores* Valero Rivera and Gonzalo Aguirre, assassinated [in the Republican zone]', providing Madrid, at a stroke, with an anti-Republican heritage. There was not a word about Sánchez Guerra.

Madrid played their first game at Chamartín on 1 October 1939, coinciding with the third anniversary of Franco's naming as *Caudillo* within the Nationalist zone. The match was preceded by a mass and a memorial service for those who had died fighting for the Nationalists. Although Madrid beat Atlético Aviación, it would not happen often in the immediate post-war era. Atlético won the first two league titles after the civil war, 1939–40 and 1940–41. In the first of those seasons Barcelona finished ninth of twelve and Madrid finished fourth. Meanwhile, Madrid reached the final of the Copa del Generalísimo. The result was celebrated in a song written by Guillermo Paylé, which projected victory as a triumph of the new regime.

The twist is that Madrid did not win, they lost. 'Two things bring glory to the colours of Spain,' the song ran. 'The *Caudillo*'s sword and Español's feat.'

Two years later Barcelona won the 1942 Copa del Generalísimo, beating Atlético Bilbao, 4-3. The final was held in Madrid – as it would be throughout the dictatorship, barring those rare occasions when Franco was not in the capital, in which case it was moved so that he could attend. For all the suspicions that surrounded the club, four thousand Barcelona fans made the trip and the cup was handed over to Raich by Franco, prompting *El Mundo Deportivo* to declare: 'Barcelona and Catalonia could not aspire to more and our jubilation could not be better expressed than like this: *¡Arriba España!* Hurrah for Barcelona Club de Fútbol! *¡Viva Generalísimo Franco!*' The triumphant team returned to Barcelona where they were met by the mayor, Miguel Mateu, and president Piñeyro dedicated the triumph to 'the glory of Spanish sport'.

It was Barcelona's first final since losing to Madrid in 1936. They did not retain the cup because the following season Madrid beat them en route. The teams met on 13 June 1943 and it finished Real Madrid 11 Barcelona 1. Yes, Real Madrid *eleven*, Barcelona one, a scoreline one paper called 'as absurd as it was abnormal'. Eleven-one remains the biggest ever victory for Madrid and an official history of the club calls it 'majestic', referring to the players as 'heroes', but there have been relatively few mentions of the game and it is not a result that has been particularly celebrated in Madrid. Indeed, the 11-1 occupies a far more prominent place in Barcelona's history. This was the game that first formed the identification of Madrid as the team of the dictatorship and Barcelona as its victims – a story still shrouded in mystery and crucial to the development of the rivalry.

It all started the week before when Barcelona won the first leg 3-0. Madrid complained that the referee, José Fombona Fernández, had allowed Barcelona's first goal to stand despite it being preceded by a foul, criticised the penalty he gave for their second and insisted that the third had been offside. Barcelona supporters were not happy either, whistling throughout. Some have retrospectively tried to infuse the fans' reaction with a romantic touch, a hint of rebellion against Franco, insisting that they were whistling the dictatorship. The truth was more mundane: they whistled Madrid, whom they accused of employing roughhouse tactics, and Fombona for allowing them to. In a letter to the football authorities Barcelona later insisted that the reaction of their fans had not been pre-prepared but was a response to Madrid's 'hard play'. Yet the fact that Les Corts whistled and booed was unusual at the time. Risky, too. The Federation fined Barcelona 2,500 pesetas.

A campaign began in Madrid. 'The press officer at the DND, and *ABC* newspaper wrote all sorts of scurrilous lies, really terrible things, winding up the Madrid fans like never before,' recalled the Barcelona player Josep Valle. But the journalist most associated with those events was Eduardo Teus. Writing in the Catholic daily *Ya*, the former Real Madrid goalkeeper described Les Corts as 'the boiling cauldron'. The fact that the phrase has become so famous gives an idea of the power it carried, however tame it sounds now. It was, he added, the ground itself that made Madrid concede two of the three goals, goals that were 'totally unfair'.

Even Teus, whose match report is even more laughably partisan than they are nowadays, a page packed with one whinge after another, admitted that Madrid had 'above all played hard, *bronco* and with edge, fighting with body and soul', employing 'courage', 'bravery and toughness'. He eulogised Madrid's 'energetic destructive play' as the correct tactic – one in which they 'closed up and sent the ball as far forward as possible at the first opportunity' – because 'Barcelona are not a team that reacts well in the face of the rough, tough, unpleasant football of cup games'. Madrid, he insisted, did not go to Les Corts to entertain but to put themselves in a good position for the return leg; they 'had not come to be gallant and refined'.

If that was fair, the fans' reaction was not. 'Les Corts thundered and Les Corts scared Fombona,' Teus wrote. 'There is no other way to explain it. Fombona, frightened, gave a goal in a scramble and a penalty and blew the end of the first half a fifth of a second before [Madrid's] Barinaga shot. And even then the imposing thunder rolled round Les Corts, tumbling down from the stands to reduce Fombona to nothing. My God! What more did they want!'

One thing Teus did *not* write in that article is the overtly political phrase that has been repeated in histories over and over again – that in whistling Madrid, Barcelona's fans had whistled the 'representatives of Spain'.

Teus censored the behaviour of Barcelona's fans but what he really did was encourage Madrid's fans to act in the same way. Far from turning the other cheek, he demanded that Madrid hit back, dressed in the language of victimhood and fair play. The tactic is a familiar one, often still employed on both sides of the Madrid–Barça divide: decry behaviour where the greatest fault is not so much the act as the actor as a justification for doing exactly the same thing. 'Madrid are not giving up the tie for lost,' Teus wrote. 'Ah, if [only] Chamartín would help Madrid on Sunday like the "boiling cauldron" of Les Corts helped [Barcelona] in the first half! We do not demand that the team from the region are greeted with anything other than the same passionate, forceful and influential support that Barcelona had . . . When will that be possible in Madrid?'

The answer, as Teus had hoped, was simple: a week later.

Reports talked up the affront of Les Corts, accusing Barcelona of preparing an 'ambush'; now it was time to prepare one back. Barça's president described the campaign as 'terrible propaganda' and sent a letter to Real Madrid seeking to calm the atmosphere. In the letter, conserved in Barcelona's archives, Piñeyro claimed to hope 'with all his heart' that Madrid's fans would show Barcelona's how to behave and insisted that 'the whistling to which Madrid were subjected in our stadium was totally drowned out by the great ovation that the 38,200 fans gave the club that, after our own, is our supporters' favourite'.

Madrid did not reply but they did release a statement. Ostensibly designed to cool passions, aware of the implications of inciting trouble under a regime obsessed with public order, it could be interpreted as seeking quite the opposite. It declared: 'The more incorrect one set of fans' behaviour, the less sporting it is to try to emulate it.

[But] let us make it clear that this does not mean that we are curbing the enthusiasm of the *Madrileño* fans, whose support we have so often missed: we just want to alert them that they should not allow themselves to be carried along by misbehaviour that could only damage Real Madrid and the good name of the *público* in the capital of Spain.'

Rather than prevent anger, the statement aimed 'to channel it.'

Madrid channelled it all right. Ramón Mendoza, Real Madrid's president between 1985 and 1995, was sixteen at the time. The memory of that game never left him. He recalled: 'The message got through that those fans who wanted to could go to El Club bar on Calle de la Victoria where Madrid's social centre was. There, they were given a whistle.' Others had whistles handed to them with their tickets: small, tin whistles that, in huge numbers, made a hell of a racket. The noise, said Mendoza, was 'extraordinary'.

Barcelona's hotel was in Aranjuez, to the south of the city, because staying in Madrid itself had been considered too risky, while their supporters had been banned from travelling. As the team left the hotel they were whistled and insulted. Stones were thrown at the bus and when they arrived at Chamartín the 'welcome' was deafening. It was the whistling that most stuck in the mind of those who were there – the sheer noise. 'The atmosphere was very strong,' Josep Valle recalled; 'no sooner were we in the stadium than the stewards were saying to us: "you're going to lose". We went out on to the pitch and there the whistling was monumental.'

'Five minutes before the game had started, our penalty area was already full of coins, five and ten centime coins that weren't even legal tender any more,' Mariano Gonzalvo remembered. Barcelona's goalkeeper Lluis Miró, rarely approached his line – when he did, he was within reach of the supporters behind the goal, armed with stones. As Francesc Calvet told the story: 'They were shouting: *Reds! Separatists!* . . . a bottle just missed Sospedra that would have killed him if it had hit him. It was all set up.'

Down in the Barcelona dugout, Ángel Mur watched events unfold: 'I genuinely thought my eardrums were going to burst,' he said. 'When I took up my place on the bench, a policeman came up to me and said: "Today you're going to lose". It was not a question. Chamartín was like the Roman Colosseum and we were the Christians. Another armed police lieutenant spent the whole game calling me a Catalan dog and a red separatist, and all the rest of it. When I got up to treat an injured player, he grabbed me and told me to sit back down again.' Eventually, Mur responded in kind, at which point Piñeyro intervened. The policeman told the Barcelona president to shut up or he would be arrested, spitting: 'Come with me . . .' 'I beg your pardon?' replied Piñeyro, who was close to General Moscardó, 'I think you'll find it's *you* coming with *me*.'

Almost seventy years later, Mur's son confirms the scene: he has heard his father tell the story so many times. It is an occasion that marked Ángel Mur senior forever. This was 1943, in the midst of the Second World War, and although the tide was turning in Europe, Franco had still not backed away fully from his Axis partners and certainly had not yet sought rapprochement with the Allies. Secret police and denouncements were common. The repression was ferocious; life was cheap and imprisonment cheaper. The fear was genuine. Striker César Rodríguez said the players were 'paralysed'; it was, remembered Valle, 'incredible'. At throw-ins, fans grappled with players and bottles were hurled. The match report in the newspaper *La Prensa* spoke of Barcelona's 'demoralisation' and their 'impotence' – 'tied up in knots by the coercion of the *público*, they surrendered'. 'I'll never forget that,' the Barcelona player Josep Escolà, said: 'they set an ambush and then what happened, happened.'

What happened was this. Real Madrid went 2-0 up within half an hour. The third goal brought with it a red card for Barcelona's Benito García after he made what Calvet later claimed was a 'completely normal tackle'. 'At which point,' Madrid's José Corona recalled, 'they got a bit demoralised'; 'at which point,' countered Mur, 'we thought:

"go on then, score as many as you want".' Madrid scored in the 31st minute and again in minutes 33, 35, 39, 43 and 44. Six goals in a quarter of an hour, as well as two ruled out for offside, made it 8-0. Basilo de la Morena had been caught out by the speed of the goals: the man in charge of the scoreboard at Chamartín had climbed up the ladder before the game and had only taken the numbers he thought he would need – one to five.

At half-time, Barcelona's players decided that they were not going out for the second half. That was when, according to an interview Valle and Calvet gave *La Vanguardia* in May 2000, a colonel appeared in the dressing room and warned that they had a duty to carry on. 'He threatened us and said literally: "Go back out on to the pitch or you're all going to jail",' Calvet said. Calvet later added an important detail when he told the story to his biographer Guillem Gómez, noting that when he questioned why there were not more police on duty given the atmosphere, he was told: 'shut up, obey, go out there and play . . . and lose!'

They had little choice. 'Obviously, we chose to play on. Those were not times for joking. All we wanted was for it to be over – and as quickly as possible,' Valle said. Three more made it 11-0 before Barcelona scored in the last minute – a goal it is tempting to read as a last symbolic act of defiance, *La Prensa* describing it as a 'reminder that there was a team there who knew how to play football and that if they did not do so that afternoon, it was not exactly their fault'.

Whose fault was it, then? The author of that *La Prensa* article was a certain Juan Antonio Samaranch – later the head of the IOC. A Catalan, yes, but an Español fan and a career fascist, a card-carrying member of the Francoist state party. It was to be the last article he wrote for almost a decade. Samaranch wrote about the 'exaggerated' press campaign that followed the first leg, Madrid's failure to act with the 'gentlemanliness' of which they always boasted and the behaviour of the Chamartín crowd. He also questioned a referee who 'saw which way the wind blew'.

'There could have been many more goals, maybe twenty,' Samaranch wrote. 'Barcelona did not exist and the same would have happened to any team. In that atmosphere and with a referee who wanted to avoid any complications, it was humanly impossible to play . . . they accepted this wealth of adversity with a smile, as if saying to their rivals: "We know we can't play, so you play any way you like".

'If the *azulgranas* had played badly, really badly, the scoreboard would still not have reached that astronomical figure. The point is that they did not play at all,' Samaranch continued. 'There is no need to look for guilty men, because there were none on the pitch. Barcelona simply were not seen all afternoon. That was the best thing they could do in the circumstances. That's the way it ended and that's the [only] way it could end.'

The Federation was furious. Both clubs were fined 2,500 pesetas and, although Barcelona appealed, it made no difference. Piñeyro resigned in protest, complaining of 'a campaign that the press has run against Barcelona for a week and which culminated in the shameful day at Chamartín'. That a man considered safe by the regime should speak out so strongly was in itself telling. As for Samaranch, to use his own rather euphemistic words, he was 'invited' by the regime to leave journalism. He did not put pen to paper again until the Helsinki Olympics in 1952. Teus, by contrast, carried on regardless.

And yet even Samaranch may have stopped short, at most hinting at the real story behind that defeat with that reference to 'circumstances' and the suggestion that there was literally nothing Barcelona could do, there being no one to blame *on the field*. In his history of Barcelona, the club secretary Rossend Calvet made an oblique reference to what might have happened. 'I was there at Chamartín watching the game and in the dressing room allocated to Barcelona,' he wrote, 'and at Les Corts [in the first leg] . . . no police agent, real or false, came into the Madrid dressing room to inhibit their players, with his recommendation of good conduct; no match official took it upon himself to warn the [players] beforehand of the severity with which he would act; and nor was there some Machiavellian type who handed out ten or twelve thousand whistles to orchestrate the performance of the Madrid players; nor were there those in the directors' box who, with an ironic smile, made a point of saying how happy that result made them.' The 'unlike in Madrid' went without saying.

The key revelation was the first one – the suggestion that someone came into the dressing room before the game and said something that affected Barcelona's performance. Someone who coerced them or threatened them. Or told them to lose.

According to some versions of the story, it was a policeman; according to others, a Civil Guard officer or even Moscardó himself. There are other versions that suggest it was only the referee who came into the dressing room pre-game – but that he was acting on behalf of the authorities, so the threat came laced with menace. At the time, it was normal for the captain to visit the referee's dressing room before the game but not the other way round. Given the tense build-up to the game, it was natural enough that the authorities should deliver a message imploring players not to cause problems. Yet, if so, it is telling that those instructions were delivered only to Barcelona not to Madrid – there has never been any suggestion of a visit to the home dressing room – and, given the context, it would hardly be surprising if such 'recommendations' provoked fear.

There are other versions of the story in which the authority that entered the dressing room reminded Barcelona's players that they had only been allowed to play professional football because of the 'generosity' of the regime, which had forgiven them for their political behaviour; in still more versions, they were reminded of their former lack of patriotism. For players like Josep Raich, who had only just returned following a ban, that was a threat that would have been very real. All the more so if, as some accounts suggest, the man who came into the dressing room was the Director of State Security, the Conde de Mayalade, José Finat y Escrivá. Finat collaborated with the Nazis during the Holocaust while ambassador in Berlin, he had been involved in the brutal beating of the gay singer Miguel de Molina the previous year and was close to Franco's brother-in-law, Ramón Serrano Súñer. He had been a prominent member of the fascistic Juventud de Acción Popular before the war. He was not a man to cross. He was also, incidentally, a friend of Santiago Bernabéu.

Whoever it was, it is impossible to conclude with certainty the message and the effect it had on the players. No film exists and drawing conclusions from photographs is fraught with risk. Not surprisingly, there is no other reference to the visit in contemporary press reports, while police files have either not survived or were never written in the first place. But something almost certainly happened to help provoke such a dramatic turnaround in the result from one match to the next and there can be little doubt that the atmosphere would have carried a threat that is virtually impossible to imagine today. Yet there is no specific mention of the visit to the dressing room in the series broadcast on Catalan TV to mark Barça's centenary in 1999 and, despite trailing the fact that they would reveal the 'true story' of that night, neither Valle nor Benito, both interviewed for the programme, refer directly to it. Another possibility arises. Memory is an imperfect tool: could the half-time visit – which may partly explain the attitude of the regime, but not the eight-goal lead Madrid already held – have been mixed up over the years? Could *that* visit, relatively frequent in public events at the time, have become remembered as a pre-match one?

Barcelona's team that day was Miró, Benito, Curta, Raich, Rosalench, Calvet, Sospedra, Escolà, Martín, César and Bravo. None of them are still alive. No one is left from the day Real Madrid beat Barcelona 11-1.

Actually, that is not entirely true. Fernando Argila is ninety-two. He has eight children and twenty-five grandchildren, one of whom plays handball for Spain, and he lives in a small flat in Castelldefells, just south of Barcelona. Although there are moments of forgetfulness and repetition, he is lucid, sharp. There is a mischievous humour about him and he is in rude health. 'I've got a dangerous past,' he laughs. It is some past: it's hard to believe that he was born way back in 1921 as he walks steadily from living room to study and back again. Black and white photographs dot the walls: team-mates from Atlético Madrid, Real Oviedo, Barcelona and Spain. He was handsome, powerful too. 'I never got injured,' he says, looking at his only battle wounds – thumbs that are bent upwards.

Argila was a goalkeeper who dominated his area. Photos show him leaping, catching the ball. Iker Casillas, he says, 'has great vision but he always pushes the ball away, to the left or the right. I didn't: I caught it. I never wore gloves. Only woollen ones if it was raining.' Admiring girls, his daughter reveals, used to knit him jumpers to wear during games and bring them to the club. Playing in Oviedo, jumpers were welcome: it was cold and it rained often. 'A slug of cognac sorted that out,' he grins. 'Those were different times.' Journeys in butane-fuelled buses took an age: from one end of Spain to another was a matter of days not hours.

He stands before a Barcelona line-up from around 1943, a black and white photograph on the wall, going through them one by one. Eleven men, hair slicked back, locked in time: 'Sospedra . . . Escolà . . . Martín . . . Balmanya . . . they're all dead now.'

At Barcelona, Argila was the *pequeñito*, the little one. Fifteen when the civil war broke out, he did not fight, and joined the club soon after the end of the war. He was a Barcelona player between 1941 and 1943 and although he did not play much, making only twenty appearances, he did win the Copa del Generalísimo in 1942. A huge leather album containing black and white photos sits on the living-room table. The triumphant team pose, leaning against the bonnet of the team bus, with big collars and bigger lapels.

Argila coincided with some of the greats. He played against László Kubala – one photo is annotated: 'Kubala scores, despite Argila's valiant stretch' – and with César, Barcelona's official all-time top scorer until Leo Messi inevitably overtook him at just twenty-four, but he rated Paulino Alcántara, their unofficial top scorer, even more highly.

He recalls Ben Barak and Isidro Lángara – 'he had some shot on him: he got the ball and practically burst it' – but, strikingly, he does not really recall Alfredo Di Stéfano, whom he briefly coached at Español. It was Alcántara who recommended Argila to Oviedo although Argila always refers to him by his nickname *Romperredes*: Net Buster.

These days, Oviedo are down in Spain's Second Division B and Argila is not confident that they will be back. An amateur at Barcelona, his salary at Oviedo was, he says, 'enough'. Exactly how much, he can't remember. 'Now, you find a kid at La Masia who is talented and he's already got a lawyer. They've got a house for him and one for his dad too.' He has met Messi, at the tennis club across the road, but never seen him play. 'I don't go now,' he says, 'and wouldn't even if they invited me.' Which they have. He wonders where Madrid and Barcelona can go next: 'they have good players,' he says, 'too many good players.'

So what of the rivalry between Madrid and Barcelona?

'There was no rivalry,' he says. Not, at least, until that game.

That day, Argila watched from on the bench – Lluis Miró played ahead of him – and the sound of the whistles is still with him. Again and again, he returns to the same theme, performing the actions: his hand to his mouth, a blowing motion: '*Peep! Peep! Peep!*'

'I was the reserve goalkeeper,' he says, 'and they put eleven past Miró. They went to the fans and gave them whistles. One of those whistles made of strips of tin, you know? *Peep! Peep! Peep!* We were there, thinking: "What are they doing?" What *is* that?' We won the first game 3-0 and then they scored eleven . . .'

Was the first game especially bad? Was it dirty?

'No, no . . .'

How do you explain the huge difference between the two scores, then?

'*Pues, políticamente.* Politically. Politically, it was something.'

There's a moment's silence and then Argila continues. 'A policeman came in and said that nothing [bad] could happen.'

Into the Barcelona dressing room?

'Yes. I was there. Who was it? I don't know. A policeman, a lieutenant or an I-don't-know-what from the Civil Guard. And he said . . . not that we had to lose . . . but that nothing must happen because there was political tension.'

Was he armed?

'Yes. I don't know if he did it [said it] to the referee or if he did it to the players, but he did it. He also told the referee: "make sure nothing happens". And he [the referee] sent off Benito. We had hardly started and he sent him off.'

What for?

'I don't know. *Because.*'

Assuming the message from this visitor was in fact directed at the referee not the players, would it still reach them?

'Of course. And the atmosphere . . .'

It is striking that it is the atmosphere, the whistling, more than the visit that sticks in the mind – and not just that of Argila. The noise must have been deafening; the impact far greater than it now appears seventy years later. It is the whistles to which he turns most readily, unprompted. The action: '*Peep! Peep! Peep!*'

Brought back to the scene in the dressing room, he continues: 'He came in, a Civil Guard, a lieutenant or something . . . I was just a kid, eh.'

Was that frightening?

'Man, of course.'

It has been suggested that Barcelona's players were warned that some of them were only playing because of the 'generosity of the regime' . . .

'It was soon [after the war], lots of people had gone [during the war] . . . but . . . I don't know.'

Did that change the rivalry?

'Of course. *Then* there was rivalry, afterwards. It was all politics. Power. *Potencial.* Economic power, too.'

Did that game make people in Barcelona see Madrid as Franco's team?

'I didn't think of it like that. Look, I'm apolitical. I see football as a sport; that's unthinkable for me. But for others . . .'

Argila's voice trails off. Again come the actions. Hand to his mouth, blowing hard. There is something almost comical about it, a look of amusement on Fernando Argila's face. *Peep! Peep! Peep!*

'And that's how it happened. Afterwards, we just wanted to forget about it. Get away from there and forget. Miró let in eleven. He had a tobacconists'. I never saw him again.'

6

DON SANTIAGO

Barcelona's bus left Chamartín on the evening of the 11-1 and headed straight to Catalonia, a policeman telling the driver: 'get on to the Castellana and don't stop for anything.' 'We did *exactly* as he said,' Calvet recalled. Four months later it was back and this time could hardly be more different – on the surface at least. Lluis Miró, the goalkeeper who conceded eleven, was no longer with them but Curta, Raich, Rosalench, Escolà, Martín and César were. When they arrived in Madrid they were met by Alberto Alcocer, the mayor, taken to the horseracing at the Zarzuela hippodrome and from there to Toledo, eighty kilometres south, to visit the Alcázar. That evening they attended a banquet at the Palace Hotel, presided over by General Moscardó, where they were joined by Real Madrid. The players ate together; there were toasts and declarations of mutual respect.

Before the match between the two sides the following day, bunches of flowers were handed out, while afterwards Madrid's president presented every Barcelona player with a cigarette lighter and gave a silver vase to the club. Two months later, Madrid travelled to Catalonia for the return match. The teams carried out a joint training session and posed for pictures together before Barça won 4-0 with the mayor of Barcelona and Moscardó as guests of honour. Madrid's players were received by the city council, taken to a performance at the Liceo theatre, presented with watches and visited the Montserrat basilica, spiritual home of Catalonia with its black Madonna, which they queued to kiss. At the end of the game a trophy was handed over. They called it the Peace Cup.

Luis Galinsoga was delighted. The man whose expressed mission as the new editor of *La Vanguardia Española* was to 'Castilianise' the paper and later wrote a gushing hagiography of Franco as the *Sentinel of the West*, declared: 'if there was an offender and an offended, after all the evidence of affection and camaraderie, that is now little more than a distant, hazy memory.' The Peace Cup was a choreographed reconciliation between Madrid and Barcelona, harmony forced and faked. The stage-managed fraternity showed just how troubled the authorities had been. A government circular prohibited newspapers from any mention of the 11-1 that could 'exacerbate passions between different regions of Spain' and the result brought immediate consequences.

Barcelona's president resigned but his replacement lasted just thirty-five days before Colonel José Vendrell Ferrer was named. Involved in a military coup against the Republic in 1932, Vendrell Ferrer fought alongside Franco during the civil war and left his post as director of public order in La Coruña to take over at Les Corts – another loyal Francoist in charge. One fellow director described his outstanding 'quality' as his 'constant desire to remain disciplined, avoiding the slightest friction with the governing bodies of sport'.

At the same time, pressure was brought to bear upon Real Madrid to change their president too and, on 6 August 1943, Antonio Peralba 'resigned'. Madrid formally requested that the Castilian Football Federation name a president and on 15 September a new man took office. He would come to embody the club, presiding over it for thirty-five years and constructing the greatest team in history.

Santiago Bernabéu was a safe option for the regime: he had friends at the Federation, was a right-winger, and had volunteered to fight during the war. Virtually the first thing Bernabéu did upon taking power was to send a telegram to Barcelona to 'extend the ties of affection and noble sporting rivalry' between the two clubs. 'I am not,' he told the media, 'going to allow the tension to go on a week longer. Where Barcelona were whistled, they'll be applauded.' If his fraternal resolve was genuine, it did not last.

Bernabéu's arrival in the presidency of Real Madrid was the beginning of a new era and he came to define the club. Imposing his personality upon the institution, creating a new structure, building a new stadium that would eventually carry his name, Bernabéu *was* Real Madrid, Vicente del Bosque referring to him as the 'moral and spiritual leader'. As Alfredo Di Stéfano says: 'Bernabéu loved the club like mad – and he knew about football. He had been everything there.'

'Everything' is no exaggeration: Bernabéu had been a ticket-seller, kit man, occasional groundsman, delegate, assistant coach, coach and secretary. A player for sixteen years, a director for nine, he would be president until his death during the 1978 World Cup – even though he claimed to have told his wife upon taking up the post that he would stay in the presidency for 'a year, no more'. Instead, he had changed Madrid beyond recognition, making it the biggest club in the world, and had presided over sixteen league titles, seven Copas, six European Cups and one Intercontinental Cup.

One of seven children, Bernabéu's father died when he was young and Santiago made no secret of his devotion to his mother. Bernabéu graduated with a law degree and did not marry until he was past forty – when he wed the widow of Valero Rivera, a board member who had been assassinated in the Usera tunnel by left-wing militias during the civil war. As a footballer, Bernabéu had taken his first steps in El Escorial where his family had moved. His brother Antonio took him to Real Madrid at the age of fourteen. Another brother, Marcelo, was already at the club and when coaches handed Santiago a pair of gloves Marcelo intervened, threatening to take Santiago home unless they played him at centre-forward. Bernabéu joined the first team squad at seventeen, made his debut at eighteen and played until he was thirty, although his career also included one season at Atlético – something he kept quiet.

Football at the time was a game based less on technique than raw power and Bernabéu had that in spades. Described as a great *shootador*, he was an inside-forward with little pace and not much skill but was powerful and could hit a ball hard. He made his debut for Madrid in March 1912 against a team of English expats and scored, got a hat-trick against Barcelona in 1916 and was part of the team that won the Copa del Rey in 1917, even though injury meant that he missed the final. He scored plenty of goals; in 1922 *Madrid Sport* made the huge claim that, the 'soul' of his team, he had scored over one thousand of them. He missed out on an appearance for Spain, though, and the experience marked him. He was told he wasn't playing only as he warmed up before a game in Lisbon in December 1922; because of a desire to have every region represented, his place was taken by the Basque forward Francisco Pagaza. 'In a national team regionalism should not win out,' he complained.

Bernabéu was not an especially rich man considering how powerful he became. He was blunt and his attitudes could be contradictory, his version of his story shifting. Catholic but critical of the Church, accusing it in one interview of 'holding back evolution for six or seven centuries', he was a religious man who, his wife said, 'did not like monks or nuns'; a monarchist who periodically claimed to be a republican; a Francoist who joked with the dictator but also publicly criticised the regime and later grew resentful towards it, after his plans to redevelop the stadium were rejected despite Franco's personal approval.

A director under Bernabéu and later president himself, Ramón Mendoza described Bernabéu as an 'archaic' man who belonged to the previous century and yet he had for so long been ahead of the game and in some aspects his attitude was curiously liberal. Gruff and uncomplicated, he talked of gentlemanly behaviour, was rigid and authoritarian, but he swore like a trooper. He could be the very model of respect but had no qualms about telling one player's wife that when her husband retired she would have to leave him in the club's hands so that they could put him out to stud.

An austere, tough man, Alfredo Di Stéfano recalls how Bernabéu used to walk round the stadium obsessively switching off the lights, yet he smoked huge cigars and his wife said he was a terrible hypochondriac. He was a proud Spaniard who took Real Madrid's patriotic ambassadorial role seriously, returning from a trip to the US, Argentina, Uruguay, Chile and Cuba in 1927 to announce 'we have carried out Spanish propaganda with great tenacity'. He was also a centralist who was obsessed by Catalonia. 'His view of the nation was unitary and centralist; he was a giant from the past,' Mendoza remarked. Bernabéu described Castilians as the most *cojonudo* of Spaniards, the bollocks. He explained: 'Those from the *meseta*, the central plateau of Spain, moulded by the cold and the heat, were sufficiently robust to be able to impose themselves on the other regions. Castile spread its language all over the world and Castile was the birthplace of all the feats that made Spain great. I'm sorry Catalans, Galicians and Basques, but the Castilians were sharper than them on the battlefield, head to head, and they beat them in every era.'

Catalans have a reputation within Spain for being thrifty, a stereotype encapsulated in the phrase *la pela és la pela*: money's money. Bernabéu joked about the Barcelona president killing a dog at customs so as not to have to pay duty on it and during a series of interviews held in 1976 he told his biographer, Martín Semprún, a story. It started with Bernabéu explaining: 'when I was a player I had a friend whose greatest defect was that he was Catalan and, worse, he boasted of being Catalan.' Bernabéu then went on to tell the tale of how he took this friend to a brothel in the capital after Madrid had defeated Barcelona 3-0. His friend requested a girl who could 'do it in Catalan', at which the madame asked her staff if any of them could oblige. After most had shaken their heads, no idea what the client wanted, a young girl spoke. Bernabéu took up the story: '"I haven't got a clue what you want," she said. "I don't even think that doing it in Catalan exists but I don't care. I'll do what you say. You show me and, if I like it, I'll only charge you half" . . .

My friend said: "You've learnt it already".'

Bernabéu had opposed the presidency of Rafael Sánchez Guerra prior to the civil war and told Semprún: 'I have never, ever, been a member of a political party, whether red or *facha* [fascist].' That was not true. He attended meetings held by José María Gil Robles' right-wing party the CEDA, carrying a pistol with him, his brother Antonio was a parliamentary deputy with the CEDA, and Santiago was at El Escorial in April 1934 when its radical youth wing, the Juventud de Acción Popular (JAP), held its most famous rally alongside the monastery palace of Philip II, Spain's sixteenth-century imperial king – an event that José Antonio Primo de Rivera, leader of the avowedly fascist Falange Española, described as 'a fascist spectacle'.

Bernabéu, a 'famous sport-man', was the JAP's sports secretary. The JAP was belligerent in its rejection of the left, regional separatism and liberalism, demanding a new state for Spain and the 'annihilation' of political opponents in its quest for the rebirth of the *Patria*, or Fatherland. Sport played a role in this programme: once in power, the JAP promised that daily physical education would be mandatory for all school children and insisted upon the need for 'pre-military' education in order to forge a new generation of patriots. It demanded: 'a youthful spirit of love of the Fatherland and harder bodies through healthy exercise, so that within every citizen there is a soldier should the Fatherland need him.'

When the Spanish Civil War broke out, Bernabéu took refuge in a Madrid hospital, pretending to be a nurse with fake papers before sheltering in the French Embassy, from where he escaped to France. He then returned to Spain, entering the Nationalist zone via Irún on the border and volunteering for service with Franco's forces, aged forty-three. He served under General Muñoz Grandes, who would later lead the División Azul on the Eastern Front during the Second World War, and was part of the forces that took Barcelona in March 1939. He described taking village after village in Catalonia where old ladies looked out from behind the curtains and old men cried in desperation. 'When a pensioner cries with hate it's because the town is beyond help,' he said.

'I took sides in the civil war and later I regretted it,' Bernabéu recalled in the 1970s. 'I don't like to talk about it, especially after so long and no longer knowing who were the good guys and who were the bad. I looked through binoculars for Muñoz Grandes but I later reached the conclusion that I chose the wrong side: the worst thing about war is that it makes more bad men than it kills.' His remarks were disingenuous and not just because the rather coy suggestion that all he did was peer through a pair of binoculars is impossible. He was awarded the Cruz de Mérito Militar, the Cruz de Guerra and the Cruz de Campaña and there was never any doubt which side Bernabéu was on, nor which side he would ever be on. He had previously insisted: 'During the war, I was a volunteer against Communism and I would still be today, despite my age.'

Upon taking the presidency at Real Madrid, he named a personal friend of Franco, Lieutenant General Eduardo Sáenz de Buruaga, honorary president and throughout his reign military men were on the board.

The *Libro de Oro*, published to mark the club's fiftieth anniversary in 1952, used the kind of tone and language invariably applied to Franco to describe Bernabéu as a 'man of iron will', for whom 'gravity and parsimony' were key qualities as a player and a director. 'Santiago Bernabéu,' it ran, 'so concise, so tenacious, so thoughtful, is to Real Madrid what Philip II was to Spain: her best King. Few words, huge works . . .' The hagiographic tone continued: 'With him at the head of our club we know that nothing bad can happen, that we will overcome all the obstacles . . . his iron fist on the controls, his eyes, forever alert, an unbreakable faith in the greatest of destinies. With Bernabéu governing, Real Madrid is living its golden age as a club in the very front row. *Better than me, no one* could be Real Madrid's currency now; a currency that Bernabéu has earned.'

Bernabéu was a pioneer, obsessed with football's power to generate revenue and determined to maximise its money-making potential with exhibition matches and tours, paying huge fees for players, determined to assert his club's predominance over the rest. Ultimately, though, this approach was costly: increased income could not match increased expenditure and the club was forced to keep borrowing. The advantage was, as Bernabéu's loyal vice-president Raimundo Saporta noted, that the Banco Mercantil knew that to call in the debt would be hugely unpopular and there were other banks willing to step into their shoes. But eventually credit dried up and Madrid were forced to face reality.

In September 1961, Saporta wrote to Bernabéu to inform him of a meeting that he was due to hold with the bank in a bid to reduce the club's debt. 'We live off the "bluff" that we are millionaires and thanks to that we still have people's trust,' Saporta noted. 'We have to keep making sure that people think we are swimming in gold, so that there is no alarm or criticism.' The following year Saporta cited a 'real battle' with the bank and the year after that, in September 1963, he described the club's financial situation as 'frightening'. They had reduced the debt by seven million pesetas but it still stood at forty-three million (£260,000) and that reduction had only been made possible by the twenty-seven-million-peseta sale of Luis del Sol to Juventus. 'And,' Saporta warned, 'there's no other Del Sol [to sell].' He told Bernabéu: 'We can't keep fighting. We're on the verge of bankruptcy.'

One of Saporta's handful of suggested remedies, which he admitted would be unpopular, was to end 'aid to journalists', which cost the club two million pesetas a year. That proposal helps to underline that Bernabéu was a man who sought to control everything, including public opinion. He oversaw every tiny detail with the assistance of Saporta – who, as time went on and Bernabéu was increasingly absent, came virtually to run the club himself. Bernabéu was to be consulted on everything from ticket prices to players' relationships and the match officials. As one former footballer at Madrid puts it, Bernabéu would know when the most insignificant referee in the lowest division had a birthday and a gift would be sent.

He talked of manners and decorum but was prepared to play tough. He 'indignantly' caught a Barcelona director trying to sign one of his players, Rafael Yunta Navarro, in a Gran Via café. Bernabéu had lain in wait with a lawyer and carefully placed witnesses. It was presented by some as the breakdown of the supposedly good relations built by the Peace Games, but Bernabéu milked it. Besides, he was capable of pulling similar tricks. He happily told the story of how he torpedoed Barcelona's signing of Luis Molowny. One morning Bernabéu picked up a paper at Reus railway station in Catalonia to be greeted with a headline announcing that Barcelona were to sign Molowny from Marino in Las Palmas, the Canary Islands. Reading that Barcelona's representative, Ricard Cabot, was travelling to the Canaries by boat, Bernabéu got on the phone and told Jacinto Quincoces to go to the bank, take out 100,000 pesetas in one-hundred-peseta notes, fly straight there and secure Molowny's signature, barking: 'stop pissing about and sign him.' By the time Cabot arrived, Molowny was a Madrid player. Marino had 75,000 pesetas in cash. In his first *derbi* against Barcelona, Molowny scored the late winner.

'Bernabéu wasn't God,' says Amancio Amaro, another Bernabéu signing who joined the club in 1962, 'but . . .'

That 'but' hangs heavy.

'We had a huge amount of respect for him.'

Fear?

'No, not exactly. But he was a proper, straight, direct man. A man used to taking decisions.'

Everyone at Madrid refers to Bernabéu as a father. A rather severe one, a strict patriarch. A man who suffered few fools and did things his way, always. 'He used to drill into us that humility was vitally important,' Amancio says. 'Sensible, serious, humble, hard-working. It was not just that you had to behave well, you had to be seen to behave well too. There could be nothing ostentatious. We wouldn't go out there, chests puffed out, thinking we were the best, even if we were. Humility, humility, humility.' No one dared defy him. On occasions Bernabéu referred to the players as 'children'. He didn't care much for fashions, either. One Madrid player recalls rushing to the bathroom to shave when Bernabéu turned up at the team hotel. Others remember the president demanding that they cut their hair. Team meals were often held in silence and he refused to let them buy cars and certainly not flash cars: it took two years for Alfredo Di Stéfano to get one.

He also prohibited them from joining unions. In 1969, when the first steps towards building a players' union were being taken, he was the most hostile of the Spanish football presidents to the idea and forced two of its instigators, Pirri and Ramón Grosso, to pronounce publicly against it. The AFE was not formally created until 1977.

An authoritarian figure, Bernabéu had a foul temper. Raimundo Saporta wrote to a fellow director to tell him of the president's fury and his own failed attempts to calm him down. That was typical, and it was not just directors who feared him. Bernabéu's harangues, gigantic cigar in his mouth, swear words tumbling out, were famous. He would go down to the dressing room and tear strips off his players, insults flying, threats too. The harangues even had a name: *Santiaguinas*.

He demanded total commitment. The first player he decorated with the club's highest award, the Laureada, was Pirri – and more because of guts than goals. Pirri played one game in 1975 with a broken jaw, even if he laughs: 'well, I took so many injections I could barely feel it.' But the game that earned him the award was in 1968. 'I had been with the national services team in Baghdad and came back to play a game with a thirty-nine or forty degree fever,' Pirri recalls. 'I took an injection and went out to play. During the game I broke my collarbone but I carried on because there were no substitutes. When they tried to take the pins out, I turned the air blue. Don Santiago came into the dressing room and gave me the Laureada because of that. You always wanted to play, no matter what was wrong with you. And that is what he wanted too. I remember another game where I played with my arm in a plaster. I couldn't feel it but I would do it all over again.'

'Bernabéu also really looked after you,' insists Ignacio Zoco, another presidential favourite who played for Madrid between 1962 and 1974.

'You weren't just a footballer to him. He wanted to know everything. He looked after you and your family. And he held me up as an example to others: I don't know why he liked me so much but he did. Probably because I was a guy who fought and battled, who ran a lot. I always gave 100 per cent and I lived an ordered life. He used to call me *Paleto* [the hick]. When I retired I was due a testimonial because I had been at the club for ten years. I said I wanted to play against the European champions, who were Bayern Munich. And he said: "what do you want to play Bayern for? For you or for Bayern?"

I said: "I want this place to be packed".

So he said: "Leave it to me to arrange." And do you know who he brought?'

Who?

'Panathinaikos.'

I don't get it.

'Nor did I at first. But Panathinaikos were cheap and their coach was Puskás. They charged two pesetas a ticket and the place was packed.'

A packed stadium: that was what Bernabéu had always wanted. It was an obsession, one that had been discussed as far back as 1931 when he was a director. If the first thing Bernabéu did when he took over was send a telegram of fraternity to Barcelona, the second was to lay down the agenda for his presidency. Item one: a new stadium with a capacity for over 100,000 people. The focus here was not Barcelona: Bernabéu would tell acquaintances in 1947 that if they had waited a year longer Atlético Madrid would have taken a lead that would have been impossible to overhaul.

It is hard to do justice to exactly how outlandish Bernabéu's proposal was. As he explained in 1961: 'the idea of a gigantic new stadium for the then "little" Real Madrid was widely described as "nonsensical!"' Real Madrid finished 1942–3 in tenth place, almost getting relegated. They were averaging only 16,000 at home matches, Europe was at war and Spain was in crisis. There was a reason why the 1940s were described as 'The Years of Hunger' and there is a reason why, however flippant it sounds, there is an entire generation of Spaniards who are short. Autarky was the chosen economic policy of the dictatorship, rationing did not end until 1952, the standard of living would not reach pre-war levels until 1954, prices were rocketing and salaries plummeting, shortages were dramatic, illness widespread and fear still gripped. There would be escape in football, certainly, circus at a time of little bread, but a stadium *that* big simply did not seem possible.

Bernabéu, though, was determined. With the regime penniless, rejecting his first approach and eventually agreeing to fund less than 5 per cent of the project, he secured a loan from Rafael Salgado, president of the Banco Mercantil e Industrial, considered close to the Falange, in return for a formal link to the club. He also organised a bond issue among supporters. 'This great and beautiful ground was made available to us without any state, municipal or institutional help,' Bernabéu told English visitors, 'it grew straight from the hearts and hopes of our loyal core of supporters, their friends and other *Madrileños* whose imagination was caught up by our plans.' That was not true: not only had Madrid been granted official funds but, as Carles Torras has demonstrated, the DND also spent 980,000 pesetas on stadium bonds. With the money, Madrid bought two parcels of land of 256,667 square feet and 93,887 square feet respectively near the old Chamartín stadium, at a cost of three million pesetas. Although they made one million on the sale of the previous ground, it was still a huge sum.

There was method in his madness: the stadium, as he knew it would, ended up situated right alongside the future extension of the Castellana and now boasts one of the most glamorous addresses in European football. Pedro Muguruza, the same architect who had overseen the renovation of the Prado Museum and much of Gran Vía, and who was building Franco's mausoleum the Valley of the Fallen, was employed to overlook the construction. Work began on 27 October 1944. The stadium was inaugurated in December 1947 with a match against the Portuguese team Belenenses, which Madrid won 3-1. Before the game it was blessed by Franco's chaplain.

Within three months, Madrid had eight thousand new members. By 1948 they had 43,000. By the mid-1950s they were the biggest team in the world, signing the biggest players. 'In Santiago Bernabéu, Real Madrid were fortunate to have a man who was ahead of his time and took risks,' says Jorge Valdano. 'In a Spain that was depressed, where there was not even cement, he constructed a stadium for 120,000 people. And then to fill it he seduced the greatest stars of his time.'

Zoco sits at the Bernabéu and waves his hand to embrace his surroundings. 'He created this stadium and they said he was mad: seven pesetas [about fifteen pence] a ticket? "Where's that madman going, this is going to ruin us . . ." And now look. He was a special man, there will never be another one like him.'

'The new Chamartín is today the best football ground in Spain,' ran the *Libro de Oro*. 'It was Bernabéu, that irresistible conductor, who galvanised the enthusiasm of the musicians to make possible the most beautiful and perfect of works. Yes, the new Chamartín could be said to be the El Escorial of this monarch capable of bringing the greatest of dreams to fruition.' That was published in March 1952. And yet even as late as 1952 it was not Madrid who really needed a new stadium, such was the clamour to see them play; it was not Madrid who packed grounds thanks to the country's finest footballer, the first real superstar of the post-war era; it was not Madrid who dominated Spanish football; and it was not Madrid who could plausibly lay claim to be the best team in the world.

It was Barcelona.

7

THE HOUSE THAT LÁSZLÓ BUILT

There is nostalgia in Josep Seguer's words, a quiet sadness. 'Barcelona has been my life, my hope and my dreams,' he says. 'I like to watch them on television. Even now I see them play and I remember my time. There wasn't much then but the hope, the enthusiasm, was huge, the *ilusión*. It was everything. I went there at the age of seventeen, one of the youngest. Now I'm the most *veterano* of the *veteranos*.' Seguer's voice is cracking. 'Time waits for no one, the years take their toll.' A momentary silence, an intake of breath. 'I came at seventeen. How can I do it justice? My era . . . we left a mark.' His voice breaks. He's crying now. 'It was different then. I came at seventeen, and now . . .'

Now Seguer is ninety and he lives in northern Catalonia in the small town of Vandellòs, Tarragona, around forty kilometres from Parets de Vallès where he was born in 1923. José Seguer as he was then – the name Josep, like names all over Spain, had been Castilianised – recalls hard times, war in Europe and confrontation with East and West, tension and suspicion. And yet he says those were good times too, the best of them. 'How,' he says, 'can you ever forget a team when you enjoyed playing with them so much?'

Seguer was twenty when he made it to the first team having joined the club at seventeen, leaving behind the barber's shop where he earned fifty centimes per shave, to become part of the amateur side, effectively Barcelona's reserves. Promoted and given eight hundred pesetas a month during the season, he joined Barcelona's first team squad the same month as the 11-1 – 'they obliged them to do something and it wasn't very correct: it was political, the man who ruled was in Madrid and things always happened because they didn't much like Catalans.' He was part of the team that played Madrid at Les Corts in the second of the Peace Games on Boxing Day 1943. It was only the eleventh game he played for Barcelona. Madrid's captain that day was Juan Antonio Ipiña. Seguer had collected cigarette cards of him.

At the start of the following season, 1944–5, Barcelona's new coach was Josep Samitier, a man with innovative ideas on training, diet, even the way of dressing. He handed out innovative silk ties to the team. Following the style of Herbert Chapman at Arsenal in the thirties, he wanted Barcelona to be dynamic, aggressive. Midway through the season, they beat Madrid 5-0 and by its conclusion they were league champions for only the second time in their history, 'We were a team made of Catalans,' Seguer recalls. 'César [Rodríguez] was from León, but mostly we were from small towns near Barcelona. We were insulted at lots of the stadiums, referees persecuted us and we had to really break our balls to win that league.'

The following season they lost the league on the final day – not that anyone let on to Barcelona's seriously ill chaplain, Lluís Sabater, who died that same evening, convinced his team had just won the title again – but soon they had two more. These were the darkest years of Francoism, the height of repression and hardship, and yet it was the start of Barcelona's golden age. Madrid did not win the league until 1953, fourteen years after the end of the civil war, by which time Barcelona had won five of them. They were champions in 1947–8 and 1948–9, beating Español on the final day. The Catalan satirical magazine *El Once* noted: 'On the desk of *Marca* the news was like a jug of frozen water and they quickly began to fill their pages with long reports on cycling, boxing and other sports.' Two leagues in a row, 'and that wasn't easy,' Seguer says proudly.

That year, Barcelona added the most significant success: the Copa Latina, a forerunner of the European Cup, played between the champions of Spain, Italy, France and Portugal. They beat Sporting Lisbon 2-1 in the final. Better still, they did so at Real Madrid's new Chamartín stadium. At full-time Barcelona paraded the trophy in front of half-empty stands. Of their first team squad, Seguer calculates that fifteen were local lads and Catalan was the *lingua franca* in the dressing room. 'One of the great feelings of the time was winning at Madrid's ground,' he says. 'It felt like a vindication.'

And then *he* arrived – the man Seguer calls 'our Messi'. The Hungarian forward László Kubala. 'He carried the team on his own and he had it all: speed and power, technique, control, charisma,' says Seguer. Today, a statue of Kubala stands outside the Camp Nou, the house that László built. It was Kubala's brilliance, his ability to pack Les Corts, that obliged Barcelona to build a new stadium, or so it goes.

In fact, Barcelona had already taken note of the construction of the new Chamartín and had bought a huge plot of land in September 1950, before Kubala had even played a game for them, at a cost of just under 10.1 million pesetas. But, having got permission for construction from the city council, and with Barcelona president Francesc Miró-Sans having been shown round Chamartín by Bernabéu in September 1953, the first stone was not laid until 28 March 1954 and it was not officially opened until 24 September 1957, day of Our Lady of Mercy, La Mercè, the festival of the city of Barcelona. It had cost just under 230 million pesetas. José Solís, the secretary general of the *Movimiento*, the political arm of the regime, attended the opening; the stadium was blessed; 1,500 people performed a huge Sardana, the traditional Catalan dance, and 10,000 doves were released.

Prohibited from naming the stadium after founder Joan Gamper – a foreigner and a Protestant who had committed suicide in 1930 following the collapse of his business interests and the ban on his involvement with the club – Barcelona opted simply for Estadio del Club de Fútbol Barcelona. Most people, though, stuck with the name that had been informally used throughout its construction: Camp Nou, new ground. And in a referendum held in 2001, 68.5 per cent of supporters voted to stick with that. When it opened in 1957, it held 93,053 people. Big enough for everyone who wanted to watch Kubala.

Seguer recalls flights in cargo planes, players tied together by ropes, the beginnings of a new era. 'When we went to other stadiums,' he says, 'it was always full; everybody wanted to see us play. They wanted to beat us but above all they wanted to see us play and at home there were even more of them, all keen to watch Kubala.' As Josep Samitier, the man who signed him, put it: 'Kubala was the foundation stone upon which the growth of support for football in Catalonia was built. With him and later [Alfredo] Di Stéfano [at Madrid], football became opera.' Kubala brought the game into a new era; he was a revelation, changing Barcelona, changing football and changing society too, becoming the first real star in grey, post-war Spain. 'Technically,' said his team-mate Gustavo Biosca, 'he revolutionised everything – our ideas and those of the whole of Spain.'

When Kubala was a child his father bought him a violin. Kubala used it as a goalpost. His father was a Hungarian Slovak bricklayer, his mother a Slovak factory worker with Polish roots. They were poor and the day that Kubala came home from the stadium with his first pay packet, his father, convinced that his son had stolen the money, dragged him back only to find that he had been telling the truth. He didn't always: Kubala faked his date of birth to play for a team at the local metal factory aged eleven, played for Ferencvaros at fifteen and was an international at seventeen. He joined Slovan Bratislava in 1946, married in 1947, and went from there to Vasas Budapest. When a Stalinist dictatorship was installed in Czechoslovakia in 1948 Kubala defected in search of professionalism, leaving his wife and newborn son, Branko, behind.

He escaped on a cold Sunday night in January 1949, in the back of a truck with Russian number plates, dressed in Russian military uniform and carrying fake Russian papers. When they were stopped he and his companions claimed to be members of the army of occupation, working in the munitions service. Ditching the truck, they walked the final few kilometres over the frozen mountains and into American-occupied Austria, taking refuge in Innsbruck. Kubala was detained there for three days but guards recognised him and arranged his paperwork to enable him to go wherever he wanted. He chose Italy.

Given a visa, he was invited to play for Torino against Benfica in Lisbon but turned down the opportunity because his wife and son, who was seriously ill, had managed to escape Czechoslovakia and eventually reach Udine and he intended to meet them there. They had swum across the Danube near Bratislava with baby Branko inside a tyre. Both made it through alive. On the way back from the game Kubala had been due to play on 4 May 1949, Torino's plane crashed into the Superga basilica, killing thirty-one people, eighteen of them footballers.

Kubala was signed up by the Italian First Division club Pro Patria but he was formally denounced as a defector to FIFA by the Hungarian Federation. Facing a year-long ban, he was released by Pro Patria. By then virtually penniless, Kubala's next team was Hungaria, which he helped form with political refugees in a holding camp in Cinecittà, Rome. The team was largely made up of Hungarians but there were also Czechs, Russians and Croatians, all of whom had escaped Communism, while the coach was Fernando Daucik, the brother of Kubala's wife. In the summer of 1950 they toured Spain, playing against Madrid, Español and the Spanish national team.

Having watched him score twice at Chamartín, Bernabéu was keen to sign Kubala but he faced three problems. First, Kubala was adamant that any team that signed him must also sign his brother-in-law, Daucik, as coach. Second, Kubala was, in the words of the Hungarian Federation, 'a deserter' who had a ban hanging over him. And third, Barcelona were interested too. At Sarrià against Español, he had received a long ball straight from kick-off, flicked it over his marker and volleyed it past the goalkeeper. Agustí Montal, the watching Barcelona president, turned to the club secretary and reportedly said: 'get him a contract right now.'

The future president of the Federation, the Falangist Sancho Dávila, noted in his memoirs that '*a* team', presumably Real Madrid, was interested in Kubala but that the Spanish Federation had warned them off, refusing authorisation. The Hungarian had Madrid's written offer in his pocket when Samitier met him after the game against Spain and tried to sign him, telling him not to worry about the ban – Barcelona would sort it out. When Madrid found out that Barcelona were pressing ahead with a transfer that they had been told not to pursue, Bernabéu was furious. Madrid's secretary later complained that Barcelona had broken a pact of non-aggression.

'It is true that Kubala was on the verge of signing for Real Madrid, but Barcelona overtook them,' Lluis Permanyer, the son of Barcelona's secretary at the time, later wrote in *La Vanguardia*. He takes up the story: 'The director [Manuel] Senillosa asked someone to urgently send an envoy who spoke Hungarian to prevent him, if possible, from accepting the contract that Real Madrid were offering. The swimmer Zolyomi did a determined man-marking job on him and on one strategic occasion even made him have a drink or two more than he should. Kubala arrived in our city with Hungaria to play against Español, without having yet signed any documents. And when Montal sat down to negotiate with him, Kubala pulled a piece of paper from his pocket and said: "Me, like this." It was the contract that Madrid had offered him.'

Another version of the story has Kubala falling into Barcelona's trap. Enrique Llaudet, who became a director in 1952 and president after that, told Jimmy Burns that Kubala arrived in Spain thinking he was going to sign for Real Madrid but because he was drunk he didn't really know where he was going or what he was doing. So Samitier was able effectively to con Kubala into travelling to Barcelona to sign a deal with the 'wrong' club. According to Llaudet, the pair were travelling on the train when Kubala turned to Samitier and said: 'Hey, we're going to Madrid, right?'

'Sure,' came the reply.

'But the sign says "Barcelona".'

'Don't worry,' Samitier said. 'We're going to the club now.'

It is a nice story; it also is probably not true. Kubala visited only two cities during that trip to Spain – Barcelona and Madrid. He could only have boarded the train in one of the two, so it seems extremely unlikely that he would be suddenly caught out by it arriving at the wrong destination and, besides, he was travelling with Samitier. The fact that his negotiating tactic was to pull out the proposal from Madrid and ask Barcelona to match it also suggests that, at least by the time he arrived, he knew exactly who he was talking to.

Kubala's tactic worked. Barcelona agreed to take on Daucik and offered to pay Kubala 1,200 pesetas (£11) a month, plus a flat 3,800 pesetas in living expenses. Signed on 15 June 1950, it was a huge deal, the biggest in Spanish history. The issue of the ban, however, remained. Kubala had officially signed as an amateur, unable to play in competitive games.

But if the bad news was political, the good news was political too. In 1955, a film was released called *Los Ases Buscan La Paz*, *Aces Search for Peace*, which tells the story of a star football player who escapes Communist Hungary after he is told by a shifty character to use an international match as cover to spy on behalf of the regime. He protests that he just wants to play football and has no interest in politics but before he knows it he is dropped from the team and newspaper headlines declare him to be out of form. He escapes in a Russian truck, kindly allowing a young girl and a baby to travel with them, before crossing the final miles on foot, evading Russian soldiers with a dash through the frozen forest. He succeeds in reaching freedom and Italy, via Austria, before heading to Spain where he signs for Barcelona, the Spanish Red Cross reunites him with his wife and son, and he is granted Spanish nationality. He is then offered the chance to return to Hungary, no strings attached, but he no longer wants to and even though it means leaving fame, fortune and his mother behind, he chooses to stay. The film ends on the line: 'I cannot let down Spain, the country that gave me peace.'

Much of the film was shot at Les Corts and includes cameos from Antoni Ramallets, Estanislao Basora, Josep Segarra and Gustavo Biosca, all of them Barcelona players. Samitier appears too, teeing up the lead role for a series of spectacular overhead kicks in a training session. The star, of course, is Kubala, playing himself – albeit the voices are dubbed – and the film tells a romanticised version of his story. It portrays an idyllic image of Spain under Franco, a haven of peace, prosperity and stability, contrasting with the Communist bloc; a place where a man who just wants to play football can follow his dream. Kubala is a victim, a fugitive of the red terror, Spain his salvation. From Kubala's point of view, it was not a portrayal that strayed too far from the truth. In an interview in 1964, he described Spain as 'hope and happiness'.

The political value of Kubala's defection from Communism to Franco's Spain, at a time when the regime was seeking to come back to the West, presenting itself as their natural ally as the Cold War began, had been realised virtually from the start. For Kubala's signing that fact would prove decisive. Samitier, Barcelona's technical director, promised Kubala that he would resolve the problem of his ban. As Kubala told Jeff King in the late 1990s: 'Samitier was on good terms with Spain's FIFA representatives, that's why Barcelona signed me. [The president of the Spanish Football Federation, Armando] Muñoz Calero was friends with Samitier and they sorted out the paperwork together so that I could play for Barcelona. Samitier also had a good relationship with General Franco, who was a fan of his as a player.

Franco personally cut through the red tape and signed the decree that meant that I could play for Spain too.' The Spanish Football Federation intervened with FIFA, adopting the kind of political 'apoliticism' typical of the dictatorship, to argue that a player should not be prevented from following his career.

Kubala played his first friendly for Barcelona against Osasuna in October 1950 and continued to play in non-competitive games even though officially he was not allowed to, Samitier giving him a false name and telling him to keep his mouth shut to put people off the scent. 'Remember,' Samitier would tell Kubala before matches, 'your name is Olegario and you're mute.' Meanwhile, the Federation presented a dossier on his signing at meetings in Brussels and Zurich in which they argued that Kubala had left the East in order to 'escape from a certain death after refusing to be a blind instrument of Communism' and alleged that the Communist regime had resolved to 'assassinate' him because he had refused to attend a Soviet seminary. The FEF even implied that if the situation was not resolved they would contemplate leaving FIFA.

The final meeting was held in London in October 1951. By then Kubala's case had been strengthened by the fact that he was officially Spanish. Formally given political refugee status in April 1951, he was granted Spanish nationality on 1 June, having first been baptised into the Catholic Church in the seaside town of Águilas, home of Muñoz Calero, who also acted as godfather. Barcelona's president, Enric Martí Carretó, had sent a supporting report to the Federation, reassuring them: 'Kubala is Catholic and profoundly anti-Communist.' The latter, at least, was true. During the London meeting, the amount of money due in compensation was discussed and eventually the issue appeared resolved, Sancho Dávila taking great pleasure in noting that while the representatives of the Spanish Football Federation could negotiate as they saw fit, their Hungarian counterparts had to consult with Budapest. This prompted Jules Rimet to confide: 'You see, they say you have to put up with an atrocious dictatorship and yet, without consulting, you can resolve this issue. By contrast, the men from the "new world" don't dare to take a single step alone.'

Kubala made his official debut for Barcelona against Sevilla on 29 April 1951, almost a year after first signing an agreement with the club. By then, it was too late to help fourth-placed Barcelona in the league, the season having finished the week before, but his impact in the Copa del Generalísimo was immediate. Barcelona won that first game 2-1 and Kubala scored in a 3-0 win in the return match. A glorious cycle had begun. Barcelona beat Atlético Tetuán 3-1 and 4-1, knocked out Atlético Bilbao 2-1 on aggregate and defeated Real Sociedad 3-0 in the final. Kubala had played seven games, winning six and drawing the other, scoring six times. Barcelona had won the Copa del Generalísimo. And it was not about to stop there, either.

Watching footage of Kubala, the first thing that strikes you is his sheer size, all rippling muscles bursting out of a tight shirt and short shorts. Even at the age of sixty he was doing over eighty kilometres a week on his bike. He had trained as a boxer when he was younger, giving up because his arms were shorter than opponents', and he could still pack some punch – as players from Brazilian side Botafogo found out to their cost in one game, literally cowering in the back of the net. Seguer recalls him, Hulk-like, scoring one goal bare-chested after desperate defenders had ripped the shirt from his body and still not been able to stop him. He could race past people on either side and finish with a real hammer of a shot, left-footed and right. 'He was a strong man: you couldn't knock him over with a cannonball,' Di Stéfano recalls.

But his game was based on finesse as much as fitness; all drag backs and flicks, running on his toes, protecting the ball, drawing players in and then slipping beyond them. He could do things that no one had ever seen before. Even his penalties were different, *paradinha* pause included – he only ever missed one, something he put down to his 'psychological study of opposition goalkeepers'. 'And no one,' says Luis Suárez, a team-mate between 1955 and 1961, 'had seen anyone curl a ball over a wall before. Kubala did it. He was an extraordinary player who brought to Spain a series of innovative improvements and perfections. He united physical power and exceptional technique. Defenders were sucked towards him and then he protected the ball brilliantly. They tried to push him over but just fell over themselves. Among the players I've seen, and I've seen a lot, he is the best of all time.'

'People talk a lot about Pelé, Di Stéfano and Puskás and more recently of Cruyff, Maradona or Schuster, but for me László was the greatest,' said another team-mate, Eduardo Manchón. 'When he rolled up his sleeves we knew we would be unstoppable.'

'He was skilful and a real leader,' Seguer recalls. 'He earned the most, he had the press on side and he was *mimado*, a little molly-coddled, but deservedly so. He thought he was better than us. And the thing is he was. He was no egotist. We all worked for him, sure, but he was a team player and we did it because he was the best and he made history for us. He worked very hard, he had such drive. He used to say to us all the time: "we don't play, we win".' When Kubala died in May 2002 Gustavo Biosca, his team-mate and his best friend, wrote a eulogy for him in the newspaper *El País*. 'When he was on the pitch we had the feeling that we couldn't lose,' Biosca recalled. 'He dominated the game and dominated the ball. He created an atmosphere of optimism, a winners' mentality, because we knew that at any given moment he could put himself one on one with the goalkeeper and score. He was extremely fast; although he weighed seventy-eight, eighty kilos no one at the club was quicker than him . . . he transformed football.'

Not that everyone was impressed, one newspaper complaining, 'we don't need footballers forged under Communism', while the brother of one of the founders of the fascist Falange, writing in *Marca*, described Barcelona 'as an association of chancers and undesirables who have come from faraway lands to eat our bread'. When Barcelona won the Copa del Generalísimo in 1953, Eduardo Teus complained that

Barcelona 'have not wanted to Spanishify themselves and have preferred to build a team that is internationalist, a word that brings so many perverse things to mind'. Opponents, meanwhile, kicked lumps out of him.

In general, though, these were rare dissenting voices; mostly, he was welcomed. Although it was a dictatorship, Spain was different from the eastern bloc and Kubala allowed his image to be used to reinforce that difference – not least because his gratitude and wonder were genuine. 'I am,' he once said, 'a man with no homeland because my country is under Communism.' When he was called up for the Spain team, the regime warned newspaper editors to 'either make favourable comments or refrain from making comments'. Kubala made much of his status as a Spaniard, later becoming the national team coach, and even appearing on television supporting Franco. His endorsement carried weight too: Kubala was a star.

With his blond hair and good looks he stood out a mile. 'He could hardly go out on to the street, because they would eat him alive,' says the son of Zoltán Czibor, Kubala's Hungarian Barça team-mate. 'There was an avalanche whenever he appeared.' Alfredo Di Stéfano had effectively lived with Kubala when he first arrived in Spain in 1953 and once jokingly said that the only thing he could not forgive his friend for was 'having more success with the women than I did and being a better actor too'. The Italian writer Francesca Petrella wrote a book about Kubala that essentially amounted to an erotic ode. 'My hero,' she wrote, 'is blond like a Viking god, strong and tall like a Greek warrior, that's why he suffers, that's why he loves.' A contemporary jokes: 'Kubala could have a hundred children in Barcelona!' Another talks of clubs closed just for Barcelona's players, of flamenco singer Lola Flores dancing on the bar, naked.

Nights out were legendary. Mornings after were too. Kubala had a taxi driver, a man from Zaragoza who took him everywhere, picking him up from his favourite haunts and taking him to training or games. Ángel Mur senior recalled the normal cure for a hangover: a cold shower, a sleep on the treatment table, coffee filled with aspirin and back out on to the pitch. Seguer cites coffee with cognac as the best way to 'get the engine running'. On one trip to Las Palmas in the Canary Islands, the then coach Sandro Puppo announced that if he caught any player going out, he would be hit with a thousand peseta fine. Kubala reached into his pocket, pulled out a thousand pesetas and handed it over. 'That's the permission sorted.' On another journey, when a customs officer asked Kubala if he had anything to declare, he pointed at his stomach and said, 'yes, two litres of whisky'.

Kubala's lifestyle would eventually bring him into conflict with Helenio Herrera, who took over as coach at Barcelona in 1958. But, for the first few years at least he was invariably forgiven. It helped that the directors often joined them in nights out, and so did journalists, but one of the reasons why Kubala was always let off was that there was no cynicism about him. Rather, there was a kind of cheerful, childlike wonder, vulnerability, an innocence. Booted out and told to go home for turning up visibly drunk a few hours before one game, he instead had a bath, a massage and returned begging for forgiveness, looking desperately sorry for himself. He did not want to have a single room when the team travelled, feeling more comfortable accompanied. He was big-hearted and looked after his team-mates. One of them, Ferrán Olivella, recalls his own five months of military service that prevented him from training with the team each morning and left him feeling depressed and removed from his friends. Kubala began training twice a day just so that Olivella would have someone to enjoy a session with in the afternoon.

People would follow Kubala everywhere. He was paid a fortune compared to his team-mates but gave most of it away. Emil Osterreicher, the former technical secretary of Honved and later a kind of informal agent for Hungarian players in Spain, noted that Kubala never worked out whether money was measured in kilos, litres or kilometres. Mur recalled taking his watch and wallet from him before he went out for the night because he knew Kubala would probably come back without either. When he had 200,000 pesetas stolen from his car he just shrugged: 'Well, I hope it does them some good.' Biosca recalls him stumbling across a family sleeping on the street: he picked them up, took them to a *pensión* and paid for them to stay. 'Kubala,' he explained, 'knew what misery was.'

Kubala, whose father had died when he was fifteen, would always insist that Samitier had become a father figure for him when he came to Spain. He had left Hungary without his mother too, not even warning her that he was planning to defect. Returning to visit was too risky and the Communist regime would not let her leave, something that depressed Kubala profoundly. Asked in 1969 to whom he felt the most gratitude, Kubala responded: Szabó, Daucik, Samitier and . . . Santiago Bernabéu. When Real Madrid were due to face the Hungarian team Vasas in the European Cup in 1961, Bernabéu intervened with the club and spoke directly to the Hungarian Football Federation on Kubala's behalf. Bernabéu's influence was decisive and just before Christmas 1961, twelve years after he had left Budapest, Kubala arrived in Barcelona on a flight from Paris with his mother. She met her three grandchildren for the first time. Together, they were greeted by players and the president of Barcelona on the runway, but it was the president of Madrid who had made it possible.

Another reason why Kubala was invariably let off was even simpler: he had a habit of turning up and still being the best player on the pitch. As Biosca noted after Kubala's death: 'It has been said often that Kubala drank a lot and played matches without having slept. And it's true too, although not that many times. He drank because he ate a lot and then he burnt it all off in training sessions. Sometimes, when he didn't make it to a session, Samitier would say to me: "Where's Olegario?" I'd go and look for him and I always knew where to find him. And then he would work harder than anyone. He hardly even noticed [the night's excesses] because he was a physical beast.' The bottom line was that Kubala won. A lot.

A lot? *The* lot. The 1951–2 season was the best in Barcelona's history. Always known as the Barcelona of the *Cinc Copes*, the Five Cups, a popular rhyme mocked Español's ditty to declare: 'there are six things that shine more than the sun: Barcelona's five cups and the shit that is Español'. League winners for the second successive season, with Kubala finishing second-top scorer behind Real Madrid's Pahíño, they won the Copa del Generalísimo too, plus the Copa Eva Duarte and the Martini Rossi and Duward trophies as the team that scored the most and conceded the fewest goals in the league.

They also claimed another Copa Latina, this time at the Parc des Princes. Barcelona players remember émigrés in Paris coming up to them, praising them for representing Catalonia and asking them to make contact with families left behind. The guerrilla resistance movement, the Maquis, had also made France their base. 'The directors told us not to speak to anyone because of the fear that there would be Maquis among them,' Seguer recalls. 'Politics never entered into the dressing room. We knew the problems we could have.' Barcelona were 1-0 winners against Nice in the final, César getting the only goal, and returned to Catalonia by train, where official estimates calculated that there were a million people on the streets for their victory parade. A telegram arrived from Franco's palace congratulating them, although when the team met the dictator at El Pardo, they were told not to talk to him too much. Barcelona's success did not end there. They won the league again in 1952–3 and, as league and cup winners, 'won' the Eva Duarte trophy for the second year in a row, this time uncontested.

The folk singer Joan Manuel Serrat was born in Catalonia in 1948. He would come to be the leading light in the Nova Cançó movement that later projected a new Catalan cultural identity in the mid-1960s. He became close friends with Kubala and dedicated him a number in which he sang: 'Pelé was Pelé/And there was only one Maradona/Di Stéfano was a fount of cunning . . . they all had their merits but, for me, none was like Kubala.' The song was an ode to a man of 'fantasy', a 'gourmet' who brought 'football into colour'. But his most famous song was 'Temps era temps', written in 1980, in which he sang of a bygone age. It is a portrayal of Catalan society during those years, a song of nostalgia and wonder in which one line stands out above all: 'Basora, César, Kubala, Moreno i Manchón.' Those were the men who formed the forward line of that *Cinc Copes* team, even though Jordi Vila actually played more than Moreno that season and Emilio Aldecoa took the inside-left role against Nice. They were the five men who represented that team in the collective conscience, the team of Serrat's childhood. Five men whose names everyone could recite by memory, 'as if it was the Lord's Prayer', in the words of Joan Gaspart.

On one wing was Estanislao Basora, known as the Monster of Colombes after he scored a hat-trick in twelve minutes against France there. Basora, whose father was mysteriously shot dead in his office by a man with a hunting rifle in July 1941, provided an endless supply of crosses: small, skilful, always willing to take people on, he also scored 153 goals in 373 games for Barça. On the other side, Moreno and Manchón were the 'Wings of a Dove', flying up and down the left. 'You see those stepovers that Cristiano Ronaldo does? Well, Manchón did those at the speed of light,' Olivella recalls. The man who took advantage was César, who they called *El Pelucas*: the Wig. 'I'm not sure if he lost his hair because of all the heading, but it would not surprise me: the ball was tough and it was hard enough crossing it, heading it was terrible,' Basora recalled. César had been signed by Samitier at the end of the civil war, joining Barcelona from the Frente de Juventudes team in León, ending his Barcelona career with 235 competitive goals. Then there was Gustau Biosca, 'The Gypsy'. And Andreu Bosch and Josep Segarra and Jaime Escudero. Behind them all stood Antoni Ramallets, still regarded as the greatest goalkeeper in Barcelona's history.

Born on 1 July 1924, over the course of his career Ramallets played 551 games for Barcelona. He won six league titles, five Copas and two Fairs Cups. Until Víctor Valdés overtook him in 2012, he had won the Zamora award as the league's best goalkeeper more times than anyone else. He collected dozens of medals, ranging from the Order of Isabel la Católica to the DND's Medal for Sporting Merit, plus over a hundred plaques and medals from supporters' clubs – all lovingly laid out on a sheet that he himself has typed up, a kind of CV of a glorious career. The sheet also notes that Ramallets played for Spain thirty-five times, including at two World Cups. At the first of those, Brazil 1950, he acquired his nickname: the Cat of Maracaná. 'That was Matías Prats, the commentator, who did that,' he says. 'Back in Barcelona there was a shop window that, for some reason, had a white cat tied up in it. The cat looked like it had wings, or maybe they'd put some on it, I can't remember for sure. Anyway, in Brazil I made a save and Prats shouted: "and Ramallets has flown like a cat with wings" . . .'

The 1950 World Cup was the tournament at which *la selección* beat England – Muñoz Calero sent a telegram back to Franco informing him that the Spanish had defeated 'perfidious Albion' – and Ramallets was a revelation. 'I made some pretty important saves,' he says, 'and the thing is, I went there not expecting to play at all.' By the time he returned to Barcelona, he had become the undisputed number one. For most fans, he still is.

'Those were difficult times,' Ramallets says. 'It was eleven years after the civil war and we began a kind of resurgence, travelling around. I remember we went to Caracas twice. Other countries looked at us with a kind of suspicion: "Spaniards!" There were some players who could not travel for political reasons. Journalists tend to mix up sport with politics but for us that wasn't an issue. There was a rivalry with Real Madrid on the pitch but not off it. From the players' point of view it is annoying that there's always the political angle but you get used to it. There are always those who, maybe not with bad intentions, try to mix up sport and politics. Esperanza Aguirre too, eh!'

Esperanza Aguirre? It is May 2012, three days since Esperanza Aguirre, the president of the Madrid government, suggested that the Copa del Rey final, to be held in the city, should be suspended if fans of Athletic Bilbao and Barcelona, Basques and Catalans respectively, decided to whistle the Spanish national anthem as they did two years before.

Ramallets lives in a small house in San Juan de Mediona, in the Catalan countryside, and he still watches Barcelona. 'One of the things that I most enjoy is watching the *canteranos*, the local kids who have come through the club at youth level because I was a *canterano* too,' he says. 'I was born in Gràcia, very near the ground. It pleases me that the *canteranos* have a key role, Valdés especially. I'm happy that he's broken my record.' He returns to his era. Asked about the *Cinc Copes* he leaps in: 'Eh, it was six, not five! No one took the Eva Duarte very seriously but we did.' He talks fondly of his team-mates. Of Serrat's forward line, of Segarra and Seguer, of Evaristo and of Luis Suárez, the man who joined Barcelona in 1955 and became the only Spaniard to win the Ballon d'Or. But it is the Hungarian who stands out.

'Kubala defined an era,' Ramallets says. 'He made Les Corts too small and he won the admiration of everyone. He revolutionised technique and tactics and he covered the entire pitch. At the start he used to come to me and say "give me the ball". I would pretend I hadn't heard him and boot it up the pitch. But then you realise it's a good idea. He stopped us giving the ball away; he could pass the ball, he could carry it, and through him others found that they could too. He was a genius, a maestro, a professor! You'd see moves in which he had three men on him, chasing him, and he would go round them all. Calm as anything. The players we had throughout that period were all great players but Kubala was the focus of everything.'

So much so that the following season, when Kubala fell ill, Barcelona's chances of winning the title appeared to have been ruined, losing to Real Madrid, Valencia, Atlético Bilbao and Málaga. In total, Kubala missed eighteen games. He had been diagnosed with tuberculosis and lost six kilos. His lung capacity dropped from seven litres to five. 'I remember the medical report,' Kubala said later: '*no apto para el deporte.*' Not fit for sports. Barcelona consulted a Dr Recasens who suggested a potential solution that turned out to be startlingly simple. Kubala was sent to the small mountain village of Monistrol de Calders not far from Montserrat, to rest. Eventually, he put on eight kilos, returning in week twenty-one of the season. Kubala had been out from late October to late February. In his first game back Barcelona drew 1-1 with Racing Santander. The next match versus Zaragoza, the first he'd played at Les Corts in four months, finished with an 8-0 win, beginning a run of eight consecutive victories, including one over Real Madrid.

Barcelona had been fifth at the halfway stage of the season. With Kubala back, they won a second successive league title then beat Atlético Bilbao to win the double. In two and a quarter seasons, the Hungarian had won two league titles, two Copa del Generalísimos, two Copa Latinas and a Copa Eva Duarte. One newspaper remarked: 'When his illness was diagnosed, such was the general anguish that it was as if the price of bread had gone up. When he was cured, it was as if everybody had been handed a pay rise.' Kubala's return was a miracle few had believed possible. Indeed, while he nursed his illness Barcelona had even begun to look for someone who might be able to fill the void. They settled on an Argentinian by the name of Alfredo Di Stéfano.

8

THE SIGNING OF THE CENTURY

Nineteen fifty-three was the turning point, the year that changed everything. Football can be divided into 'Before Alfredo Di Stéfano' and 'After Alfredo Di Stéfano'. Countless players have earned winners' medals, produced moments of magic that linger forever in the memory and even carried teams to glory, but few can truly claim to have changed history. Perhaps none can claim to have changed history quite like the man who signed for Real Madrid in September 1953. 'Nothing,' says Paco Gento, the only player to have won six European Cups, 'would have been the same without him.' Without Di Stéfano, much of football does not make sense. He propelled the game into the modern era and contributed more than anyone to making the European Cup the most prestigious competition there is and Madrid the biggest club in history.

Real Madrid's culture and identity are bound up in what Di Stéfano brought. Without him there would be no *galácticos*, no packed stadium, no sense of grandeur or entitlement, and little of the success that makes them what they are. Without him, they would not be the most popular club in Spain and possibly the world; on the other side of the divide, nor would they be so hated. Barcelona would be different too and so would the relationship: Di Stéfano's transfer to Madrid lies at the very heart of the rivalry. One single player may never have symbolised so much. A case can even be made for saying that, without Di Stéfano, Spain would have been different too.

The coincidence is certainly striking. Nineteen fifty-three was the year Madrid signed Di Stéfano; it was also the year Franco signed a concordat with the Vatican and a military bases agreement with the United States. All that happened within just four days. The concordat was signed on 27 August; the Madrid Pact with the USA was signed a day earlier; and Di Stéfano made his debut for Madrid three days before that. *Arriba*, the newspaper of the state party, later declared that the country had become the 'decisive axis of world policy'. It was a wild exaggeration but Spain was about to become the centre of world football and that was a shift that would have a political meaning too, helping to change society and projecting 'Spain' towards a world that had turned its back.

According to former striker Emilio Butragueño, now a director at the Bernabéu, 'the history of Madrid starts with Alfredo'. The blunt truth is that when he arrived Madrid were not very good. Atlético Madrid had won four league titles since 1940, while Barcelona had won five, including the last two. Since the end of the civil war, Atlético Bilbao, Atlético Madrid, Valencia and Sevilla had all won the league but Madrid had not. In total, there had been fourteen post-war competitions. Madrid had won two – the 1945–6 and 1946–7 Copas – while Barcelona had won nine. 'Madrid hadn't won the league for years,' Di Stéfano recalls, 'but they were a prestigious club from the capital with an extraordinary stadium and great players. That obliged us to be the best. I came to do something great. I didn't come for the money alone, I came to win.'

He won immediately. Madrid claimed the league in Di Stéfano's debut season – their first since 1933 – and went on to win eight of them in eleven seasons. The momentum had been shifted for ever. In their entire history, Madrid had won just two league titles before Di Stéfano but since the day he arrived in 1953 they have won thirty. They have eleven more than Barcelona, twenty-three more than Atlético, twenty-four more than Athletic and twenty-six more than Valencia. Betis and Sevilla, only one behind when he arrived, now trail by thirty each. Madrid also won the first five European Cups with Di Stéfano scoring in every final, and played in seven of the first nine finals, establishing an unrivalled dynasty. No team has ever been as synonymous with a trophy, still less the greatest club trophy of them all.

No wonder Barcelona fans can't help wondering what might have been. After all, they had signed Di Stéfano too.

As Estanislao Basora, then Barcelona's captain, put it fifty years later: 'With Di Stéfano, there would have been a huge difference between Barcelona and the rest. Maybe we would have won the five European Cups in a row that Madrid did.' When Di Stéfano turned out for Barcelona in a charity match in January 1956, playing alongside László Kubala at the Camp Nou, *El Mundo Deportivo* declared the pair of them 'flares of a thousand colours lighting up the sky'. There was a hint of melancholy in the remark, a forbidden desire: *we should have seen this every week.* They had been denied the chance – by Madrid and, so the argument goes, by the Franco regime. The historian and former Barcelona director Jaume Sobrequés describes Madrid's signing of Di Stéfano as 'a manoeuvre from the paladins of *franquismo*'. In the Spanish capital, meanwhile, talk of the transfer is swiftly glossed over or presented merely as evidence of Catalan paranoia.

'*Nos lo robaron*,' said Narcís de Carreras, Barça's vice-president during the affair and later president between 1968 and 1969. The words are simple and often repeated: *he was stolen from us.* The theory has it that Madrid robbed Di Stéfano and, by extension, a glorious future too. Madrid's European Cups, their status as the twentieth-century's greatest club, the aura that surrounds them, is 'rightfully' Barcelona's. Di Stéfano's signing is symbolic, definitive 'proof' of the 'fact' that Barcelona were victims and Madrid beneficiaries of the Franco dictatorship.

Di Stéfano's transfer was a complex story of intrigue, interest and accusation. Put in very simple terms, Di Stéfano played for the

Ronaldo, Messi; Messi, Ronaldo.
The world's best players score
two each as Real Madrid face
FC Barcelona at the Camp Nou
in October 2012.

When Madrid meet Barcelona it is
never just football,
but this was billed as the most
political *clásico* of them all.

17 minutes, 14 seconds, and the
chant went up from the Camp Nou:
'Independence! Independence!'

The north end of the Camp Nou towers over the walls of the cemetery of Les Corts, resting place of some of Barcelona's greatest players and a source of inspiration on *clásico* morning.

The most famous photo in Spanish football history: Ricardo Zamora's last minute save in the 1936 cup final gave Madrid victory against Barcelona. The Spanish Civil War broke out less than a month later. Madrid and Barcelona would not meet in the final again until 1968.

Barcelona's American tour in 1937 allowed them to raise money and escape the war. Afterwards they were accused by the Franco regime of having been 'sent to Mexico as a propagandist of the red cause'.

Barcelona president Josep Sunyol (*right, centre*), assassinated by fascist troops on the Madrid front on 6 August 1936.

A memorial stone to Sunyol (*above left*) was placed in a small, unremarkable park in the nearby town of Guadarrama in 1996 after a long campaign to have him formally remembered. The point on the road where Sunyol was shot (*above right*). The stone staging post has gone now and his body has never been recovered.

Rafael Sánchez Guerra (*left*), the Real Madrid president arrested and tried by the Franco regime as a 'dangerous' man, closely identified with the 'reds'.

Patriarch and president: for forty years, Santiago Bernabéu (*right*) *was* Real Madrid.

The last survivor of Real Madrid's infamous, politically charged 11-1 victory over Barcelona in 1943: reserve goalkeeper Fernando Argila.

The 11-1 is still Real Madrid's biggest ever victory but it has a more prominent place in Barcelona's history.

The hidden file, lost to history, that sheds new light on Alfredo Di Stéfano's contested transfer to Real Madrid.

'I earnestly request the approval of an order prohibiting the signing of foreign players as proposed by this delegation. I consider this measure necessary for the satisfaction and decorum of national football and to avoid uncomfortable attitudes and situations.' The regime intervenes to prevent the signing of Di Stéfano by Barcelona ... or Madrid. 1953.

The forbidden fantasy. Alfredo Di Stéfano and László Kubala, together in the Barcelona side. Di Stéfano and Ferenç Puskás pull on the *blaugrana* shirt for Kubala's testimonial against Stade de Reims.

Madrid's finest hour: the 7-3 victory over Eintracht Frankfurt at Hampden Park – Madrid's fifth European Cup. 'We almost achieved some kind of footballing perfection,' Puskás recalled.

1960. Evaristo de Macedo's diving header knocks five-time champions Real Madrid out of Europe for the first time ever. After the game, Madrid's players tried to beat up the English referee.

Ferenç Puskás. 'That bugger played pregnant,' laughs team-mate Amancio Amaro. But he was still arguably the best striker they had ever seen.

Alfredo Di Stéfano changed Real Madrid for ever, leading them to the first five European Cups and scoring in every final. Madrid's history starts with him.

Helenio Herrera, the original Special One, took Barcelona to two consecutive league titles but it was not enough. He was sacked after Real Madrid knocked the Catalans out of the European Cup.

Franco hands the Copa del Generalísimo to Barcelona captain José Antonio Zaldua after the controversial 'Bottles Final' in 1968.

1970, Copa del Generalísimo quarter-final. Over 30,000 cushions were thrown onto the pitch in protest after the referee Emilio Guruceta gave Real Madrid a penalty for a foul outside the area.

Colombian side Millonarios but was owned by River Plate. Barcelona struck a deal with River, Madrid struck a deal with Millonarios. And then the Spanish football authorities and the government stepped in to break the deadlock by proposing that he alternate between the two clubs – at which point Barcelona renounced their rights. It is either the biggest mistake in their history or the biggest robbery, depending on your point of view. Either way, it is *big*. It remains the key moment in the rivalry, a turning point that continues to be an obsession, still argued over and debated more than half a century later.

As for Di Stéfano, the man who meant everything to Real Madrid, for ever identified with its greatest glories, he is startlingly blunt, disarmingly honest. 'I always said that I didn't care if I played for Barcelona or for Madrid,' he wrote in his memoirs. 'It was all the same to me. I just wanted to play.'

Alfredo Di Stéfano is eighty-seven now. He is also gloriously grumpy. He does not suffers fools – he never did. Nostalgia is laced with a tough edge of realism, not viewed through rose-tinted spectacles, and you can still see the determination that helped make him what he was. There remains a spark about him, spikiness and shafts of humour, some of it sharp and genuinely funny. He is a proud man, prickly too. If there is little sentimentality, there is real warmth towards his team-mates. Sixty years after leaving Argentina, he's still here. And so, he says with satisfaction, are many of them.

Di Stéfano sits behind a desk in his 'office', in the bowels of the Santiago Bernabéu, looking through a small match-day programme: Stoke City versus Real Madrid, the English club's centenary match in April 1963. 'Stanley Matthews,' he says slowly, almost reverentially, 'now *he* could play.' His walking stick leans against the side of the desk as he runs his hands gently over the paper, lifting his glasses to gaze at the pictures, going through the teams, player by player, picking out the names that mean most to him. '*¡Que barbariedad!*' he says, *Wow!*

He waves his hand in the rough direction of the rest of this hidden corner of the stadium, home to the veterans' association – founded on the recommendation of Josep María Fusté, who had done the same at Barcelona. 'They're all here,' he says proudly. 'Emilio . . . Pachín . . . Amancio . . . Zoco . . . a family. If there's one with a money problem, he gets looked after. I know: I went through that myself.'

Di Stéfano's conversation is occasionally rambling, sometimes contradictory and often disconnected, trailing off at one point ready to return somewhere else entirely, but it is penetrating too and some of the memories are crystalline. The way he speaks is uncomplicated, unaffected, and his voice is gruff and gravelly, the Argentinian accent not entirely lost. He talks about his team-mates – 'one hundred and twenty-one of them, at least, and all great players' – and he talks about travel. He talks about games, pressure and money. He talks about Madrid and about Barcelona, about the president, Santiago Bernabéu, and about the fans. He talks about Spanish society and about what it was that moved him and his team-mates.

'It had to be a spectacle; it was not enough to win. But the word is *win*,' he says. 'Nothing else was good enough. Every time we lost, it was a disaster, a huge problem at the club. Our mission was to win – and we *had* to win. We were all good players but it was hard, eh. There had to be unity and mutual affection. If you didn't win here, you were nothing. In the rain, in the snow . . . People want to win always – and when they don't . . . well, it was bitter. We wanted to win for the fans and the players wanted to win for the financial interest it had for us too, of course. Our hobby became a job, an obligation. But we didn't get tired of it; football is to be enjoyed – even though we knew our responsibilities . . .

. . . Oh, we knew.'

You can sense the weight as he says so – and pressure and pay, hardly staples of misty nostalgia, are themes he returns to often. But you can sense the enjoyment too. There is no stopping him, memories flooding back, emotions and ideas, snapshots running into each other, a stream of consciousness. 'We were an attacking team: what we did was attack for seventy-five minutes and then maybe we could spend the last fifteen or twenty protecting the result, playing . . .

'We were professionals, working for the club. We would do tours, lots of them: Rio, Buenos Aires, Alaska . . . we went everywhere, literally all round the world. And in the middle of all the travelling, we'd play a bit. The people were always pleased to see us. The club would get thirty or forty thousand dollars a game. Money. Buenos Aires, Caracas, wherever, then it would be off to Rio, maybe $50,000. They said they'd give us a bonus, a *prima*. A thousand pesetas for each goal we won by. So the next game we scored six and they said: *prima suspendida*. No more. *Nada más.* There's no more money. We scored too many.'

'Back home,' he continues, 'Spain was changing: I don't know if we improved Spain . . . we improved Spanish sport, though.'

And European too?

'The European Cup has changed a lot,' he says, starting up again and returning once more to the pressure, that sense of vindication and the competitive edge. 'Now it's forty-odd teams; then it was just the champions. If you didn't win, you didn't play. There weren't many games but you had to win every time, any way you could. And the moment you lost, you were *liquidated*. It's dangerous because if you have a bad day, just one . . . there was always a great pressure on the team but we knew we could play and we worked too. You have to have the strength of character to put up with that: to put up with the pressure and everything we had to put up with. We used to fly to European games and . . .'

Now there's a longer pause, a break in the monologue, the hint of something darker. Eventually the penny drops. You were afraid of flying?!

'And how!' he exclaims. 'There were mountains there alongside you. We felt pressure and fear. We didn't want to fly. But we had to.'

Di Stéfano talks about all that – and more. But the one thing he's not keen to talk about is the thing others most want to talk about.

'The rivalry with Barcelona?' he says, barely pausing to ponder. 'It was sporting. We had friends in their team. Kubala was a *crack* and a good guy, a good lad. He was a real friend. A great player too. And Barcelona had a good team then: very, very good. But for me the rivalry at the time was with Atlético Madrid. They were a good team and they were right here next to us. When they won, they suddenly sprang up like mushrooms and started shouting. Barcelona? They were six hundred kilometres away – we couldn't even smell them.'

They didn't see it like that, though. Not least because there was a political dimension to it . . .

'Yeah, but that's the fans, not the players. You're a footballer. Someone kicks you, you maybe kick them back. But you don't worry. We're football players not political warriors.'

Barcelona see themselves as more than a club and some fans accused Madrid of being Franco's team.

'Everyone's free to do the propaganda they see fit . . . it's a buzz-word, but anyway . . . Look at the competitions we won.'

You signed for Madrid. Barcelona thought . . .

This time the response is sharper. '*Pero eso dejarlo.*' Yeah, but leave that.

Di Stéfano continues: 'I'm *hasta las pelotas*, sick of it. So, that's it. They shouted all sorts of things at me in the stadiums but . . . *nada*. I didn't have any problem. People are cowards. When there are loads of them, they shout and they talk and they throw bottles. When they're on their own, they're all timid and quiet. Off the pitch, they don't shout any more. And if I see one, *lo reviento!* I'll smash him in! I ended up laughing at it all. Battles, wars, attacks. In the end, they drop like flies.'

One sunny spring morning in May 2012, there it is. A government file, old and greying, a little dusty, hidden away for years and lost to history. It dates from 1953 and it is tucked inside a white archive box numbered 51/19035 in Alcalá de Henares, the university town to the north-east of Madrid. The front of the file is embossed with the yoke and the arrows, the symbol of the Francoist state party, Falange Española Tradicionalista y de las JONS, and the department: General Secretariat/Political Secretariat/Technical Section. In the top right-hand corner it says 'no. 519-' and across the bottom a subject line. Typed on to the dots, it reads: 'Di Stéfano'.

The file contains documents that shed new light on Di Stéfano's transfer to Madrid, including the telegram with which General José Moscardó, the head of the Delegación Nacional de Deportes, requested that the regime place a blanket ban on signing foreign players and an exchange of letters between the president of the Spanish Football Federation Sancho Dávila, the secretary-general of the state party Raimundo Fernández Cuesta and Moscardó. The documents provide a long-awaited official glimpse of the transfer and confirm that Di Stéfano's signing did indeed reach governmental level and that the final resolution was imposed against the initial judgement of Dávila, who had dismissed *Madrid's* agreement to sign Di Stéfano as worthless.

It starts with a letter Dávila wrote to Fernandez Cuesta on 17 August 1953, bemoaning 'a press campaign that completely lacks foundations around the Di Stéfano case', which had reached an awkward and ugly stalemate. In it, Dávila wrote: 'in the summer, as there are no news stories, they have to invent them and employ a sensationalist tone that confuses the readers and creates general disquiet and anger.'

In a letter to General Moscardó, Dávila was more explicit, describing the situation, on one level at least, as simple: the legal claim over Di Stéfano resided with Barcelona. 'There has been an extraordinary fight which has been even greater than for Kubala,' Dávila informed Moscardó. 'Millonarios cannot transfer [Di Stéfano] without agreement from River Plate, who won't give it, and River cannot sell him to Barcelona now. [The newspaper] *La Hoja del Lunes* even ran a story of the player "signing" for Madrid as if it was Spain's treaty with the

United States. But the signing is not worth the paper it is written on because they do not have an agreement with River or authorisation from the Federation.'

'It is,' he concluded, 'a mess.'

That much was certainly true. By then, Alfredo Di Stéfano had been stuck in Spain, and in limbo, for three long months, not knowing who he was going to sign for or even if he would be able to sign for anyone at all.

The saga began over four years earlier with the Argentinian players' strike. Denounced by his club River Plate, Di Stéfano took the unilateral decision to leave for Millonarios, a Colombian team playing in a pirate league, not recognised by FIFA. There was no formal transfer, no fee paid, no certificate, no official registration and River were up in arms. When the case was treated by FIFA, the Lima Pact ruled that the renegade players could stay in Colombia for the time being but that ownership would automatically revert to their original clubs on 15 October 1954. To make matters even more complicated, during Christmas 1952–3 Di Stéfano returned to Buenos Aires without telling Millonarios and did so with the $4,000 chunk of his salary they had already advanced to him. Now, like River before, Millonarios denounced him. Tired and disillusioned, Di Stéfano decided to call it a day.

But if retirement beckoned, so did Spain's biggest clubs. Barcelona moved first. President Enric Martí Carretó charged Josep Samitier with organising the transfer and Samitier sent two emissaries to convince Di Stéfano to give the game another go. Soon, Madrid became involved too. Bernabéu was still furious about missing out on Kubala and itching for revenge. According to the minutes of a board meeting held in April 1953, he insisted: 'Madrid cannot let its territory be trampled on . . . [we must] do whatever is necessary to sign the best players.' But by the time Madrid reacted, Di Stéfano had, as he himself recalls, 'already given my word to the Catalans'.

Madrid would not give in so easily and a communiqué from the Catalan Football Federation had told Barça to abstain from signing

Di Stéfano because Millonarios's formal complaint could leave them in a 'delicate position with FIFA'. The Federation warned that Barcelona should not make any 'surreptitious' attempt to sign him, noting: 'Di Stéfano has disappeared from [Bogotá] with an unknown destination, although it is supposed that it is Barcelona.'

The supposition was correct and the biggest tug-of-war in history was about to begin. Di Stéfano arrived at Madrid's Barajas airport in the early evening of 22 May 1953. Samitier was waiting and a car drove the Argentinian, his wife and his daughter to Barcelona, where he was set up in a flat on Calle Balmes. A blue plaque could go up outside the flat: 'Here was born the Barça–Madrid rivalry'. Barcelona agreed a four-million-peseta fee with River but Di Stéfano would not revert to being a River player for another sixteen months so Barcelona also needed to reach a deal with Millonarios if they were to push the transfer through earlier. Di Stéfano recalls Barcelona telling him they were waiting for a 'third man': they had the player, they had River, but they needed Millonarios. Instead, it would be Madrid who struck a deal with the Colombian club. The stalemate was served.

Di Stéfano began training with Kubala and the rest of the Barcelona team until a ruling from the DND prevented him from doing so. 'Barcelona's directors told me to wait,' Di Stéfano recalls, 'it was always wait, wait, wait.' He also played in three friendlies in Masnou, Palafrugell and Sitges, but at that point Barcelona's first team were on a summer tour of Caracas, Venezuela, and calling the side that played those games 'Barcelona' might be a stretch – in one match Di Stéfano's side even wore white shirts. 'When we came back from Venezuela we expected him to be a Barcelona player,' recalls Josep Seguer. But as Di Stéfano remembered it: 'June passed, July, and . . . *nada*.'

Barcelona dispatched a Catalan lawyer called Ramón Trias Fargas to Bogotá to strike a deal with Millonarios at the start of July. It was to prove a frustrating trip. The Millonarios president Alfonso Senior asked for $27,000 and Barcelona refused. Another deal was verbally agreed by Trias Fargas but when the Barcelona president Martí arrived in Bogotá five days later, the offer was withdrawn. Martí informed the Colombians that he wouldn't pay a high price and that, if needs be, he would leave Di Stéfano inactive until October 1954 when he automatically reverted to being a River player and would be sold, unopposed, to Barça. Senior later told reporters: 'we gave Barcelona lots of chances, even the chance to not pay any money ["paying" with friendly matches instead] and we were always treated with disrespect. Now that they realise we do have rights, it is too late. I would have liked it to have ended well but Barcelona's directors took a step backwards and that's when Millonarios negotiated with Real Madrid. After that we kept our word to Bernabéu.'

Senior's remarks may be disingenuous. Saporta had been sent to Colombia to tell Millonarios that Madrid would beat any offer from Barcelona and Bernabéu later boasted that winning over the Colombians was 'easy'. And yet Barcelona's complacency and division at that key point is startling and was quite probably fatal. Had Barça paid Millonarios what they wanted – and Trias Fargas later insisted that the series of deals he lined up for the approval of the board were bargains – Di Stéfano would have been theirs. 'We lost out on Di Stéfano just at the moment when it was easiest to sign him,' Samitier remarked.

One possible explanation is simple: that despite subsequent and largely retrospective complaints once Madrid began building a dynasty, the reality is that Barcelona were no longer especially bothered and that, while they cooled on the transfer, Madrid stepped in. Kubala had recovered and there was no pressing need to sign Di Stéfano now. There have also been suggestions that reports prepared on the Argentinian following the friendlies were not entirely positive. In his autobiography, Di Stéfano himself notes, displaying an arresting lack of self-confidence: 'they had a great team. Kubala was a veritable machine. The stadium, 45,000, was full every week and I thought: "if these guys are champions, why do they need me?" They said that Kubala had a lung problem but I didn't think so . . . I always felt they went a bit cold then [after the friendlies].'

But no reports on those games have been found and there is a flaw in that theory: if Barcelona's interest really had waned, why did Trias Fargas keep on resisting? Why did the saga continue into September? Barcelona's refusal to pay Millonarios was an appalling mistake but it was an understandable one – a negotiating tactic that failed but one that had been founded on a certain logic. From 15 October 1954, Di Stéfano would legally have been Barcelona's player anyway. The Catalans were essentially being asked to pay 1.35 million pesetas for a little over a year, having already committed to spending four million pesetas. Madrid were a threat but, without a deal from River, at most they could sign Di Stéfano for sixteen months only. Moreover, because Di Stéfano had refused to return to Millonarios and threatened to retire if he was not allowed to join Barcelona, the Colombians' position appeared as weak as Madrid's.

Martí's communiqué back to the Barcelona board said it all: 'Di Stéfano says he will not go back to Bogotá so sooner or later they'll have to accept our offer.'

Or did it? As time went on, Trias Fargas grew ever more exasperated. Every time he thought he had reached an agreement with Millonarios, the Barcelona board rejected it, and he arrived at the baffling conclusion that they were being deliberately obstructive. Trias Fargas wrote a report after Di Stéfano joined Madrid in which he effectively accused Martí of torpedoing the deal. The question is: *why?* Self-justification is one reason – Trias Fargas certainly did not want to carry the can for the failure – and Barcelona's possible cooling on Di Stéfano is another, but a further possibility emerged many years later.

In 1980, Lluis Permanyer, whose father was the vice-secretary at Barcelona between 1948 and 1953, wrote in *La Vanguardia* of 'a whole array of pressures applied to Barcelona to make them renounce their claim'. Two years later in an interview with *El País*, Narcís de Carreras claimed that Martí had been pressured into ceding the rights to Di Stéfano and insisted that Barcelona's board members had been followed by detectives and their premises bugged. 'Martí even had a call from a high-level civil servant from the Ministry of Commerce who said to him: "up until now you've had no problems with the Institute of Foreign Currency but if you persist with Di Stéfano we don't know what might happen".' And, in 1997, the Barcelona director José María Azorín told Jordi Finestres and Xavier Luque, the Catalan authors of an impressively researched account of the signing: 'Martí didn't have any other way out. I didn't give details [at the time], I couldn't! If I had, I would have gone to jail. Something far worse would have happened.'

According to the former Barcelona director Josep María Minguella, a friend apparently warned Martí: 'Be sensible, you have family.' And even Di Stéfano remembered: 'I heard that Enric Martí had received threats because he had business interests in Morocco. That's the kind of thing they said: there was talk of them investigating where he got his money from, of pressure from Madrid.'

It is impossible to verify the claims or to establish what form the threats took, if they really did exist, or *where* exactly they came from. If they came from within the regime, how high up? And how serious were they? It is also not clear at which points the threats were made – whether during Trias Fargas's frustrated attempts to get the Barcelona board to back his offers to Millonarios or later on when the regime became involved in trying to break the deadlock, although the latter is more probable. It is also legitimate to ask why it took quite so long for anyone to speak out, even though silence naturally reigned during the regime and a circular in October 1953 prohibited the media from talking about Di Stéfano in anything other than strictly sporting terms.

The summer wore on. Raimundo Bernabéu told Saporta to offer Di Stéfano a million pesetas just to walk up the Castellana and the vice-president travelled to Catalonia to convince the Argentinian that Barcelona was not big enough for two superstars: he and Kubala could not play in the same team. At first Di Stéfano was furious at the temerity, berating Saporta for complicating the situation still further and spitting, 'are you trying to ruin my career for me here, or what?'

Saporta insisted there was a genuine chance of making the move happen, showing Di Stéfano the paperwork from Colombia.

'And?' replied the player, 'I'm still here, aren't I?'

He had little faith in Madrid and increasingly little faith in Barcelona either. He even told the Barcelona board he had had enough of waiting – he was heading back to Buenos Aires, throwing in the towel.

Barcelona made one last try – hardly the action of a club that was no longer bothered about signing Di Stéfano – and Narcís de Carreras, the vice-president, met Senior in Madrid in the hope that he would connect better with the Colombian than Martí had only for Senior to tell him him that he had an agreement with Madrid. The pressure told on the Barça board, where there were recriminations and splits. Bernabéu gleefully wrote in August of 'an enormous mess at the Catalan club and a ferocious hatred between the president and his friends and the vice-president and his friends'.

The conflict had escalated. In mid-August, Madrid's vice-president received a letter from a friend in Barcelona, telling him: 'the passion and anti-Madrid phobia here has reached superlative levels and now, with this transfer, it is even more inflamed. [Di Stéfano] has no problem announcing at supporters' clubs or on the radio and in the press that he will never play for Madrid, that he will only play for Barcelona or he will go back to Argentina . . . Every Sunday they take him round like an exhibit, an act of propaganda. He goes to town *fiestas* and plays in friendly matches. If we don't get the "Phenomenon" I'll be so disappointed.'

The letter reflects just how much of a public battle this had become, played out in the press. It was a political issue in which both sides were in the hunt for popular support, seeking to apply pressure and present the signing as a *fait accompli* – something that deeply embarrassed the regime, prompting the authorities to intervene. A ban on all foreign imports was announced on 24 August. In the course of his correspondence, Dávila rightly noted: 'I assume that it is the Di Stéfano case that has motivated the ban.'

In Catalonia, the ban has been seen as part of a long-term, ongoing strategy to engineer Di Stéfano's move to Madrid. But to judge by the content and the tone of the exchange of letters, it seems clear that the regime had decided that the best way to resolve a situation not of its making was to say: *ok, forget it, neither of you can have him.* Moscardó's request for a ban had explicitly stated: 'in order to avoid embarrassing situations.'

That should have been the end of it. Barcelona, conscious that there was no other solution, 'sick of it all' in Di Stéfano's words, tried to sell their rights to Juventus. But Di Stéfano would still be confronted by dual ownership. Madrid had to agree to relinquish their rights to Juventus too and they did not. Barcelona then tried to undo the deal with River and get their money back: after all, they weren't going to get him and, thanks to the ban, nor were Madrid. But River refused. Back to square one. Madrid would not shift, Barcelona *could* not shift. The ban was no solution for either Madrid or Barcelona and it caused problems for other clubs too. Letters soon arrived at the Federation and the DND from Español and Valladolid, both preparing foreign transfers of their own, pleading for the ban to be lifted.

Faced with continuing stalemate, Madrid and Barcelona had little choice but to accept mediation from Armando Muñoz Calero, the man who had helped Barcelona sign Kubala. A member of the FIFA Executive Committee and a former president of the RFEF, Muñoz Calero was also in constant contact with Moscardó. Together, Madrid and Barcelona wrote to Moscardó to request that the ban be lifted in preparation for a mediated resolution, arguing that Di Stéfano's arrival would be 'hugely beneficial to Spanish football given the extraordinary quality of the player and as a source of education'. He would strengthen the national team and bring financial reward via increased gates and prestige.

The letter signed off: 'Knowing your sense of justice and humanity, we trust you will do this service for Spanish football as you have done so many services for the nation, for which we are already grateful.' If it was genuine, that trust was misplaced.

Eventually, another solution was imposed upon the two clubs – one that was the exact opposite of the ban and yet similar in its conception. From *neither* club having Di Stéfano, *both* clubs would have Di Stéfano. Rather than resolving in favour of one club or another; rather than ruling on the legality of their respective deals; rather even than making Di Stéfano a Madrid player until 15 October 1954 and a Barcelona player thereafter, which might at least have been faithful to the two deals in place, Muñoz Calero proposed a share. Di Stéfano would play for Real Madrid in 1953–4, for Barcelona in 1954–5, for Real Madrid again in 1955–6 and then for Barcelona in 1956–7. The costs would be shared equally and after that the clubs would come to an agreement about his future – as if *that* was going to be easy. Speaking on Catalan television in 1999, Di Stéfano insisted: 'whoever suggested that knows nothing about football: how could I score goals for one team one day and for the other the next?'

The final clause of the agreement, (e), read like either the ultimate act of cynicism or the ultimate act of stupidity. It ran: 'both presidents promise to make the greatest effort to consolidate the friendly sporting relationship that have always and must always exist between their respective clubs, clubs with such deep roots amongst football fans in Barcelona and Madrid.' The deal was signed: Enric Martí, Santiago Bernabéu and Muñoz Calero, 15 September 1953. It was followed by the DND's resolution to lift the ban on foreign signings for those players, like Di Stéfano, who had embarked upon the transfer process before 22 August.

It was a ridiculous decision but, having accepted mediation, the clubs had little choice but to swallow it. There was still not a final, long-term resolution, though, and Barcelona were furious: they felt they had miscalculated and, more importantly, that they had been played. Trias Fargas's suspicions relating to Martí never truly went away. On 22 September, Martí resigned and a temporary commission took over the running of Barcelona until elections were held. Francesc Miró-Sans became president on 22 December 1953, by which time Barcelona had lost what would prove the most important battle in their history.

Although the vast majority of the details were inevitably omitted and the real reason never revealed, if there was one, Martí's resignation letter briefly laid out what had occurred over the previous six months – from the original FIFA/RFEF ban to the agreement with River, from the 'vicissitudes' in dealing with Millonarios to the DND ban on foreign players 'which we respectfully accepted' and discussions to transfer Di Stéfano abroad. Given that to do so also required Madrid's agreement, Martí explained, he travelled to the Spanish capital to be confronted with a different potential solution: Muñoz Calero's intervention and the plan to rotate Di Stéfano.

'Immediately after telling the board of directors of the club and knowing that many *socios* would have preferred things to have been handled differently, I presented my irrevocable resignation, of my own volition, which has been accepted by the Real Federación Española de Fútbol,' Martí wrote. 'Having not been able to bring to fruition all that I wanted for the benefit of our club, I do not have any reason to feel satisfied.'

Martí's choice of words is intriguing. His statement that the decision to resign was reached 'of my own volition' was a public obligation but it was also one that may just have hinted at the opposite, an implicit suggestion that ultimately the decision – or the *decisions* – had not been his alone. That feeling is increased by mention of his own dissatisfaction and, as he rightly suggested, many Barcelona members would have preferred things to have been handled differently. Above all, they would have preferred them to have ended differently.

Barcelona's culpability is unavoidable. Had they been more determined and less complacent, had they handled Millonarios differently, they would surely have signed Di Stéfano. If they had been able to reach a deal with *both* clubs it is hard to believe that the move would have been blocked. And yet the pressure was intense and they were entitled to think that, legally, they trod firm ground.

The president of the Federation had explicitly dismissed Madrid's deal for Di Stéfano as *papel mojado* – literally, 'wet paper', an agreement that was worthless. He had also recognised that a share deal was unworkable. Yet a month later those considerations no longer mattered. It was Madrid who had their man and Barcelona who went empty-handed. The Federation, the DND and the state party had all been involved in the deliberations. The regime had played a central part in making it happen and, without its involvement, it is likely that the saga would have ended with Di Stéfano joining Barcelona. But that is not the same as saying that the regime systematically engineered Di Stéfano's signing for Madrid; even suggestions that pressure was brought to bear upon Barcelona, and particularly on Martí, do not necessarily signify that – at least not to start with, not as part of a premeditated plan.

The regime was confronted with an uncomfortable and embarrassing problem; as the Catalan Federation circular suggested right at the start, they would probably have preferred Di Stéfano never to have come in the first place and Barcelona had been warned to desist even then. Faced with a stalemate and the absence of FIFA intervention later, the authorities acted. The regime was more favourably predisposed towards Madrid and the influence they could exercise upon the authorities is likely to have been greater than that of Barcelona, while Saporta and Bernabéu appeared more determined, more ruthless and better equipped to resist. There has been no suggestion that the regime pressured Madrid to relinquish their claim on Di Stéfano as it is alleged to have done with Barcelona.

For all the background machinations, though, it *is* possible to take the ban and the share deal at face value. Those decisions were consistent with the way the Franco regime proceeded on a number of issues, and fitted with the prevailing military mindset: Solomonian 'equality' of punishment and treatment was typical; the desire to not be seen to favour one party or the other, even if in doing so that was exactly what was achieved, was characteristic. Even siding with Madrid may have been seen, by the regime, in the same terms after Barcelona had got Kubala. According to Carles Torras, Martí told his grandson how Bernabéu said to him one day: 'You robbed Kubala off me, I robbed Di Stéfano off you and that's that. 1-1.' When the ban was enforced, it almost certainly was intended as a way of shutting the problem out of Spain: *if neither side signs Di Stéfano, neither side can complain.* When the share issue was proposed, it really is plausible that Moscardó, Fernández Cuesta and other dictatorship figures in the regime thought it workable or at least preferable to the alternative and the potential fallout. 'Whoever suggested that knows nothing about football,' Di Stéfano said. That is a fairly accurate judgement of many within the regime.

The day after the share deal was signed, Di Stéfano arrived in Madrid. This was the first year of his share deal; he would never reach the second. The new Barcelona board agreed to sign him over to Madrid entirely, renouncing all claim to him – a decision that Saporta rather cynically described as 'quite unexpected'. Barcelona's last chance to resist was passed up. An agreement was reached straightaway and then formalised on 23 October. Miró-Sans later told Saporta that Barcelona could still fill the stadium with Kubala. Madrid paid Barcelona 4,405,000 pesetas, plus interest, covering their costs thus far. 1,225,000 pesetas were paid by cheque immediately; 1,500,000 on 31 July 1954; 750,000 on 1 January 1955; and 930,000 on 31 July 1955.

In total, Madrid paid Barcelona, River Plate and Millonarios 5,750,000 pesetas (c. £53,000) as well as 1,350,000 to Di Stéfano as a signing-on fee, 650,000 a year basic salary, and 16,000 a month. He was also promised double the bonus earned by all of his team-mates: 250 pesetas per home win, 500 per away win. In total, over eight million pesetas. No one had ever been paid so much: no one had been *allowed* to be paid so much. The Spanish Football Federation had set a limit of 150,000 a year plus 3,000 a month. Saporta described the deal as 'cheap', writing, 'we have achieved a sensational victory over Barcelona after all the shenanigans with Kubala'.

Di Stéfano had first arrived at Madrid's Atocha station on the overnight train from Barcelona a month earlier, at 10.30 a.m. on 23 September. It was the morning after Martí's resignation. He went for a medical, ate and was at the stadium for 3.30 p.m. Madrid had hurriedly organised a match against Nancy, which kicked off just after 4 p.m. and which earned Madrid half a million pesetas. Di Stéfano was unfit, he hadn't trained properly and he was almost five kilos overweight – 78.9 kilos compared to his normal playing weight of seventy-three or seventy-four kilos. He was nervous. But still he scored. '*Veni, vidi, vici* . . . the mother that gave birth to me!' as he put it in his memoirs. Two days after the final deal was agreed on the very afternoon that those remaining details were ironed out and the Argentinian permanently signed up at Chamartín, Real Madrid beat Barcelona 5-0.

Di Stéfano scored twice.

9

BLOND ARROW

Juan Santisteban gets up from his chair and walks towards the exit at the Santiago Bernabéu stadium. He's been talking for over an hour, reminiscing about his time at Real Madrid, his seven years as a player and thirteen as a coach of the first team and Castilla. He has talked about the four European Cups he won, about twenty years managing Spain's youth teams, about working with Cesc Fàbregas and Gerard Piqué – 'good kids,' he says – and even about his brief spell as a player in the United States with the Baltimore Bays. He has talked about a tough and sometimes miserable childhood, a very different era, and about how he found a family at Madrid, about Santiago Bernabéu, Ferenç Puskás, Paco Gento and Héctor Rial. He has had much to say but before he bids farewell there is something to add. He does so quietly, with an almost conspiratorial air. 'Whatever people have told you about Alfredo Di Stéfano,' he says, practically whispering, 'ignore it.'

Ignore it?

'It is not enough. However good they say he was, he was better.'

And the thing is that they do say he was good. Ask team-mates and opponents about Alfredo Di Stéfano and virtually every word drips with deference.

Di Stéfano was denied the opportunity to exhibit his talent at the

World Cup. In 1950 and 1954, Argentina did not go; in 1958 his adopted Spain did not qualify and in 1962 a muscle injury prevented him from travelling. His absence is one of the tragedies of the game, meaning that recognition has not been universal. In England, Maradona and Pelé are followed by Best or Charlton; in France, by Platini or Zidane; in Holland, by Cruyff; in Brazil, by Garrincha; in Germany by Beckenbauer; across the world, by a combination of them all. Yet in Spain, where he played, it is not that Di Stéfano follows Pelé and Maradona, it is that he matches them. Exceeds them, even. Those who saw him, or played alongside him, invariably concur.

'I coincided with both Pelé and Alfredo,' says Darcy Silveira dos Santos, 'Canário', the Brazilian who joined Real Madrid in 1959. 'And they were the best. But Alfredo was more complete. He was the number one.'

Better than Pelé?

There is no hesitation. 'Yes.'

If FIFA did not know who to pick as the twentieth-century's best player, they had no such doubt when it came to picking the best club: it could not be any one but Real Madrid. And without Di Stéfano it could not have been Madrid; he made them the greatest club in the world. Ramón Calderón likes to tell the apocryphal anecdote of a father and son strolling through a park and coming across a statue of Di Stéfano. 'Daddy,' says the boy, 'was he a player?' 'No,' says his father, 'he was a team.'

In his debut season, Di Stéfano was Spain's top scorer, as he would be four more times, finishing his career with 216 goals in 282 league games for Madrid, 418 in 510 overall. 'Scoring goals is like making love,' he once joked, 'everyone knows how to do it but no one does it like me.' Di Stéfano wore no. 9 but to call him a centre forward is woefully inadequate. Nicknamed the Blond Arrow, twice he won the European Footballer of the Year award and, watching videos, he is far more than a finisher. There is a smoothness and grace to his game; he almost seems to be floating. He is also everywhere. It is hard not to think of Leo Messi when he says: 'I played differently to others, as a *delantero atrasado*, a withdrawn striker. I came back to look for the ball.' *L'Equipe* dubbed him *l'Omnipresente*. 'He played like three players put together,' says his biographer. 'He was a midfielder who won the ball and started the play, a no. 10 who controlled the game and delivered the final pass, and a striker who put the ball in the net. If you put together Redondo, Zidane and Ronaldo, you might just get close.'

'Pelé was amazing twenty metres from goal,' says Santisteban, 'Alfredo played in one hundred metres. I don't think there is a player who has been born or will be born who can match him. Physically he was incredible. People compare him to Pelé but he played in every position. In. Every. One. I saw him save a goal inside his own penalty area once – against Real Sociedad, I think – and in the same move end up at the other end and score. He was a beast. No one could stop him. You've never seen anyone like him and you never will either.' Amancio adds: 'He was a defender, a midfielder and a striker. He was a fucking robot! He did everything and he never, ever tired.'

Helenio Herrera famously claimed that if Pelé was the lead violinist, Di Stéfano was the entire orchestra, while Bobby Charlton, whose Manchester United team were knocked out of the European Cup by Real Madrid, remembers: 'He totally controlled the game. Every time you looked, he had the ball. Everything happened around him. You looked at him and asked yourself: "how can I possibly stop him?"'

The answer, much of the time, was that you could not – and Di Stéfano knew it. Ten minutes into one game, he turned to Fidel Ugarte, a young defender, and said: 'Are you going to follow me everywhere, sonny?'

Nervously, Ugarte replied: 'Yes, my coach told me I have to.'

'OK,' shrugged Di Stéfano, 'sure, you can follow me about. You might even learn something.'

The remark reveals something else about Di Stéfano: he had a sharp, withering wit, absolute confidence in himself and a dismissiveness that could destroy. 'He was not always very nice,' as one former team-mate diplomatically puts it. Puskás recalled card games where he, Di Stéfano and Raymond Kopa cleaned up, noting: 'Alfredo would rage if he lost at cards (and he would only bet the smallest Spanish currency he could find).' He was, they say, a man in a permanent bad mood. As one contemporary chronicler put it: 'He always seemed to be angry. He smoked naked in the dressing-room post-game, would let out a grunt and everyone saw it as some wise statement. He was serious, sombre and almost sad but he sprang into life on the pitch, where he had the ability to be ubiquitous and the dubious privilege of being allowed to have a go at his team-mates.'

The word *pesado* – heavy going, hard work, difficult, relentless – comes up over and over again. 'He was,' says Pachín, 'a born champion: he was obsessed with winning, winning, winning.' He could not abide those that did not think the same way and he was frightening too, the undisputed leader. More than any coach: between Di Stéfano's arrival in 1953 and the fifth European Cup in 1960, Madrid had five different coaches across seven spells. 'There were always mistakes and Di Stéfano would have a list of them in his head,' recalled Puskás. Canário says: 'He shouted and swore for ninety minutes, always trying to get the best out of you. The coach would give a team talk before the game but we had players who changed things once we were on the pitch and knew how to lead. Alfredo, above all.'

'He'd be at you all game: "Son of a bitch, run!",' says Santisteban. 'And I'd respond: "Don Alfredo, if only I could run a quarter as much as you could". That's the thing: he never demanded you ran for him; he demanded you ran as much as him, but that was impossible. Nothing was ever enough for him – he always wanted more, in training sessions, in games. His demands were huge on himself and on his team. He had such drive.'

Rarely was that made clearer than when he turned on Amancio Amaro, who had signed for Madrid for twelve million pesetas (£71,500) from Deportivo de La Coruña in 1962, a colossal fee. One day very early in his first pre-season with Madrid in Ghana, Amancio noted that his training top did not have the Real Madrid badge on it, unlike everyone else's. Di Stéfano famously snapped: *hay que sudarla, chaval.* 'You've got to sweat [to earn] it first, sunshine.'

Laughing now, Amancio takes up the story: 'You have to bear in mind the age difference and who he was. I noticed that the shirt didn't have the Madrid badge on it and I mentioned it. I was twenty-one or just turned twenty-two and had joined from a Second Division team and he . . . well, he's Alfredo Di Stéfano. He just happened to be passing by there at exactly the same time. If he hadn't been there, I'm sure someone would have just said "well, change it then". But it was Alfredo and he said that. How about that for bloody bad luck! *Joder*, I stopped cold. He was thirty-four, thirty-five, and I had so much respect for him. My first game and the first blow is right between the eyes. Bang!

'Unforgettable? That's one word for it. Ultimately, though, I think that helped me. Our attitude was very serious – and that started with Di Stéfano. First we work to win the game; then, if there's time, you can show your skills. It was all sacrifice, effort, sweat. We were eleven workers. But not just workers, specialists: engineers, surgeons, people with talent. Alfredo was a strong character: if he did anything, he had to do it well and he demanded the same of others. But he never ordered people to do things that he wouldn't do himself.'

Puskás joked about the time that he and Di Stéfano were level on twenty-one goals each: 'I thought to myself: if I score here, he'll never speak to me again.' Puskás had a point, and some found the Argentinian hard to live with, but Di Stéfano's discourse always focuses on the team. Even now he talks about himself as '*uno más*', just another player. It is not only his talent that won him such success and admiration from those around him but his temperament too: his determination and desire to win, even if it meant sacrificing himself. The Italian Gianni Rivera recalled one occasion when Inter put two players on him, so Di Stéfano ran around the most pointless areas of the pitch, sprinting about the full-back areas, seemingly running blind, tiring them out and leaving space for his team-mates. 'He drove us mad,' Rivera sighed.

Team spirit and unity was everything, even if it was always on Di Stéfano's terms. Few players express that better than Santisteban. Santisteban's mother and father died when he was six and he was placed in a school for Civil Guard orphans: 'I don't even want to think about that school,' he says, 'we're talking Spain in 1946 and *that* kind of school. We went hungry, we . . . well, everything. I was quite good at football and Madrid took me out of there but I was small and weak. If I tell you how much I weighed the day I made my debut, you won't believe it . . .

Go on.

'. . . fifty-two kilos . . . in the First Division, eh.'

Fifty-two kilos is just over eight stone.

'So they sent me up to Navacerrada, to the *sierra* north of Madrid.'

To get fit?

'To get fat. Everyone looked after me. I think because I was the little one, the youngest, and because they knew what had happened to me. Bernabéu wanted us to all be team-mates – he wanted us to be friends, to eat together. No envy. He wanted to know everything. He was a patriarch. Playing with them was like playing at home. *Run lad! Wait lad! This and that.* Alfredo would shout at me and Zárraga always used to say to me: "if anyone gives you a kick, you tell me". We'd swap wings and Zárraga would give the guy something back. I can't find the words to say what that team was like.'

Di Stéfano was not alone; no player can achieve so much success without a decent team around him. In fact, it is the sheer amount of talent that so stands out from that era. The current Real Madrid president Florentino Pérez likes to present the *galácticos* policy as finding inspiration in Di Stéfano's time, claiming to take Bernabéu as a role model. In 1961, Bernabéu explained his approach: 'Our policy up to now has been to contract a great international figure each season.' Quite apart from important players like Manuel Sanchís, Emilio Santamaría, José Mariá Zárraga or Marquitos Alonso, Bernabéu signed stars and lots of them, one a season for six seasons. After the European Cup final in Paris against Stade de Reims in 1956, Gabriel Hanot wrote in *L'Equipe*: 'Di Stéfano is the most complete player we have ever seen . . . he eclipsed Kopa completely.' Within weeks, Kopa, a brilliant inside-forward, had joined Madrid. Then there was Paco Gento, who joined in 1953, Héctor Rial in 1954, Puskás in 1958, Didí in 1959, Canário the same year and Del Sol in 1960.

Madrid were unable to sign Pelé and Bobby Charlton, two men Bernabéu became obsessed with, but the roll-call of players was astonishing. 'Raymond Kopa did magic, amazing things that you didn't think possible,' recalls Santisteban. 'And Rial was incredible. He worked so hard, was strong in the air, had vision. He more than anyone else was the person who used to play those balls through, putting Gento into space. Not many people talk about Rial but he was fantastic.'

Paco Gento signed from Racing Santander the same year as Di Stéfano. Still just a kid, he was slow to settle but it was the only thing about him that was slow. Nicknamed the *Galerna* after the howling wind that races through his native Cantabria, he was astonishingly quick on the left wing, 'the devil' in Canário's words. Gento was so fast it was funny: at first fans laughed at this player who was for ever running out of pitch, hurtling into the hoardings beyond the by-line. Di Stéfano complained that he was too quick, telling team-mates, especially Rial, not to play the ball into space for Gento too soon. 'I'd be there shouting "stop, stop",' he remembers. The reason was simple: the rest of the team could not catch up.

Bit by bit, though, Gento gained in control and became a central part of Madrid's armoury. Zoco recalls: 'Gento's speed was terrifying. It was impossible to stop him and as fast as he went he could stop – in a metre, while the other guy kept on running, skidding past, trying to put the brakes on. He's out of the game, and Gento's going the other way.'

Gento recalls his first game against Barcelona. 'I was being marked by Seguer, their full-back and he was chasing behind me, sweating seas. At one point he stopped in front of me and said: "are you ever going to get off your bike, lad?"' Puskás remembered: '[Gento] had a tremendous shot but it could be wildly inaccurate sometimes, disturbing the birds in the trees round the training ground and we could never find the ball afterwards.' And yet he was vital. Puskás again: 'Our game was fairly simple – we knew that in Gento we had the quickest thing on two legs down the left wing.'

Ah, Puskás. Nicknamed the Galloping Major in the UK, *Cañoncito, pum!*, *Little cannon, bang!* in Spain, he recalled: 'Bernabéu didn't seem keen [on signing me]. He was not impressed. He also thought that Puskás argued too much with referees.' He was wrong. The reality was that Bernabéu signed him in 1958 even though the board had voted against it. It was the right decision, even if Rial – the man shifted out of position to accommodate him – didn't always think so.

While there is admiration and gratitude when former players talk of Di Stéfano, when it comes to Puskás there is warmth, almost a childish pleasure, in having known him. 'Puskás had the biggest heart I have ever seen in my life,' says Zoco. 'Puskás?' replies Amancio, giggling, 'I feel like standing to attention every time he is mentioned.' Little cannon, big belly, as Di Stéfano used to put it. When Puskás arrived at Madrid he was eighteen kilos overweight. Banned by UEFA for having escaped from Hungary in the wake of the 1956 anti-Soviet uprising like Zoltán Czibor, who went to Barcelona, he had not played competitively for two years but he had been part of the wonderful Hungary team the Mighty Magyars; the side that shocked England 6-3 at Wembley, won Olympic gold in 1952 and then beat Germany 8-3 at the 1954 World Cup, only to lose the final to the same country, with Puskás having what would have been an equalising goal ruled out two minutes from the end.

The Budapest side Honved had been in Austria playing Athletic

Bilbao in the European Cup when the Hungarian uprising took place and Puskás and his team-mates defected, going on a tour of Spain, Italy and Portugal. Eventually, despite opposition from FIFA, Madrid paid $100,000 for him. 'It wasn't much to pay for a fit Puskás, but it wasn't bad for a fat one,' his agent said.

Puskás recalled the conversation with his new president:

'"I'm too fat, I can't possibly play." I was the size of a large balloon. I threw my hands up and gestured: "listen, this is all very well but have you looked at me? I'm at least eighteen kilos overweight."

Bernabéu replied: "That's not my problem, that's yours."'

A similar conversation took place with the coach, Luis Carniglia, who asked Bernabéu what he was supposed to do with him.

Bernabéu replied: 'get him fit.'

Puskás trained with plastic wrapping around his body and layers of jumpers in Madrid's August sun, with temperatures consistently soaring towards forty degrees. It worked. Besides, the talent never left him. As Zoltán Czibor, the son of Puskás's international team-mate of the same name, puts it: 'He was the best there has been. There are no videos from those early years but he was as good as Pelé or Di Stéfano. The thing is, by the time he was at Madrid he was thirty-one. Not what he was, but still brilliant.' 'He had a left foot that . . . wow!' says Santisteban. 'I remember him picking up ten balls and lining up ten posts twenty yards away. He ran along the line hitting these balls, left foot. Bang! Bang! Bang! Bang! He knocked all ten posts down. And don't think that he was floating the ball at the posts – he was thumping it.' Canário adds: 'He didn't have a left foot, he had a hand.' In his garden at home, he had goalposts. Hanging from the crossbar on ropes of different lengths were plastic rings in different sizes. He spent hours striking the ball through them.

'That bugger played pregnant,' smiles Amancio, 'he was fat but he had a left foot that was *un escándalo*. I've played football and I know what it means to be able to hit the ball like that. It was prodigious. He used to swear at me like you wouldn't believe out on the pitch.

We called each other every name under the sun. I used to dribble too much. He'd call for it at his feet and if I didn't give it to him exactly where he wanted it, he'd "remember" my family. He only ever moved in a five-metre space but we let him because those five metres were golden.'

Puskás scored more than twenty goals in his first six seasons for Madrid and was top scorer four times. In thirty-nine European Cup games he scored thirty-five goals. When he died in November 2006, he was given a state funeral. Amancio was there. 'It was different, incredible. He just transmitted so much warmth and humanity to everyone,' he says, adding wistfully: 'Pancho was a genius.'

Madrid won the league in 1953–4, Di Stéfano's first season, and again in 1954–5. Barcelona were no longer the champions. Madrid won the championship again in 1956–7 and although Barcelona reclaimed the title two years running between 1958 and 1960 by then Madrid's attention had been drawn elsewhere. International friendlies between clubs had begun to take place and were taken seriously. When Wolves beat Honved the *Daily Mail* declared the English team the best in the world. Gabriel Hanot of *L'Equipe* was not impressed. He came up with the idea of formalising those claims with a European club competition. Enthusiastic about the idea and seeing this as the perfect opportunity to parade his team, Santiago Bernabéu travelled to Paris to take part in its organisation in the spring of 1955, before hosting final meetings in Madrid. The Spanish Football Federation was keen; the president was equally pleased that 'my good friend' Bernabéu was so enthusiastic. Eventually, UEFA came on board. Not every national federation did, though: the English FA did not give its backing for the competition, turning its nose up. This meant that Chelsea were not included in the first European Cup.

Nor were Barcelona included – and they could have been. The Catalan Carlos Pardo was *L'Equipe* correspondent in Spain and he contacted Barcelona about taking part. They, after all, had won the closest thing there was to a European Cup in 1952 – the Copa Latina, a trophy Madrid would win in 1955, the year the first European Cup began, and again in 1957, the last time it was held. According to Pardo, Barcelona's secretary had not heard of the newspaper and was not interested, insisting that he could not see the project getting off the ground. It was only after Pardo had returned home that his wife suggested he speak to Raimundo Saporta, Bernabéu's vice-president at Real Madrid, who also saw the chance to steal a march on Barcelona. Once the door had been opened to him, Saporta ensured that his position could not be usurped.

As Pardo told the story: '"Barcelona aren't interested?" "And you're inviting us?" . . . Saporta asked me to fly to Madrid the following day. Bernabéu's car was there to pick me up at Barajas, and he was waiting at the stadium with Saporta and [general manager Antonio] Calderón. The next day we all went to Paris where the European Cup was founded. Real Madrid were always grateful to me.

Rightly so. Barcelona, like many clubs, had not anticipated that the European Cup would be so successful, seeing it as a potential distraction. Barcelona successfully competed in the Inter-City Fairs Cup, albeit formally as a representative city team rather than the club, winning it in 1955–8, 1958–60 and losing to Valencia in 1960–61. Bernabéu disparagingly called it the 'town cup' and it went on to become the UEFA Cup while the European Cup became the most prestigious competition of them all. Barcelona certainly had not anticipated that Real Madrid would be so successful in the European Cup – or that it would serve so decisively to cement their status. As one English account put it, in the international tournaments 'Madrid have been unchallenged and in most continents have come to represent Spanish football almost exclusively in the minds of millions.'

Madrid won the first final against Stade de Reims, having beaten Servette, Partizan Belgrade and AC Milan en route, with centre-back Marquitos scoring a vital goal. 'Some of us shouted anxiously at him – "What are you doing? Quick, give it to so-and-so! Get back in the middle for heaven's sake!",' recalled Zárraga. '[but] Marquitos kept his head down and ignored us . . . scoring with as glorious and exciting a drive as I will ever wish to see.' In 1955–6 Madrid defeated Rapid Vienna, Nice, Manchester United and Fiorentina, this time in Madrid. In 1956–7, Royal Antwerp, Sevilla and Vasas fell before Milan were beaten in the final – Madrid won 3-2 with an extra-time winner from Paco Gento. The *Galerna* won twelve league titles and six European Cups but ranks that as his finest moment for Madrid. 'We were nervous, we were into extra time and because we had won the competition twice before, the pressure was enormous. Everyone was relieved as much as delighted.' The following year, 1958–9, Madrid knocked out Besiktas, Wiener Sportklube and Atlético Madrid – 'Real's great rivals', as Puskás put it – before defeating Stade de Reims again.

'Those games were not easy,' recalls Santisteban, 'and we always had the attitude that the other team were better than us – why shouldn't they be?' It was not just the opposition that were tough. Madrid's trip to face Partizan Belgrade was the first time a Spanish team had travelled to a Communist country – and it was snowing. Madrid were down to ten men through injury (there were no substitutions at the time), Rial missed a penalty and Madrid's coach, Pepe Villalonga, was hit by a snowball with a rock hidden inside it. Madrid had won 4-0 in the first leg but only after Partizan had two goals ruled out that even Di Stéfano describes as blatant mistakes; in the second leg the Yugoslavs won 3-0; 'I thought they were going to turn it round,' Di Stéfano admitted. Madrid did not trust the food either; they were obsessed with the possibility of being poisoned or laid low, so travelled with their own, refusing even to drink coffee in hotels that they did not know.

That was not the only trap laid for them. Di Stéfano tells the story of a trip to Bucharest in the 1959–60 season: 'They'd put a girl in all of the adjoining rooms. They told us later on that it was common for the Romanian teams to do that to the visitors. We had a meeting, we talked about it and we decided to act as if we hadn't noticed:

"We've come here to play football and, after the game, whoever wants to go out, go. But first, think about the match." They were pretty girls, twenty-two or twenty-three years old. We didn't fall into their trap. When the game finished, some of the players said: "let's get changed quick and get back to the hotel." They went running off thinking that the girls would be there, but those doves had flown . . . we didn't get the girls, but we beat the Romanians home and away.'

By 1960, Madrid faced their greatest challenge yet. The team was getting older – Di Stéfano admits that the search had begun to replace him – and Barcelona were widely considered to be the stronger team, a fact which for those outside Catalonia appears implausible half a century later, not least because 1960 would also include Madrid's greatest hour, the culmination of five years of brilliance. Barcelona had taken two consecutive league titles off Madrid and faced them in the semi-final of the European Cup. But Madrid found a way through.

The final was against Eintracht Frankfurt at Hampden Park, Glasgow. It only went ahead after Puskás wrote a formal letter of apology to the German football association for having accused their 1954 World Cup-winning team of being on drugs. The attendance was given as 127,621 and, as Eintracht had beaten Glasgow Rangers in the semi-final, almost all of them wanted Madrid to win. Before the game, Bernabéu spoke to the players, telling them: 'man has five senses and five fingers on each hand . . . you have four European Cups.'

Eintracht went 1-0 up; they then hit the bar. Canário recalls the shock. 'We were looking at each other thinking: "can this really be happening?" But once we got into our stride, I remember the Scottish fans applauding us.' Madrid ran out 7-3 winners, with four goals from Puskás and a hat-trick from Di Stéfano.

Di Stéfano admits that one of the three was a fluke that came off his shin, but there was nothing fortuitous about the team's performance. One history of the European Cup calls it the greatest final ever and many would agree. It was a match that the BBC in Scotland continued to show every Christmas for years, one that continues to sell, in black and white, on DVD; a game in which, according to one report, Madrid had 'played like angels' in front of the highest ever attendance for a European Cup final. A young Alex Ferguson, watching from the stands, remembers it as the finest game he has seen; one in which, according to a news report the following morning, 'Real flaunted all that has made them incomparable.' 'To list Real Madrid's team,' added this scribe, 'is to chronicle greatness.' *France Soir* called it a 'magisterial ballet'.

'We'll never see a game like that again,' Canário says. 'Football is different now, a business. Back then, it was fun, a spectacle. Now people go to games happy not to suffer too much. Then, they went to enjoy it. I liked that football more. That was our best game. I was in Scotland recently and I went back to the stadium. A man came running towards us. "Oooh," he said, "when you played I was just a kid but that was amazing." It turned out he was the president of the Scottish FA.'

'We almost achieved some kind of footballing perfection,' remembered Puskás. 'At the end, the Scottish fans came running on to the pitch in sheer delight . . . We were paraded through the centre of town and then on to the town hall. You would think it was *their* team.' Marquitos had made a promise: if Madrid won, he'd 'turn Scottish'. He travelled back in a kilt and tartan jacket, carrying bagpipes down the steps of the plane. 'He was a lovely guy, Marquitos. Tall too: the kilt was a mini-skirt on him,' Canário laughs. Puskás, by contrast, was empty-handed. He had not taken his booty. 'I had glanced at the ref's watch and I was counting the last minute in my head to make sure that the ball was at my feet when he blew the whistle. [Erwin] Stein came up to me [wanting the ball]. I thought: "I really want this ball, but this guy has scored two and lost the match. It's the least I can do".'

Juan Santisteban was watching the game from his hospital bed back in Madrid, where he had undergone an operation on his thigh. He had played throughout the tournament but missed the final. 'People talk about the best forward line ever from time to time, about this team or that, and I think: "Really? Are you *really* trying to compare that team with our one?",' he says. '*Really?* With Kopa, Rial, Di Stéfano, Puskás, Gento, Del Sol, Canário . . . ? Some of those players were just extraordinary. And that final was marvellous. I have never seen anything like those men: they were a wonder. I felt proud of them, delighted too. I did feel part of it and they involved me as much as they could when they came back. But I was also cursing my luck. Imagine being alongside those phenomenal men. It was the most incredible thing I have ever seen, just the most beautiful thing. And I was lying there in the sanatorium, crying. Thinking to myself: "If only I could have been there".'

'A cemetery.'

Alfredo Di Stéfano falls quiet for a moment. It is as if he can still see it, still feel it. The sadness, the silence. The moment it all came to an end.

A cemetery?

'*¡Sí! Muerta, la gente.*' Yes! Everyone was dead.

Again, the quiet.

'Look,' he says slowly, 'people always want to win, and when they don't . . .'

And when they don't there are consequences. That night at the Prater stadium in Vienna there were certainly consequences. Knocked out of the European Cup for the first time in 1960–61 by Barcelona, Real Madrid reached the final again in Amsterdam in 1961–2, where they lost 5-3 to Benfica, and they were defeated by Anderlecht in the preliminary round of the 1962–3 campaign, but those latter games did not have quite the impact that this one did. It was 27 May 1964 and Real Madrid had reached another European Cup final

– their seventh in nine editions of the competition – against Internazionale. Coached by Helenio Herrera, Inter had Sandro Mazzola, Jair da Costa and Mario Corso and the former Barcelona player Luis Suárez, while their president was Angelo Moratti. 'Bernabéu didn't like Moratti,' Di Stéfano later recalled. 'He always said that if we handed out pens or pennants to referees he handed out gold medallions.'

Inter also had a left-back by the name of Giancinto Facchetti. Madrid's coach, Miguel Muñoz, was obsessed with him. Facchetti had a reputation for bombing up the wing from full-back and Muñoz had decided that he, and only he, was the man to stop. Some of the players were not so convinced; there had been tense discussions during the team meeting. Everything was set up to prevent Facchetti causing Madrid problems, leaving other men free, altering Madrid's approach. 'He drove us mad with Facchetti, giving him an incredible importance,' Di Stéfano remembered. 'Anyone would think he was Gento. So what happened? Facchetti never attacked us once.'

Playing on the break, others did. Inter controlled Madrid. Tarcisio Burgnich marked Paco Gento, Facchetti controlled Amancio Amaro and Aristide Guarneri stuck close to Ferenç Puskás. As for Di Stéfano, Carlo Tagnin followed him everywhere. It was a frustrating night. Madrid had more of the ball but they were tracked all over the pitch. Inter were surprisingly comfortable: 'The only thing their sweeper didn't do was grab a chair and play the violin in the middle of the pitch,' Di Stéfano complained. Mazzola scored twice, Milani once and Inter won 3-1, claiming the first of two consecutive European Cups under Herrera. For Madrid, it was another European Cup final lost, the golden era coming to an end.

Ignacio Zoco had signed two years earlier and was Real Madrid's centre-half that night. He points at the video recorder in the corner of the room. 'We must have watched that game eight times,' he says, 'and every time we watch it, it gets harder to explain how we lost. I still don't understand it. None of us do. But we lost; no matter how often we watch it that score's not going to change. We came second and in football second is nothing, especially at this club.'

'The reaction afterwards was like it is now: when you play well you're a phenomenon and everyone is patting you on the back; as soon as you play badly you're worthless,' Zoco continues. 'It was always hard to live with the pressure at this club but you had no choice because otherwise you wouldn't live at all. You'd climb in the back of a taxi and worry in case the driver said: "about last night's match . . ." When things went wrong, that was it. Everyone wants changes; "that guy's no use any more." It's like they're changing the oil in the car: "This is burnt out, get rid of it!" They want to retire you.'

Almost bang on cue, Di Stéfano shuffles into the room, hunched over his walking stick, gently lifting a hand as he passes slowly by. 'Don Alfredo,' Zoco says by way of greeting. 'Here we are, putting the world to rights.'

They want to retire you? In Di Stéfano's case, quite literally.

The 1964 European Cup final was the last official game Alfredo Di Stéfano ever played for Madrid. He could not get away from his marker and on those rare occasions that he did was confronted by Armando Picchi, 'one of those sweepers,' he remarked, 'who played so deep that if there was a bit of fog and you thought you'd gone past all of them, another one would appear: where did that bloke come from? Are they playing with twelve or what?' Di Stéfano was not impressed by the tactics, insisting that he had been obliged to run aimlessly all game and that Madrid had effectively played a man short. There was smouldering tension, frustration and anger. At one point, he claims Muñoz swore at him from the touchline, telling him to fuck off. To which Di Stéfano replied: 'You fucking fuck off. We're playing for our lives here, going at a hundred miles an hour, and you tell me to fuck off?'

'At that moment,' Di Stéfano recalled, 'I found out who Muñoz really was.'

If Di Stéfano thought he had run too much, others thought he had not run enough – and might never do so again. He was, after all, coming up to his thirty-eighth birthday, his hair receding and his pace diminishing. As one contemporary put it, the Blond Arrow had lost the two things that made him the Blond Arrow: he was no longer blond and he was no longer an arrow. 'Di Stéfano did not exist. He lacked speed; he didn't have the strength to cover the whole pitch,' wrote one newspaper. 'Sadly, we have to recognise that he's reached the sunset of his career.' His angry response to Muñoz had not exactly helped. The conflict had been growing for a while; Di Stéfano had long been the *de facto* coach and he could be overbearing, difficult to live with. In truth, he was not the player he had been either. Yet the ending was still abrupt and unexpected. Before the match, Bernabéu had insisted, 'old soldiers never die'. After it, he insisted: 'If you want to act like a star you have to know how to be a star. It's not enough to say: "I'm so-and-so, the best in this position." Yeah, and?'

If anyone doubted that the so-and-so in question was Di Stéfano, the doubts did not last long. Real Madrid's next game was against Atlético Madrid and Di Stéfano was left out, for the first time in eleven years. When he asked Muñoz why, the coach replied: 'I don't have to give you explanations.'

Di Stéfano was offered a role at the club but, his pride hurt and convinced he could still perform on the pitch, he turned it down. As he recalls it, Bernabéu told him that he wanted him to stay and work for the club in 'any position'; 'any position,' Di Stéfano countered, 'what's any position? I'm not going to be a doorman or an administrator . . . Renew my contract and if by October or November I'm not playing how I should, I'll go home and you can offer me a job and if I like it, fine. There won't be any problems. But at least talk to me after so much blood, sweat and tears.'

Bernabéu was not for shifting. Muñoz, who the president made a point of describing in the media as 'honest and thoughtful', had written a report in which he recommended that Real Madrid's greatest ever player go into retirement, insisting that he could no longer play in the club's system. That was not the only reason. 'I am not for or against Di Stéfano but what we cannot have is a lack of discipline,' the president announced, disguising how much it hurt him. 'Di Stéfano is leaving but it's not a problem. Others left too. We cried but it didn't matter at all.'

Di Stéfano joined Español, where he teamed up with his old friend László Kubala and he scored nineteen league goals in two seasons. Bernabéu saw his departure to another club as a betrayal; so did Di Stéfano. Others were equally unimpressed with the club's behaviour after all the Argentinian had done, Marquitos insisting to the secretary during an argument not long after: 'half of this ground belongs to Alfredo.' Di Stéfano thought he knew where it all started: 'Muñoz told me to fuck off,' he later wrote. 'And they kicked me out of the club because I told him to fuck off back.'

It was the end of a beautiful friendship. Bernabéu had named the small fishing boat on which he idled away the hours off the coast of Santa Pola after Di Stéfano but the Blond Arrow never returned to Real Madrid. Bernabéu's wife later complained that Di Stéfano did not even ask after her husband when he was seriously ill. And yet Bernabéu himself might not have welcomed the enquiry. Di Stéfano earned his coach's badge, finishing his exams at the top of the class with Kubala, both of them gaining full marks, and became a successful manager, winning the league and the Cup Winners' Cup with Valencia as well as leading River Plate to the Argentinian title. But when the media suggested he was the perfect man to take charge at Real Madrid his former president did not want to know, reportedly vowing that Di Stéfano would not return to the club as long as he, Bernabéu, was still alive.

Di Stéfano became the elephant in the room, a man whose name Bernabéu virtually refused to utter. 'I lost a son', someone heard him say. Di Stéfano eventually came back at the start of the 1980s, coaching the club's youth team and then the first team. In 1983, his Madrid side were runners-up in five competitions and he was later, in 1990, caretaker manager with José Antonio Camacho. Florentino Pérez made him the club's honorary president at the start of the new century. But by then Bernabéu had been dead for more than two decades, his vow fulfilled.

10

HH: THE ORIGINAL SPECIAL ONE

Helenio Herrera arrived in Barcelona on a mission: to knock Real Madrid off their perch. It was the tail end of the 1957–8 season and a kind of psychosis had taken hold. Madrid had won four of the last five league titles and the first three European Cups. Barcelona, not long ago Spain's dominant force, had claimed the 1957 Copa del Generalísimo but hadn't won the league since 1953, before the arrival of Alfredo Di Stéfano. The timing couldn't have been worse: by failing to win the domestic title as they had done in 1948, '49, '52 and '53, they hadn't set foot in the recently created European Cup. In their absence Madrid embarked upon a run that secured a position as undisputedly the Continent's best team and eclipsed their rivals, leaving Barcelona forgotten and frustrated.

Barcelona wondered what might have been, looking at their rivals as usurpers and through conspiratorial eyes. 'Real Madrid's success both inside and outside Spain had the Catalans intimidated,' Herrera recalled, 'but we had the team to compete with them – and that was what I wanted to show them. The fact that an extraordinary team like Barcelona still hadn't played in the European Cup needed rectifying immediately.' Herrera was the perfect man for the job, the Special One fifty years before the Special One – called into the Camp Nou half a century before Jose Mourinho was called into the Santiago

Bernabéu on a startlingly similar mission, employing similar methods and ultimately ending in a similar way.

The Italian novelist Gianni Brera later wrote when Herrera was working for Internazionale: 'clown and genius, vulgar and aesthete, sultan and believer, boorish and competent, megalomaniac and health freak . . . [Herrera] is all this and more.' The son of Andalucían parents who had met in Gibraltar, Herrera was born in Argentina and raised in Casablanca, played football in Morocco and France, and first became a coach at Puteaux. Later nicknamed *Il Mago*, the Magician, he managed in Portugal and joined Barcelona from Os Belenenses, having previously coached Valladolid, Atlético Madrid, Málaga, Deportivo de La Coruña and Sevilla. Winner of the league title with Atlético in 1949–50 and 1950–51, Herrera led Sevilla to second place in 1956–7, and was obsessed by detail: a deep tactical thinker, often wrongly accused – and in Spain 'accused' is the word – of being the father of *catenaccio*, the ultra-defensive 'door-bolt' system.

Charismatic, bullish and determined, never afraid to speak up, the author of a thousand legendary phrases, some of which he never actually said, no coach had ever enjoyed such a huge media profile. The press hung on his every word and he sought them out as much as they did he. 'It is not what he says that matters,' one newspaper wrote, 'it is the fact that it is he who says it. If HH says "it's windy", the newspapers say: "HH attacks the Met Office."'

Abbreviated to HH, something that enhanced the aura surrounding him, by 1955 a survey showed that Herrera was the most popular coach in Spain. Those that didn't like him, meanwhile, *really* didn't like him. He revelled in the attention. The blurb on the cover of his memoirs sums it up: 'This Herrera is the devil! Now he's writing memoirs! May God forgive us! As if he hasn't made enough noise already! As if the papers don't dedicate him enough attention already! As if his words weren't already invading every home, every office, every workshop and every public place! As if he wasn't admired enough already! As if he wasn't hated enough already!'

Madrid's players certainly came to hate him: provocation was his currency and on the day he became Spain coach in 1959, while still in charge at Barça, Madrid's internationals refused to shake his hand and discussed staging a boycott of *la selección*.

It was hardly a bed of roses at Barcelona either, where jealousies in the dressing room and the boardroom only increased over Herrera's two years at the club. Josep Samitier, the departing technical director, told a delighted Santiago Bernabéu that his former club was a 'disaster'; Herrera later wrote of 'the intrigue of the great circus', 'a disagreeable atmosphere [of] rancour inside and out'; and after one *derbi* the previous season, the Madrid forward Héctor Rial commented: 'the attitude of the [Barça] fans is strange: they don't support their team.' There had even been punch-ups between supporters of the club's two stars: Kubala on one side, Luis Suárez on the other. In short, Herrera encountered what Johan Cruyff would later call the *entorno*, or entourage – the political and social maelstrom that swirled round the club with its fantasies and phobias.

No phobia was greater than the fear of Madrid. Barcelona's board were obsessed that Madrid had bought journalists, referees and other teams. Herrera had his own suspicions, leaving his dugout during one game in Granada to shout at the official, 'you wouldn't dare do that to Madrid!', but his response was remarkably pragmatic. If Madrid are buying people, he said, Barcelona must do the same. No moral outrage, just matter-of-fact. Herrera, who had been approached by two men offering to pay him to throw matches as Barcelona battled it out with Madrid at the end of his first campaign, admitted to offering bonuses to Madrid's opponents at key moments in the season – even if he always insisted that his club could not match the 'generosity' of the team from the capital.

There were other problems too. Herrera found players who lacked confidence and trust in each other and in the club. And, the truth was, he did not entirely trust them either. Some were fond of life, one hiding cigarettes, cognac and erotic French magazines in his bedside table in the team hotel while another with a voyeuristic streak got locked in his 'hide' on a hotel balcony and had to escape by clambering down a drainpipe and through another bedroom on the floor below. The board of directors feared that another player was being led astray by his girlfriend, a singer. Worse, they told the new manager, when he's away with the team she goes off with other men. The club had tried to split the couple up but without success; they had hired private detectives to follow her and gather proof of her infidelity but she was too clever. Again, Herrera's response was direct and to the point. That's simple, he told the board: we'll hire someone to sleep with her. There was a momentary silence and a young director put up his hand. *I'll do it.*

The way Herrera dealt with that was symptomatic. He left the meeting and took the player and his girlfriend for a meal. In tears, the couple told him how their lives had been made impossible in Barcelona: they were followed everywhere, the rumours never ended, the pressure was unbearable. There's only one way to reverse the criticism, Herrera told the player, and that is to win something. He turned to the girl, looked her straight in the eye, and said: 'and that depends on *you*.' As the Brazilian striker Evaristo de Macedo puts it: 'Herrera did not just take care of the team, he took care of absolutely everything around it.'

Not that it was easy, and getting through to László Kubala proved rather more difficult. Not least because some members of the squad suspected that Herrera never truly wanted to. Kubala was thirty-one by then and, in the words of one team-mate, 'was on the way down'. He was treated with a reverence that Herrera distrusted. It was not that Kubala had an ego as such – and certainly not compared to Herrera – just that his status eclipsed everyone else and his lackadaisical, playful approach to the game, the almost child-like way that he acted, clashed head-on with the ideas of his coach. One journalist who covered Barcelona during that era describes it in simple terms: 'HH didn't like *kubalismo* because *he* wanted to be the *prima donna*.'

Another potential problem was that Kubala was the team's highest earner. In 1956–7, he earned 1,308,025 pesetas (£11,120); the next highest earners were Eulogio Martínez on 378,500 and Basora on 371,637 pesetas. By the time Herrera arrived, signing the Hungarians Sándor Kocsis and Zoltán Czibor from Honved, both of them on over 300,000 pesetas, Evaristo earned 682,500 pesetas but Kubala was on 2,471,950. Barcelona's total wage bill of 10,886,062 pesetas (£92,400) in 1957–8 climbed to 17,373,853 (£148,000) the following season – a millstone that eventually weighed them down. Herrera was hardly cheap himself: Barcelona had been forced to pay a million pesetas compensation to Sevilla after Herrera walked out on them. In the short term, he was worth it: in the long term, though, some thought he wasn't.

Herrera bemoaned the fact that he had not been able to coach Kubala at his peak, when the player had been probably the best in the world. Herrera also believed that the Hungarian's end came too soon. He complained that Kubala did not look after himself – even though, powerfully built, he really *could* look after himself, once punching four American Marines into the sea during a boozy argument. Herrera used such episodes to justify removing Kubala from the team but, instead of creating the unity he sought, it deepened the conflict. When he encouraged the Barcelona board to issue a public statement accusing the Hungarian of having repeatedly missed training and of refusing to play, alleging 'illnesses that are hard to demonstrate', seven directors resigned in solidarity with Kubala. And yet, far from thinking that he was too harsh on his star, Herrera came to blame himself for not having the nerve to go further.

As far as Herrera was concerned, Kubala was slow and his habit of turning back on himself, taking an extra touch, broke the momentum of the moves that the new coach wanted to impose – high-speed, direct, aggressive. Kubala, he alleged, was playing to the gallery, 'more spectacular than effective'. He became obsessed, attacking Kubala as the 'cancer' of the team in front of his *compañeros* and later writing about 'myths and idols fed by the magazines', complaining that 'fans did not see that victories would not have been possible without others like Segarra, Rodri, Gràcia, Olivella, men from the *cantera* with a genuine love for the club's colours'.

Herrera was convinced that he could win without Kubala, but to do so he needed to impose absolute authority, a new mentality and approach, a new style. When Herrera arrived at Barcelona at the end of the 1957–8 season, the team he inherited had just played the first leg of the final of the Fairs Cup and had finished second, second, second, third and third in the previous five league seasons. An impressive team but one that lacked *something*; one that suffered an anxiety crisis that only defeating Madrid and winning the European Cup could resolve.

There was no shortage of ability. Herrera called that group the best he had ever worked with – better than the Internazionale players with whom he won two consecutive European Cups. It was probably the most talented team that Barcelona had ever had, even ahead of the *Cinc Copes* side. Apart from Kubala, they had Sandor Kocsis, Eulogio Martínez, Just Tejada, Ferran Olivella, Ramón Villaverde and Evaristo de Macedo. Antoni Ramallets was still in goal and they had Galician playmaker Luis Suárez. Then there was the lightning fast Zoltán Czibor.

Czibor came to Spain following the Hungarian uprising in 1956, joining Barcelona in 1958. Ten thousand people were killed in the first week of the uprising as Soviet tanks rolled in and the Hungarians desperately defended themselves by pouring washing-up liquid on to the streets in the hope of sending the invaders slipping off course. Like Puskás, Czibor was playing in Austria at the time and took advantage of a European game to escape. His club, Honved, hired smugglers to help his family sneak across the border to be reunited with him. During the escape, the small group reached a fork in the road where they split up, Czibor's wife and child going one way with one group. Those who went the other way were mown down by machine-gun fire.

Czibor's son Zoltán sits at a restaurant table by the waterside at Barceloneta. 'The babies had been given a slug of alcohol to stop us crying,' he says with a mischievous smile that belies the drama of the moment. 'For the players, arriving in Spain was a liberation. People talk about the Franco dictatorship, but we had escaped Communism. We were given Spanish nationality as refugees from a Communist country; the process was sped through, basically on the grounds that Franco felt like it. My dad later set up a bar in Barcelona called Kep Duna, which acted as a refuge for Hungarians. Defectors would come looking for the bar – they'd stay there or at Kubala's house. My dad was one of the best players there has been, a skilful left-winger. Justice hasn't been done with that team.'

Suárez recalls: 'We had attacking players of the very highest level, really world-class players.' Suárez himself was probably the best of them, a man who Herrera said was a 'great organiser of teams' who 'led an exemplary life'; Di Stéfano described him as the 'architect'; and Evaristo insists: '*Luisito* was the greatest player I ever saw. He was intelligent and could really pass – he left me one on one with the goalkeeper time and again.' 'I was the *organizador*,' Suárez says, 'I started deep but covered a lot of the pitch and I had a wide perspective, vision. I had a change of speed, good technique and could shoot from outside the area.' Some have likened him to Xavi Hernández. Xavi is a player Suárez himself has championed but he's a man who enjoys winding people up and, anyway, he's not convinced. A cheeky grin stretches across his face. 'I hit forty-yard passes, and could switch the play from one side to the other,' he protests, laughing. 'My game was *much* more varied than Xavi's.'

Herrera's task was to make them a team, to get them to do things his way, imposing himself on players and directors. Sound bites and motivational speeches spewed forth. Slogans were slapped up on walls, words like Speed, Technique, Teamwork. Before games the players would pass the ball round shouting 'win!' at each other. Promises were made. Before one tour, Czibor complained that he didn't want to be away for so long, so Herrera told him he could go home if he scored three times across the games. Czibor got a hat-trick in the first match. 'To the Catalans I talked "colours of Catalonia, play for your nation",' Herrera told Simon Kuper in the early 1990s, 'and to the foreigners I talked money. I talked about their wives and kids. You have twenty-five players, you don't say the same thing to everyone.' Actually, Herrera often did. What he didn't do was say the same thing to everyone at the club. He actively sought to create a bond between himself and his players – up to a point, *against* the board, buying their loyalty by telling them they could make more money than they had ever made before and fighting to get them ever-bigger bonuses. Promises of cash had the squad cheering and chanting his name; a *show-me-the-money* moment decades before *Jerry Maguire* brought sporting cynicism to the cinema.

If there was cold, hard cash, there was hard slog too. Herrera's first training session ended with players vomiting. Three sessions a day were common to start with and he was tough, aggressive. He sent one player back on despite protests that he was sick, broke the plaster cast off another and refused to allow any respite. Amid countless rumours, Barcelona's doctor was forced to deny that the 'sugar' supplements that Herrera handed out were something else altogether and players complained that they couldn't sleep after games. Others, concerned about the content, refused to take the supplements or simply threw them away when the coach was not looking. According to Lluís Lainz, one player, suspicious about the tea Herrera handed out, gave it to a doctor friend to analyse. Tests showed that it contained amphetamines and Kubala challenged Herrera to drink it himself. Some players deny this took place.

Herrera's search for success was relentless. Ramallets calls him a genius. 'He had files on everything. He could tell you about the parents of some Italian or German, what day he was born, everything. He had great tactical vision and he knew how to wind his players up. He was a man on a mission and he knew the other team from *pé* to *pá*. He said to me: "Antonio, if there's a penalty and so-and-so takes it, he's going this way or that." I never took any notice! But he knew players inside out.' 'There was always great intensity, conviction, and concentration. He was extremely professional – and totally different from anyone else,' recalls Suárez. 'The work was harder, stronger, quicker and more aggressive; the approach, direct. There was no joking – it was very serious.'

The contrast in style to Madrid could hardly have been greater. Barcelona had to find a way of counteracting the European champions and Herrera did just that; his tactics were conditioned by theirs. His antidote to Madrid's technical game was to adopt a direct, physical approach. It worked: Barcelona and Madrid met in October 1958 at the start of Herrera's first full season in charge. Madrid had *that* forward line – Kopa, Rial, Di Stéfano, Puskás and Gento – but Barcelona won 4-0, with an Evaristo hat-trick, a result that knocked Madrid off the top of the table. 'The secret was to play extremely fast, while Real Madrid like a calmer style which benefited their undoubtedly superior technical game,' Herrera said proudly. And although Madrid beat Barcelona 1-0 when they met again later in the season, Herrera's side took the title for the first time since 1953.

The final game was away at Racing Santander. The press attributed quotes to Herrera in which he said his side would win 'without getting off the bus', and, although he denied saying it, it did not stop him receiving abuse throughout the game or the expression slipping into Spanish footballing lexicon to describe any easy victory. Racing's players were allegedly on a car apiece to beat Barcelona, courtesy of Real Madrid; Barcelona, meanwhile, offered a bonus to Madrid's final-day opponents. Barcelona won and the league title was theirs at last – and they had broken a points record to get it.

That was not all they won. Barcelona faced Madrid in the semi-final of the Copa del Generalísimo, just days after Madrid had won their fifth European Cup in Glasgow with that stunning victory over Eintracht Frankfurt – there had been a homage to the European champions before the game. Puskás had scored twice and Barcelona were 2-0 down at half-time but Ángel Mur senior remembered Herrera, who had loudly announced before the game that his team was going to win, coming into the dressing room and shouting at his players. 'They're ours now! They're knackered! You're slaughtering them! Carry on like this and we're going to hammer them!' He couldn't believe his ears but Herrera was right: Barça won 4-2 and the second leg finished 3-1, taking them to a final where they secured the cup to go with the league title and the Fairs Cup, plus the Copa Duarte and the Martini Rossi trophies.

In other words, everything going. Except the European Cup.

And that was the thing. At the banquet to celebrate the league title, Herrera didn't speak – he claimed that the directors were jealous of his popularity and later bemoaned a 'ferocious campaign', insisting he was 'sitting on a barrel of dynamite' – but the president and other members of the board did. Every speech made some reference to Madrid. The title was the first step: Madrid were overhauled at home. Now they had to do the same abroad. Barcelona would go into the European Cup for the first time; an opportunity to right the wrong.

'Had it not been for Real Madrid, we could have won it all,' recalls Luis Suárez. 'History has been unjust with us.' At the time, only the champions of their respective leagues entered the European Cup. Madrid's former players argue that that gives greater significance, increased value, to their success: it wasn't just any team that played in the tournament. Barcelona's former players, and fans, offer an alternative view. Because only the champions could enter the tournament, many of the best teams in Europe did not get the chance to compete. Barcelona had won four of the eight pre-European Cup league titles. In the five years that they won the European Cup, between 1955 and 1960, Madrid won the league only twice. As many times, ultimately, as Barcelona. A case can be made – and in Catalonia it has been made – for saying that Madrid might not even have been the best team in Spain; Helenio Herrera's Barcelona were.

As Puskás put it: 'While we were winning the European Cup in 1959 and 1960 Barcelona were winning the league twice on the run.

They had a great team and seemed to be able to "do" us any time they wanted. The Hungarian lads took the piss mercilessly . . . even phoning me up to rub it in.'

But Europe was where teams were judged and legends built. 'We wanted to overcome them,' Suárez says, 'but we didn't even get the opportunity. The problem was that there were two great teams. We were a great side but, bloody hell, only one team could be in it. Until we won the league we never even participated. If you were second, you had done nothing. Imagine the Champions League now and Madrid not even being allowed to take on Barcelona for three years because Barcelona had won the league. That's what it was like.'

It is a recurring theme. For some Barcelona supporters, Madrid's historic supremacy is partly built on a fallacy. The joke ran that, until 1998 at least, Madrid had never won the European Cup in colour, only in black and white, and they had won it because they had played it; Barcelona would have done so too had they been competing, but when they won the European Cup in 1992 it was only the fifth time they had ever set foot in the competition. Madrid's aggregate score over the first five European Cup competitions was 70-8 but, this argument goes, the opposition were not up to much – and certainly not as good as Barcelona. Domestically, of ten trophies available between 1956 and 1960, Madrid won two: the league in 1956–7 and 1957–8. The problem was that the European Cup eclipsed all else and continued to do so, way beyond the Di Stéfano and Kubala era and into the 1970s. That, says Charly Rexach, is unfair.

The former Barcelona player, coach and manager, an attacker who won the Cup Winners' Cup and two Fairs Cups, explains: 'if you look at it, Madrid and Barcelona are practically the same. Barcelona won the Fairs Cup and the Copa Latina, they won three UEFA Cups and three Cup Winners' Cups, because they didn't play in the European Cup. To win it you had to play it and Barcelona had a kind of veto against them. But what they did was as impressive during those years. They won harder competitions, competitions in which there were three teams from every country. Real Madrid played against four decent clubs and then maybe a Swiss team or a Hungarian one. We had Roma, Juve, Milan from Italy; Hamburg, Cologne, Leverkusen from Germany . . . there's more *mérito* in winning three or four UEFA Cups than four European Cups. The number of Spanish Copas are similar [Barcelona have twenty-five, Madrid eighteen] and the numbers of league titles are too, twenty-five versus seventeen or eighteen [in fact, Madrid have thirty-one, Barcelona twenty-two]. But the European Cup had a brutal significance.'

The first year Barcelona *could* win the European Cup was 1959–60, by which time Madrid had won four in a row. But at least now, having won the 1958–9 title with Helenio Herrera, the Catalans at last got the chance to compete. Barcelona won the 1959–60 league title again, this time on goal difference, having lost in Madrid and won at the Camp Nou, but it was all about Europe. There, they hammered Wolves 4-0 in Barcelona and 5-2 in Wolverhampton, prompting the home side to line up and give them a guard of honour, applauding them from the field. Then they beat AC Milan 2-0 in Italy, 5-1 at home. And then it happened: they drew Real Madrid in the semi-final on 21 and 27 April 1960.

And that's where it went horribly, horribly wrong.

The referees were two Englishmen whom Herrera suggested were 'influenceable'. Barcelona's board had decided that Herrera's old trick of offering a huge bonus to his players was not appropriate this time – Herrera makes the unlikely claim that they told him 'this game doesn't matter', but they did later publicly denounce his and the players' 'unacceptable demands' – and the atmosphere was tense. In the build-up to the game an impeccably timed offer reached Herrera to coach Real Madrid the following season. Bernabéu could not bear the thought of Barcelona being better.

The first leg finished 3-1 to Real Madrid, with Di Stéfano scoring the third in the eighty-seventh minute. Herrera insisted it had been a fluke and that Madrid were scared. In the second leg, Barcelona went for Madrid but Puskás caught them on the break after twenty-one minutes. It was over. There were tears in the dressing room at half-time. Madrid added two more in the second half and played wonderfully, 'dancing round us' in Herrera's words, but by then it was irrelevant. It finished 3-1 but the scoreline could have been greater had it not been for Ramallets. For the first time in two years, Barcelona had been beaten at home and nothing broke the silence afterwards. Madrid were on their way to *that* final at Hampden Park, Barcelona were out. 'The whole of Europe witnessed Herrera's Waterloo', declared one headline gleefully.

The following day, Herrera was driving down the Ramblas with a French journalist. As they passed Canaletes, they saw a group of Barcelona fans discussing the game. The journalist thought the scene would make a good photograph and asked Herrera if he was prepared to talk to them. At first the conversation was amiable enough with the coach explaining how Barcelona had been beaten and the photographer snapping away. But as the crowd grew, so did the tension. Someone grabbed at the coach. Herrera backed off and into the reception of a hotel on the Ramblas, which turned out to be Real Madrid's hotel. The shouting began, the accusations too. *That's right, go and collect the money they owe you!* The media portrayed it as an assault. Barcelona still had the Fairs Cup final to play but, by now, Herrera had brokered a deal with Internazionale behind Barcelona's back. The board got wind of it, acted and kicked him out before he could walk. His parting shot was classic Herrera: 'you won't last long without me!'

Helenio Herrera was right. Sort of. A year later, he signed Luis Suárez for Inter for twenty-five million pesetas. Barcelona felt they had little choice but to sell: the division between Suárez and Kubala had widened, in the public eye at least – some players insist that the pair actually got along fine – and the economic reality was inescapable, with the club confronting the cost of constructing the Camp Nou and the cost of Herrera's time there. The players Barcelona did sign – such as Alcides Silveira, Tibor Szalay and José Cubilla – mostly didn't succeed and, post-Herrera, the decline set in. Barcelona had won two leagues in two seasons under Herrera and four of the previous ten – as many as Madrid. They'd won seven league titles since the end of the Spanish Civil War to Madrid's four. But they finished the 1960–61 season *twenty* points behind Madrid and wouldn't win another league title until 1974. In the same spell, Madrid won nine titles.

Barcelona stopped winning; Herrera didn't. Together with Suárez, he won three Italian leagues between 1963 and 1966. He also won the European Cup twice – a trophy Inter would not claim again until Jose Mourinho took them to the 2010 final at the Santiago Bernabéu. And in 1964, it was Herrera's Inter team that didn't just knock Real Madrid out but ended Alfredo Di Stéfano's career at Chamartín.

Yet, before their former manager's success at San Siro, before Suárez had gone and Inter beat Madrid 3-1 to take the 1964 European Cup, and just months after Herrera's departure, Barcelona did have their moment. Inter might have brought Di Stéfano's career to an end, but it was Barcelona who became the first team ever to knock Madrid out of Europe.

Barcelona's second league title meant a second attempt at the European Cup, a second opportunity to break that hegemony and bring the empire to its knees. And this time, under the Yugoslav coach Ljubiša Bročić, they took it. It was the last sixteen. In other words, the second round. Barcelona had beaten the Belgian team Lierse Sportkring 5-0 on aggregate; as champions, Madrid had been given a bye in the opening round. The first team they faced in the European Cup since Hampden Park, less than six months after that night and just two after winning the first Intercontinental Cup with a 5-1 second-leg victory over Uruguay's Peñarol, was their biggest rivals. Real Madrid versus Barcelona.

One hundred and twenty thousand people turned up at the Camp Nou for the second leg. In Madrid, one correspondent observed, 'something unusual was happening'; streets were quiet, but bars and cafeterias were packed. The lucky few who owned televisions had invited everyone they knew to watch. Crowds pressed against the windows of TV shops. 'They were always games of great tension and rivalry,' remembers Suárez, 'especially during that period when people considered Madrid Franco's team; as a battle it always had a political edge and although that mattered more to the fans than the footballers, the Catalan players did take that seriously.' Not least because as Suárez adds – and this lies at the heart of the rivalry – 'Madrid and Barça were the [world's] strongest teams. It wouldn't have been so big otherwise.'

The first leg, played in Madrid on 9 November 1960, had finished 2-2. The second leg was played in Barcelona on 23 November and Barcelona won 2-1. After five years and twenty rounds, Madrid had been beaten in the European Cup. For the first time ever there would be another winner. 'The King is dead, long live the King!' wrote *La Vanguardia Española*. On the other side of the divide, it hurt as no defeat ever had. The editor of one of Spain's leading sports newspapers recently described it, even now, as the most painful loss in Madrid's history. It was also the game that undermined two of the persistent myths that surround the Madrid–Barça rivalry, particularly during the late 1950s and early 1960s when their popular identities were first being forged. One, that the referees always helped Real Madrid; two, that only Barcelona, taking the loser's way out, sheltering behind a victim complex, ever complained about referees; that Real Madrid, by contrast, were a *club señor* who never protested.

The second leg was, said the match referee, 'a sensational game, in which the stars were the best players in the world'; a game that one paper declared, 'deserved two winners'. Barcelona's goalkeeper Ramallets had kept his side in it with a series of excellent saves while, in the words of *El Mundo Deportivo*, Kubala, who needed a painkilling injection to complete the match, had turned the clock back to his finest years: 'he alone tipped the balance away from the great things that the *whites* did last night . . . this is without doubt one of the most emotional and brilliant pages that he has written into his service record.'

If some thought this Herrera's team and Herrera's victory *in absentia*, *La Prensa* claimed the opposite, reopening old wounds and revealing again the depth of feeling and mutual mistrust between star player and star coach, media and manager: as far as they were concerned, Kubala had not just beaten Madrid, he had beaten his former coach too. They turned it into a fairy tale in which an angelic blond boy, loved by all, had been attacked by a jealous 'terrifying howling wolf called HH'. Now the boy was back – 'impressive, unstoppable, heroic, like in an oriental tale'. When the battle was over, *La Prensa* wrote, 'a white giant took the magic wand, a white ball, and Kubala asked for it . . . and the opponent, made greater still by a gesture so beautiful, handed it to him as if to say: "victory is always reserved for true giants".'

But it was not Kubala or even Ramallets who was for ever associated with that moment. Rather, it would be two Englishmen and a Brazilian who two years later left for Real Madrid, the striker who scored the winning goal in the sixty-eighth minute – 'flying like a plane' to meet Olivella's cross-shot, in the words of his team-mate Vicente. For three decades Evaristo de Macedo's diving header was arguably the most important and most emblematic goal in Barcelona's history. A famous photograph of him, horizontal, connecting with the ball, lit up against the shadows, gave the goal an even more mystical feel.

Evaristo remembers it perfectly: 'Madrid were playing for their sixth European Cup and we were obliged to beat them,' he says. 'They had a great team, but people forget that we did too. We were overlooked – the second best team in the world, maybe even the best by then. But few people talked about us. We were the *two* biggest teams in Europe. The thing is, Madrid always won the European Cup. I remember our fans pleading with us – literally pleading, eh – not to let them win again, coming up to us and saying: "please, *please* stop them." Catalonia had problems with Madrid that came from the [civil] war. It's still there even now, something that's never been fully overcome. We were so nervous before the game, but not as nervous as the fans. I can still see the ball coming across, diving for it . . .' Evaristo hardly need say more.

'There was happiness,' he says, 'but there was a kind of relief too.'

For Real Madrid, there was anger, and lots of it. Canário does not even wait for the question to be finished. 'We lost *malamente*,' he says. '*I* got kicked in the chest and the referee ruled it out!' Juan Santisteban was at Madrid for thirty years as a player and a coach. He is too even-tempered, just too nice, to rant. But, he says: 'Something strange happened that day.' He falls silent and adds with a knowing, slightly sad smile: 'Too strange.'

Even now it stings. Much has been made in Madrid of the fact that victimism and conspiracy is not written into Madrid's DNA, but here it is writ large. *Marca* revisited the game in 2011 under the headline 'Barça take revenge with the referee's help', presenting it as a 'shameful' occasion in which Madrid had lost purely because the referee had been Barcelona's 'greatest ally'. A video produced a few years before is narrated by the current Radio Marca broadcaster, Paco García Caridad, in a tone that half a century on is so indignant, so furious, as to be almost funny – the report opens with the exclamation 'what bad refereeing!' and at one point García Caridad responds to a disallowed goal by decrying '*hombre, por favor!* What a brass neck you have!'

Two men are instantly recalled whenever anyone mentions that knockout tie – and they are not even players. Arthur Ellis and Reg Leafe were the referees: Ellis in the first leg, Leafe in the second. In England, Ellis was considered the best referee in the world and became famous for his participation in the comedy game show *It's A Knockout*; in Spain he is considered one of the worst and is famous for his role in knocking out Real Madrid. Ellis & Leafe for ever go together in

Madrid's collective conscience, like partners in crime, symbolic of their suffering. Barcelona have Guruceta; Madrid have Ellis and Leafe.

Like an angler's fish, the injustice gets bigger every time the story is told. From one goal correctly disallowed, to two disallowed, to three, to four, to five . . . correct or not is no longer an issue. Nor is it noted that not all the decisions went against the same team: instead, the headline figure rises and the injustice too. In the first leg, Barcelona had a goal ruled out for offside, scored by Villaverde, and their late equaliser was a penalty, scored by Suárez. Madrid complained that the foul on Kocsis by Madrid's goalkeeper José Vicente was outside the area – and that, in any case, Kocsis was offside. In the second leg, Madrid had a goal disallowed when Canário, escaping a high karate kick of a challenge, brought the ball down and Del Sol scored, only for the referee to rule it out for handball. Almost immediately after Evaristo's goal, Puskás crossed for Di Stéfano to score with a header but Leafe said he was offside and Pachín then scored another one for Madrid, which was again ruled out. And finally, a shot from Gento was cleared off the line by Gràcia. Off the line? Over the line, according to the legend.

After the game, the Falangist newspaper *Arriba* wrote: 'Real Madrid have died. A double-edge knife slit their throats. One, the great play from Barcelona; the other, the unexpected, cruel refereeing of Mr Ellis in Madrid and Mr Leafe in Barcelona – an unfair penalty, two goals unfairly disallowed and other black arts have thrown the invincible gladiator to the floor.' As for Eduardo Teus, he insisted: 'In all my years I have never seen a refereeing display so resolutely adverse for a team as that of Mister Leafe at the Camp Nou.' Forty years later, in 2001, the official chronicler of the city of Madrid, the veteran *ABC* journalist Luis Prados de la Plaza, published a history of Madrid, with a prologue from Alfredo Di Stéfano, to coincide with the club's centenary. In it, he described Leafe and Ellis as 'crows with English accents'. The chapter ends on the line: 'once the rage had died down, Real Madrid took the decision to accept all that [had happened] with

Christian resignation. *Pero, ¡los jodíos ingleses!* But, those fucking Englishmen!

Christian resignation? Enrique Mateos played for Madrid between 1954 and 1961. He is blunt: 'Real Madrid's success stung; that's why we were knocked out unfairly. In the squad we thought they had clipped our wings. Winning five in a row irritated more than one European club, especially the powerful ones, and more than one UEFA director. Mr Leafe was Barcelona's best player.'

One of the striking things about the images that have survived from the game is the relative tranquillity at the end of it, the way in which players shake each other's hands. The official comments in the media too mostly comprised good wishes and good sportsmanship, just as the regime demanded. Paco Gento, the Madrid captain, offered 'sincere congratulations to Barcelona'. 'It has been an honour to get knocked out by Barcelona, a team that has shown it deserves to compete in the European Cup,' added Santiago Bernabéu, 'we offer them our hand and congratulate them with all our heart.' But beyond platitudes that reflect not only the mores imposed upon the protagonists but also upon a heavily controlled press – Barcelona were a Spanish team too and the regime publicly wished to project harmony and patriotic unity – the reality was very different, Bernabéu later bemoaning 'one of the greatest injustices in the history of football'.

Despite the censorship, Gento told reporters, 'There are no adjectives to describe the fact that he ruled out three goals' and Di Stéfano called it 'scandalous'. At the post-game banquet – attended, as always, by both teams and the match officials – Madrid's players tried to beat up the referee and his linesmen. 'We had to hold back Del Sol: he wasn't exactly going up to the referee to offer him a drink,' Di Stéfano recalls. 'Gento, Del Sol and me were still pretty furious. Because we had made mistakes ourselves, we were even more wound up. We felt offended by the way we had lost – and we considered it our competition.' It was Barcelona's players who intervened to calm their opponents down.

'Yes,' Canário admits, 'we wanted to punch them. I have never wanted to believe that it was premeditated but that night it felt like it. We were very angry. We wanted to win the sixth European Cup and if there had been a decent referee . . .'

At a Madrid game later that season, supporters carried a banner with a picture of skulls embossed with the names Leafe and Ellis crossed out and even at an institutional level the anger was intense. Their official publication, the *Boletín del Real Madrid*, reproduced comments from the international press complaining about the referees' decisions and ran a bitter editorial that, even fifty years on, is briefly reminiscent of Jose Mourinho's rant in 2011 when he claimed that he, a proud, clean winner in 2010, would be 'ashamed' to have won the Champions League in the way that Barcelona had won it two years before. One line particularly encapsulates that sensation: 'May God bring Barcelona luck and hopefully they can gain the same laurel in this edition of the European Cup as the clean efforts of Madrid did in the five that went before.'

The fact that *L'Equipe* saw fit to insist 'Mr Leafe, the referee, has knocked Real Madrid out of the European Cup', suggests that there was something in the complaints and that much of the anger was justified but drawing definitive conclusions is difficult. Footage of the games is dark, incomplete and occasionally shot from angles that do little to clarify the moves, often from behind the goal and low down. Even the lines on the pitch are not clearly visible and the film doesn't carry commentary except in the state NODO newsreels, put together retrospectively. There are some plays not normally included in the historic narrative that suddenly appear in shot and are unexplained. In the second game, for example, there appears to be a Barcelona goal disallowed – one that curiously goes unmentioned in the accounts.

In the first game, it is impossible to see if Barcelona's goal was correctly ruled out or not but Pedro Escartín, a columnist, former referee and briefly Spain coach in 1952–3, insisted that it 'could not be offside'. There is no way of judging for certain whether Kocsis was offside – Escartín insisted it was 'flagrant' – or inside the area on the penalty given three minutes from full time but decades later José Vicente told Television Española that he had been outside the area and Puskás recalled: 'Kocsis was brought down on a run just outside the area. My one-time Hungarian striking partner did his famous forward roll. I could see that [Kocsis] didn't want to meet my eyes.'

The evidence from the second game is similarly inconclusive. Del Sol, the first Madrid player to have a goal disallowed, insisted: 'when the referee blew the whistle, we assumed he was either giving the goal or a penalty. But he didn't give anything.' Canário, the player who had brought the ball down and then tumbled to the turf, was convinced he had been kicked in the chest. In fact, the referee gave a handball, which is clear. What's not clear is what came first: the kick in the chest or the handball, but it looks very much like the former. The third goal – the one in which García Caridad accuses the referee of having a brass neck – was given for offside against Pachín, who later admitted to the journalist Alfredo Relaño that it was correctly ruled out. When Di Stéfano scored his header, Barça's players immediately appealed for offside and Di Stéfano does appear to be behind the last defender. And Gento's shot is one of the few decisions that seems clear: it was cleared *off* the line, not *over* it.

Asked if he was satisfied with his performance, Leafe replied: 'frankly, yes.'

'But what about the goals that you disallowed?'

'I didn't doubt for a second,' he responded, 'because they were scored illegally. And I blew at that very instant.'

'This was not as Barcelona dreamed it during days, weeks, months, years,' *L'Equipe* insisted. 'They didn't expect to go into the Capitol through the service door.' Barcelona didn't agree and didn't care, *El Mundo Deportivo* hinting at domestic frustrations to insist that they had witnessed two refereeing displays 'without prejudice from which there is more to learn than to criticise'.

'Bah!' says Barcelona's goalkeeper Ramallets, 'there's always an excuse, always someone to blame. We beat them well. Maybe there's a goal . . . they were celebrating, hugging and Mr Ellis ruled it out. But we would have won anyway.'

'Madrid complained a lot,' says Evaristo, 'because they lost.'

After the game, Gento said: 'I can only hope that Barcelona have better luck in the final than we had here.' They didn't. Di Stéfano said: 'I hope Barcelona don't have the same bad luck that we've had.' They had worse.

A few weeks later, Madrid defeated Barcelona 5-3 at the Camp Nou and went on to win the league by twenty points. Around the same time, Madrid's vice-president Raimundo Saporta wrote to Bernabéu. His report, as they did often, included a rundown of what was going on at Barcelona as well as at Madrid. Barça, he told Bernabéu, had problems: Kubala, Czibor, Kocsis, Segarra and Ramallets were all out of contract at the end of the season, there had been doubts about the manager and Alfredo Di Stéfano's renewal with Madrid 'has hurt them'. He concluded: 'Only winning the European Cup can save them but I don't know if they will be able to hang on in there until then.'

Barcelona did hang on but they got no reward. By now under another coach, Enrique Orizaola, they reached the European Cup final at the Wankdorf Stadium in Berne on 31 May 1961. They had defeated Spartak Kralov and Hamburg, beating the Germans in a replay held in Brussels and settled by Evaristo. In Switzerland they faced Benfica and lost 3-2. Benfica had the same team, minus Eusebio, that would defeat Real Madrid in the final the following season and their third goal was a wonderful volley from Mario Colona, but in Catalonia that game has come to be known as the Square Posts Final. Barcelona hit them four times, Benfica cleared two off the line and at the other end Ramallets dropped an easy catch into his own goal.

It still hurts.

'And how! And how!' Ramallets says. 'I went out on to the pitch before the game and the posts hadn't been put up yet. And when they were, they were square. They scored three goals and we gave them two of them – one of them was my fault. The other one was a long ball and I shouted "Diego, mine!" He didn't hear me. They had five chances and they scored three times. Three goals and two saves that I made. We hit the post five times. *Just* five. One, fine. But five! After the game, Alberto da Costa Pereira, their goalkeeper, said to me: "Antonio, that's football. Sometimes the best team doesn't win." That hurt us all. It was a real kick in the teeth.'

Among the crowd was the future Barcelona president Joan Gaspart. 'We didn't win that game because of pure chance, a miracle,' he says. 'The sun was shining in just the wrong place, Ramallets missed an easy catch, the posts were square – the ball hit one, then the other . . . You've never seen anything like it. If that team had won the first European Cup it would have made history. They had beaten Real Madrid when Real Madrid used to win without having to get off the bus.' 'We were so up for it, so excited, but we didn't have any luck at all,' remembers Evaristo. After the game, Orizaola told the media: 'we're the champions . . . of bad luck.' Luis Suárez's recollection is eloquent in its incredulous simplicity: '*madre mía*,' he says. 'It's impossible for something like that ever to happen again.'

For the Hungarians, who had lost the World Cup final against West Germany in the same stadium, it was especially hard to take. 'My dad told me that at half-time in 1954, when Hungary were winning 2-0, the Germans took this drink that they used to give to the pilots who flew Stukas in the war so that they wouldn't feel fear,' Czibor's son says. The allegation has not been proven, but he continues: 'Hungary had beaten them 8-3 in the group and were 2-0 up in the final. But the Germans came out for the second-half flying. Some of them didn't know their own names. He always talked about that and then Barcelona went and played in the same stadium.'

Czibor and Kocsis changed in the corridor because they didn't want to set foot in the same dressing room. It made no difference. 'That's the reason why justice wasn't done with that Barcelona team,' Czibor's son says. 'Because they didn't win the European Cup; because they lost in Berne and that game tore them apart.' For Czibor, 1954 had been worse but Kubala described Berne 1961 as the saddest day of his life. Three months later he played his last game for Barcelona in a testimonial, joined by Puskás and Di Stéfano – a forbidden fantasy that was repeated when Kubala and Di Stéfano, older now, slower too, played together at Español.

On 23 November 1960, Real Madrid – *that* Real Madrid – were defeated for the first time in Europe. It had to be Barcelona that knocked them out. Mr Leafe and Mr Ellis would never be forgotten in Madrid; Evaristo's diving header would never be forgotten in Barcelona. Ultimately, though, victory had a strangely hollow feel. Barcelona had finally ended that long wait, but they had finished up without the European Cup, without definitive proof that they were as good as their rivals, that all they had needed was the chance to prove it. The trauma of defeat was overwhelming. Within twelve months, Evaristo had gone – to Real Madrid. Barcelona had to wait thirty-two years to win the European Cup: the same wait that Madrid would endure. The difference was that Madrid waited until 1998 for their seventh; in 1992, Barcelona were still waiting for their first. The Catalans beat their greatest rivals but Berne and its square posts beat them. A historic fatalism was born.

11

THE BEST EMBASSY WE EVER HAD

In the veterans' association at the Santiago Bernabéu there are nine team pictures on the wall – one for each of the club's European Cups. There are others, of course, small photographs dotted around, plus pennants and banners, trophies in glass cabinets, books and videos, notice boards with cuttings on them. But those are the teams that really mattered. Nine of them in over a hundred years of history: posters from 1998, 2000 and 2002, borrowed from magazines, and team photos in black and white from almost forty years earlier, the first five European Cups between 1956 and 1960. Then there is *la sexta*, Madrid's sixth in 1966.

Ignacio Zoco looks at the pictures proudly, hovering over the one in which he appears. 'The European Cup fell in love with Real Madrid and Real Madrid fell in love with the European Cup,' he says. 'We still have something special with it, a connection. It happened to us with *la sexta*, that feeling. We had been waiting for it; it was deep in our soul. And then it came . . . at last!'

At last? It had been only six years since Madrid had won it and they had played two more finals since 1960, but that 'at last' makes some sense. Six years is some wait for a team who had won the first five, provoking fear that the European Cup might have deserted them for ever. All the more so because in late 1962 Madrid had been virtually bankrupt and Alfredo Di Stéfano's departure in 1964 was the end of an era. He was followed over the next two years by Ferenç Puskás and José Santamaría and by the time they reached the 1966 final Paco Gento was the only player left who had started against Eintracht Frankfurt at Hampden. Madrid had bought Amancio Amaro from Deportivo de La Coruña for twelve million pesetas in 1962, the man who would lead them into the future, but he was the club's last really big signing and had not yet been able to win the European Cup either, losing the 1964 final to Internazionale – Di Stéfano's final game.

'In 1964 Inter had a great team,' Amancio says, sitting at the bar that doubles as a trophy room, hundreds of cups lining the walls. 'But we were still obliged to win – and after we lost the game the club began a renewal process. It was a time of transition, more *casero*, home-made. And in truth over the next few years there were some fairly average players brought in. In fact, it was the start of a pretty bad era for Spanish football in general. It's fine if you sign someone like Alfredo but that just wasn't the case.'

Madrid did have good players, though. Amancio was as talented a footballer as Spain would produce in a decade, Manuel Velázquez, Pedro De Felipe and Ramón Grosso came through the youth system and Madrid had signed Zoco from Osasuna the same summer as Amancio. José Martínez Sánchez arrived in 1964. Better known as 'Pirri', his playing career ran until 1980, when he qualified in medicine and became the club's doctor. 'I was the youngest there, just a kid,' he says. 'And it was a totally new era. The truth is I had never actually seen Di Stéfano play: I lived in Ceuta in North Africa and I didn't have a television, but still you knew: they'd won five consecutive European Cups and Di Stéfano was everything. The structure stayed the same – Miguel Muñoz was still there as manager and Bernabéu and Saporta – but it was a new period. There is a "Before" and an "After Di Stéfano". It was hard for us because they constantly compared us to that team. Looking back, it was the most difficult period in Madrid's entire history.'

If Di Stéfano's retirement seemed to herald a collapse, it did not work out that way. Madrid's success, in Spain at least, remained largely unchecked – certainly by Barcelona. Atlético Madrid, by contrast, won the league in 1966, 1969, 1970 and 1973 and the Copa del Generalísimo in 1960, 1961, 1965, and 1972; Real Madrid won the league in 1965, 1967, 1968, 1969 and 1972 and the cup in 1970, 1974 and 1975. If that diminished the Barça–Madrid rivalry on one side of the divide, it deepened it on the other. 'Barcelona mattered of course but for us back then the bigger rival was Atlético Madrid,' Pirri says. 'They were a very good team at that point. Barcelona? I was friends with some of their players and there was a sporting rivalry but we didn't . . .'

Pirri stops for a moment. He seems to be looking for a polite way of saying what follows. 'In my era as a player I think we won ten leagues in sixteen years. Barcelona won one. Barcelona were also very *pendiente del* Real Madrid, hanging on what Madrid did. We didn't care what they did. We just got on with winning. I don't like the fact that these days Madrid are so *pendiente del* Barça because there's no need. In my era, I remember they were always looking at us. But always from a distance.' One member of the footballing staff at Madrid, a man who was at the club for over three decades, insists: 'We didn't care about Barça. We didn't even look at them. My dad used to say the only time it's worth looking at them is down the barrel of a gun.'

The problem was that domestic dominance was one thing, European excellence another. And if by 1966 the pressure had become huge, after 1966 it would grow to be unbearable. Despite insisting that he was so young that he did not realise how big it was, Pirri describes winning the final as a 'relief'. It was also unique. 'That was the chance to show people that Madrid were still there. And with an entire team of Spaniards, too,' Pirri says. 'I have said lots of times that '66 is the European Cup with the most merit of all of them,' insists Zoco. 'Eleven upstanding Spaniards, not one foreigner. That was something special.'

Madrid defeated Partizan Belgrade 2-1 in the final in Brussels. Effectively the Slav army team, Partizan were the first side from the eastern bloc to make the final. They had knocked out Manchester United in the semi-final, and scored the opening goal in the final. But Zoco speaks for everyone when he insists that the semi, when Madrid beat Internazionale 1-0 at the Bernabéu and then drew 1-1 at San Siro with Amancio getting the goal, was 'much bigger'. Before the game Inter coach Helenio Herrera had declared that Madrid's definitive eclipse was nigh. He had also booked the hotel for the final, only for Madrid to end up taking Inter's rooms. 'Inter were the *coco*, the bogeyman,' Amancio says. 'They were the holders, champions two years in a row. They had Helenio Herrera at the height of his prestige and they were an *equipazo*: Suárez, Joaquín Peiró, Jaír . . . No one gave us a hope in hell at San Siro.'

'By contrast we really didn't know much about Partizan,' Amancio admits. 'Those were different times. So different that I never even saw the game for years – I think I got the tape from Dutch television in the end. And when we got back to Madrid after the final it was explosive. There was some party! We had a meal with Bernabéu and his wife, went to a *sala de fiestas* and went dancing. Well, I didn't. I never danced. The next day we went to the stadium. There were so many people waiting: Madrid went mad for us. We had come from an age of splendour and famous players to a team with five players from the youth system, two brought from the Second Division, all of us Spanish, and we won the European Cup.'

Spain was changing. In 1959, the dictatorship shifted policy, formally confirming a trend towards economic liberalisation and the opening up of the Spanish market, which slowly brought with it a gigantic shift in society, consumerism emerging for the first time since the war. Per capita income doubled between 1963 and 1971. In 1961, there were just twelve cars per thousand people; that figure could be multiplied by six ten years later, although it was still well below the rest of Western Europe. When Madrid and Barcelona played each other on

15 February 1959, it was the first televised game in Spain's history and there was a sudden rush to buy TVs, despite costing an enormous 2,000 pesetas (£12). From 600 sets in 1956, there were 2,125,000 in 1966.

Madrid's players got a privileged view of the shift. 'We travelled and we could see that Spain was not the same,' Amancio says. 'You could see the difference between, say, Spain and Italy or other European countries. They had more of everything: more light, more commerce, more clothing . . . although when it came to food no one could beat us. But then we would go to the east and think: *joder macho*, bloody hell, this is a disaster. If you think our situation isn't good, look at this. You'd go to Romania, Yugoslavia, Hungary, and it struck us the same way that maybe other countries were struck by Spain. And at home we could see that was changing.'

What most drove the change, propelling Spain's economy, was movement in the other direction. Tourism. One million people visited Spain in 1954; that figure doubled by 1957, reaching three million at the end of the decade. Just over ten years later it stood at thirty million. And not only did tourists bring money, they brought different attitudes, different behaviour, different aspirations. This was a regime that had painted vests on to boxers' naked torsos and dubbed Hollywood lovers into brothers and sisters. Sonia Weinberg recalls arriving in Madrid in 1954, a city of 'great poverty', with her husband – the Real Madrid player Héctor Rial – and being stopped on Gran Vía by a Civil Guard officer who took offence at her low-cut top. That was just one challenge; by the late 1960s there were thousands of them and by the 1970s it was irresistible. The Bishop of the Canary Islands declared the bikini a 'symbol of the delinquency and degeneration of today's women' and much has been made of the image of Civil Guards patrolling beaches, ordering topless bathers from abroad to cover up. It has been exaggerated but a challenge to some of the regime's mores had been brought into the open – one that had social and political consequences.

In 1966 the dictatorship wrapped itself in a pseudo-democratic cloak. Juan Carlos was named as the king-in-waiting, groomed for the task of following the Generalísimo, while censorship was both slightly relaxed and repackaged within the Ministry of Information and Tourism under Manuel Fraga Ibarne: it was now punitive not preventative. Publications did not have to pass by the censor first but could be sanctioned afterwards, meaning that some began tentatively to push the boundaries, taking risks. *Spain is Different* ran Fraga's famous tourist slogan. Mass tourism meant that Spaniards got to see just how different, acquiring a taste for some of the freedoms and comfort their European visitors enjoyed and serving to close that gap.

And in the midst of it, Madrid won the European Cup. Photographs have a power that resists all else and that team will always be locked in its time because of one particular picture. Spain was certainly not impervious to the charms of the sixties, even if they were less swinging than elsewhere. The Beatles played at Madrid's Ventas bullring in July 1965 and when the European Cup came round in 1966, a photo appeared on the cover of *El Alcázar* with Grosso, Antonio Betancort, Sanchís, De Felipe, Velázquez and Pirri all wearing Beatles wigs. Paco Gento had been asked to take part too but had refused. The picture was the idea of a photographer by the name of Félix Lázaro. Never mind that the wigs were so lamentable, so scraggy, that they looked more Incredible Hulk than Fab Four, Manuel Sanchís bearing an uncanny resemblance to Carlos Tévez, the players, all beaming smiles and goofy grins, were presented as Madrid's *ye-yé* – a transliteration of the Yeah, Yeah chorus from 'She Loves You'. 'Introducing Madrid's *ye-yés*: perfect camaraderie and a contagious, youthful happiness' ran the caption.

The meaning was inescapable but were they even Beatles fans?

'Of course,' protests Amancio with a grin. '*Sí, sí, sí*. It was ingenious of Félix to get the wigs. A couple of people got in there that probably shouldn't given their age – Betancort or Sanchís, maybe. The rest of them were young, twenty-one, twenty-two. I don't know if Bernabéu liked that title. Maybe it expressed something that didn't really fit with Real Madrid, like the *galácticos* tag years later, but it was a reflection of a new era that we could all sense. A different generation.'

Zoco recalls: 'The Beatles were in fashion at the time and they made it easy for the photographer. The wigs, the euphoria, everything: it is hard to explain what it feels like to win the European Cup. Those guys felt like what they were: young, happy, healthy, strong, handsome.' He stops himself and starts laughing. 'Well, handsome? One or two of them were a *long* way from handsome. That win represented Spain, its resurgence. We had no reason to have a complex, no reason to feel inferior. That helped Spain. It was a way of saying: "hey, over here we too can do things that people over there can do".'

Real Madrid returned to Spain with their sixth European Cup and José Sebastián de Erice, the ambassador to Brussels, wrote: 'I wore Madrid's badge with pride and happiness because, as a representative of my *Patria* [Fatherland], I consider the presence of the *Merengues* in cities across the world to be a genuine expression of our reborn, virile Spain, young and enthusiastic.' His was a familiar narrative. Madrid as standard-bearer for Spain, its sole representative in a hostile world, was a portrayal that had been made often with the success of their first five European Cups, and two years later in 1968 the president of the Madrid Press Association told his audience at a banquet in the capital: 'As you're young, you probably don't remember that during the diplomatic blockade of Spain, when from every corner of the world they strangled us, there were three embassies: the girls from the *Coros y Danzas*, the [bullfighter] Manolete and the goals that Real Madrid scored; together they made up the best Diplomatic Corps, Spain's great counterattack.'

By 1968, it was natural that they might not have recalled it or recognised it; this was a different society now and for many it felt like a different state too. Madrid's ambassadorial role had become less important, less obvious, its symbolism shifting. But it had long been highlighted and it had been genuinely important too. At a time of isolation – from which, by the mid-1960s, Spain was slowly emerging – the success of Real Madrid was a significant tool of legitimisation and patriotic pride. And for the Franco regime, the last outpost of European fascism, legitimisation was fundamental.

Madrid's early European Cup victories dovetailed with the opening of Spain and the beginning of a rapprochement with Europe, breaking down boundaries: there could be few better demonstrations of Spain's worth than the five- and then six-times European champions, giving the country an allure absent before. In late 1960, there were plans to hold a match to honour Madrid's success in winning the first five European Cups and the Intercontinental Cup. When it looked like the plan might fall through because of difficulties in putting together an opposition, Barcelona's president, Francisco Miró Sans, wrote to Bernabéu to plead for the chance to arrange the match on Madrid's behalf, insisting: 'who could deny Real Madrid a public display of respect from supporters after you have brought so much prestige to Spanish football?' In the end, Madrid faced a national XI, with Franco watching from the directors' box. Kubala played despite having been in Chile two days before the game and having arrived at Barajas airport just two hours before kick-off. The proceeds went to a regime-sponsored charity and Di Stéfano, Kubala, and Gento were received at El Pardo. Franco gratefully gave them all signed photographs.

His gratitude went beyond relative formalities such as this. Franco's status as a political pariah and the image of Spain as a downtrodden, miserable place was palliated by footballing success and the joy it brought; popularity was intangible, impossible to measure, but Di Stéfano, Gento, Puskás et al, certainly helped. As the journalist Francisco Cercedo put it in *Posible*: 'Real Madrid were a flying embassy. Without doubt the three great events of the period between 1950 and 1960 were the Concordat with the Vatican, the [Madrid] pact with the United States and the five European Cups. Pío XII, Eisenhower and Bernabéu were the men who made Spain a full member of the international community. Not even all the gold in Mexico and Moscow could have paid for the satisfaction of being able to parade round Europe, heads held high.'

Conscious of the value of sporting success, the regime celebrated Madrid's feats, even if they were invariably packaged as patriotic rather than explicitly political. 'When in other fields, in other spheres, Spain has been denied bread and water, people surrender to the dazzling play of Madrid. Real Madrid have unfurled the Spanish flag,' wrote the Francoist historian Luis de Sosa. According to Alfredo Sánchez Bella, ambassador to Italy between 1962 and 1969, Madrid were 'one of the best, if not the best instrument we have had to cement our popularity beyond our borders'. As Fernando María Castiella, the foreign minister between 1957 and 1969, put it: 'Madrid have carried the name of Spain round the world with the greatest decorum. Their players have acted like veritable ambassadors, bringing prestige to our Fatherland.'

Madrid were not reluctant contributors to the promoting of Spain's image although to what extent this can be read as a whitewashing of the regime is another matter entirely. In 1953, the front cover of the club's official publication, the *Boletín del Real Madrid* carried a reproduction of a telegram from the head of the Spanish state's overseas service describing their successes as 'a stupendous sporting and patriotic campaign'. The *Boletín*'s headline was eloquent: 'This is the glory that matters to us'. A front page editorial insisted: 'this is what Madrid represents and symbolises.' It was no one-off: the *Boletín* invariably and proudly reproduced the eulogies, often uttered at official receptions when the club arrived in foreign countries to play matches, and after the 1966 final Madrid's players posed for another famous photograph. Taken from above, looking down on them, fourteen players and the coach stand in formation on the Bernabéu turf holding a Spain flag, Francoist imperial eagle at its centre; in front of them, six more players, each holding one of the club's six European Cups.

The idea of Real Madrid representing Spain was an obsession for Bernabéu, one he drilled into his players constantly, particularly when

Spain played in cities with a large Spanish expat community. At the 1966 final, one set of fans attended with a banner that declared: 'Madrid: abroad you play with twelve men'. Zoco paints a portrait of the president, thumping the desk Bernabéu-style to underline the point. 'We played games all over the place – the European Cup, tours, friendlies – and Bernabéu always said: "we have to win, we have to make the thousands of Spaniards over there happy." His obsession was making Spaniards abroad proud.' Bernabéu himself insisted: 'As a Spaniard I think the greatest achievement is to have made Madrid admired overseas.'

For those who see in Real Madrid's ambassadorial status a vehicle of Francoist propaganda, this particular obsession poses a problem, offering up a contradiction. These fans were Spaniards who had left the country, economic migrants and in some cases even the exiled. There was in Bernabéu's obsession a populism that was not merely cheap demagoguery: these were normal people who missed home, even if the fact that it benefited the regime is incontrovertible. 'We stumbled across them in hotels and airports,' says Amancio. 'They used to come and find us when we played abroad, especially in France, Germany or England. There was always someone from your home town. They took pride in our success. A friend of mine used to joke about how after we had won he would go back to the hotel where he worked, feeling like the star washer-up.' Bernabéu recalled: 'We were more important at the Foreign Ministry than we were at the DND. All over the world we were met as if we were from another galaxy and the regime took advantage of that.'

Castiella called Real Madrid 'the best embassy we ever had' and the word 'embassy' could hardly have been better employed: receptions were common, the exchanging of gifts too, in the name of the nation. Before every trip, Madrid obligatorily informed the Foreign Ministry of their travel plans and reported back afterwards – impressions, experiences, what they noted. Bernabéu jokingly told Franco of a trip to Yugoslavia in which he informed Real Madrid's hosts: 'Yeah, we have a dictator too, and better still he's Galician.'

But it was more than off-the-cuff remarks. Trips to the UN in 1959, Morocco in 1964 and Cairo in 1969 all had a political value, and in 1961 Castiella asked Madrid to go to the Council of Europe in Strasbourg while they were there for a match. Saporta gave a speech in which he insisted that Madrid's presence there 'shows that even in this council, where Spain is not represented, we are considered Europeans'. When Madrid visited Communist countries where there were no Spanish embassies, the reports they sent back were formal ones. This was effectively a mission of discovery and information, a genuine ambassadorial role. At one game in Germany in 1971, late in the dictatorship, vice-president Raimundo Saporta noticed that the banned Spanish Communist Party in exile was distributing leaflets in both German and Spanish. He kept one and sent it to the ministry of the interior on his return as a way of warning them of what was happening.

The exchange of information was not entirely one-sided either. If Madrid played politician, Spain's diplomats played scout. Before the 1960 European Cup final, the Spanish consul in Frankfurt sent a report to the Bernabéu on the Eintracht Frankfurt team and foreign office files show that colleagues in other cities provided similar reports. On an informal level, that trend continued well into the democratic era: as late as 1986, eleven years after Franco's death, the ambassador in Rome sent through information on a potential new manager for the club – the Swede Sven-Göran Eriksson.

During the 1950s and 1960s Madrid travelled with a Spanish flag and a copy of the national anthem just in case. They were trusted to defend and project Spain as the state wished. Bernabéu's concept of the nation was shared by the regime. By contrast, in one government archive there is a secret police file preserved alongside ones on the Basque terrorist organisation ETA. Dedicated entirely to Club de Fútbol Barcelona, it contains résumés of board members and presidents. However carefully chosen and vetted its presidents, Barcelona were by definition suspicious; Madrid were not. Madrid were natural potential partners for the regime in a way that a Catalan club could not be. Exorcism and control never fully washed away the suspicion and Barça retained and later recovered its Catalanist identity, partly cohering against the regime.

Castiella was a *socio* at Real Madrid. He was not the only one. According to Duncan Shaw in his book *Fútbol y franquismo*, so were Manuel Fraga Ibarne, José Solís and Gregorio López Bravo, all of them significant ministers within the regime, while Muñoz Grandes, Luis Carrero Blanco and José Millán Astray were also Madrid fans. The latter wrote one letter to Bernabéu in which he signed off with a 'Ra! Ra! Ra! And *viva* Madrid!'. The board of directors invariably contained military men and even the coach who won Madrid's first European Cup was from the army: José Villalonga had been an infantry captain and gym teacher at the Toledo military academy.

Requests for tickets to Madrid games were constant and the club did what it could to satisfy representatives of the armed forces, police and Civil Guard. The president of Atlético Madrid, Jesús Gil – the same Jesús Gil who was handed a personal pardon by Franco after an apartment complex he built collapsed, killing fifty-seven people – famously complained that the 'the directors' box at the Bernabéu is worse than the General's hunting trips'. In other words, a kind of informal court where everybody jostled for favour and influence, a place of business and politics. A glance at directors' boxes all over Spain, and Barcelona and Madrid in particular, suggests that the basic principle has not changed, even if the regime has.

Franco himself visited on occasion but Saporta always claimed that he gave little away, sitting through games largely impassive and, when it came to return visits, the club's general manager claimed that Bernabéu tried to avoid going to El Pardo at all costs. The dictator was a football fan, his doctor claiming that he never missed a game on television, and he even won the pools on one occasion under a false name. But if that sounds suspicious, which it may well be, it was not because he controlled the results: the games on the coupon that week were played in Italy's Serie A. Paul Preston, Franco's biographer, says that the *Caudillo* was a Real Madrid supporter while the regime's official historian, Ricardo de la Cierva, whose duty it was to rehabilitate the dictator, insists there is no indication that he supported them.

Franco's cousin Francisco Franco Salgado-Araujo recalls talking to him about the 1958 cup final between Madrid and Atlético Bilbao, but while Franco noted that Madrid missed Gento and Kopa, and that it was a 'pity' Di Stéfano had not played at his best, his remarks are mostly anodyne: he had enjoyed Bilbao's 'enthusiasm' and, in a comment more revealing than it first appears, expressed satisfaction that the fans had been 'worthy of the capital of Spain, quite impartial for games of this nature'. Franco's grandson, meanwhile, told Carles Torras: 'He never said "I'm a Madrid fan" but I'd say he was. He was a Madrid fan like almost everyone was a Madrid fan then, because Madrid was something you could be proud of.'

That Madrid counted regime figures among their fans was hardly surprising: they were, after all, the most successful side in Europe and located in the capital, a simple fact that by definition aroused suspicion in Catalonia. Bernabéu was right when he said that the regime took advantage of Madrid. It almost certainly would have done the same had Barcelona been the winners of the first five European Cups. This was a chance to be identified with success. Regime figures began arriving en masse in the directors' box when trophies began arriving en masse in the cabinet. This was the best ticket in town. Madrid did not become the best because they were the regime's team; they were the regime's team because they became the best. Prior to 1955, Madrid's only reception with Franco had been when they handed him a copy of their fiftieth anniversary book. And while it would be naïve to suggest that the state could not intervene to aid a football team, and much as the Franco regime began with totalitarian aims even in sport, this was a chaotic state. Influence could undoubtedly be exerted and on occasion probably was, but the regime did not really act systematically any more.

There are other flaws in the popular notion of Madrid as Franco's team. The suggestion that Real Madrid the club, or Madrid the city, were the victors of the civil war is mistaken and offensive. During the Second Republic, Madrid had won two leagues in 1932 and 1933, before the right was in power, and two cups in 1934 and 1936. After the civil war, with Franco's dictatorship established, it took them until 1946 to win anything at all, when they claimed the first of two cups, and they were twice on the verge of relegation. Their city rivals Atlético, merged with the air force team, won the first two league titles but it took Real Madrid until 1953, when the most repressive phase of the regime was drawing to a close, to win the championship. By then Barcelona had won it five times during a period when the DND actively aspired to control football. When they won, Barcelona too were granted receptions with Franco.

When Madrid's greatest success came, it came in Europe – where Franco was a pariah. Revisiting Madrid's matches through the international media, there is no bitterness, no suspicion and no controversy, just admiration for a team that redefined the game. Here, Barcelona's complaint is that they too had an impressive team that was rarely given the chance to compete in Europe and, of course, that Alfredo Di Stéfano, the player who had made it all possible, had arrived at Madrid in the first place because of the regime.

'When I hear that Real Madrid were the regime's team, I feel like crapping on the father that says so,' Bernabéu said in the early 1970s. By then he had become irritated by the regime, after his planned development of the stadium had been turned down, although it is wise to tread carefully with his contradictory and self-justificatory remarks later in life. He would have been aware too that the debt Barcelona incurred in the construction of the Camp Nou was eventually resolved when Franco belatedly authorised the reclassification of land around the stadium in 1965, and Bernabéu also complained at Madrid's failure to secure more money from the football pools, about Barcelona's influence at the DND, about the size of Madrid's television deal with the state channel, even though it dwarfed Barcelona's, and about the ban on foreign players – a ban that was eventually lifted just in time for Barcelona to sign Johan Cruyff.

Raimundo Saporta was in step with the Falange and the regime: he admitted 'Franco liked me' and his personal correspondence, much of it overtly political, reveals him as a committed supporter and a man who showed an interest in the shifting dynamics of the dictatorship. But Bernabéu was a little more ambiguous, probably closer to the regime's military men and monarchist sympathisers than the fascists of the Falange, and there had been the occasional clash, albeit not as many as he liked to boast about later. There were moments in which the government bemoaned problems of Bernabéu's making. In 1955, during a trip to Switzerland, Madrid's players were visited by the exiled royal family: the former Queen Victoria, the pretender Don Juan and the Prince Juan Carlos. The prince even came into the dressing room at half-time where he told Di Stéfano 'you're not doing much'. The succession question was a live issue at the time and the regime did not thank Bernabéu for his actions.

Madrid's president described the under-secretary of the treasury as 'Madrid's number one enemy' after he had called Puskás a 'Communist' and the minister for agriculture, Rafael Cavestany, bitterly complained to the Francoist council of ministers that he had not been given a central seat in the directors' box, Bernabéu telling him: 'that is where the president of Real Madrid sits.' Bernabéu also moved to have José Millán Astray expelled from the directors' box after he groped a lady there. The founder of the Foreign Legion, Millán Astray, a sadistic, bloodthirsty psychopath with one arm missing and a hole where his right eye should have been, was a veteran of the Moroccan wars famous for a clash with the philosopher Miguel de Unamuno in Salamanca in October 1937 in which he had shouted 'Long Live Death!' He was not a man you contradicted. But when Millán Astray insisted on returning, Bernabéu held firm, enlisting the help of General Muñoz Grandes to intervene.

This can be read in two ways: far from revealing a serious confrontation with the regime and still less a political resistance, it probably signifies the opposite. Unlike his counterparts in Catalonia, Bernabéu felt entirely secure in his position, certain enough that there was no suspicion about his fundamental convergence with the dictatorship to challenge those he did not like. This was a rebellion against an individual not the state and, moreover, he had the backing of influential regime members, belying his oft-made claim to carry no weight at all. It is a claim that is emphatically disproved by the sheer number of letters Bernabéu received asking him to intervene on behalf of members and former players and his ability to satisfy such requests – albeit usually with low-level regime functionaries. One example is a letter in which he personally contacted José Finat, by then mayor of Madrid, to secure a taxi driver's licence for a former player. Curiously, Saporta also pulled strings to get another player a car to which he should not have been entitled – Barcelona's Ferran Olivella.

These were complaints from the regime about Bernabéu's behaviour, not rejections of Madrid's entire identity. But they also pose questions that can, and should, be extrapolated to both clubs: what were Madrid supposed to do? What were Barcelona supposed to do? Bar the way to regime figures? Not let them into games? What politician, fascist, Communist or democrat of left or right has not sought political capital in sporting success? And who really represents the club? The directors' box was open to them and so were directors' posts but if Madrid's board was full of military men so was Barcelona's. Presidents and directors had been approved by the state.

Every club necessarily accommodated the regime, even if that accommodation existed on different levels and was undertaken with differing degrees of enthusiasm. In 1977, one member wrote privately to Bernabéu praising the president for 'maintaining Madrid's independence from the totalitarian organs of the state'; achieving this during 'such difficult times' was, Bernabéu's correspondent claimed, 'as important as the six European Cups'. But it is true that the two clubs later took divergent paths. Barcelona felt like an outsider and by the late 1960s became a focus of resistance and discomfort for the regime in a way that Madrid never did, albeit usually at a social rather than institutional level.

Madrid were awarded the Order of the Yoke and Arrows in 1955 after winning the Copa Latina, a distinction not bestowed upon Barcelona in 1949 or 1952. Bernabéu was handed the Gran Cruz de Mérito Civil in 1959. And Di Stéfano was given the Order of Isabel la Católica in 1960. All were important state decorations. But Bernabéu was also awarded the Légion d'honneur by democratic France, where his contribution to the European Cup was never forgotten, and Barcelona gave awards to Franco too, in 1971 and 1974. The difference perhaps lies in the fact that there were campaigns in 2003 and 2012 to revoke those that Barcelona handed over whereas no one at Madrid later proposed they withdraw awards made during the dictatorship. Unlike Barcelona, they saw no shame in it, or perhaps they saw no need. Times have changed; that was simply another era with another state.

'Madrid,' Saporta famously claimed, with a touch of pragmatism that bordered on cynicism, 'is and always has been apolitical. It has always been so powerful because it has always been at the service of the backbone of the state. When it was founded in 1902 it respected Alfonso XIII and in 1931 when the Republic was proclaimed, the Republic; in 1939, the Generalísimo. And now it respects his majesty Juan Carlos. It is a disciplined club that accepts with loyalty the institution that runs the nation.' This is reflected in the sheer number of letters sent to congratulate or offer platitudes to politicians of all creeds, both during and after the regime. Indeed, the earliest mention of current president, Florentino Pérez, appears to be, curiously enough, a letter sent to him by the club's general manager, congratulating him on becoming Madrid council's delegate for sanitation in 1976. The historian Ángel Bahamonde suggests that Bernabéu fostered political relations as a means of protecting the club from political interference. The paradox here is that Real Madrid's supposed apoliticism, the claim to be simply a football club with no other deeper meaning, served to make the club one of the great symbols of Spanish nation-alism, infusing it with a political meaning from which it has largely shied but not explicitly rejected.

The image of Madrid as the regime team endures, as does the notion that they are favoured by the Establishment: a right-wing club. There is a version of the club's anthem that has been adapted by opposition fans – not just from Barcelona – and runs: 'Madrid, the government's team, the national disgrace!' You can't ask a Barcelona fan why they hate Madrid without Franco's name being mentioned, without some reference to power and centralism. The myths matter even when they are myths because they come to inform football fans' perceptions of their clubs, even as times shift. Whether or not it is fair is another issue.

Madrid count left-wing politicians among their supporters too. Gregorio Peces-Barba joined the clandestine Socialist Party in 1972, became secretary-general of the party in 1977 and was president of a Socialist-led parliament between 1982 and 1986. In an interview with Madrid's *Boletín* in 1989, he insisted: 'My father was imprisoned by the regime after the civil war and one of two things that he did as soon as he came out was to make me a *socio* at Madrid, just as he had been before. He was a freedom fighter during Francoism and so was I.'

His experience is a reminder that football clubs are not monolithic blocks. A political scandal broke out in October 2005 when it emerged that a prominent club director, close to the players and the father-in-law of the president, was a member of the Fundación Francisco Franco, an organisation dedicated to celebrating the memory of the director. Alejandro Echevarria was a director at Barcelona. Similarly, Paul Breitner was a pipe-smoking Maoist who donated 500,000 pesetas to striking workers at the Standard factory; he played for Real Madrid. So too did Manuel Fernández, 'Pahíño'. Scorer of 108 goals in 126 matches for Madrid between 1948 and 1953 and a reader of Tolstoy and Dostoyevsky, whose contraband books he bought under the counter in Barcelona, he claims he didn't go to the 1950 World Cup because he was 'too left-wing'. He had openly laughed when a military man came into the

Spain dressing room before a game in 1948 and demanded 'balls and Spanishness' from the players.

Vicente del Bosque spent virtually his whole life at Real Madrid. His parents were left-wing trade unionists and his father spent three years in Murgia in a Francoist prison camp. Del Bosque defended the controversial Law of Historical Memory, which sought to investigate the crimes of the Franco regime and recover the bodies of its victims, while in the 1970s he had been one of a number of Madrid players who lent their support to strikes, and he was among the founders of the players' union, the AFE. 'Madrid,' he says, 'represents all of Spain. The idea that it is Franco's club is totally off the mark. It doesn't make any sense, any at all. It is a plural club.'

Now even more so. Joan Gaspart makes a similar point and he personally supports the right-wing Spanish, anti-independence Partido Popular. 'Facing Real Madrid always represented something beyond football for us, beyond those ninety minutes, but that is diminishing and I'm convinced that a high percentage of Madrid's fans don't even know who Franco was and don't or wouldn't like him,' the former Barcelona president says. 'They're not the regime team any more. Spain's a democracy and we don't even talk about Franco. There are different types of Madrid fans and different types of Catalans. Some want independence, some a Catalonia within Spain, some more autonomy, some less, some feel Spanish. When Barcelona score a goal, you can turn round to celebrate and find yourself embracing a separatist, a Spanish nationalist, a right-winger, a left-winger, extreme left, extreme right. When you're supporting your team together, you forget everything else. You might not even know the name of the person you embrace; you have no idea who he is and for a moment you forget who you are.'

Yet according to a 2009 poll carried out by the Centro de Investigaciones Sociológicas, in general terms Barcelona fans *are* more left wing than Madrid fans. Among voters of the left, 41 per cent claimed to be Barcelona supporters, twice as many as claimed to be Madrid supporters, while half of right-wing voters declared themselves Madrid fans compared to under 20 per cent who said they were Barcelona supporters. Of those who vote for the Partido Popular, currently in power in Spain, 50 per cent are Real Madrid fans, 13.7 per cent Barcelona fans. Among supporters of the centre-left PSOE, 25 per cent are Barcelona fans, 33 per cent Real Madrid. And among supporters of the left-wing Izquierda Unida, 30 per cent are Barcelona fans, 25 per cent Madrid. Among voters of the Catalan left, the Esquerra, less surprisingly 93 per cent claim to be Barcelona fans – and none claimed to be an Espanyol supporter. Curiously, one in ten voters of Catalan nationalist parties claims to be a Madrid fan. The differences even stretch to religion. According to a 2011 poll, 60 per cent of Madrid fans are practicing Catholics compared to 38 per cent of Barcelona fans.

The nationalist question, in particular, can be a complex one. Madrid fans will almost to a man sing 'Y Viva España' when Barcelona come to town but they see that as a tool to wind them up and as an expression of a patriotism that is apolitical; on the other side Barcelona say much the same, even though their nationalism is usually judged by others to be overtly political. 'We share the DNA of Catalan society; the history of Barcelona is directly linked to the history of Catalonia and it represents a nation without a state,' says Carlos Villarrubí, the current vice-president. '[But] politically we do not choose sides.' Joan Laporta insists he did not act politically; he instead chose *fer país*, make a country.

In Madrid, some left-wingers came to support other teams because of Real Madrid's identification with the regime, but those statistics also show that, while the proportions are eloquent, there are huge numbers of left-wingers who support Madrid. Some of them feel a kind of implicit guilt at their choice of club. During Madrid's centenary in 2002, Jorge Valdano, then the club's director-general, sponsored a book of stories for precisely that reason: every one of the writers was a left-winger, an intellectual . . . and a Real Madrid fan. Valdano wanted to show that these men had a place at Madrid too.

Valdano's former assistant Ángel Cappa makes the point eloquently:

'Real Madrid has at its heart a contradiction. It represents Spanish nationalism and the Spanish Establishment, the right. But at the same time, it is the most popular club in Spain, with all that that entails. There's a difference between the top and the base. People used to say to me: how can a left-winger like you work for Real Madrid? And I always said the same thing: "you show me a left-wing club." Socrates's Corinthians apart, there isn't one. Barcelona represent Catalonia but at board level it is also a right-wing vision of Catalonia. At an institutional level, Madrid represents Spanish centralism, a right-wing ideological current, but there are many nuances. There is no doubt that Franco used Real Madrid but any government would have done so – when Miguel Induráin won the Tour de France, politicians were elbowing each other out of the way to get to him. They all use sport and Real Madrid is *very* popular.'

So too is Barcelona. With a mixture of incredulity, amusement and disgust, the former player Josep María Fusté tells the story of his decision to form part of a candidacy for the Barcelona presidency. As soon as the news was out, the phone started ringing and within forty-eight hours he had been called by every major political party.

At its inception, the decision to support a team is stripped – at least at a conscious level – of those considerations; the decision is about something less tangible, about enjoyment. Fans flock to Madrid or Barcelona because of success, visibility, importance, players and proximity. It is later that they 'rationalise' their support with something deeper. The internationalisation of fandom also changes the panorama. Although it is so often used as a weapon, the Franco team argument has a different currency for a Madrid or a Barcelona fan in, say, the Middle East or North America. 'The Englishman who sees Madrid as Franco's club probably thinks Spanish women dress as Flamenco dancers,' says former Madrid winger Michel.

For the players themselves, it is different again. 'All players think about is football, not politics,' says former Madrid winger Santi Solari, who also turned out for city rivals Atlético, a club with a very different self-identity. Then he adds with a knowing smile: 'And who's to say we're not the truly wise ones?'

Those Real Madrid players who represented the club during the Franco years protest that they were not political animals, that there was little they could have done: this was a dictatorship, remember. They also feel most keenly the accusation that their success, hard fought, is somehow sullied. 'People used to throw the Franco thing at us,' Amancio says. 'But it made no sense. If Madrid was anything it was that politically it belonged to no one. It's stupid. Jealousy. I don't think politics influence the European Cup – if there was one thing that Europe didn't exactly like it was Spain's politics, but Madrid won five European Cups and then ours in 1966.'

'Did the regime take advantage of that?' he ponders. 'Yes, for sure. But us? We were never political. We would get some award and it was done, just like that. Someone would say: "We've got to go to El Pardo to meet Franco." You go, you go. What else are you going to do? You can't do anything about that. Besides, in most cases we're hardly the right people to be carrying out political analyses. We were foot-ballers, we weren't qualified for that. And we were born into that Spain, that regime, that era. We didn't know anything else.'

'Twaddle,' says Zoco, when asked about the accusation that Madrid were Franco's team. 'Absurd, totally absurd. That Franco thing just rolls off me. I'm not bothered.'

Actually, he does seem quite bothered.

'When did Barcelona win the most trophies? Under Franco and under [the Socialist government of José Luis Rodríguez] Zapatero. They can't complain about anything, anything at all. Look, I know the Barcelona people. I have a home in Cambrils on the Catalan coast, I've got them sussed. I buy *Sport* every day to know what they're saying in Barcelona and I laugh my head off. Happy as anything.'

Zoco continues: 'Excuse me, but in sixteen years as a professional I met Franco just once and that was when I was playing for Spain and we won the 1964 European Championships against the Soviet Union . . . Actually no, sorry, twice – the other time was when he handed the Copa del Generalísimo to me in 1974 after we had beaten Barcelona at the Calderón. That day he didn't say anything. He was poorly, he had thrombophlebitis and he could hardly talk. So, I only really met him once, in 1964. He held a reception for us, the Spain team, at El Pardo. He came down the line and greeted us one by one. "Congratulations", "congratulations", and five minutes later we were all outside. Over.'

Not quite. That day, Barcelona's Josep Fusté was there too, a team-mate of Zoco's in the Spain side. Spain had beaten the Soviet Union at the Santiago Bernabéu, a game of gigantic political significance that Fusté calls 'a war'. Two years before, Franco had banned Spain at the last minute from travelling to Moscow for a game; diplomatic relations between the two countries did not exist and the Spain team had been forced to disembark the plane as it waited on the runway. By 1964, Franco had been persuaded of the potential benefits of defeating the Communists, especially at home, and reluctantly gave the go-ahead. The decision paid off. Spain defeated Hungary, Communists and favourites, in the semi-final and then the Soviet Union in the final.

'I am Catalan, but I want to win, whether I am playing for Russia, Hungary or Spain,' Fusté says. 'I was playing football and enjoying it, trying to win. They were better than us but we got lucky.'

Not as lucky as he was going to get.

Fusté was one of two single men in the Spain team, along with the Atlético Madrid defender Isacio Calleja. 'And the two of us were *puteros,*' Fusté grins. They liked the ladies. After the game the coach, Lieutenant Colonel José Villalonga had told the players to be in the hotel reception at nine o'clock the following morning, suits on, shoes shined, ready to travel to the official reception at El Pardo, Franco's palace to the north-west of Madrid. 'I was against the regime,' Fusté says, 'but there was the euphoria of the win and anyway you didn't have any choice.'

First, though, Fusté and Calleja had their minds set on a night to remember. Assuming they could remember it at all come the morning.

As it turned out, they couldn't.

'We went to this flat and when we woke up the next morning it was already late. It was eleven o'clock, we didn't know where we were. *Hostia! Hostia!* Fuck! Fuck!' Fusté recalls with a mischievous grin. 'We almost didn't go at all but we decided we had to: it was Franco! So we bundled into a taxi and headed straight to El Pardo. We didn't have time to go back to the team hotel and our stuff, our suits and ties, was all there. We were a mess and we were dressed like clowns. I had a polo shirt on and trousers. Jeans, maybe, or tracksuit bottoms. We hadn't showered and we hadn't changed. You know, there might even have been a picture. Had that ever been published it would have been the bomb. I was wearing sandals, bloody hell. Calleja was a bit better dressed than me – although he still wasn't wearing a tie.

'And we got there: they're all looking at us thinking: "what the . . . ?" The manager says: "Bloody hell, where did you two get to?"

"We overslept."

"But how the hell . . ."

"We didn't hear the alarm."

We looked a mess so we thought we had better stand at opposite ends; two of us together would have screamed at them.

So Franco turns up and he goes along the line, shaking everyone's hand. "Well done" . . . "Well done" . . . "Well done" . . . "Well done" . . . He reaches me and he looks at me and he says:

"Ah, Señor Fusté, we have to talk."

I say to myself: "the mother that gave birth to me . . ." I'm terrified. This is during the regime. I'm a Catalan nationalist, my dad was in the Esquerra, and I'm dressed like that. I look like that. I have sullied Spain's great moment. This is a problem. A real problem.

Afterwards we go into his office and I'm thinking: "I'm in so much trouble here". And Franco comes in and says:

"So, Señor Fusté, I gather you still have military service to complete?"

Back then, you could be sent to Africa for military service – and for three years. If you got the wrong man in charge he could make your life hell, especially if he had orders from above. I've *really* done it.

"Er, yes, General."

And he looks at me and says:

"Not any more you don't: you've served your duty to the Fatherland".'

12

THE WHISTLE-BLOWER

They called Charly Rexach *el Noi de Pedralbes*, the boy from Pedralbes
– one of the smartest neighbourhoods in Barcelona, across the Diagonal
and up the hill from the Camp Nou, lined with huge houses and
depicted in Joan Miró's 1917 painting. Rexach was born in 1947 and
raised there, always kicking a ball around the streets. He joined
Barcelona at twelve and almost never left. 'I will go down in Barcelona's
history,' he jokes. He doesn't say that because of the seventeen years
he spent in the first team between 1965 and 1981, blond locks flowing
on the right wing, or the half-century he has dedicated to the club
as player, assistant coach, coach, technical director and presidential
adviser, but because one day he turned up at a training session and
saw a tiny, thirteen-year-old Argentinian kid. 'After two seconds, I
knew,' Rexach says. He signed Lionel Messi on a paper napkin.

'Barcelona is a feeling, the love of my life,' he says easing on to a
sofa in the *antepalco*, the area just behind the directors' box at the
Camp Nou. It is packed and noisy but not nearly as noisy as it is through
the doors to the right. There is just under an hour to go before kick-
off in another *clásico*, Barcelona versus Madrid in the quarter-final second
leg of the Copa del Rey, and outside the atmosphere is building. By its
rise and fall, by its pitch and intensity, you can tell when the warm-up
starts and when it finishes, when Jose Mourinho makes his first

appearance, when Ronaldo does too. You can tell when Messi emerges from the tunnel, ambling on behind his team-mates. The clock ticks down fast. Too fast. Charming, funny and committed to his cause, his conviction unshakeable but worn lightly, Rexach has much to say. So much so that by the time he has finished, the room has emptied. The others are all outside now and they have taken their seats. The game is just about to kick off: time to make a run for it. To step beyond that door and into an arena few know like Rexach.

'There's no escaping the political aspect,' Rexach says right at the start. 'Barcelona was a refuge, a way of expressing ourselves for *Catalanistas*, separatists, nationalists. Even people who did not like football gathered round the club. Barça-Madrid is politics and football wrapped up together and what we are is also hung on Real Madrid, measured against them. Their identity is totally different to ours.'

Madrid were the regime team, in other words? '*Hombre*, no doubt, no doubt.'

Rexach says that once the golden age of Kubala and Di Stéfano had passed, there were two matches that really marked the rivalry between the two clubs, both of them in the Copa del Generalísimo. He played in both: one at the Bernabéu in the 1968 final, the other at the Camp Nou in the quarter-final second leg in 1970. Barça prevailed in the first, Madrid in the second, but that doesn't begin to tell the story. These were matches that reflected, shaped and defined the rivalry. They represented a shift, not just in the sport but also in society. For Barcelona, they were a catalyst for a kind of reawakening, fostering an identity that, if latent, had not always been explicit. And at the heart of both games was the supporting actor so often stepping into the lead role: the referee. Antonio Rigó in 1968 and Emilio Guruceta in 1970.

Rexach is not alone in recalling those games as if they were yesterday. Back at the Bernabéu, asked for his memories of the 1968 final, the Real Madrid centre-back Ignacio Zoco pulls a face and says simply: 'bad.'

He continues: 'First because we lost and second because we were the victims of some catastrophic refereeing. Mr Rigó's performance was unbelievable. I cannot let myself think that a referee would deliberately go on to the pitch to get it wrong but there are times when you think that either they are very, very bad or . . .'

Or?

'Or . . .' he continues, 'I don't know.'

'I didn't say anything at the time,' Madrid midfielder Pirri agrees, 'but he was against us all the way through.'

The game was awful and it was ugly: 'terrible, terrible, terrible,' says Josep Fusté. 'These days it would finish eight-a-side,' adds Rexach. Barcelona won it 1-0 thanks to a ridiculous own goal from Fernando Zunzunegui and Madrid's greatest complaints centre on two possible penalties, while everyone else's memories centre on what came next. It became known as the Bottles Final and led directly to the ban on glass in Spanish football stadiums, after hundreds of bottles were thrown by furious Real Madrid supporters. The players were taken off but when they came back on it started again, especially when Eladio Silvestre and Amancio Amaro tangled near the by-line, leaving the Barcelona full-back within reach of the fans. Pirri and Manuel Velázquez appealed for calm, to no avail, and afterwards a news agency remarked: 'it's frightening to think what could have happened had it not been for the sedating presence of Franco in the ground.' Rexach could not disagree more. He sees Franco's hand in the trouble, not in its pacification. 'It was all controlled by the regime, orchestrated,' he claims.

Rexach recalls the abuse, shouts of *polacos*, or Poles, at the Barça players, the name used to refer to Catalans. He can even see a bottle flying through the air and hitting the cup following the presentation. There was no lap of honour. A pity, says Rexach, because the Copa del Generalísimo, named after and handed out by Franco, brought with it a special kind of dirty thrill for the Catalans, that hint of rebellion. 'Back then the idea of pulling out of the cup as some kind of protest was impossible. If anyone said "let's not play the cup", he would have had serious problems. So the only thing you could do, the only option you had, was not just to participate in it – it was to win it and *joderlos*, really piss them off. Just as we didn't win many leagues we *did* win a lot of cups. It was *their* cup, it was *his* cup, and we went there to piss them off.'

That night, Barcelona certainly pissed them off. But Amancio insists that the mythology surrounding the game has been exaggerated. 'It wasn't so bad. There were no fences but still no one ran on the pitch. There are a hundred thousand fans: there is always someone who ruins it,' he says. 'No one actually got hit by a bottle.'

'Oh no?' asks Fusté when he's told what Amancio said. He reaches down and starts to roll up his trousers. Across his knee is a scar, three or four inches long. 'That was one of only two times in my life that I was actually frightened in a football stadium,' he says. 'The other time was in Mallorca sometime in the 1980s. I was working for the radio and some Ultras tried to get into our commentary box to attack us because we were speaking Catalan. In 1968, I was afraid too. Some of those bottles were broken *before* they were thrown. I could see it coming and I tried to step out of the way. It bounced and hit me on the knee, slicing it open.'

Afterwards Barcelona dashed for the safety of the dressing room. 'And after that everything was fine,' Fusté admits. 'We were always treated well in Madrid . . . better than they were here.'

It had in fact just begun. 'After the final they were supposed to give [the officials] a cup but they said they had lost it. I think no one liked the score,' the referee Rigó said years later in an interview with the *AS* journalist Pedro Pablo San Martín. 'We left for Barajas airport surrounded by five jeeps full of armed police and I had a plainclothes policeman with me right up until I boarded.' He was vetoed by Madrid, meaning he could not officiate their games again, and six other clubs quickly followed suit. 'I think the majority did because they were under Madrid's orders,' Rigó claimed. Rumours, which he denied, soon circulated that Barcelona had bought him a flat and set him up in business. His refereeing career was as good as over. For those Barça fans of a suspicious mind, his refereeing career was over because he had favoured Barcelona; had he favoured Madrid, he would have been fine. 'That game made me anti-*Madridista*,' Rigó admitted.

Up in the directors' box, where Santiago Bernabéu was brooding over the sight of his team losing the cup final in their own stadium and against Barcelona, chewing over the injustice, a different conflict was being played out. At the end of the game, the wife of Camilo Alonso Vega, the interior minister, turned to Bernabéu and exclaimed: 'Santiago, we lost! What a pity!'

Her husband heard the remark and, conscious of his diplomatic role, intervened. 'Ramona,' he said, 'congratulate the president of Barcelona at once,' to which she replied: 'Ah, that's true, of course'. She then turned to the recently elected president Narcís de Carreras and added: 'I congratulate you because Barcelona is Spain too, isn't it?'

Narcís de Carreras's response, delivered in Catalan, has become legendary: '*Senyora*,' he said, '*no fotem!*' Lady, let's not piss about.

A few days later, Bernabéu agreed to an interview with the newspaper *Murcia Deportiva* in which he praised Joan Vilà Reyes, because 'just the fact that he is president of a club in Catalonia that is called Español is worthy of admiration'. He also claimed: 'When I first arrived in the presidency twenty-five years ago, we had the same problems with Barcelona, the only thing that has changed is that they have got bigger'. And he delivered his most famous line: 'It is not true that I dislike Catalonia. I admire and love Catalonia . . . in spite of the Catalans.'

The comment caused a huge storm. Bernabéu received a telegram from Manuel Fraga, the minister for information and tourism, telling him to take it back, but he refused. Meanwhile, the secretary-general of state television, Juan Rosón, essentially a regime apparatchik, devised a confidential plan to minimise the impact of Bernabéu's 'unfortunate words' and contain the fallout. Rosón blamed Barcelona as much as he did Madrid, noting that many football fans were 'antagonistic towards them' and that the Catalans suffered a 'complex when it came to Madrid'. Barcelona, he said, 'tend to act according to their Catalanism' and wondered whether Narcís de Carreras had 'politicised this issue premeditatedly, in search of some objective'. His plan demanded tougher sanctions and outlined a day-by-day course of action for the following fortnight. It proposed that Bernabéu write a letter to fans lamenting the 'misunderstanding' and calling for sportsmanship, especially against Barcelona. De Carreras should then request that fans join in honouring Bernabéu's silver anniversary as Madrid president. And, in a suggestion that echoes the 1943 Peace Match, Rosón recommended that gifts be handed out and public statements of fraternity made.

The plan wasn't put into practice but it is revealing of the mindset of a state obsessed with maintaining a public façade of unity and the loyal media did demand that Bernabéu apologise, one newspaper insisting: 'the president of Real Madrid cannot be allowed to offend [Catalonia] with impunity when he holds a position of such responsibility, still less perturb the harmony and respect that Barcelona and Madrid profess to each other.' Eventually, Saporta claimed that Bernabéu's words had been taken out of context: he had in fact said he loved Catalonia, despite the fact that not all Catalans loved him.

The regime always sought publicly to silence Barcelona's differential status, its identity as a representative of an unrecognised nation, and now that had been brought out into the open – not by Barcelona but by Real Madrid. Spanish nationalism too was often exclusionist: that Barcelona were different had often been projected *on to* the club rather than, or as well as, projected *by* the club, and now this had been made explicit. Gabriel Cisneros, a member of the Francoist Council of Ministers, complained, 'there is no worse separatism than centralist separatism, manifest in attitudes like that of Don Santiago', while Barcelona's president insisted: 'separators are worse than separatists.'

A club that had, at an institutional level, done little to confront the regime, now found a voice. Although such complaints had to be carefully couched in terms of hurt patriotic pride – *Spanish* patriotic pride

– there was opportunity here too. As Carles Santacana notes in his superb book *El Barça y el franquismo*, the secret police reported that Bernabéu's attack had caused the regime problems because it was used as a pretext for a Catalan nationalist agenda, the chance to 'reveal' and take advantage of 'the [supposed] hatred that Spaniards feel towards Catalans'.

It was Real Madrid's fans who threw bottles and Real Madrid's president who launched the insult but there were no sanctions, no fines and no bans, merely an investigation into the newspaper that ran the quotes, and on the pages of the Catholic daily *Ya* it was Barcelona who were reprimanded. The essential message, and the tone, could have come straight from Franco's El Pardo residence. In an article that said nothing of Spain's refusal to play the USSR in 1964 but criticised the city of Barcelona for its plans to hold the abortive Popular Olympics as an alternative to Hitler's Berlin Games, calling that 'a black page in Spanish history', it wrote:

'Whoever seeks to carry out political acts through sport should leave sport . . . the idea of sport as an escape valve for political passion is only ever defended by those who are anti-sporting. You do not have to go to stadiums to shout nor to let loose your resentment, quite the opposite. Sport is proud of uniting and not separating, and the thing that Real Madrid feels most proud of in recent years is having contributed to breaking down the international wall that for twenty years was constructed around us by our enemies, to the point of becoming, as has been officially recognised, an extraordinary embassy. That is the path.'

Barcelona were finding their own path and it was heading in a different direction. Barcelona and Madrid met again two years later, this time at the Camp Nou, and it became probably the most famous scandal in Spanish football history. Because this was the first season since 1951 when neither side finished in the top three in the league, and because it was potentially the first season in which Madrid might not make it into Europe, the Copa del Generalísimo took on special significance and the rivals met each other in the quarter-final. Madrid had won the first leg 2-0 at the Santiago Bernabéu, then Barcelona went 1-0 up in the second leg with Rexach scoring the goal. 'We were dominating them,' he says, 'absolutely all over them. They could barely get out of their six yard box.'

Then, fourteen minutes into the second half, Amancio broke away and found Manuel Velázquez who, dashing through, was brought down by Joaquim Rifé. Velázquez tumbled into the area and Guruceta, sprinting up behind, gave a penalty. When the Barcelona defender Eladio applauded sarcastically, Guruceta sent him off. Amancio scored the penalty and any chance Barcelona had of a comeback was extinguished. 'That day Guruceta put his foot in it, right the way down to his liver,' Zoco admits, 'I was close to the play and Velázquez was a metre and a half outside the area at least.' Rexach reckons more like three metres. He was certainly outside, even if Bernabéu claimed it was 'a penalty the size of a cathedral'. After the game, Fusté spoke to Guruceta. 'He told me: "I don't think I made a mistake." I said: "bollocks, yes you did."

'But,' Fusté adds, 'that doesn't mean you do something stupid, for Christ's sake. It's a football match not a war.' A handful of Barcelona players made as if to walk off the pitch in protest, encouraged by fans. The coach, Englishman Vic Buckingham, had to push them back on to the pitch to continue playing. Fusté was unimpressed. Even now there's incredulity about his tone as he tells the story, remembering the conversations: 'What the hell are you walking off for?' A bottle was thrown that hit the Madrid coach Miguel Muñoz but mostly they just threw cushions – according to Guruceta's official match report, almost 30,000 of them. The air was full of cushions and soon the pitch was covered with them, a mosaic strewn across the turf. It became increasingly difficult to play and with five minutes still to go Guruceta blew the full-time whistle.

There was a pitch invasion and Barcelona's fans were charged by police – a charge that one Falangist writer described as 'beautiful'. The lights were turned out and fires started. According to the police,

69 seats had been ripped out, 169 broken, 5 benches burnt and 11 windows smashed. As fans carried on their protests down the Ramblas to Canaletes, Madrid's players were still in the stadium. 'We spent two hours in the dressing room unable to come out,' recalls Amancio, 'and then in our hotel in Castelldefells we had to be surrounded by the Guardia Civil to protect us.'

'Guruceta,' he adds, 'was sentenced there and then.'

'This is the kind of thing that happens in any town,' muttered Antonio Calderón, Madrid's general manager. The choice of the dismissive word *pueblo* rendered the town tin-pot. 'If the press had a terrible go at us [in 1968], then only the worst possible adjectives can be applied to Barcelona tonight,' he said. The referee and his linesmen needed police protection, sleeping in a cell overnight. The scandal was monumental, the fallout nuclear. 'We were the three most famous men in Spain,' one of the linesmen told the British writer Phil Ball during a chance encounter in a San Sebastián bar. Barcelona went for Guruceta; it was not just that they put him on their veto list, as was a club's right, it was that they demanded his withdrawal from the game. The cover of the *Revista Barcelonista* asked: 'Guruceta . . . Inept? Unconscious? Irresponsible? Impudent?'

Or, many asked, downright crooked? The fact that he was seen driving a new BMW did not go unnoticed and almost twenty years later the president of Anderlecht admitted paying Guruceta a million Belgian francs to beat Nottingham Forest in the 1984 UEFA Cup. That does not of course mean that he was bought or even corruptible in 1970 and Guruceta could not defend himself against the claim: he had been killed in a car crash in 1987.

Guruceta had become Barcelona's antichrist. Another sports paper, this time from Zaragoza, wrote: 'Barcelona were literally kidnapped by the dictatorial whistle of a man who was obliged to wear black but who on the inside is so white he could make detergent companies jealous.' Bernabéu claimed that in two days he had received over two hundred death threats. This issue was not going away. The Barcelona president Agustí Montal junior appeared before the media to read out a statement, the solemnity of his tone giving it a grave, dramatic edge: 'Members and supporters of Barcelona feel deeply hurt and mocked by the unjust and shameful performance in which Mr Guruceta gloried,' he said. 'You simply cannot give a non-existent penalty in front of 100,000 spectators for no reason and with impunity. Although it is always disagreeable and reprehensible to see people throw cushions on to the pitch and to see the field of play occupied by those that should not be there, I understand that the emotional dyke should break and overflow when supporters felt so hurt by Mr Guruceta's unjust act.'

Francesc de Carreras was close to the clandestine Catalan Socialist Party, the PSUC. He wrote in *Destino*: 'From that moment, the rivalry was total. The history of Barcelona–Madrid is packed with penalties in Madrid's favour that are not, goals disallowed for Barcelona, insulting declarations made towards Cataluña by high-ranking Madrid directors, measures that are clearly biased from the Federation [and] the referees' committees, bottles thrown at Barcelona players for having won the cup, etc. A sad, disagreeable history, symptomatic of the things that happen in this country.' Some sections of the Catalan media ignored the potential consequences to demand resignations. That they felt emboldened to do so speaks of the shift in society and in politics, where Franco was growing older and increasingly withdrawn.

Barcelona were hit with the maximum 90,000 pesetas fine, Eladio was banned for two games and an investigation was announced into the conduct of Montal, which only aggrieved Barcelona still further. As for Guruceta, he was suspended for six months. He would never referee Barcelona in a competitive match again. The head of the referees' committee, José Plaza, resigned in solidarity, insisting: 'we need more Gurucetas.' For some time, whenever a referee made a bad decision against Barcelona the chant went up 'Guruceta! Guruceta! Guruceta!'

Watching the incidents again, the response appears ridiculously overblown. Velázquez was fouled well outside the area but he did tumble into it. The decision was a bad one but not *that* bad, hardly warranting the furious reaction that it provoked or such intense mobilisation. But it was not just about Guruceta and it was not just about that decision; it was about the context, about the 1968 final and beyond. Guruceta became Catalan shorthand for every referee in Spain, shorthand for injustice. For some, he had become shorthand for the football authorities, for Real Madrid and for the dictatorship.

'During those years we always felt that we couldn't win the league, we would always lose three or four games in the last minute, or lose leagues in the last game,' says Rexach. 'It was like there was a veto. I'm not saying that Madrid didn't deserve to win those leagues but something always happened. In a hundred games there would be thirty-five penalties: thirty for Madrid and five for Barça. And the same thing always happened. Sometimes that became an excuse for us but it's also a fact.'

If that night deepened that sense of victimhood, adding to the problem, it also ratcheted up the rivalry a notch and brought Barcelona into the open. It became another strand of an emerging Catalan movement and Barcelona's part in that movement, their self-identification as a kind of resistance. Few had dared challenge the regime openly before. The *Revista Barcelonista* gave thanks to Guruceta for helping the club 'to be conscious at last of what it is and what it represents'. 'Mr Guruceta,' it said, 'has proven the injection we needed.' The newspaper *Informaciones* added: 'more than a sporting protest, it was a manifesto.' Joan Colomines was active in the Catalan cultural resistance. In his diary he wrote that the protest, 'one of those collective moments that you have to know how to channel', had causes that 'go well beyond sport': 'neither the goal that was ruled out, nor the sending off of a Barcelona player, nor the attitude of the Real Madrid players justify such a remarkable disturbance. It was more the visible manifestation of an internal tension long suppressed.'

Cuadernos para el diálogo, later *the* cultural magazine of Spain's transition to democracy, a meeting point of intellectuals and opposition, a reflection and a motor of change, noted how Guruceta's appearance had prompted the emergence of almost revolutionary theories on the significance of football in general and Barcelona in particular. They would soon dedicate an entire issue to the social meaning of sport. 'That day many secret admirers of Barcelona – who previously could not profess themselves publicly because of political, social or intellectual constraints – finally raised their heads above the parapet,' it wrote. 'Barcelona's Divine Left is now one of the most fervent supporters of Mr Buckingham's boys.'

Guruceta became the spark that ignited Barcelona, that penalty an awakening. Montal's statement made the point that this was not a one-off, the memory of 1968 still present and now brought to the surface. Instead, he claimed that this was another manifestation of the differential treatment to which Barcelona were subjected, the first formal public expression of the club's conviction that it was consistently a victim. A call for justice according to Barcelona fans, a sign of their paranoia according to Madrid fans, it evolved into a full-scale attack on the football authorities – for their handling of referees, for their refusal to allow the signing of foreign players, and for the supposedly unequal manner in which policy was implemented. 'We do not want special treatment,' Montal concluded, 'we just want fair and just treatment, something which, sadly, we do not always get . . . with very rare exceptions, Barcelona have suffered calamitous refereeing season after season. Mr Guruceta is the last straw . . . the statistics are clear.'

Jordi Medina and Joaquim Molins have the statistics. Indeed, their statistics go beyond the point at which Montal made his statement, running right up to 1985. Medina, twice a presidential candidate, and Molins, founded the group Un Crit Valent, A Valiant Cry. Sitting in the café at the ice hockey arena alongside the Camp Nou, they explain that among the group's aims is the recovery and protection of Barcelona's historical memory. They are, they say, determined that 'the truth will out' and are active in ensuring it does. In March 2009 they prepared a report entitled 'The great fraud of R. Madrid's nineteen leagues'. The report focuses on the 'robbery' of Alfredo Di Stéfano; the disastrous economic impact of the construction of the Camp Nou, which they say was exacerbated by the delays in approving the reclassification of the land occupied by the old Les Corts stadium and the refereeing 'abuses' Barcelona faced. The report focuses particularly on the period when José Plaza headed the national refereeing council.

According to the report, Plaza was in charge of naming the referees for games over the course of thirteen seasons, in 1967–70, 1975–80 and 1985–9. During that period, Real Madrid won eleven league titles, Atlético Madrid two and Barcelona none. In the ten seasons between 1970 and 1985 that he did not designate the referees, Real Madrid won two league titles – the same number as Barcelona, Real Sociedad and Athletic Bilbao – while Valencia and Atlético Madrid won one each. During the thirteen-year period with Plaza in charge Real Madrid earned thirty-four penalties more than Barcelona while Barcelona had seventy-eight more yellow cards and fifteen more red cards than Madrid. Without Plaza, Madrid's advantage in penalties drops from thirty-four to fifteen and in yellow cards from seventy-eight to eighteen, while the red cards shift entirely: from fifteen more Barcelona red cards to ten more Real Madrid ones. Un Crit Valent's report then cites the famous claim by the referee Antonio Camacho, who once insisted: 'as long as Plaza is president, Barcelona will not win the league.'

The absence of definitive proof of a refereeing conspiracy is not definitive proof of the absence of a refereeing conspiracy. But there has never been sufficient convincing evidence offered up – and it is not for want of trying. Rexach suggests that is because there was not so much a conspiracy as conditions. 'The referees were against us,' he wrote in his book *Ara Parlo Jo*, 'and I say that totally consciously.' He wrote of permissive referees and hostile stadiums, of extra time being added to order, and of TV highlights packages cut to taste, incriminating evidence mysteriously disappearing. He believes that Madrid's social power, acquired through television and deals with the state channel TVE, was important in creating the social and psychological conditions that favoured them.

It is an argument he expands upon now: 'when I was a kid Madrid were Spain's team. Barcelona would be on telly maybe once for every twenty times that Madrid were. So kids supported Madrid. Now there are lots of Barcelona fans. Why? Because, under democracy, they can watch them. These days you can *choose* who you want to support. The social and political reality matters. Beyond the fact that we were living during a dictatorship that didn't have much sympathy for Catalans, most Spaniards were Madrid fans who filled grounds wherever we went and that continued after the regime. Referees could not remove themselves from that entirely. If a referee helped us, he couldn't leave the ground. We got destroyed in the small grounds where leagues are decided and where there was no television and no evidence.'

Johan Cruyff, who didn't even arrive at Barcelona until 1974, echoes the point. 'One of our problems was that they did not televise the games. So if you said "yes, but", they said "Ah, you're always complaining." Once everyone had television, things were much better because people could see what happened. Since we have had television, results have been much better.'

One current Barcelona board member admits that there was not a systematic campaign and that conspiracy claims have been exaggerated but says: 'The referees didn't need orders. It was more a current, a trend. Was there the occasional order in a match? For sure. But it was more that in the two or three cases where a referee blew in Barcelona's favour, Rigó for example . . . well, that day he stopped being a referee. So other referees know that if they want to continue being a referee they have to look the other way.'

This argument bears a certain similarity to the theory put forward by the pro-Madrid newspaper *AS* to explain Barcelona's success in the new century under Frank Rijkaard and, particularly, Pep Guardiola.

They call it *Villarato* after the president of the Federation, Ángel-María Villar. According to the theory, Madrid are paying for their failure to back Villar in presidential elections while Barcelona did, and as a consequence of that there is a trend towards favouring Barcelona based on referees' fears for their own career, which remain in the hands of their superiors. Make a mistake in favour of Barcelona and you're fine, the theory runs; make a mistake against Barcelona or in favour of Madrid and you can forget about refereeing the big games or being put forward for international matches.

There is one problem with this theory: it just does not stand up. Certainly not in the terms in which it is presented and considering who it is presented by. These days, every game is televised, every decision scrutinised, pawed over and debated endlessly. Before every game, statistics are presented to show that referees favour Madrid or Barcelona, depending on which newspaper you read. The referee who takes charge of one Barcelona/Madrid game in which they win 8-0 is deemed to have a 100 per cent record in favour of Barcelona/ Madrid. Must be suspicious, then. Even when the decisions are analysed, so often the 'evidence' presented to 'prove' the conspiracy is laughable – lines have been drawn crooked, conveniently rendering players offside – while the claims of *AS* and their counterparts in Madrid and Barcelona to be the guardians of objectivity are comical. The same challenge in a different penalty area draws an entirely different judgement. It is not the *referees* who are biased.

So far, so good, and it is tempting to reach the same conclusion of the complaints made by *culés* during the regime years. But it is impossible to make similar judgements on decisions going back further. Footage is not available, there are not countless camera angles and replays with which to clarify decisions. It is not possible to sift through the evidence, to sit in judgement on the referees or on those who judge them, to analyse the theories. And the context *is* different. Yet there are still flaws in the claims made by Un Crit Valent and many Barcelona fans. Un Crit Valent's claim that Plaza alone designated the referees is not entirely true: two of the seasons included are 1967–8 and 1969–70, the years of the Bottles Final and the Guruceta match. At that point, while Plaza designated the referees, the system was based on the ranking put together by the clubs themselves which theoretically ensured that everyone got a ref they rated highly – and Barcelona too had the power of veto. Before Guruceta's big night, he had been considered one of the best by everyone, including Barcelona.

Then there is the fact that without more profound analysis the use of statistics to prove the point is problematic. Put simply: it is perfectly plausible that one team wins ten penalties while the other team earns none because one team has been fouled in the area ten times while the other team has not been fouled in the area at all. Statistics on decisions do not necessarily prove anything about the predilections of referees, still less the system; even statistics on *wrong* decisions do not, although they would be an improvement. Equidistance is not objectivity; five red cards and five penalties each is not the definition of fairness.

The popular idea of Madrid as a team favoured by referees was widespread, and embodied in the chant that first appeared in 1979 and is now repeated at stadiums everywhere: whenever Madrid benefit from a decision, the crowd launches into '*¡Así, así, así! ¡Así gana el Madrí!*' – that's how Madrid win. It was not Barcelona fans who invented it but Sporting Gijón ones and Madrid's supporters have appropriated it for those moments when their team plays especially well. But just because it is a popular perception does not make it necessarily true and it is an assumption that especially irritates Madrid's players. It is also striking that Madrid's older generation, talking in 2011 and 2012, turn their backs on the trend of seeing pro-Barcelona conspiracies at every turn adopted in the capital.

Just before their centenary, Madrid handed out a written code of conduct to every player imploring them to uphold Madrid's tradition of never talking about referees; but a few years later, still under the same president, their official website ran an article entitled 'The Seven Deadly Sins of Sánchez Arminio', the country's head of referees. At the same time, their TV channel complained of the officials' 'clear attempt to damage us', opening one news bulletin with the line: 'We have one more opponent to beat in this year's league: the referees.'

'In the time I played for Madrid, I think we won nine leagues or something while there were two for Atlético, one for Valencia, only one for Barcelona,' Amancio says. 'Their anger, their disgust, their phobia towards Madrid starts with that basic fact. They saw something political. I just don't see it. And I don't see it now with Barcelona either. "You get more penalties." *Joder*, that's because I'm in the area more. That's normal. We knew that we won because we were the better team.' Zoco agrees: 'It's like the Villarato now – completely and utterly ridiculous. Barcelona won a lot under Guardiola because they were the best team, full stop. They have been helped by referees on occasions just as we have been helped by referees on occasions. We would be in the penalty area eighty times; the opposition would be in ours two. Of course we got more penalties.' 'If they have a go at you it is because you win,' says Pirri. 'We won then and Barcelona win now – because we were better, nothing more. And now they are. I don't like Madrid's behaviour in that sense.'

Among men of their generation, that opinion is largely shared six hundred kilometres away. The bottom line is that during the 1960s and early 1970s Barcelona were not good enough and for the most part they know that. One journalist jokes with friends among Barcelona's ex-players about the possibility of writing a book on their era. His suggested title? *When We Were Shit*. 'In my day, Madrid had a better team than us,' Fusté says. 'Their squad was the bollocks, eh. We beat them sometimes but they were better than us, more consistent. Now they seem to have a complex with us; back then we had one with them; victimism. When they went out to buy a player he really made the difference. We seemed to go out and buy *lotes*, value packs. That didn't exactly help.'

Rexach does see hidden interest and he does believe that Barcelona were victims, but he too refuses to leave the analysis there or seek all-encompassing excuses. 'There was a kind of fatalism. "There's nothing we can do about it", "something always happens". I've always attacked that idea – not just in sport but also in society. It became a smokescreen. The Catalans suffer: we pay a lot and have little say, but we don't do anything about it. Look at the Basques: they'll join forces. Not here; here, there are internal conflicts. Barça is the one thing that unites everyone but even there we haven't always got it right. I had twelve coaches in seventeen years, some of them twice. There was a huge instability. Madrid didn't need to trip us up; most of the time, we tripped ourselves up. Over the years people would say "*coño*, the thing is, Madrid . . ." and I'd say: no, a lot of the time, *we're* the problem.'

13

JOHAN CRUYFF SUPERSTAR

Franco's secret police entered the parish of Santa María Mitjancera on the morning of 28 October 1973 and broke up a meeting called by the clandestine resistance movement the Asamblea de Catalunya. A hundred and thirteen arrests were made and most of the suspects were imprisoned in the Modelo jail, where they continued to conspire and to plan for the post-dictatorship era. Among them were many of those who would later became significant political figures in Catalonia, including Josep-Lluís Carod-Rovira, the future leader of the Esquerra Republicana and vice-president of the Catalan government. When they reached the police station Josep Solé Barberà, one of the key members of the outlawed Catalan Communist Party, complained that the arrest could not have come at a worse time. In his pocket were two tickets for that night's match at the Camp Nou.

It was not just any match either. Barcelona versus Granada featured the long-awaited debut of Johan Cruyff. Like Solé Barberà, the Communist intellectual Xavier Folch was also arrested on the morning of the game but at least he was compensated: a few days later an envelope arrived for him in prison containing a signed photograph of Barcelona's new star signing. Solé Barberà and Folch had missed some performance. The Camp Nou was packed and Barcelona won 4-0. Cruyff scored twice and ran the game. *La Vanguardia* declared Barça 'revitalised', its match report opening by inviting fans to 'imagine what Barcelona would have achieved if they did not have Cruyff in the side'.

Actually, they had a pretty good idea. Before the match, Barcelona were fourth from bottom. They had won just two of their seven league games, drawing 0-0 at home against Real Madrid and Racing Santander, and losing at Elche, Celta de Vigo and Real Sociedad. They had already been knocked out of the UEFA Cup by Nice. In the meantime, Cruyff had played five specially arranged friendlies as he awaited his competitive debut and had scored six times, including a hat-trick, in his presentation. One cover story depicted him in flares and a striped jumper, huge shirt collar, jacket draped coolly over his shoulder. 'Cruyff: the only hope to avoid the chaos', it declared.

It was more than just the 1973–4 season, too. 'We had got to the final game with a chance of winning the league for three successive seasons but in the end we hadn't won any of them. In total, we had gone fourteen years without winning the league. What with bad luck and referees, *culés* had started to despair,' team-mate Charly Rexach recalls. 'And then Cruyff arrived.'

A single signing changed everything. 'History repeats itself sometimes. There are men sufficiently talented to repeat the phenomenon of the Kubala–Di Stéfano, Di Stéfano–Kubala era,' claimed *El Mundo Deportivo*. They were only half right: Cruyff was right up there with Kubala and Di Stéfano; what he did not have was another player who was his match. For Barcelona, he became practically a deity. Joan Laporta would later become Barcelona's president. In 1974, he was eleven and he wanted to be Cruyff, cutting his hair like the Dutchman and copying his moves. Even now, there is a kind of child-like wonder when he hears the name. Mention Cruyff and Laporta interrupts, in English and with a smile: 'the best.'

He continues: 'If I was born again, I would like to be Pep Guardiola . . . And I say that because I wouldn't dare to say that I would like to be Johan Cruyff.'

Cruyff was the son of a fruitseller who died when Johan was twelve and whose mother cleaned the dressing rooms at Ajax's stadium. His idol was Alfredo Di Stéfano and he led Ajax to three successive European Cups and won the Ballon d'Or in 1971. He would win two more as a Barcelona player. He was different: graceful, elegant, clever. He had a swagger about him, a drive, natural leadership. Already recognised as the world's best player, even before the 1974 World Cup, Barcelona were determined to have him.

They also had an advantage. Barcelona's coaches at the time were, first, Vic Buckingham, the Englishman who had given the seventeen-year-old Cruyff his debut at Ajax and then Rinus Michels, credited as the inventor of 'Total Football'. Their secretary, meanwhile, was Armand Carabén, a lawyer and economist who also happened to be married to a Dutch woman, Marjolin van der Meer, and counted Cruyff among his friends.

Not that signing him was easy. Getting Cruyff was, in Rexach's words, like 'giving birth'. He had first posed in a Barcelona shirt for the magazine *Barça* as far back as 1970 but it would take three more years for him actually to join. And when Barcelona declared their interest, they found that a familiar foe had become involved too: Real Madrid had reached an agreement with Ajax.

Santiago Bernabéu later claimed that he didn't sign Cruyff because he didn't like his *jeta* – his cheek, his attitude. Another version of the story goes that Cruyff didn't sign for Real Madrid because they were Franco's club. Both are false. Bernabéu made excuses to explain away his failure, employing typical bluster, and Cruyff never said anything of the sort. Only later would he become aware of the political implications of the rivalry, adept at tapping into Catalan sensibilities, embracing its cause.

Not that it stops him enjoying people thinking that the story *might* be true, even forty years on. Asked about it, Cruyff grins from ear to ear. 'No, no, no, no . . . no, that's not true,' he laughs.

So?

'So, first of all, Michels was here and Buckingham was here before him. I knew them both, so there was a relationship, but the reason why I went to Barcelona was that Ajax sold me to Madrid.'

Again, a mischievous smile. 'The people from Ajax sold me to Madrid and that's unethical. I said: "*I* decide." It was not because I was against Madrid; I didn't really know about the political situation, I didn't really know the difference. The reason I came here was obvious: the coach, the coach before, Buckingham, a very good friend of mine and that they tried to tell me what to do. It really was nothing to do with politics. I was not going to let anyone else decide for me.'

Cruyff told Ajax that he would only join Barcelona, threatening to retire if he did not get his own way and announcing his willingness to end up in court if needs be, but Barcelona had another problem to overcome. Foreign players had been banned following Spain's failure at the 1962 World Cup. The ban had led to mass abuses; foreigners were prohibited but *oriundos*, those with Spanish roots, were allowed. In many cases their ancestry had been entirely made up. Stories of Latin Americans claiming that their grandparents were from Osasuna or Celta, the equivalent of announcing, 'yes, my family originally hail from the town of United', became legendary. Both Barcelona and Madrid had lobbied for the ban to be lifted, but had not succeeded.

The breakthrough came when Barcelona's bid to sign the Paraguayan Severiano Irala was blocked. Furious that they had been prevented from signing a player despite the widespread abuse of the system, and sensing an opportunity to undermine the policy that prevented them from buying Cruyff, Barcelona employed a legal firm to investigate. When Miguel Roca delivered his report it revealed that of sixty *oriundos* playing in Spain, forty-six did so under false papers. The pressure brought to bear on the DND was intense, particularly from Barcelona, and on 26 May 1973 the ban was lifted. Clubs were now free to bring in two foreigners each. Immediately, Barcelona signed the Peruvian Hugo Sotil and Real Madrid signed the German Gunter Netzer. Then, on 14 August, Barcelona and Ajax agreed a deal and four days later Cruyff formally signed a five-year contract.

Barcelona paid six million guilders, three million to Ajax and three million to Cruyff, making him the first $1 million player. It was paid for via a loan from the Banca Catalana but there would still be significant bureaucratic delays in a system that was not ready and a sleight of hand was needed when his paperwork was put through. 'If I understood the stories well, they needed to buy me as some sort of one hundred tractors,' Cruyff says, smiling. Almost. Eventually he was registered as a *bien somoviente*. Livestock. At one hundred million pesetas, his was the highest transfer fee in history, almost three times what Madrid paid for Netzer.

It was worth it. Cruyff represented a radical departure at Barça, and not just on the pitch. As team-mate Juan Manuel Asensi puts it: 'With Cruyff, everything changed – the club as well as the team.' 'With Cruyff, Barcelona entered decisively into the world of 100 per cent professional football, the world of show business,' recalled club secretary Carabén. His arrival represented a challenge, coinciding with a shift in Spanish society. Cruyff was acutely aware of his value – when he later returned to Holland to play for Feyenoord, he waived a normal salary in return for a share of gate receipts and came out a winner – and saw no reason why others should cash in without him benefiting. He charged for interviews, had a boot sponsorship deal with Puma – one of the very first players to do so – and advertised underwear with Netzer. On the morning of his greatest triumph, Cruyff's smiling face looked out from a full-page advert, holding a pair of pants in a small box.

'They said I was difficult but I was not difficult, I just fought for justice,' Cruyff says. 'I'm from the post-war era; I was born in '47. And all the people from my age were renewing everything – take the Beatles, all those kinds of people. I have always been renewing, always challenging. When I started, "football player" was not a job, so even though you earned money you were not [actually] a worker. The job didn't exist and you had all these problems. Then you had a time when your image was important and a lot of people took advantage

223

of it. I said: "it's *my* image." When things change you have to change with it and sometimes it is a battle. When I was eighteen or twenty years old, they could pay you one euro and ask for ten million. There's no balance. So you had to fight; I was part of the union in Holland and part of it in Spain – all the things that are normal now didn't exist then. We had to fight for everything and we fought for it.'

Barcelona were quickly aware of Cruyff's value. His presentation game alone generated twenty-two million pesetas, nearly a quarter of his cost, and the number of *socis* rose from 58,000 in 1972 to 64,130 before the following season, his first, had even begun. On the pitch he was even more valuable. Cruyff's two goals against Granada were just the start. 'That season,' says Silvio Elías, a Barcelona director under Sandro Rosell, 'Cruyff was enormous. *Enormous!* I cannot remember anything like it. He was miles better than Maradona. His change of speed was incredible.' The team's physio, Ángel Mur, insists: 'Cruyff was an artist. Even those people who didn't like football stopped to watch him – he always left you with something, he marked you.' The crafty fags, puffing away when he thought no one was looking, just made him somehow even more attractive, more artistic, more bohemian. Almost impossibly brilliant.

When Cruyff made his debut Barcelona were fourth from bottom; at the end of the season they were champions for the first time since 1960. Cruyff missed just one game that season when international duty forced him to pull out of the trip to Zaragoza – his place was taken by Migueli Bianquetti, who was supposed to be on military service but slipped out of the barracks to play – and with him in the side Barcelona didn't lose a single game that mattered. They went twenty-two unbeaten, having lost three of seven prior to his debut, before losing two irrelevent matches after the title had been clinched. At last they could look Madrid in the eye, the fatalism was washed away. Temporarily, at least.

'They were always thinking about inferiority: they had *madriditis*, they had "yes but",' Cruyff recalls. 'We were always thinking we were the victim but in my way of thinking there was no victim. I said: "let's look at ourselves, let's think about how we can be better. Let the rest do whatever they want; we know what we want".' 'Cruyff was a sensational player,' says Asensi. 'He was also a winner. The change in mentality was *brutal*. Suddenly, from always losing we saw that we could win, it was as if we had been drowning and now we were pulled out of the water. We could swim.'

Rexach says the change in footballing terms was 'radical' too, while Asensi adds: 'these days you'd call it Total Football.' Rexach explains: 'We were much closer together, there were fewer spaces; it was a revolution and opponents didn't know what to do. Back then football was "right, out we go: come on lads, in hard" and that was it. No one studied the opponents, it was: *fight, run, jump*. Then it was: "no, let's play better football." There was a method, an idea. We brought that to the game and other teams couldn't handle it.'

Football and psychology. Together, they worked. Players talk about feeling different once Cruyff appeared: their mindset had changed and so had that of their opponents. 'I remember going to places like Santander, Burgos or Granada and sometimes even their own fans would have a go at their players when they fouled us. For the first time in their lives they had the chance to see a world-class figure like Johan Cruyff in the flesh and they didn't want their centre-back to ruin the spectacle,' Rexach recalls. 'The team felt as if they could never lose, like he had come from another planet, fallen to earth for our sake,' Carabén wrote. Barcelona stormed the league: they scored more goals than anyone else and conceded fewer, finishing eight points ahead of Atlético in second. Real Madrid were eighth.

Eighth and humiliated. On 19 February 1974 the cover of the *Revista Barcelonista* depicted an elephant, its foot hovering over a tiny defenceless chick, just about to be brought down upon its head. There was no headline, just a red strap across the bottom: 'R. Madrid, 0 – Barcelona, 5.' Madrid had begun the season in desperate form, it was a cold night and the Bernabéu was only about a third full and some of them had come to see the opposition. Emilio Butragueño, a Madrid *socio* and later the eponymous character of the most emblematic generation of players the club had had since the late 1950s, was just a young kid that night and admitted that Cruyff was his idol. 'And I wasn't the only turncoat in the stadium,' he confessed.

Madrid were torn apart. Cruyff was the catalyst. The speed of foot on the second goal, in particular, is extraordinary, undiminished by the passage of time. Barcelona had beaten Madrid 5-0 just twice before in their history, in 1934–5 and in 1944–5, and yet it could have been even more, *Marca* describing the home side as 'puppets in Barça's hands'. Asensi scored the first, Cruyff the second and Asensi the third, while Hugo Sotil got the fifth. The fourth was scored by the captain Juan Carlos Pérez, whose father had been imprisoned by the dictatorship and who later stood as a Socialist candidate at the 1977 general elections, the first since Franco's death. In the military coup of February 1981, Pérez hid. He later found out that, as he had feared, his name was on a list of left-wingers to be purged.

Asensi calls that night 'historic': we played the kind of football no one had ever seen before.' Rexach describes the 5-0 as '*the* moment'. He explains: 'That was the beginning of the current Barcelona model: pressuring high, attacking constantly, pushing the defence into midfield, the style Barcelona still play now. Rinus Michels laid the first stone with the "Clockwork Orange" and Dutch "Total Football" and then Cruyff put it into practice – first as a player and later as a coach. The way he played rubbed off on all of us and it started to work so smoothly. Everybody wanted to show that they could play a bit too.' The Real Madrid midfielder Pirri describes the match as a 'fluke' but there was more to it than that. The victory was a watershed, the promise of a new beginning. 'It was strange: we just weren't used to that: it was a real beating,' recalls Amancio Amaro. Barcelona were not used to it either. Fans poured down the Ramblas, barely able to believe what they had seen. Police later dispersed them.

'That night,' recalls Cruyff, 'I started to understand the rivalry.'

'The happiness was not just sporting,' Asensi admits. He says he would prefer politics to play no part in the rivalry but recognises that it is unavoidable. In February 1974, especially.

As Enric González writes: 'the 0-5 is a whole story on its own, it was as if *franquismo* had come to an end. It is a game that has a brutal semantic power. That night the defenders of the *culé* cause turned the victimism on its head.' It was like a collective catharsis. In a poll in 1999, 60 per cent of fans described the 0-5 as a victory against Franco. Even the local Falange newspaper called it 'a triumph over centralism', insisting: 'of course football is more than football! And even if dark times do return, history will never wipe out the five goals scored past García Remón.' Much to the delight of *culés*, the *New York Times* declared that the result had done more for the Catalan cause than any politician or resistance figure ever could. Everyone was clambering to get on board. Intellectuals and social commentators were writing about football for the first time, seeking deeper meanings. 'Beneath this 5-0 at Madrid's ground, beneath the passion and everything . . . hides that 11-1 from the 40s,' claimed *La Vanguardia*. 'Subconsciously [Barcelona fans] know that football is politics. They know that if Cruyff and Netzer advertise the same underpants, one of them's pants are immaculate and the other's dirty . . . Barcelona is more than a football team; it is a hope.'

What made it even better was that Cruyff had been able to play only after he and his wife had decided to bring forward the birth of their son precisely so that he would be available for the game. Jordi Cruyff, originally due on 15 February 1973, was born by Caesarean section on the ninth. 'Jordi' (George) is also the name of the patron saint of Catalonia, the dragon slayer of legend whose saint's day is celebrated every year with stalls springing up all over the city of Barcelona, draped in the *senyera*, selling roses for the women and books for the men; stalls that invariably overflow with books on Barça players.

These days, there are countless Jordis in Barcelona; back then, there were none below the age of forty and even those over forty usually found themselves forced to adapt their name. Under Franco, it was forbidden to name a child by a non-Castilian name so when Cruyff went to register his son he was told he had to call him Jorge. Cruyff was having none of it. He simply would not back down, practically bullying the registrar into writing his son's name the Catalan way. He was Johan Cruyff, after all.

He takes up the story, a smirk stretching across his face.

'It is probably because we're Dutch: we're like that. Jordi was born in Holland, then we came here . . . Jordi was a name we liked. Not because of any political thing, we just liked it. When we went to the civil [registry] people in Holland we wrote him down as Jordi. We liked the name, we didn't know anything about consequences or anything, but then I came here and they said: "he's not allowed here."

I said: "What's not allowed? I decide: I'm Dutch. I decide the name of my son."

They said: "We can't write it here."

I said: "Well, just don't write it then. It's your problem, not my problem. In all my official books it's there. If you want to copy that, perfect. If you don't, don't."

Then I said: "Do it or I leave."'

A triumphant grin.

'And they did it . . . in the end.'

'I was the first Jordi officially registered in Barcelona,' Jordi says, thirty-nine years later. 'That was the week of the 5-0. There was that touch of rebellion in the air, a kind of release. When people talk about Real Madrid versus Barcelona, it tends to get reduced to the political question, to Franco, to Madrid being the government's team, even though that's debatable. There is a very direct relation [between football and politics] and when you're young in Barcelona you're very aware of that sense of rebellion towards the government. Also Barcelona is a club that carries you with it.'

Jordi was born into that. His surname guaranteed it; so, thanks to his father's determination, did his first name. 'You know what?' he says. 'I never actually asked why he called me Jordi. I imagine it was just that he liked the name. Gratitude to Catalonia? Maybe but I doubt it. He hadn't been there long. I don't know if there was that element to it [yet]. Mind you, my dad definitely had that rebellious streak. And that episode resonated with the feeling of the time.'

It certainly did. What's in a name? Quite a lot. Cruyff's actions drew displays of gratitude from Catalonia. The world's best player calling his son Jordi was met as if it was a small victory for Catalonia against the dictatorship; beating Madrid 5-0 ten days later was a big one. 'It was not just Barcelona fans,' Joan Laporta insists. 'Progressive people developed a sympathy for us because of Cruyff. He represented modernity, a revolution.'

The 5-0 was the most outstanding performance in a triumphant march towards the title that was celebrated with a 4-2 victory over Sporting Gijón with five weeks of the season still remaining. 'We won the league because we were so far ahead so quickly that they had no time to react,' says Rexach – and "they" doesn't mean the other teams. Twenty-five thousand supporters were waiting for Barcelona at El Prat airport. 'You know what most struck me?' Cruyff asked Frits Barend and Henk Van Dorp as they strolled round the Camp Nou conducting an interview for Dutch television in 1977. 'They didn't say "congratulations", they said "thank you". That was really something. That will always stay with me. It was all they said: "thank you", everywhere. One time we were shopping on the Costa Brava and an old woman came up to me and said over and over again: "thank you, thank you". That made a very deep impression.'

It still does; it did stay with him. Asked for his memories of those title celebrations now, Cruyff smiles. '"*Gracias*,"' he says.

The Catalan comedy music trio La Trinca, who traced their roots to the *Nova Cançó* movement, reflected the impact of Barcelona's success with their song 'Botifarra de pagès'. The song insists that 'one hundred million [pesetas] are nothing, because we've got money, we'll bring to Barcelona the best legs around', jokes about how 'true

Barcelona fans' were now spending their money on 'records, dolls, pictures and pants', and includes a chorus in which they leap up and down not so much chanting Cruyff's name as ribetting it like frogs, *Cruyff! Cruyff! Cruyff!* Sung in Catalan, it begins with the end of the agonising fourteen-year wait and takes great joy in the season's defining moment, the destruction of Madrid: 'Five bells toll/At the Puerta del Sol/Five times Cibeles cried/Madrid was in mourning/ And on the streets they said:/"The sun has set on Flanders" . . .'

Flanders is a reference to Spain's imperial power, the heart of its empire under Philip II and 'Botifarra de pagès' climaxes on an even more overtly political note – even if the *Long live a free Catalonia!* is cheekily beeped out, both a nod and a middle finger to the censor. It draws a conscious parallel to the Catalan nationalist song 'Santa Espina' with its reference to being *gent catalana* (Catalan people) whether *they* like it or not, by ending on the line: 'We are and we will be Barcelona people, whether they like it or not!'

All over Spain people were positioning themselves, preparing for the new political order after Franco's imminent death. Barcelona were not immune to the process; the club could not be divorced from its context. These were the final years of Francoism as the dictatorship confronted its own mortality and Franco grew increasingly ill. Bit by bit a future could be glimpsed and momentous events seemed to be occurring daily, from the Burgos Trials in 1970 when, having called a state of emergency in the face of waves of national protests and international condemnation, Franco was forced to backtrack on death penalties handed down to six ETA prisoners, to the assassination of Admiral Luis Carrero Blanco in December 1973, less than two months before the 5-0. The man Franco had entrusted with continuing the dictatorship after his death was killed by a bomb so powerful that it sent his car sailing over a five-storey building in central Madrid and on to the courtyard on the other side. The veneer of invincibility held by the regime had been literally blown away.

That was the latest in a line of attacks from the Basque separatist group ETA and the following day Spanish television showed Johan Cruyff signing an autograph, scrawling his name across a newspaper front page that declared: 'Carrero Blanco Assassinated'. The fact that it was coincidence did not diminish its power for those who wanted to see meaning in it. The chances of the dictatorship resisting Franco's death had been dealt a definitive blow.

Within the administration there were those who pushed for a policy of *apertura*, or opening up, others who saw no need to change and still more who simply accepted the regime's collapse as inevitable and sought to secure their own political future, repackaging themselves as life-long democrats. Among those bending in the wind but essentially determined for the dictatorship to continue was the man to whom Franco next handed power, Carlos Arias Navarro. He announced some tentative liberalisation as a way of maintaining the regime post-Franco. Meanwhile, Juan Carlos, the king whom Franco had groomed to succeed him as head of state in a restored monarchy, was quietly listening to advice convincing him that the regime was an anachronism that could not continue. The public debate centred on *¿ruptura o reforma?*. Should there be an evolution of the state towards a more democratic system or a clean break with the past? There was little debate now that the dictatorship would not survive in its existing form.

Catalonia was not the sole crucible of change – the regime faced greater challenges from the Basque Country, where ETA killings had stepped up, from the *Costas*, and from Madrid, where political manoeuvring had begun – but it was one of its key motors and the Catalan movement was finding its voice too. The 1960s had already seen a cautious stressing of the *fet diferencial*, the distinctiveness of Catalonia, in language and culture. As early as May 1960, the 'Cant de la Senyera', the expressly forbidden Song to the Catalan flag, had been played at the Palau in the presence of a number of government figures. Among those arrested was Jordi Pujol. Imprisoned in Zaragoza for two and a half years, he became active in promoting, through culture and society as much as politics, what he called a policy of *fer país* – making a country. Barça represented a social mass that obsessed Pujol. He later became the head of the Catalan government.

These shifting attitudes, already partly apparent in and echoed by the Copa del Generalísimo meetings with Real Madrid in 1968 and 1970, soon took on greater significance for Barcelona – reflected in and maybe even encapsulated by the famous phrase *mès que un club*, more than a club.

The concept was first employed by the incoming president Narcís de Carreras in January 1968 when he was reported to have said: 'Barcelona is something more than a football club, it is spirit that is deep inside us, colours that we love above all else.' During the 1969 presidential elections the man who would emerge as winner, Agustí Montal junior, had hinted at a similar conceptualisation of the club by insisting: 'Barcelona is what it is and represents what it represents.' And the phrase was given currency when the advertising executive Javier Coma was asked to come up with a slogan that expressed what Barcelona was for the World Football Day held at the Camp Nou barely forty-eight hours after Cruyff's debut.

On page two of *La Vanguardia* the morning after Cruyff's debut was a full-page advertorial. The headline, written in Castilian, said: *El Barça es más que un club*. 'Barça is more than a club: it has an emotional and cultural significance beyond what is normal for a sporting association,' ran the text. That the two events – Cruyff's debut and the appearance of this slogan – stood side by side did not feel entirely coincidental, football, politics and culture converging.

The slogan came to be the embodiment of Barcelona and remains so today. Written in Catalan, *mès que un club* is now a trademark, present on official club literature, from communiqués to team sheets, and splashed across press room backdrops and stadium meeting points. Asked how he would define Barcelona, Laporta sits back on the sofa in his offices just off the Plaça Francesc Macià, sucks deeply on a huge cigar and smiles with the satisfaction of a man who is about to deliver the perfect answer:

'*Mès que un club.*'

What it actually means is harder to nail down. At the time, what it meant went unsaid. By not expressing it openly, *culés* shared a kind of secret – something that 'they', the regime and their opponents, could not participate in. From a contemporary perspective it is easy to forget that this was a definition first arrived at during the dictatorship: you did not articulate what Barcelona was, you *knew* what Barcelona was. When asked, those who did not wish to utter the politically incorrect often unconvincingly justified it with a literal explanation: it is more than *a* club, it is many. Barcelona, after all, have basketball and handball and roller-hockey teams too.

There remains a certain vagueness, a sense just of Barça being something *good*. The decision to make UNICEF the club's first ever shirt 'sponsor' was explicitly designed to express the idea of *mès que un club* internationally On the walkway that connects the stadium to the Paris Room at the Camp Nou, electronic rotating billboards carry words such as 'liberty', 'democracy' and 'solidarity' and Laporta talks about Barcelona's 'values', about resistance, social responsibility and Catalanism, about a belief in the *cantera* – the youth system. 'Summing up,' he says, 'Cruyff, Catalonia, Masia, UNICEF.' His predecessor, Joan Gaspart, says: 'For many years you couldn't express yourself except via Barça, so it was the defence of a country, of a language, a kind of flag to express Catalan sentiment; it was more than just football.'

Cruyff soon saw that for himself: 'Barcelona is not just a football club, it is social. In Franco's times, or maybe even before, it was some sort of a protest; everybody could be part of the club, part of a movement.'

For Madrid supporters, *mès que un club* was something to be mocked. They saw in Barcelona's desire to be something more than a football club their failure to be much of a football club and adapted it to: *más que un club, un puticlub.* More than a club, a brothel. It is also, especially now, a phrase that irritates *Madridistas* intensely. If once they saw in it a victimism that was offered up in lieu of success, an excuse for failure at a time when Madrid were better, now they see in it the occupation of the moral high ground, a self-satisfied angelic smugness.

The Catalan writer Manuel Vázquez Montalbán complained that the creation of the slogan *mès que un club* had been attributed to him and a group of left-wing intellectuals in the late 1960s and 1970s when it had in fact been 'two directors, men of order like Messrs Narcís de Carreras and Agustí Montal, that first spoke of the fact that Barça was "what it was and represented what it represented" or "more than a club".' Besides, he insisted, they had not invented it either: 'Ever since 1939 lots of *Catalanistas* fulfilled their quota of patriotism by joining Barça and beating Madrid was like overturning the Nueva Planta Decrees [in which Castile took control of Catalonia in the early 1700s]. That was already there when we started to theorise about [Barcelona's identity] within the popular aesthetics of the end of the sixties.'

The *Divine Gauche* was the name given to this coming together of intellectuals, artists and writers which turned its attention to football and to Barcelona, formulating and articulating theories on the club's meaning. And despite his protests, Vázquez Montalbán was the most significant of them, doing more than anyone to articulate Barça's identity, providing the club with a narrative. He helped give Barcelona a literary voice that Real Madrid do not have, creating a set of foundational myths – an ideological framework that could then be built upon. Barcelona have protected and projected their identity, writing a story, a *relato*, in a way that Madrid have not. It is one in which the former Barcelona director and historian Jaume Sobrequés admits the mythology of heroism, suffering and resistance has been overplayed but one that remains powerful and seductive.

It began with an article entitled 'Barça! Barça! Barça!' which was published in *Triunfo* in 1969, and it continued throughout Vázquez Montalbán's work, right up to his death in 2003. Vázquez Montalbán

called Barcelona Catalonia's 'unarmed symbolic army' and his position is defined by statements such as: 'Barcelona owes its meaning
to the historic disasters of Catalonia since the seventeenth century,
in perpetual civil war, whether armed or metaphorical, with the
Spanish state'. And: 'Catalans feel misunderstood and oppressed or
rejected by the rest of Spain'. His articles invariably invoke the
closure of Les Corts, the assassination of Sunyol, Franco, the Di
Stéfano case, Guruceta and the Bottles Final – key exhibits in
Barcelona's case.

Real Madrid are also ever-present of course. One of Vázquez Montalbán's literary characters declares: 'Our club represents Saint Jordi and
the dragon is the external enemy: Spain in other words . . . or Real
Madrid.' The fight must be epic. 'We *barcelonistas* need a strong
Real Madrid to feel sure of our victories and our defeats,' Vázquez
Montalbán wrote. 'There could be nothing more tedious than imagining
a future with a depressed Real Madrid. If that happened Barcelona
would languish and would end up accompanying Madrid further down
the table.' In another article written at the turn of the century he
insisted: 'A world without Madrid–Barcelona would be unthinkable
. . . the confrontation between them has been the escape valve for the
irreconcilable antipathy between Madrid and Barcelona, a bank of
historical bad blood that has distracted us from abysmal radical acts.'

And so the story rolls on. The sheer number of books on Barcelona
is colossal compared to the number on Madrid; their focus and perspective is more varied too. There is far more of a literary and political
pretension about Barcelona than Madrid. In 1970 *Cuadernos para el
diálogo*, noted: 'these two clubs reveal something about society right
now but Catalonia has done more than Madrid to express this political
voice for football.' Four decades later, nothing has really changed.
Jorge Valdano expresses it well. 'Real Madrid is a football club that
has defined its social relevance through its results. Real Madrid is as
great as the number of titles it has won and the number of star players
it has seduced to become part of its history. Barcelona's identity has

more to do with the size of its enemy which represents a centralist force, and that gives Barcelona a dimension which is not just sporting but political and which provides it with a tremendous social power. Madrid's social power starts and ends with football.'

Madrid fans would say that's a good thing. At the entrance to Real Madrid's trophy room a huge sign used to declare: 'Trophies tell the whole story. They are concrete facts that define the holder without the need for cliché. The end result is the sum of these trophies and the well-deserved title of the Best Club of All Time – the Best Club in History.' The word *cliché* could be read as a sideways glance at Barcelona but Madrid have missed the opportunity to offer an alternative. Madrid's history is strangely and sadly neglected. For all the talk of *grandeza* and success, for all the human stories, for all that there is much around which they could and possibly should construct an identity, Madrid have failed to do so. Even the accusations have rarely stung them into action: there has been little real interest in redressing the balance, in correcting some of the widely held falsehoods.

That's one of the reasons why Madrid fans often feel like they have lost the 'ideological' battle: they resent the good guy–bad guy dichotomy and with some justification. After a documentary shown on television in Spain in 2001 uncritically repeated the usual lines, the editor of *AS*, Alfredo Relaño, lamented: 'Madrid might have won the footballing war but Barcelona have won the propaganda war' and, despite his own role in a modern-day battle between the clubs, he was right. In the summer of 2013 the Madrid president Florentino Pérez claimed: 'all our lives it's been Barcelona as the good guys, Madrid as the bad guys.' He complained but he did nothing about it. Madrid do not react; instead, they close the doors.

The difference is visible in their respective museums; Barcelona's presents a more social and overtly political story than Madrid's does. It is an exaggeration but it is tempting to suggest that if Madrid and Barcelona sought to explain what they were in two books, one would be huge, page after page of story and anecdote and meaning, layer upon layer explaining what Barcelona are. The other, Madrid's book, would contain a single page. There would be no words: just a photo of the European Cup.

A few days after beating Real Madrid 0-5, Barcelona visited El Pardo. One director, Raimón Carrasco, excused himself from the trip on the grounds that he had to travel to Paris; in fact he had refused to take part in an audience with the dictator who had ordered the shooting of his father in 1938. Franco told the players that he had watched the game and was impressed. Barcelona gave the dictator the club's gold medal to mark their forthcoming seventy-fifth anniversary. According to Montal, they had little choice. The Catalan president of the DND, Juan Gich, had told Barcelona's president that not doing so would not go unnoticed. 'And those kind of recommendations were more than just recommendations.'

'The day arrived, we put on our jackets and we went to El Pardo,' Montal recalled. 'They took us to a room and five minutes later Franco came in, dressed in military uniform. He shook our hands one by one, the man in charge of protocol handed me my speech, I read it, we gave him the medal, and the Generalísimo said thank you and disappeared from whence he came.' When a petition was launched to persuade Barcelona to withdraw the medal in 2003, a commission was put together by the club to investigate and it ruled that Barcelona could not withdraw what was not voluntarily handed out in the first place, an argument founded upon the fact that when the club's board returned to the Camp Nou that day in 1974 they did not include the presentation in their *Libro de Actas*, as if to say: *let the record state that . . . nothing happened.*

This episode demonstrates that while the regime was losing its grip, there was still a limit to the actions football clubs could take. Another example came when Barcelona were warned after announcements over the Camp Nou loudspeaker were made in Catalan for the first time in 1972, the interior minister describing it in dark terms as 'the most *anti-18 July* act in memory' and warning Montal: 'be careful or next time I'll be telling you in a different way and in a different place'. The risks were still significant. Resistance and collaboration, whether passive or active, is always a complex subject, difficult to judge with certainty. What is voluntary and what is forced? What do people really want? Beneath the fear and coercion, what do they really think? Shifting regimes bring shifting stories – and not all of them are true. Identities are rebuilt, pasts rewritten. It is true at societal and political level and it is true of football clubs.

Throughout the later years of the dictatorship, virtually the whole of Spain was on a kind of active stand-by, waiting for Franco to die. Real Madrid maintained an expectant silence while Barcelona had begun to push the boundaries. With Franco's impending death *mès que un club* would become explicitly framed in political terms, expressed as a manifestation of liberalism, nationalism and democracy. In 1972 Joan Josep Artells published a book entitled, like Vázquez Montalbán's article, *Barça! Barça! Barça!*, which was a political and social history of the club, the first of its kind. It portrayed Barcelona as a collective identity incarnated in a club. A certain defiance was growing in the face of the regime. The captain's armband was embossed with the Catalan flag and in 1974, when Barcelona celebrated their seventy-fifth anniversary, they did so with a new anthem, still played now, that refers to a 'flag that unites us all'. That flag is the *blaugrana* one but the double meaning is not entirely coincidental. The anniversary poster was painted by the Catalan artist Joan Miró, Catalan nationalist songs were played, and supporters hiked up to Montserrat. A group of politicians took advantage of the numbers to blend into the crowd and meet, founding Convergència Democrática de Catalunya, Jordi Pujol's new political party.

The far right, clinging to Francoism, saw in Barcelona an enemy. As Carlos Fernández Santander's book shows, in January 1975 a letter to the political party Fuerza Nueva claimed: 'Barcelona is a massive political party of separatist tendencies, with enormous weight in social, economic, cultural and sporting spheres. Everything is in Catalan: announcements, magazines, membership cards, atmosphere, etc. Who's behind this institution? The great majority of its members are recalcitrant separatists from the generation of the Catalan Generalitat; others, recently arrived from other Spanish provinces, are absorbed into these same separatist doctrines . . . El Club de Fútbol [sic] Barcelona fulfils a political mission more than a sporting function . . . Fuerza Nueva and a whole load of good, conscious Spaniards know who we're up against.'

The following month, Barcelona's official magazine suggested that the RFEF should be democratised in order to 'faithfully reflect the feeling of the country'. And yet Barcelona was not engaged in a frontal battle with Francoism. Its resistance to the regime was not as significant as that of Athletic Bilbao, for example, where there were protests during the Burgos Trial in 1970 and police were called into San Mamés. But even Athletic waited until Franco's death for the most symbolic of statements: the Basque derby in December 1976 was marked by the captains of Real Sociedad and Athletic Bilbao, José Luis Iríbar and Ignacio Kortabarría respectively, holding aloft the still-banned Basque flag, the Ikurriña.

Franco died on 20 November 1975, after a lengthy illness. He suffered internal bleeding, Parkinson's, kidney failure, stomach ulcers, thrombophlebitis and bronchial pneumonia. The life-support machine was switched off a little before midnight on the nineteenth and he finally passed away after 5 a.m. His voice cracking, Carlos Arias Navarro delivered the news on television: '*Españoles, Franco ha muerto.*' Almost half a million people filed past his coffin as it lay in state. Black cloth sold out and so did champagne. There were celebrations, some of them wild, most of them wary. The future was by no means secure – there would be two military coups in 1978 and 1982 led by nostalgic Francoists determined to turn back the clock and prevent democracy from being implanted. Both explicitly bemoaned the emerging power of regional nationalism and demands for autonomy. 'Champagne corks soared into the autumn twilight,' Vázquez Montalbán wrote of Barcelona's reaction to Franco's death, 'but nobody heard a sound. Barcelona was, after all, a city which had been taught good manners. Silent in both its joy and its sadness.'

At the Camp Nou, a Barcelona board member by the name of Antoni Portabella excused himself claiming to feel unwell, overcome by sadness. The club sent out two telegrams: one to Franco's household expressing their condolences for the 'irreparable loss', the other to King Juan Carlos, the man who had become the new head of state. The letter expressed the club's loyalty as it looked forward to 'a future of peaceful and democratic coexistence'. The magazine *Barça* would mark its first issue after Franco's death by looking ahead rather than back, printing a photograph of Montal and Juan Carlos under the headline 'a king for the future'. The club's official bulletin meanwhile described the new king as a breath of 'fresh air that means democracy'.

Real Madrid's official *Boletín* took a different approach. It led on a photograph of Franco and his wife, Carmen Polo, with Juan Carlos and Sofia, above a subheading that noted that the Bernabéu had welcomed the dictator 'many times'. In these 'hours of pain', the *Boletín* declared Real Madrid's 'sadness at the death of Franco, who for forty years guided the destiny of the state and brought the peace and tranquillity necessary for the social development of the country. As Spaniards, as a people and as sportsmen, beyond [political] banners, we will always remember him with immense respect, as befits a man who sacrificed himself for Spain from the first years to his last breath.'

When it came to Juan Carlos, 'King of all Spaniards', Madrid's bulletin presented him as a man of continuity rather than change. 'The age that ends and the one that begins are joined in the same desire for order, peace, work, concordance and union among all Spaniards who, regardless of ideology, want to participate in an optimistic future.'

In one of the boardrooms back at the Camp Nou, the secretary and the director general, Joan Granados and Jaume Rosell, reacted to the news of Franco's death by picking up the obligatory bust of the dictator and throwing it to each other across the room, laughing. The bust fell to the floor and smashed into tiny pieces. When Barcelona met Madrid a month later, almost a thousand hastily-stitched Catalan flags were smuggled into the Camp Nou.

Within three years of Franco's death, political parties and trades unions had been legalised, a new constitution passed by referendum, regional autonomy granted to Spain's 'historic nationalities', a two-chamber parliament constructed and democratic elections held, facilitated by an unwritten pact of forgetfulness that left key issues unresolved but allowed for a smooth passage towards a new era. Franco's dictatorship was dismantled from within as a peaceful transition to democracy was completed. Juan Carlos did not represent Francoist continuity after all. In fact, two Madrid directors pulled out of an audience with him in 1977 complaining that he was too left wing.

As John Hooper explains, because Franco was a centralist and many of his most powerful opponents were separatists, the public mind formed a strong association between regional nationalism and freedom on one hand and national Spanish unity and repression on the other: towards the end of the regime a dislike of totalitarian rule was frequently expressed as distaste for centralism, even away from the regional communities. When Josep Taradellas returned in October 1978, it was a huge event not only in Catalonia but across Spain. The former head of the Catalan government, in exile since 1939, Taradellas had refused to return until the Generalitat was re-established; now Adolfo Suárez, the president of the Spanish government overseeing the transition, contacted him and when he flew back he did so as the head of the provisional Generalitat, the embodiment of Catalonia's 'national' survival and revival.

Taradellas had been a Barcelona fan of the first hour. He famously announced his arrival from the Plaça San Jaume, a huge crowd waving Catalan flags below, by making a declaration that became celebrated: *'Ciutadans de Catalunya, ja soc aquí!'* Citizens of Catalonia, I'm here now! That weekend he attended his first match at the Camp Nou.

The biggest ever Catalan flag had been made for the occasion and he was given a standing ovation. A sign declared: 'welcome home, president'. Taradellas gave a speech recalling his days as a Barcelona fan over sixty years earlier. 'There were not many of us but we had the same faith as you do today,' he said. 'That is the Barcelona you have inherited, the Barcelona rooted in its Catalanism.'

The following year, Barcelona won the Cup Winners' Cup in Basilea, beating Fortuna Düsseldorf 4-3 in extra time. It was the first huge demonstration of their social power abroad. Thirty thousand fans made it to Switzerland, a thousand kilometres away; more than a million waited on the streets of Barcelona when they returned, chanting '*Visca Barcelona! Visca Catalunya!* We want a [Catalan autonomy] statute!' According to the Barça winger Lobo Carrasco, it took three hours for the bus to make it from the airport to the Plaça San Jaume. Catalan flags were everywhere. Four years earlier that would have been unthinkable.

But by then Johan Cruyff had gone and democracy did not prove to be the new sporting dawn that Barcelona had hoped for – at least not immediately. After the 0-5 in February 1974, in a report that seemed to have echoes of Franco's own inexorable demise, *La Vanguardia* had announced: 'Today was the definitive death of a giant of world football. The great Real Madrid, whose slow agony we had been watching for some time, finally died on Sunday 17 February, at the hands of Barcelona, who emerged as the new giant of Spanish football – a team whose name will reverberate around the world.'

In fact, Real Madrid went on to win the league in 1976, '78, '79 and 1980 and the following year they were back in the European Cup final at last. Real Madrid midfielder Vicente del Bosque describes that era as 'grey', while Pirri calls it 'virtually forgotten', but the success continued. It would take Barcelona until 1985 to win the league again, ten years after Franco's death, and they did not win another one until 1991 when Johan Cruyff returned as coach. In the first sixteen years of democracy Barcelona won a solitary league title.

As a player, Cruyff won just one league title at Barcelona, plus the newly named Copa del Rey, the King's Cup, in 1978. For all his impact, for all his brilliance, for all that he seemed to change everything, for all that he appeared the perfect fit, he had not been as successful as expected. In 1974–5, Barcelona returned to the European Cup for the first time since the Square Posts Final in Berne but they were defeated in the semi-final by Leeds United. In the *derbi* against Real Madrid that season, a young Murcian defender by the name of José Antonio Camacho marked Cruyff out of the game, the photograph of the two men side by side becoming one of the most emblematic of the Madrid–Barça rivalry. And in February 1977 Cruyff was sent off for protesting to the referee after Málaga had taken the lead, pointing at the linesman and whispering: 'I think it might be a good idea if you consult that man over there.' The referee's report said that Cruyff had sworn at him repeatedly. At first Cruyff refused to leave the pitch and was eventually led off by a police force that was still a hangover from the dictatorship. The image became a symbolic one – a uniformed figure escorting the Catalan icon away, the writer Francisco Umbral later dismissively noting how some treated the sending off as if it was a 'democratic act'.

Cruyff's performances had dipped from the second season on. Johan Neeskins had been brought in to join him as the club's second foreigner and although Neeskins was extremely popular, the marginalisation of the Peruvian attacker Hugo Sotil struck many supporters as unfair and did not help the team. Asensi explains: 'Sotil was an extraordinary player – one of the two most talented foreigners I have seen at Barcelona, with Cruyff. But he was sacrificed in the second year. They thought that they could get him Spanish nationality so they signed Neeskins but the nationality didn't happen and we really missed him up front. Neeskins was a good player but Sotil was vital. Marciel didn't play much in the second season either, or Rifé, or Gallego . . . Of the team that won the league there were five or six changes. Normally two or three changes are more than enough but they didn't see it like that and destroyed a team of champions . . . and for nothing.'

At the same time, Cruyff, whose growing power some saw in the decision to sign Neeskins at the cost of Sotil, stood accused of going missing – especially away from home. Certainly he was inconsistent. There is a curious, unexpected glimpse of this when Real Madrid's forward Amancio is asked about his Dutch opponent.

'Yes, he was a good player,' he replies flatly.

There's a long gap and then he adds: 'remember that I played with Alfredo [Di Stéfano] and Puskás.'

Mention of them allows Amancio to recall his team-mates, fond memories, seemingly happy for the conversation to head in a different direction. It is time to insist. But what about Cruyff?

'He was good, yeah,' Amancio says. He sounds unconvinced.

He *is* unconvinced.

Good?

'He was good at Ajax and in the national team.'

And at Barcelona?

'For a year. One year. The rest of the time *no tocó bola*. He hardly touched the ball. He would come and get it off the goalkeeper, take the throw-ins, the occasional corner. He didn't want to take any risks. He won the league in that first year and he was very good, although he also had a good team around him that everyone forgets about. In the other two years he didn't do anything.'

There is no escaping the brilliance of the 5-0, though. No hiding from its impact, its symbolism.

'Yeah,' Amancio admits, 'that hurt. So much so that Ignacio Zoco retired at the end of the season.'

Ignacio Zoco, Madrid's captain, retired? Because of Cruyff? Twelve years, gone? Because of one night?

It sounds like an exaggeration. It is not.

Zoco remembers it as if it was yesterday. And it looks as if it still pains him.

'After the game we were in the hotel – Pirri, Velázquez, Grosso, Amancio and me – and I told them. I called the bellboy up to the room, we ordered a glass of something each and I said a toast. "Lads, this is my last season: on 30 June I'm gone. I'm retiring." And that was because of that game. That shame I felt that day . . . I decided I was never going to feel shame like that on a football pitch again. 5-0, *joder*.

'The next day I came to the Bernabéu and I spoke to Don Santiago . . .'

Zoco affects a gruff, Bernabéu voice. You can almost picture him chewing dismissively on a colossal cigar.

'He said: "What? You're pissed off? So am I. And? Take your wife out, go and eat, relax, and we'll speak tomorrow."

I came back the next day and I said: "We ate yesterday, Don Santiago, and it was a lovely meal but I'm retiring on 30 June."

He said: "You're staying here, even if all you do is go to the Ciudad Deportiva every day for a spot of sunbathing."

I said: "I'm sorry, you're not going to convince me. I'm retiring."

He could see that I was being so stubborn, so bloody-minded, that he didn't argue. And a few weeks later I said: "Don Santiago, it's still the same."

Sometimes you know: that night against Barcelona showed me. When you can't do it any more, it's time to go. Out on the pitch there's no forgiveness.'

There was, though, one last waltz. A chance for revenge. At the end of the 1973–4 season, the season when Johan Cruyff seemed to take Barcelona into a new era, Real Madrid reached the final of the Copa del Generalísimo. Their opponents? Barcelona.

Barcelona had gone into a process of '*mucho relax*' after winning the league and the cup was 'secondary', Asensi insists. On top of that, foreigners were not allowed to play in the cup, so Barcelona were without Cruyff. In any case, he had travelled to the 1974 World Cup in Germany, where Holland revolutionised the game, delighted the world but ultimately lost the final to Germany. Rinus Michels, who was Holland's coach as well as Barcelona's, had travelled to Germany too. The difference was that Michels did make a flying visit back to Madrid for the final.

He might have wished he had not bothered. With seven minutes to go, Real Madrid scored their fourth goal. Four-nil up, manager Luis Molowny made a substitution. Zoco, no longer a regular starter after the 'shame' of that 5-0 defeat in the winter, came on for the last five minutes of his career. As he trotted on to the pitch, Grosso ran over and unexpectedly gave him the captain's armband. When the final whistle blew, Zoco went up and collected the cup from Franco, the tenth trophy he'd won with Real Madrid.

Zoco smiles. 'We wanted another goal to make it five like they got,' he says, 'but, still, we got revenge. It was wonderful.

And then it was over.'

14

THE VULTURE SQUAD

They called it the *Movida Madrileña*. Franco's death and the arrival of democracy brought with them a cultural revolution. A different society emerged, a new generation too, liberation expressed socially as much as politically. Repression was followed almost inevitably by excess and nowhere more so than in Madrid. *Solo se vive una vez* ran its unofficial motto – a slogan that eventually became song, one whose chorus is still belted out at discos with a collective defiance that's almost evangelical. *You only live once.* Spain's equivalent of the Swinging Sixties, an outpouring of creativity and imagination, arrived in Madrid in the 1980s. It was an explosion in music, in literature, in film, in art.

And in football.

Spain's first free elections for forty-one years were held in 1978. Less than three years later a military coup sought to overthrow the new regime. At 6.30 p.m. on 23 February 1981, the mustachioed Lieutenant Colonel Antonio Tejero burst into parliament, pistol in hand, shooting and shouting: 'everybody on the floor!' The entire chamber of parliamentary deputies was taken hostage while four hundred kilometres away tanks were sent on to the streets of Valencia by Captain General Jaime Milans del Bosch. Across the country, fearful people prepared to depart. But while the attempted coup was televised live, so was its ultimate failure. King Juan Carlos appeared at 1.14 a.m. to denounce the conspirators and it began to unravel, with Civil Guard officers clambering out of parliament windows to hand themselves in. The coup lasted little over twelve hours.

In response, pro-democracy marches were held all over the country, the biggest civic mobilisation ever seen in Spain. For some, the coup's collapse marked the end of the transition and the arrival of democracy proper. The last assault had failed, Tejero and Milans del Bosch were imprisoned and in 1982 Felipe González's Socialist Party swept to power. Freedom, which had been so graphically threatened, bullet holes in parliament's ceiling serving as a permanent reminder, was embraced with even greater feeling. The *Movida Madrileña* reached its peak in the mid-1980s and is often considered synonymous with the film director Pedro Almodóvar who ditched La Mancha, land of Don Quixote and the arid plains of *la España profunda*, to make for Madrid where he packed kitsch movies with sex and drugs.

But Almodóvar was not the new Spain's only icon. And if Almodóvar was vice, Emilio Butragueño was nice – fresh-faced, blond and angelic. Butragueño was polite and softly spoken, shy, the kind of boy every mother wanted for her daughter. He was also a footballer. Nicknamed *El Buitre*, the Vulture, the striker gave his name to the footballing expression of a new era and to Real Madrid's finest team since Alfredo Di Stéfano had left twenty years earlier – a team Jorge Valdano, who formed part of it, goes so far as to call 'the sporting arm of the *transición* to democracy'. 'Just as the *Movida* existed,' Valdano says, 'so the *Quinta* existed.'

The *Quinta* in question is the Quinta del Buitre, the Vulture Squad, a team that defined its era and was defined *by* its era, a side one Spanish newspaper claimed had dragged Madrid out of the darkness.

Emilio Butragueño grew up working in his father's *perfumería* out by the Casa del Campo on the west of the city. He had been a Madrid *socio* from birth, joined the club while he was still doing military service – leaving for the barracks at 5.45 a.m. and finishing training at 10 p.m. every day – and made his first team debut in Cádiz on 5 February 1984, aged twenty. Madrid were losing 2-0 when he came on, his legs trembling. By the time the match was over, Madrid had won 3-2. Butragueño had scored two and made the other. A star was born. Suddenly, he was everywhere and on everything, his cherubic looks and blond hair proving a marketing man's dream. Even now, a Butragueño table-football game takes pride of place at the Spanish Football Federation's museum, his boyish face smiling out from its box.

Butragueño was a revelation and yet fans had been waiting expectantly for him for some time. Two and a half months, to be precise. One of the most striking things about the Quinta del Buitre is that, even if it took a while to cement its place as one of the finest sides in Spanish football history, it is easy to locate the *exact* moment it was born. On 14 November 1983, Julio César Iglesias wrote an article in *El País* about the kids coming through Real Madrid's youth system – ninety lines that introduced a new generation of players and a new style. A new hope too. Ninety lines and a headline: 'Amancio and the Quinta del Buitre'.

Fans clung to that hope. Madrid were struggling, embarked upon a desperate search for lost hegemony on and off the pitch. Immediately after Franco's death, Madrid won four of five league titles but Santiago Bernabéu had died in 1978 and Real Sociedad took the league from them in 1980–81, a late goal clinching the title on goal difference and heralding a period of Basque dominance in which they and Athletic Bilbao shared four consecutive championships. Madrid had also lost the European Cup final in 1981, denied the chance finally to recover the prestige that defined them. And yet they had never expected to be presented with the opportunity at all, and few gave them a chance in the final against Liverpool at the Parc des Princes.

Mariano García Remón, Rafael García Cortés, Antonio García Navajas and Ángel García Pérez earned that generation the nickname the Madrid of the Garcías, the equivalent to being the Smiths'

Manchester United. It was a title, the midfielder Vicente del Bosque says, that was employed with a combination of *aprecio y desprecio* – fondness and dismissiveness. Largely products of the youth system, a tough, no-thrills side, their two permitted foreigners were the German Uli Steilike and the Englishman Laurie Cunningham, who had cost just short of £1 million in 1979. But goalkeeper García Remón was injured, Ricardo Gallego had only just got out of plaster and was in the stands, Steilike played despite a bad knee and Cunningham wasn't fully fit either. Besides, Liverpool had a great team, European champions twice in the last four years.

It was fifteen years since Madrid had last been in a final and when it eventually came it was ugly, dirty and desperately dull. On a pitch full of holes and ridges, the grass long and dry, the passing was embarrassingly poor. 'Liverpool bad, Madrid worse,' as the full-back Alan Kennedy puts it. Madrid's only real chance fell to Camacho, the last person they would have wanted it to fall to, and in the eighty-first minute Kennedy dashed forward for a throw-in: 'I wasn't even trying to score: I was running to try to make space for others,' he remembers. 'But Ray [Kennedy] threw it to me, I ran into the area, García Cortés made a wild challenge and tried to take me and the ball out of the game. Agustín Rodríguez went to his left, thinking I would cross and . . .' Kennedy laughs at the absurdity of it all. García Cortés swung and missed everything: the ball, the player, his moment. The Liverpool defender ran straight through and scored. Madrid's chance had gone.

Juan Santisteban was assistant coach. 'The European Cup is the one you most want and we were so close,' he says. 'It was to our enormous credit that we reached the final at all but when you lose it is like something has been snatched away from you. It eclipses all else.' 'When you take a step back, that European Cup has to be looked on as a success,' insists Del Bosque, playing in the middle of Madrid's midfield that night. 'That was a team based almost entirely on the *cantera* and it reached a European Cup final and although it hurt I think people at the club understood that. Other presidents might have demonised us for losing it and there might have been a depression – which there was of course – but Luis de Carlos had a cool head. He rewarded us for reaching the final: we got a [525,000-peseta] bonus anyway. That was one of the very few times I ever got a bonus for losing.'

'The very few,' he adds, thinking for a moment . . . 'or the only.'

It was little consolation. Rafa García Cortés's family had recorded the final for him. When he got home, he took the tape from the video recorder and threw it out of the window.

Defeat knocked Madrid sideways. They didn't win the league again until 1985, the six-year drought their longest since before Di Stéfano's arrival. In the meantime, 1983 had seen them finishing as runners-up in every competition: defeated in the Cup Winners' Cup by Alex Ferguson's Aberdeen, second in the league, and beaten in the Copa del Rey by Diego Maradona's Barcelona, a dramatic injury-time diving header from Marcos Alonso sealing victory for the Catalans. Jorge Valdano arrived the following year. He recalls 'a club in decline where players' papers were kept in shoeboxes; there was a sense of a club that had fallen asleep and was slowly getting smaller and smaller'.

The good news, Valdano insists, was that 'the sheer size of Madrid's history meant that just by applying a cloth to it, the Rolls-Royce could shine again . . . and that was when the Quinta emerged'. This was the generation that would bring the glory days back.

Julio César Iglesias was not the only one who came to fix his attention on Castilla. So much so that Madrid's striker Juanito Gómez complained bitterly that during one match at the Bernabéu fans showed their discontent with the first team by chanting the name of the second team. Madrid's *cantera*, or academy, had proved successful before. In 1981, Juanito had been part of the Madrid side that played against their own youth team in the final of the Copa del Rey. Castilla, as the youth team is known, were beaten 6-1 but had knocked out four First Division teams en route – Hércules, Athletic Bilbao, Real Sociedad and Sporting Gijón – and the following season they competed in the

Cup Winners' Cup, defeating a West Ham side – that included Billy Bonds, Frank Lampard senior and Trevor Brooking – 3-1 at the Bernabéu. But by 1983, Castilla were an even better side, top of the Second Division and drawing huge crowds to the Santiago Bernabéu – sometimes in excess of 60,000.

Iglesias would go and watch Castilla train at the Ciudad Deportiva. One day, Paco Gento was sitting alongside him, chewing on sunflower seeds. 'See that kid?' he asked, nodding towards the pitch. 'He's Sanchís's son – and he's better than his dad.' Manuel Sanchís senior had won four league titles and the European Cup with the *ye-yé* team in 1966 and Manolo Sanchís junior recalled family arguments that would end: 'Have you ever won a European Cup? I have. Now go to bed!' Iglesias watched the young centre-back and started to wonder if Gento was right, but he was even more impressed by Miguel González 'Míchel', Miguel Pardeza, Rafa Martín Vázquez and Emilio Butragueño.

Small, balletic, graceful, always on tiptoe, Butragueño was the one who most caught the eye; the former Madrid player and coach Luis Molowny had called him a 'genius' and Iglesias named the group after him. Quinta referred to the number of them – five; to the speed with which they played – they had a fifth gear; and to their shared generation – the word 'Quinta' comes from military service but is also applied to school and refers to those who come through the same year as you; a bunch of mates who graduate at the same time. A gang, a squadron. They came through the youth system together and made Madrid great together.

In truth, the name was a little arbitrary both in its conception and in its longevity. There's a reason why the most famous picture of Sanchís, Míchel, Vázquez, Pardeza and Butragueño comes from a game between Real Madrid and Real Zaragoza and it does not take a genius to spot the deliberate mistake: in it, Pardeza is wearing white, the other four are in blue. Pardeza, the only one of the Quinta not from Madrid, couldn't stake a consistent claim to a place and departed for Zaragoza. That meant that the five players only appeared in the same Madrid team once – in a Copa del Rey game against Atlético Madrid in June 1987. Pardeza had always been the least likely to make it, Iglesias later admitting that he wanted the group to have five members for the sake of the story and that he hadn't been sure whether to include Pardeza or Francis as the fifth.

The name stuck anyway, forever identified with those five men, their era, their team and the ideal they represented. 'The great fortune that [Castilla] team had was that practically all its players spoke the same footballing language,' Pardeza recalled. 'Short passing, touch, technique, one-twos . . . that idea was translated into the first team because lots of players took the step up from below and shared it.'

Their coach at Castilla was Amancio Amaro while the man who gave them their chance in the first team was Alfredo Di Stéfano. 'You could see that they were special,' Amancio says. 'We had to teach them to compete but they had so much quality; they were artistic in the way they played. Martín Vázquez could dribble like Garrincha. Míchel, whose father and grandfather had played for Atlético Madrid, had incredible precision in his passing and crossing. Butragueño was electric, and very cool. Sanchís was anticipation, character, serenity. I'd suffered his father often enough as a player, but he was even better. Pardeza was a scurrying player, quick and clever, an intuitive striker. Bernabéu always said that it was great if one player came through the *cantera* every year or so, but five! That's a *filón*.' A rich seam.

'People expect players to come out like *churros* but it doesn't work like that,' says Di Stéfano. *Churros* are the strips of sweet, doughnut-like batter that are churned out of a machine like a sausage-maker. This time, though, it did work that way. 'We were weak and when you're weak, you look behind you, at the kids coming through. I saw kids that played well and I put them in, that's all.'

That's all?

'Well, you have to have the bollocks to put them in and keep them in.'

Míchel was the first to officially make his debut in the 'first team', when Castilla replaced Real Madrid during a players' strike in April 1982 – something he now regrets – but he didn't make a 'proper' first-team appearance for two more years, well after his contemporaries had done. When Butragueño made his first appearance against Cádiz, Sanchís and Martín Vázquez had already been given their debut at Real Murcia in December 1983, three weeks after that *El País* article, and Sanchís had even scored the winner. Three weeks later, Pardeza got a few minutes as a substitute against Español. And Míchel eventually appeared on 2 September 1984, not bowing out until 1996. The Quinta del Buitre was born.

They were not immediately successful. The 1984–5 season started with Barcelona defeating Real Madrid 3-0 under new manager Terry Venables and it ended with the Catalans winning their first league title for thirteen years and with summer signing Steve Archibald finishing as top scorer. Barça had laid on a private jet – 'big soft seats, full service, the whole shebang', as the Scot recalls it – just so that Archibald could stay for the celebrations in which over a million people took to the streets. But, with the Quinta settling in, something was slowly building. Madrid won the UEFA Cup, defeating Videoton in the two-legged final, and the following season they took the league title back for the first time in six years. A second successive UEFA Cup joined it and four more league titles followed. In total, the Quinta del Buitre won five league titles in a row under three different managers, Di Stéfano and Amancio having given way to Luis Molowny, Leo Beenhaker and John Toshack. It was a run of success only achieved once before, when Madrid won the league every season between 1960–61 and 1964–5. It also dwarfed anything Barcelona had achieved: their best run up to that point had been two consecutive titles, between 1958 and 1960, 1951 and 1953, and 1947 and 1949.

But it was not just that Madrid won; it was the way they won, who they were and what they came to represent. In 1988, the year the Quinta produced arguably their finest football, they beat Bayern Munich, Porto and Napoli in the European Cup – the last one a game that was famous for Chendo, Madrid's rugged full-back, nutmegging Maradona, prompting Valdano to remark: 'the birds are shooting at the rifles.' Domestically, their achievements are perhaps best illustrated by the time they defeated Sporting Gijón 7-0 and Atlético Madrid's president Jesús Gil scoffed 'that was an accident, they won't do that again' only for them to follow it up by beating Zaragoza 7-1 the week after. That season, they finished eleven points clear of Real Sociedad in second, *twenty-three* ahead of Barcelona. Míchel described it as the finest football anyone had seen at Madrid for twenty-five years and insisted that another twenty-five would have to pass before they saw its like again.

What made their style so significant was the way it seemed to fit perfectly with what was happening in society: it felt like a product of their time, a footballing reflection of a new era, another strand of an artistic new wave led by the capital. 'With Franco dead, it was a good idea to bury that archaic identity of the *Furia Española*,' Valdano wrote. The *Furia Española*, or Spanish Fury, was a footballing concept based on aggression and power, not talent. Or, to use the journalist Santiago Segurola's words, 'a fascistoid racial myth that had been forged and promoted during *franquismo*'. 'We had a very specific style that wasn't really in line with what had happened in the previous years or the general current,' Butragueño says. 'And we all had the same interpretation of the game: it was very harmonious. We were lucky, we all emerged at the same time, we were all from Madrid and the talent was innate. We complemented each other perfectly.'

With his intelligence, playfulness and lightness of touch – slim and short, he is far from an imposing figure even now – Butragueño was always different. Initially told he would not make it, he broke the mass-produced mould that was all about athleticism and strength. In the penalty area he was cold, as if there was never any hurry and no doubts. A famous goal against Cádiz sums him up: reaching the byline, he cut back inside in the space of barely a couple of metres, left two defenders on their backsides and walked the ball in by the post. It was precise and expressive. 'I try to be creative on the pitch,' he told one interviewer. 'Instead of novels, I sometimes read art books; I like the lives of artists. Art is any creation.'

His position has not changed at all. 'Having the ball, playing, feels better,' Butragueño says. 'It is not the same watching the clock run down and never getting a touch. You compete to win, that's the bottom line, but it is a game. You begin playing any game with the intention of enjoying yourself. If you win, you might feel satisfied but that doesn't necessarily mean that you have enjoyed yourself. When you win and enjoy yourself, it's marvellous.'

But with all the pressure, the demands, the *need* to win, isn't that a utopian vision? Do players really enjoy football? The response is immediate.

'Yes! On the pitch, it's a delight. You like having the ball. I understand football as a way of expressing yourself, of inventing something. It is all about creation. Enjoyment, fun. When that comes off it is wonderful.'

His words could be a manifesto for the *Movida*. According to Valdano, *El Buitre* was 'poetry', a player who showed the value of seduction. The Argentinian once wrote that 'to defend Butragueño is to reinforce an attitude, to choose between fear and daring, boredom or happiness, talent or muscle . . . the grace, the invention, the fragility of Butragueño left our feelings, our sentiment, contented'. And for those, Valdano added, 'who believe in things and not ideas, I have this to say: with Emilio it's easier to win.'

Valdano believes that the passage of time has served to reveal the Quinta's contribution to have been even greater than it appeared then – Spain have become the world's best team in the twenty-first century by explicitly embracing a more talent-based approach. He is not alone in seeing a certain parallel between the Quinta del Buitre and modern-day Barça: local and likeable, exponents of a technical game; packed with kids from the youth system. 'In Madrid's case that emergence was more spontaneous, at Barcelona it was more planned, but the similarity is certainly there,' he says, adding sadly: 'The problem is that if you praise Barcelona you get treated like some kind of traitor in Madrid, even though the best way to value your own achievements is to value your opponent.'

Míchel agrees: 'Di Stéfano and Amancio were to Madrid what Guardiola became for Barcelona. People say it is a one-off, but it depends on having a coach that plays them [the kids] and understands them. That Madrid, this Barcelona? They come together. Sanchís would be Puyol; Iniesta, Martín Vázquez . . .'

And you?

'Me? I was Xavi.'

Míchel leaps to break the silence. 'And before people say "bloody hell, he thinks he's Xavi", I'm talking about the way it all fitted together . . .'

He continues: 'Winning was taken as read. The difference was that we were aesthetic too. And precisely at *that* moment. At Real Madrid, people want you to go through four puddles and still come out the other side with clean shoes. Spain was changing and football does not live on another planet; it's not played in a vacuum. Looking back it is clear that the social, economic and cultural change that Spain, and especially Madrid, was undergoing included us too. We had a style, a creativity, and we felt free to express it. We were allowed to try something new.

'That brought us into the mainstream. Suddenly, we mattered. We were somebody: people asked our opinion on things. Footballers became social figures – there was a sea change in our image. We were innovators.'

When it came to deciding the captain, Manolo Sanchís recalls that he wanted the decision to be democratic and put it to a vote. Valdano could see the shift: 'Even then I thought that they represented a generation that could benefit football. A group of local boys who took the game into another dimension. That had a political element: I remember people chanting: '*¡se siente, se siente, Butragueño presidente!*'

257

Until then, football was an *expresión animalesca de la sociedad* – a savage, wild, animalistic expression of society. They started to change the status of football. Bit by bit they became part of popular culture, of a society that didn't necessarily need to be ashamed to be an intellectual. That was down to the Quinta.'

Not that the *expresión animalesca de la sociedad* Valdano mentions was entirely left behind. There is a contradiction that lies at the heart of the Quinta legend and has become more pronounced as time passes. Many Madrid supporters, confronted with the current Barcelona team, now cling to the Quinta's other qualities instead – and by extension to an identity they prefer to see as somehow more eternally theirs, stretching beyond the 1980s and into the 1960s and 1970s. One that was based as much on testosterone as talent. And the Quinta had plenty of that. It wasn't just Butragueño, Míchel and Martín Vázquez, the artists; there was also José Antonio Camacho, Madrid's captain and the emotional heart for whom one team-mate recalls 'every game was an act of faith'; the striker Carlos Santillana, whom some consider the finest header of a ball they had ever seen; and the Málaga-born Juanito, who famously claimed: 'If I had not been a footballer I would have been an *Ultra Sur*.'

And then there was Hugo Sánchez, signed in the summer of 1985 from Atlético Madrid, where he had finished the season as *Pichichi*, the league's top scorer. It was almost exactly a year after he had posed, thumbs up, for the Catalan newspaper *Sport* and given an interview in which he talked about his excitement at joining Barcelona – only to find that Barcelona's new coach had other ideas. On the day that Sánchez found himself in the Rey Juan Carlos hotel, preparing to sign, another striker was in another room with exactly the same idea. Barça's vice-president Joan Gaspart had lined up Sánchez but Terry Venables had just become coach and he was determined to sign Steve Archibald instead. Eventually, Barcelona reluctantly backed their coach. And 'reluctantly' is the word.

Archibald recalls the scene.

'I went into the room and Gaspart said to me: "Are you sure you want to sign for us?"

"Yes."

"But . . . Really sure?"

"Yes."

"And are you sure you want to accept these terms?"

"Yes."

"Okay, then."

He goes away. Five minutes later he's back with the president. "Everybody happy?"

"Yeah."

And then we signed the deal. Maybe the president had been upstairs with Hugo, I don't know. They wanted Hugo, they didn't know enough about me.'

Madrid took advantage, signing Sánchez the following summer. He was an instant hit, finishing top scorer in 1985–6, '86–7, '88–9 and '89–90, becoming arguably Madrid's best player during the Quinta era and possibly their most important too: the run of league successes did not start until he arrived and no forward was more feared than he was. He could not have been more different from the ethos of those who define that team in the collective conscience, right down to the fact that Sánchez and Míchel hated each other and the Mexican proposed that the team be renamed the *Quinta de los Machos*, reclaiming for himself the eponymous role. He was aggressive, nasty, athletic and almost ridiculously effective, utterly deadly. And, of course, idolised by the fans.

Nor was Sánchez the only counterbalance to the aesthetic of the Quinta. Apart from the artistry, if there is one thing that Madrid supporters hang on to from that era it is the *remontada*, or comeback, the ultimate in epics. The words of the forward Juanito in April 1986 are now the stuff of legend, trotted out every time Madrid have to overcome a first-leg defeat. Whenever Madrid are up against it they invoke the 'Spirit of Juanito', a phrase given all the more meaning because Juanito, one of the most emotional and best-loved of all Madrid players, died in a car crash in 1992. Madrid had been beaten 3-1 by Inter in a UEFA Cup semi-final first leg. At the end of the game Juanito warned that it was not all over, insisting in Italian that was half invented, half-Spanish with an 'Italian' accent: '*noventi minuti en el Bernabéu son molto longo*'. Ninety minutes in the Bernabéu are very long.

He was right but for one thing – the game lasted even longer than that. There was method in his madness, a reason for his bullishness. Madrid had beaten Anderlecht 6-1 after a 3-0 first-leg defeat in 1984 – a comeback they later attributed to a team outing to the cinema to see *The Karate Kid* – and in 1985 they beat Inter 3-0 having lost the first leg 2-0. That same season they had got through to the last sixteen by coming back from a 5-1 defeat in Germany against Borussia Moenchengladbach with a 4-0 victory at the Santiago Bernabéu. Now, just as Juanito warned, they won 4-1 after extra time, going on to beat Cologne in the final.

Remontadas formed part of Madrid's mystique going back years – they had beaten Derby County 5-1 having lost 4-1 in a European Cup first-leg tie in 1976 – but it was the Quinta that made the mythology all the more powerful. They added to the trepidation visitors felt upon setting foot in the Bernabéu, described by Valdano as *miedo escénico* – stage fright. The fear factor was something Madrid worked on; the stadium alone was not enough. One member of the squad reveals the methods employed: the first three fouls, the first three shots and the first three corners had to be Madrid's. Immediately after kick-off, wallop, the opposition's best player was taken out and even as he hit the ground Madrid players were surrounding the referee accusing him of diving. They called it the Code Red.

One German opponent recalls Madrid's players in the tunnel before the games eyeballing them through the fence, spitting at them and shouting abuse, gesturing that they were going to kill them. If the rest of the Quinta's story broke with the past, that chapter had always been part of Real Madrid's genetic make-up. 'You'd never get away with it now,' admits Santillana. 'These days with twenty cameras in the stadium they would have caught everything,' says Ricardo Gallego, 'we were a kind of Dr Jekyll and Mr Hyde.' The damage done, it was then up to Butragueño to tiptoe past the defence and deliver the killer blow.

If opponents were supposed to feel paralysed, defeated, Madrid felt invincible, no matter what adversities they faced. They have a taste for the epic and for sacrifice that does not play a central role in Barcelona's discourse. Last-minute goals and barely believable victories were their thing. That's the legend, anyway. The reality is different. Even Juanito had experienced the other side of the coin: in 1983 he had been walking back to the dressing room on his knees as he'd promised to do if Madrid won the league, only to find out just before he reached the tunnel that a late, late goal for Real Sociedad meant they had not won the title after all. When Madrid had to overcome a 4-1 first-leg deficit against Borussia Dortmund in the Champions League semi-final in 2013, the Spirit of Juanito was again awoken. But although they were close, Madrid failed to come back – just as they had done the last fourteen times they had sought to turn round a first-leg deficit, going back twenty-seven years.

And yet the identity remains, the belief, the hope. 'The history of Real Madrid is full of games won in the last minute and the opposition knows that,' says Míchel. 'Whether or not it really is full of last-minute wins is another matter; it feels that way. Maybe the last minute is actually the seventieth, or maybe the stats show that Madrid have lost as many as they have won late on, but that doesn't matter: Real Madrid's indomitable character is an identity. "Rebellion". "Strength". "Sacrifice". "Last minute". History matters, history plays. No one knows why but you pull on that Real Madrid shirt and you become a mini Incredible Hulk.'

Emilio Butragueño looks back on his career from a suite at the Santiago Bernabéu, dark brown walls dotted with paintings in frames, footballing themes made art. On the table in front of him sits a photograph of himself as a thirteen-year-old, all fresh-faced and wide-eyed. On a plinth just across the room sits the European Cup: Real Madrid's identity and their obsession. As Butragueño sits there, metres away from the trophy, there is something a little cruel about the scene. Taunting. Glancing over at the trophy, its long handles looping up on either side, he admits: 'Real Madrid wouldn't be Real Madrid without it. This club is so prestigious because of its nine European Cups – that is what defines us.'

The Quinta del Buitre were set to be the generation that ended Madrid's long wait in Europe too; no one doubted that they, unlike the Madrid of the Garcías, were good enough. Instead, it was the only competition that the Quinta del Buitre did not conquer; in fact it was the competition that conquered them. And when the European Cup left them dying, Barcelona arrived to deliver the final blow, like a bullfighter plunging his sword between the shoulder blades of an exhausted, disoriented animal.

Asked about the Quinta, Di Stéfano notes: 'they played well', pausing to add simply, as if it was the ultimate judgement: 'they never won the European Cup.' In a way it *is* the ultimate judgement. They never took the prize they wanted most of all. Valdano puts it well: 'That was a generation that never set foot at the summit and for Real Madrid, the only summit is the European Cup.'

Of the five players who made up the original Quinta, only Sanchís would win the trophy – and that was as captain at the head of a very different team in a very different era, fifteen years after he made his debut, eight days before his thirty-third birthday and long after his erstwhile team-mates had departed.

'We are the only Real Madrid team that remains in the memory without winning the European Cup,' counters Míchel. 'Look at the emblematic teams, the ones that have marked an era, those whose names immediately locate them in a time and place, and they are all European Cup-winning teams: the Di Stéfano side that won the first five, the *ye-yé*, the *séptima*, even the *galácticos* to some extent. We didn't win it but *still* we're remembered, *still* we have a special place in the club's history. We still claimed an era as ours. Football is about legacy and, even without the European Cup, we left one.'

He is right. And yet . . . And yet, he concedes: 'the European Cup was a necessity.'

One of the main reasons Madrid never won the trophy that defines them during the 1980s was simple: they were unlucky enough to encounter Arrigo Sacchi's AC Milan, complete with Ruud Gullit, Marco Van Basten and Frank Rijkaard. It was not only Milan who knocked them out but, according to some members of that squad, they were at the heart of the Quinta's crisis. 'Psychologically, they damaged the Quinta so much as to make them disappear completely,' says Valdano. Milan had created what he calls a kind of Stockholm syndrome in which Madrid were so dazzled by the Italians' revolutionary brilliance, their sheer invincibility, as to shrink before them, developing a complex. For Míchel and Butragueño, by contrast, the team that really destroyed them was Guus Hiddink's PSV Eindhoven. 'It was not that Milan pushed us aside, it was that they pushed everyone aside,' Míchel says. 'And when they beat us too, we were already wobbling.' By the time Madrid faced Milan in 1989, he says something had already been broken on the inside; failure had eaten away at them.

In 1986–7, Madrid were knocked out at the semi-final stage by Bayern Munich: beaten 4-1 in the first leg, this time there was no *remontada*, a solitary Carlos Santillana goal securing a futile 1-0 win. In 1987–8, they were knocked out by PSV Eindhoven, again at the semi-final stage. In 1988–9, they reached the same point only to be beaten 5-0 at San Siro by Milan. The following year they met Milan again, this time in the last sixteen, and went out once more.

One of the reasons European failure mattered so much was that by then winning the league was not enough. Spain was too small, the domestic title too easy; continued success served to undermine that very success in the minds of fans who had come to take it for granted, Míchel being moved to note: 'we should stop winning the league so that they value it.' His opinion has not changed greatly. 'We won three or four in a row and people criticised us because there was no emotion, no fight, no epic. They wanted more: the European Cup.' He in particular was a victim, a player of touch and technique more than temperament, he felt forever in the firing line: a team-mate describes him as living a 'constant torture' and he once admitted: 'it's reached the point that the referee whistles and I think it's the fans whistling me.'

'We reached four successive semi-finals. First against Bayern, then PSV, then Milan. We should have gone through the first two and won the European Cup, especially against PSV. We were the better team; we drew in Madrid 1-1 and then drew 0-0 away. That was our chance,' says Butragueño sadly. 'Then Milan turned up and they were a better team than us, tactically and physically. That did not hurt so much. They created a dynasty: they played four finals in five years. But the previous two, we felt like we blew a great opportunity. If you lose against Milan you think: "hey, kid, it happens". But when it is a team that is not better than you . . .

'That night in Eindhoven was just terrible, without doubt the worst night in my career. It was devastating. When I joined Madrid, the desire to win the European Cup was palpable. The last time had been 1966; we're talking about 1988, twenty-two years later. We beat Napoli, with Maradona; Porto, who were the reigning European champions; Bayern Munich, finalists the previous season. And then in the semi-final we were favourites. When you're a player sometimes you know it's your moment – and that was ours. We were an extra-ordinary team; we had veterans that were near to retirement but still in great shape and contributing. We, the young players, had been there for three years. We had Hugo at his peak, Gordillo was playing. It was a great side. It was our time.'

So what happened?

'Hans Van Breukelen happened.' The mere mention of the PSV goalkeeper sticks in Butragueño's throat. 'In Madrid, we played badly.

Away in the second leg, we were clearly better than them. We had five or six clear chances but he was splendid. That year we failed to score in just two games out of sixty-odd and one of them was there.' PSV were experts: defensive, dull and astonishingly effective. They went through to the quarter-finals on away goals after drawing 1-1 away at Bordeaux and 0-0 at home; against Madrid the results were exactly the same and they won the final 6-5 on penalties after a 0-0 draw with Benfica. It summed them up. Five games, two goals, no wins and they were European champions. Madrid got nothing.

'We have just knocked out the best team in Europe,' Hiddink said after the semi-final. Míchel sat on the toilet sobbing. As they flew back they heard a call for a flight to Australia: 'Let's get that one instead,' Butragueño said to Sanchís. He was only half joking. Madrid returned to win the league but the players had little appetite for celebrating. They felt they had failed. Madrid's most talented team in a quarter of a century left without the trophy that would have immortalised them, reinforcing their superiority over their great rivals, just two years after Barcelona had blown their own big chance against Steaua Bucharest in the 1986 final. Instead, it would be their rivals, slowly finding their feet and building an artistic, epoch-defining team of their own, who reached that summit first in the modern era.

'PSV created a conflict of identity in us so great that that's where we disappeared, or at least where the decline began,' remembers Míchel. 'I don't know if it killed us but it took us out of circulation. No one likes to talk about, "luck" or "last minute" or what might have been, but in that European Cup you can't help it. We didn't do anything badly. *Anything*. Van Breukelen saved one in the last minute but the thing is he had saved ten like that. We went out. Why? I don't know. Did we do anything wrong? No. We really didn't. There was no explanation. And that destroys you emotionally.'

So did other factors. Míchel reels them off: 'there were lots of changes of coach . . . players . . . signings . . . money was wasted . . . then there was no money . . . and we were alone, completely alone.

When we lost against PSV we started a decline and the people whose job it was to make sure that there wasn't total collapse didn't do so.' He then adds something with which Johan Cruyff, Bobby Robson and Louis Van Gaal, long-suffering coaches at the Camp Nou, might disagree: 'At most big clubs when you don't win everyone pushes in the same direction, but Real Madrid is different – it is a far more difficult, far more complex club than Barcelona. There are cynical interests, you almost wonder if there are people who want to lose for their own benefit . . .'

Certainly, there were internal battles and political manoeuvrings behind the scenes. Beenhaker had been replaced by John Toshack not long after leaving Butragueño out, prompting president Ramón Mendoza to warn him: 'you're playing with our patrimony.' Half the stadium, he warned his coach, had come to see *El Buitre*. Johan Cruyff, the Barcelona manager, stuck his oar in: 'in my team,' he said, 'it would always be Butragueño and ten others.' Toshack's relationship with the squad was hardly idyllic. He later described meeting Sanchís as 'one of the great disappointments of my life'. Toshack also complained: that he 'sweated more on the bench than some players do on the pitch', prompting Paco Gento's nephew, the defender Julio Llorente, to respond: 'he sweats more because it's hot . . . and because he's fat.' One player describes Toshack as 'a magnificent coach who came across badly'; another told the media that the one thing the squad couldn't do was 'silence the mister with a pistol'. Some of them would not have minded.

Yet Toshack was an effective and talented coach. Under him, Madrid won the 1989–90 league in style. It was the culmination of a brilliant cycle, the fifth season for the Quinta. Hugo Sánchez called it 'the best version of a team that marked an era'. It was also a team that had become more aggressive, and more expensive, as Mendoza sought the European Cup Madrid so desperately craved, with Fernando Hierro, Bernd Schuster and Sánchez now at the forefront. This was the least *Quinta* of the Quinta teams, but still astoundingly talented. 'We had an ambitious dressing room that had made the spirit of Juanito and Camacho our own,' Gallego says. They lost just two games – 3-1 at the Camp Nou and 2-1 at Anoeta against Real Sociedad – and they steamrollered teams, winning the league with five weeks to spare. They scored 107 goals, a new league record, and Hugo Sánchez reached thirty-eight – equalling Telmo Zarra's all-time benchmark. Thirty-eight goals, all of them scored with a single touch.

But for some players on the inside, the sense of decline lingered. It was inescapable. Meanwhile, on the other side of Spain's footballing divide, something was shifting. Madrid's dominance had not diminished the rivalry. Not least because Real Madrid's new president, Ramón Mendoza, who had come into office in 1985 and remained there for a decade, had no intention of letting it be diminished. A man who had made his fortune in Russia, accused of having connections with the KGB, Mendoza stood out more for his luxuriant hair, cigars and outspoken manner. He was, says Valdano, 'one of those men who didn't knock on the door before coming in.' A president who thought nothing of TV cameras filming him leaping up and down with the *ultras*, chanting anti-Barcelona songs, boinging away as they sang: 'whoever doesn't bounce is a *polaco*.'

Mendoza took Barcelona on at every turn, despite being friends with Gaspart and having initially signed a non-aggression pact with the Catalans in which they promised not to muscle in on each other's signings and to work together on issues such as TV rights and merchandising. He always claimed that one of his most enjoyable moments was winning the 1989 Spanish Super Cup against Barcelona and going on a lap of honour of the Camp Nou, and hinted at the fact that the rivalry was part invention, a profitable pantomime that was good for the clubs. He spoke openly about the value of promoting the idea that Barcelona were copy cats, moved by jealousy and bitterness. He wanted to create, as he put it, 'a sporting story that works'. Madrid and Barcelona were two superpowers and Mendoza insisted: 'that means we have to both have the nuclear bomb. You have to have missiles: you can't combat permanent terror or blackmail with your hands behind your back.'

When the Barcelona president, Josep Lluis Nuñez, told Mendoza that he did not like going to the Bernabéu, Mendoza responded: 'they don't exactly chuck flowers at me at the Camp Nou.' Going there, he said, 'was like going to the battlefield to inspect your troops'. In his memoirs he wrote: 'I'd had enough of the fact that they always talked about Madrid as the regime team: that really wound me up because Real Madrid have always been a hugely popular team under any regime. I couldn't accept their constant envy. They always had the advantage in manipulating [the arguments] with nationalist feeling. If there was a penalty, a simple penalty, in favour of Madrid, they would be talking about the oppression of Catalonia, about the regime team, about centralism and the lack of liberty . . . Madrid and Barcelona are two cities, two worlds.'

Those worlds were about to collide. Madrid had the chance to prevent their rivals' rise, but they could not. Instead, their rivals consummated Madrid's decline and, unlike Madrid's greatest team in a generation, Barça *would* win the European Cup. Real Madrid and FC Barcelona met in the final of the Copa del Rey in April 1990, a repeat of the 1983 final. Madrid were favourites, while Barcelona's coach, Johan Cruyff, in the job since May 1988, was under intense pressure. He had won the Cup Winners' Cup in his first season but the Copa del Rey was his only chance of winning anything in the second. 'Johan was a revolutionary,' recalls Luis Milla, the Barcelona midfielder who later left for Madrid, 'but after two years the club wanted to see something. A title. That final was vital for him to continue.'

Lose and Cruyff would be out of a job. 'On the inside, who knows if Cruyff was shitting himself,' recalls one player of that final, 'but on the outside, the tranquillity was startling. There was no panic at all. Barcelona could have finished out of Europe for the first time ever and he could have been out of a job but he barely flinched.'

Fernando Hierro was sent off just before half-time; Real Madrid full-back Chendo accused the referee of needing Barcelona to take out a gun and shoot Butragueño for him to give a penalty; Aloísio Pires took out Sánchez, only to injure himself; and Guillermo Amor scored for Barcelona. So, in the ninety-second minute, did Julio Salinas. Barcelona won 2-0 and their goalkeeper Andoni Zubizarreta was hit by a missile during the celebration, which split his head open. Afterwards Chendo sniped: 'this cup has been won by a foreign team.' Mendoza made him apologise, which he reluctantly did, explaining: 'I won't accept anyone insulting me by calling me Spanish.'

Cruyff's job was safe; Madrid's collapse was about to become complete. PSV and Milan had started the job; now an emerging and brilliant Barcelona would finish it off. Míchel could see it coming. 'When Milan beat us, you look back on the lost chances: on Bayern and PSV and them. You know it is your time to go. We didn't make it in the end because we were mentally weak. We were already wobbling: we didn't need to be pushed that hard. You look back on the European Cup, and you think "shit". We didn't get there. And then, suddenly, on top of it all a super team appears that tips you over the edge.'

15

DREAM TEAM

Joan Gaspart undid his belt, pulled down his trousers and took a deep breath. It was nearly five o'clock in the morning. He knew the time because he could see Big Ben from where he stood in garish swimwear, a Barcelona shirt and nothing else. Slowly, he started off down the stone stairs, treading uneasily, until he got to the bottom. Up on the road above, a crowd gathered, peering down and wondering if he was actually going to do it. Photographers had followed him all the way there and two friends joined him, one wearing a Barça scarf to go with the trunks. Reaching the bottom, Gaspart paused, poked out a toe and then ducked under the surface, briefly disappearing into the filthy green water of the Thames.

'I didn't find out until later that the river has an incredible under-current,' Gaspart says, looking back on that moment twenty years later. 'It wasn't especially cold but it was dirty and afterwards I was told that it's dangerous. You can get dragged in and vanish until, a few centuries later, they find your body. Well, your skeleton.' Back at the top, towels were waiting and so was his taxi. 'The driver asked if I wanted to go for breakfast with the Queen. He probably thought to himself: "some madman goes swimming in the Thames at 5 a.m.? I wonder what else takes his fancy? Why not pop to the Palace?" I said: "No thanks, I'm soaking." The driver could see we weren't drunk and we were being followed by cameramen but he didn't turn round once. I never even introduced myself.'

If he had done, he might have told the cabbie that he was the vice-president of FC Barcelona and that he was honouring a debt. He might also have told him that this was the greatest night of his life.

'I realise that the vice-president of Barcelona probably shouldn't be doing something like that,' Gaspart admits with a grin, 'but then I've always been a fanatic, since I was little. I'd promised to go swimming in the river if we won that night. I thought no one would remember but when I came out of the stadium there were coachloads of fans there and they were all knocking on the window making gestures.' Gaspart stops and does a diving action. 'I knew then that I couldn't get out of it. Besides, I don't regret it.'

Why would he? May the twentieth 1992 was the night Barcelona finally won the European Cup, beating Sampdoria at Wembley.

On the morning of the game *El Mundo Deportivo*'s cover ran with Hristo Stoichkov dressed in a London bobby's helmet, thumbs up, Big Ben behind him. 'The biggest day', read the headline. As if they needed reminding. Goalkeeper Andoni Zubizarreta recalls debates on the pitch the night before, Barcelona's players arguing how many steps there were up to the royal box. Others remember the silence on the team bus. Some retreated into their music, Pep Guardiola among them. The dressing room was so small that the kit man was forced to leave bags in the corridor and the players were practically sitting on top of each other, literally all in this together. Barcelona had arrived two hours before kick-off. The wait felt eternal. The striker Julio Salinas paced up and down, up and down. His team-mate José María Bakero talked a lot. But a lot was far less than normal. Immediately before the game, coach Johan Cruyff told his players '*salid y disfrutad*'. Go out there and enjoy it.

Enjoy it? There was no way they could enjoy it. The tension was too great. The winger Txiki Beguiristain talks about a pressure that was 'oppressive'. One newspaper declared them closer to *that* moment than they had ever been – closer than in Berne in 1960, closer than in Seville in 1986. But they had been expected to win those finals too, only to lose both, and no one could get them out of their minds. Seville had been just six years earlier and even if the players had gone, most of the staff remained. Fans were nervous. 'People stopped us on the street and told us they didn't want to experience another night like Seville,' defender Ronald Koeman remembers.

That night in Seville, 7 May 1986, was perhaps the greatest ordeal in Barcelona's history. There appeared to be no way they could lose. Their opponents, Steaua Bucharest from Romania, were playing their first ever final, the game was held at Sevilla's Sánchez Pizjuán meaning Barcelona were practically playing at home with 70,000 supporters setting up in the city, and they had luck on their side for once. In the semi-final a hat-trick from third-choice striker Pichi Alonso had seen them overturn a 3-0 first-leg deficit against Gothenburg, eventually going through on penalties. Goalkeeper Javier Urruticoechea, whose penalty save had won them the league the previous season, saved one and scored another, Víctor Muñoz took the decisive spot kick to send Barcelona into their second European Cup final twenty-five years later, and, as Muñoz celebrated, a delirious ballboy in a Barça tracksuit sprinted over, grabbed him by the arm and pleaded for his shirt. The ballboy's name was Josep Guardiola.

'People thought that we were going there to pick up the trophy, not to fight for it,' Ángel Mur junior, the club's physio and kitman, says. 'No one had heard of Steaua. We were in the hotel watching bus after bus go past full of Barcelona fans. The ground was ours, all ours.' According to many in Barcelona, the Romanians even offered to throw the game. The offer was turned down – not so much because it was deemed unethical as because it was deemed unnecessary. As Pichi Alonso remembers it: 'It was so clear that we would win: they had no reputation, no prestige. There were 47,000 in the stadium in Seville and 46,700 were Barcelona fans. *What the hell are they going to do?* Throw in enough ingredients and you create a brew that turns things against you. Unconsciously I think even we thought it was done.'

Seville was Barcelona's darkest hour: 'a terrible trauma, horrifying, desperately sad', in Gaspart's words, while Steve Archibald admits: 'It still haunts me to this day.' Manager Terry Venables says that he has 'never been so depressed'. 'I carry that pain inside of me; it will accompany me forever,' says the winger Lobo Carrasco. So bad is the hurt for Carrasco that he recently refused to travel to Bucharest for an anniversary event and subsequent successes have made it even harder to take: 'Every time I see Barcelona in a final a little devil leaps into my mind and tells me that we could have been the first . . . it's a *putada psicológica*, it fucks with your mind.'

A truly dreadful match ended 0-0. The Romanians never attacked. 'They didn't cross the halfway line for Christ's sake: they don't want to come forward and be free, they want to be the winners,' Archibald notes. And Barcelona never found a way through. '[Bernd] Schuster, our main playmaker in midfield, had already told us he was leaving straight afterwards,' remembers Pichi Alonso. 'We thought he was joking but he said his wife had arranged a private plane. "What about the celebrations?" *Fiestas, cojones*. Parties, bollocks to that.' As it turned out, Schuster fulfilled his threat. Substituted on eighty-five minutes, he walked straight out of the stadium without a word and climbed into the back of a taxi. In open conflict with Barcelona for his actions, he did not play a single game the following season and in 1988 he left for Real Madrid.

When it got to penalties, the pressure was intense yet Barcelona still thought they had a chance: they had Urruti after all and they'd reached the final thanks to a shootout. This was opportunity and responsibility wrapped into one. Score and Barcelona's players would be heroes forever; miss and . . . well, what would happen was what did happen. Schuster was off, Archibald was off; there were no penalty takers left; tiredness and frustration had taken a hold. 'There was,' remembers Pichi Alonso, '*a desbandada*, a desertion. Suddenly everyone disappeared. Whooosh! Gone. No one wanted to take a penalty. Terry said: "Pichi?" I said okay. I should have said: "tell your mother to take one! I've been warming up for one hundred minutes, waiting, I'm pissed off, you can't ask me to take one." But of course I think we can win; I think we can still be heroes. But I'm invaded by doubts . . . and I took an awful penalty.'

Alonso was not alone. No one could score in ninety minutes, no one could score in thirty minutes more and no one, it seemed, could score from the penalty spot. Steaua Bucharest won the final 2-0 on penalties. Urruti saved two, but Helmuth Duckadam saved all four he faced. Not so much because he made brilliant saves but because Barcelona took such bad penalties – 'piss poor' in Archibald's words. After the final, the goalkeeper disappeared for two years. Rumours circulated that he had been given a car by Real Madrid but the truth was more depressing: a thrombosis pushed him into retirement and, penniless, he was forced to sell the gloves he wore that night. All he has left from the final is a tatty poster taken from a magazine.

Analysed coldly, Barcelona's achievements under Terry Venables between 1985 and 1986 were huge: they had won a first title in eleven years and then reached the final in Seville, losing only on penalties. But it did not feel that way. 'The European Cup would have reinforced the league title, given it value; by not winning the European Cup, we threw mud over the league title,' one player says. 'We broke an eleven-year drought but it is the final that everyone remembers,' says another. The passage of time has eased the pain – in 2011 the club paid homage to that team on the twenty-fifth anniversary of winning the title and most of the players insist that now, at last, the good is remembered with the bad. But at the time, the sensation was the opposite.

'What should have happened is that the team that won the league and reached a European Cup final should have been lauded and encouraged to go on,' says Archibald, 'but that's not what happened. It should have been the start of something. We were just a penalty away from winning the European Cup but there was no proper clear thinking.' 'Once we had lost people were looking for someone to shoot,' says Mur. 'That final killed everyone.'

Barcelona could not have been offered a better opportunity finally to stand up to Real Madrid. They did not take it and it hurt. The man who missed the final penalty was Marcos Alonso, the son of the former Real Madrid central defender Marquitos. 'That final scarred us. I missed the last penalty. After Seville, I went a long time . . .' he says, his voice trailing off, the sentence left unfinished. Then he adds: 'That was a chance to say to my dad: "look, Dad, I've got one too. We've won the European Cup as well. Yes, you've got five, but I've got one now." And in the end, I couldn't.' A banquet had been arranged at the Alfonso XIII hotel in Seville after the game. Three hundred people were there; every coach Barcelona had ever had was invited. But there was not a sound. Venables remembers being 'virtually ignored'. Archibald describes it as 'brutal . . . nothingness', Marcos Alonso as 'just horrible; everyone was *dead*'.

The pain of Seville hung over Barcelona; it was still there in the Wembley dressing room in 1992, lingering. The pressure, the weight of history. *Salid y disfrutad*. 'You knew what Cruyff meant: there might not be another chance and we had to make the most of it,' Danish forward Michael Laudrup recalls. 'We were part of the occasion: it's far worse to lose a semi-final than a final. He wanted us to relax and play, to forget all that. That was the right thing to tell us. But we couldn't go out there and enjoy it because we wanted to win so much.'

Striker Julio Salinas admits: 'We were all *cagados*, shitting ourselves. We couldn't enjoy it until afterwards.'

Sampdoria played with nine men behind the ball, looking to catch Barcelona on the counterattack. And although Stoichkov hit the post and Salinas missed a wonderful chance – 'it should have been my boots in the club's museum,' he says – the Italians were dangerous on the break. Albert Ferrer man-marked Roberto Mancini, Gianluca Vialli missed two good chances, but there was no way through and no goals. Laudrup puts it simply: 'it wasn't a good game.' The match went into extra time. Barcelona had hit the post, as in 1961, and now they seemed to be heading for penalties, as in 1986. *Not again*. Down on the bench Txiki Beguiristain was fretting: 'We can't, we can't, no, no, no . . . we just can't. We'd had chances and wasted them and you think: "shit, this can't be".'

But then, in the 111th minute, Eusebio Sacristán was fouled just outside the area. A free kick. Stoichkov rolled it, Bakero stopped it and Koeman hit it hard and straight. The wall opened and the ball speared through. As the headline in *El Mundo Deportivo* had it the following morning: 'Minute 111: Koooooooooeman!' 'Every year people call me to ask if I remember it,' Koeman says, 'how could I ever forget it?' He was off and running before the ball even hit the net; he could see it heading into the corner.

On the bench, they couldn't. 'It's a moment, a feeling,' says Beguiristain. 'You can't actually see anything.' At the other end of the pitch, nor could Zubizarreta. For Barcelona's keeper, the most important goal in the club's history arrived in three stages. He starts to visualise it. 'I can see Ronald take it,' he says. 'I can see the wall move and the ball disappear behind it. Then I can see the stadium go up . . . That's when I knew it was in; I didn't see the ball, I saw the fans. I heard them too.'

So did Gaspart. Barcelona's vice-president had left his seat in the directors' box in the first minute, walking out of the stadium, unable to take the tension. He kept on walking for forty-five minutes and then headed back, reckoning the final whistle would arrive about the same time he did. But the nerves made him walk faster and when he returned there were fifteen minutes left of the ninety and then extra time. Still terrified, the game still in the balance, he locked himself in the toilet, too scared to watch. When the ball hit the net he could tell from the direction of the roar that it was Barcelona who had got the goal. Seconds later a policeman hammered on the door: 'You've scored, you've scored.'

Gaspart was still not coming out. 'There were eight minutes left and they were eight very tense minutes,' remembers Beguiristain. 'But Cruyff transmitted real calm and the goal changed everything. Now it's different. You think to yourself: "Bloody hell, we're close." The delirium of the fans, the madness, the atmosphere. And that immediate fear has gone. You've eliminated the risk. You're scared of them taking the victory from you but you're not *right* on edge any more. Even if they do score now, there's still penalties, you still haven't lost.' Eventually, the final whistle went and the policeman came running back to tell Gaspart that it was all over. 'I was able to go out and watch [José Ramón] Alexanco lifting the European Cup for the first time in our history.'

First, though, a change. Barcelona had played in orange. *Orange.* Now they pulled their traditional *blaugrana* shirts over the top. 'I don't know whose idea that was: probably Charly Rexach or Cruyff's,' remembers Mur. 'We didn't take the shirts to be able to do that: we took them because we had to have them. I always take all the kit just in case, it wasn't a question of: *we're going to win, let's take these.* But changing was the right thing. That kit has a sentimental value. It's important you keep your identity and that comes from the colours. I remember one time Barcelona went out in white shirts – to warm up, eh, we're not even talking about white shirts to play in – and there were whistles. *Off! Off! Off!* It was some friendly, I think, I can't remember, and we had to change our shirts *por cojones*, just because. Bloody hell, of course! You don't change colours. Not for money, not for anything. No. Never. Your colours are what you are.'

Barcelona are what they are now because of Wembley; no game has ever been so important for the club. Long after the final whistle had gone, after the visits to the dressing room had ended – 'it gets pretty tiresome after a while, all these people pretending to be your friend,' one player admits – Mur sneaked back out on to the pitch and pulled out a chunk of the turf, placing it in the makeshift museum he built over generations in the Camp Nou dressing room. When Wembley closed for redevelopment, Barcelona spent 4.5 million pesetas at an auction, buying up what for them were virtually religious relics, from the goalposts to the team benches and even seats from the royal box, mementos of the place where they had been born again.

'Normally after a game like that you go crazy,' recalls Laudrup. 'But after Wembley we didn't. The players were all there, their wives too, but we just had a couple of glasses of wine and went to bed. Maybe it was just relief more than anything else.' Charly Rexach, Barcelona's assistant coach that night, calls it a 'liberation'. 'There were lots of people waiting for us to screw it up again,' he says, 'and the feeling was, man, we've won it now. It might be only one but we've done it. Another life starts. We were released.' Or to put it in the words of the man whose family had been the guardians of Barcelona for sixty-six years: 'I want you, I want you, I want you . . . I've got you!' That, says Mur, was just the greatest feeling. 'The responsibility was colossal. It was an obligation, the pressure was huge. I didn't enjoy it, but afterwards the sense of release was enormous.'

A celebratory dinner was held, a huge event with countless people invited. The 1986 team was among them but the contrast was cruel. The team from Seville had been given the worst table of the lot – behind a pillar. Pichi Alonso recalls that night: 'Look what we could have been and look what we are. We could have been the first to lift the European Cup, which would have been historic. When I went on in Seville the substitute goalkeeper grabbed me. He could see that I was pissed off but he said to me: "score and you'll be in the museum for ever, the most important person in the club's history." I did but it was ruled out. And then we lost. That defeat marked us out. Berne, Benfica, the posts and all that . . . Seville was another chapter, only even crueller. We were *el equipo maldito*.' The damned.

The 1992 team broke the curse. César Luis Menotti, coach when Diego Maradona was at the club, had always talked of Barcelona's *urgencias históricas*. That paralysis finally seemed to have been cured.

Barcelona's European Cup success in 1992 put them level with Aston Villa, who also had one. Madrid fans joked that Barcelona had won two European Cups – their first and their last – and crowed that they were miles behind Madrid who were on six at the time. Barcelona fans countered that at least they had won it in colour. Now they could begin. 'Until 1992, Barcelona were a small club,' admits Beguiristain. 'It had always been a great club because of its size and what it represented, because of forty years of dictatorship and that unique identity. But Bayern Munich, Milan, Liverpool . . . they had I don't know how many European Cups. Madrid? You can't even start counting theirs. We didn't have one. Wembley changed everything. It was a liberation, a sense of *at last*. It was overcoming Seville. That had been trauma, trauma, trauma. No one who had been in Seville could forget it, but something new was set in motion: now instead of Seville, fans remember Wembley and Paris and Rome and Wembley again.'

For Gaspart, it went back further. He had been in Berne at the Square Posts Final in 1961; thirty-one years later he had been in a toilet. 'Wembley finally meant removing that thorn from our side,' he says. After the game, Cruyff announced: 'that was for ninety years of suffering.'

Twenty-five thousand fans had travelled to London and millions watched the game on television in Catalonia. According to Barcelona's municipal police, when Barcelona returned to the city over a million people were out on the streets to greet them. The significance started to sink in. Barcelona's players gathered on the balcony of the Plaça San Jaume, *senyeras* waving. Stoichkov grabbed Jordi Pujol, the president of the Catalan parliament, and made him bounce up and down as supporters chanted. The fact that this was the same balcony from which Josep Taradellas had announced his return to Catalonia after exile in 1978 was not lost on some of Barcelona's players and the symbolism of the moment certainly did not escape Pep Guardiola. Lifting the European Cup, Guardiola offered the trophy to the fans below, choosing his words carefully. The association was immediate.

'*Ciutadans de Catalunya,*' he announced, '*ja la tenim aquí!*' Citizens of Catalonia, now we have it here!

Nineteen ninety-two was Barcelona's year. That was *the* year and that was *the* team, one against which all others would be judged. The Olympic Games, held in Barcelona that summer, were the showcase for a dynamic, modern, successful city, confident, artistic and international. The Games symbolised a new era and, although only 18 per cent of the funding had come from the Generalitat, the rest of the public money provided by central government, polls showed that by July 50 per cent of people saw them as a Catalan success while only 14 per cent credited the Spanish state. The Generalitat had funded a six-hundred-million peseta media campaign that described the Games as taking place 'in Catalonia, a country within Spain with its own culture, language and identity', while Jordi Pujol explicitly advised: 'the more the Games are Catalanised, the more they will appear as something Catalan.'

The Olympics seemed to reflect a new rapprochement too, a kind of Catalan–Castilian harmony; the opening ceremony brought Spanish and Catalan anthems and symbols together. 'We have proudly recovered a plural Hispanic identity,' announced Pasqual Maragall, the city's mayor. Fermín Cacho's victory in the 1,500 metres was roared on by the crowd at Montjuic, while Spain's Olympic football team won gold when Atlético Madrid striker Kiko scored the ninetieth-minute winner against Poland. European champions Pep Guardiola and Albert Ferrer, both of them Catalans, were in the Spain team on that warm night in August. When the goal went in, the Camp Nou, a stadium that had seen just five Spain international matches before, in 1960, 1963, 1969, 1980 and 1987, and has yet to see one since, erupted. Spain flags were everywhere.

But the team that most marked that Olympics was American. For the first time, basketball at the Olympics welcomed the professionals; for the first time, fans would see Michael Jordan, Magic Johnson and

Larry Bird together, the most ludicrously talented team in history. Unstoppable, gifted, oozing class and confidence. Different. They were called the Dream Team. The name was quickly applied to FC Barcelona. There was a kind of symmetry to it; it fitted somehow. It was not just that Barcelona finally won the European Cup in 1992, it was that they won four consecutive league titles between 1990–1 and 1993–4 having never won more than two in a row before and having won just two in the previous *thirty-one* years, claiming a solitary title since Franco's death sixteen years earlier. It was also the *way* that they did it, changing the club's identity.

When Johan Cruyff took over as coach at Barcelona in 1988 they were a club in debt and in crisis. Results were bad and performances worse, the atmosphere terrible and attendances down, while even the relationship between the president of the club, Josep Lluís Nuñez, and the president of the 'nation' they represented, Jordi Pujol, had deteriorated. The relationship between Nuñez and the players was even worse. In April, the Mutiny of the Hesperia had broken out. The scandal started when Bernd Schuster's contract was leaked by his agent, Jacint Soler, because of an ongoing legal battle that went back to his walkout following the 1986 final. The leak revealed that Schuster, like a number of other Barcelona players, had part of his wages paid as image rights as a means of avoiding higher tax rates. When Spain's Inland Revenue investigated and demanded back payment, the players insisted that it was the club's responsibility, sparking a public battle.

On 28 April, led by captain José Ramón Alexanco, Barcelona's players sat before the media in the Hesperia Hotel. Only three members of the squad did not sign the statement or attend the meeting: Francisco López López, who was recovering from an operation; Gary Lineker, who was on international duty with England in Hungary; and Schuster, who had already prepared his departure for Real Madrid. In a statement that talked of 'the values of this club which have always represented the idiosyncrasies of the Catalan people', Alexanco and his colleagues called for the resignation of the president. Coach Luis Aragonés backed his players, believing he had no other option. The result was effectively a purge. Muñoz was the first to go. Pichi Alonso and Lobo Carrasco were not far behind him. In total, thirteen players departed and by the end of the exodus there were just nine members of the squad remaining while Aragonés walked too, his position untenable.

Cruyff's appointment as coach was announced on 4 May, coinciding with Español's first appearance in the UEFA Cup final, meaning that Barcelona's city rivals *still* did not occupy the front pages. The Dutchman had not been Nuñez's first thought but he was a popular choice. A populist one too – a remedy to the crisis, a shield behind which the president could hide. Among Cruyff's first decisions was to keep captain Alexanco at the club, contradicting Nuñez's determination to force him out as the ringleader of the mutiny. The following summer Lineker departed, despite his popularity with fans and having scored in three *derbis*, including a hat-trick on his debut. José María Bakero and Txiki Beguiristain, signed from Real Sociedad, were joined by Ronald Koeman from PSV Eindhoven, Michael Laudrup from Juventus, and then Hristo Stoichkov from CSKA Sofia.

Koeman ended up scoring the most important goal in Barcelona's history and Laudrup was impossibly elegant, the Magic Johnson of Barcelona's Dream Team, all clever assists without looking and soft touches. As for Stoichkov, Carrasco described him as the best forward in the world, a striker who could 'run like Carl Lewis, pass like Ronald Koeman, and finish every bit as well as, or better than, Gary Lineker – and on top of it all, he's got *mala leche*.' *Mala leche* literally means bad milk; edge, a fearsome temper, aggression, competitiveness, a touch of madness. It is also exactly the point. Cruyff had focused on Stoichkov as much for his temperament as his talent. 'We needed him. We had too many nice guys.'

During his first ever game against Real Madrid, Stoichkov was sent off for stamping on the referee, who later called him 'an angel off the pitch but the devil himself on it'. A further red card came for two yellows – just six minutes into another game. During a pre-season friendly, a referee approached the Barcelona bench to warn Cruyff: 'either calm that bull down or I'll send him back to the *corral*.' Cruyff replied: 'what am I supposed to do?' 'If he'd been an actor, Stoichkov could have been Mel Gibson in *Mad Max*, Clint Eastwood in *Unforgiven* or Harrison Ford in *Blade Runner*,' noted one Catalan columnist – and the fans loved him for it. The willingness to embrace *barcelonismo*; the fact that he lived every match so intensely and boasted a hatred of Madrid so visceral, so public, that he once kicked a seven-year-old boy out of training when in charge of the Bulgarian national team because he turned up in a Madrid shirt, made him a hero. *La Vanguardia* hit the nail on the head when it declared: 'We're all Stoichkov; his story could be the story of the millions of Barcelona fans who are transformed when they come to the Camp Nou.' 'Every game against Madrid was life and death for me,' Stoichkov says himself, 'the injustices of the past became mine, too.'

If they look like obvious signings now they did not then and nor was joining Barcelona the natural career choice for all of them. 'It was the beginning of 1989 and Cruyff had been there for only six months,' Laudrup explains. 'Before him Barcelona were in chaos. In the door, out the door constantly – coaches as well as players. The last league they had won was in 1985 and they were running at a league every ten years or so, plus a cup here and there. I had seen the penalty shootout where they missed them all in Seville. And I came from Juventus. So, no, it was not an easy choice. Real Madrid were bigger. Much, much bigger. But Cruyff wanted me: he came to see me. I had always admired him and his style was my style.'

Persuading Hristo Stoichkov was a little easier. Rumour has it that the Bulgarian asked for just one thing: a red sports car.

He grins. 'Yes, correct,' he says in brilliantly idiosyncratic English. 'Red. Only red. I wanted a red car. I signed for that. Audi. I had a licence, but only Bulgarian so I couldn't drive it. But the first thing was: "red car".'

Do you still have a red sports car?

'Maybe one, yes.'

Cruyff changed every facet, from the style to the mindset, but he was under pressure. The Copa del Rey success against Real Madrid at the end of the 1989–90 season gave him a stay of execution. 'And after that,' the central midfielder Luis Milla concludes, 'they won four leagues in a row.'

The 'they' is well chosen. Milla left that summer for Madrid. 'Johan was a *grandísimo* coach but he acted like he was a director,' Milla says. 'I had a number of difficulties with him. I was twenty-three and I was aware of the potential reaction to me going from Barça to Madrid but you have to decide what's best. Fans do not want to see your reasons but I had them. When we didn't reach an agreement on contract negotiations, Cruyff left me out of the team and that ruined my chances of going to the 1990 World Cup. He thought he had to be tough and it turned unpleasant in the end. I left.'

Milla grins. 'And then Pep appeared in my place. It's not a bad swap for Barcelona!'

Pep Guardiola became Barcelona's metronome, the man who defined Cruyff's approach perhaps better than anyone else: intelligent and visionary, *different*. Few were talking about Guardiola as a potential star when Cruyff first saw him play for the B team, told the coach to switch Guardiola's position to the middle of midfield and then brought him up to the first team and put him in charge. But Cruyff was counter-cultural, imposing a new model throughout the club whose roots could be traced to Rinus Michels and whose continuity could be seen with future coaches Louis Van Gaal, Frank Rijkaard, Guardiola himself and even the Spanish national team.

Not that everyone is convinced. 'Everything is the work of God and God is Cruyff but Barcelona existed before Cruyff,' says Pichi Alonso. 'In fact, it was Terry Venables who invented the pressing game, for example.' This is an issue that eats away at Alonso's team-mate Steve Archibald; there's a tone of vindication as he insists: 'The system we used is still used now. We put a lot of pressure on the opposition, very high up. We were the first to do that. You'd think that Barcelona started with Cruyff, but we laid the foundations and won the league at last. We brought Barcelona out of the darkness, not Cruyff. It irks me that we are not recognised for that.'

There is, though, a 'Before Cruyff' and an 'After Cruyff'. In Barcelona's entire history before 1990, they won ten league titles and no European Cups; since 1990, they have won twelve league titles and four European Cups. Over the last two decades they, not Madrid, are Spain's most successful club. The victimism no longer makes sense. When Cruyff's Barcelona won their third successive title, the president Nuñez provided the prologue for a book entitled simply *Dream Team*. 'Barcelona,' he wrote, 'no longer live on edge, waiting on the results. We have forgotten the bad moments of the past.' Pessimism gave way to confidence, dynamism. 'I'm never afraid of making mistakes and I tried to put that idea on to the pitch,' Cruyff says. 'I told players not to be afraid: "if you have an idea on the pitch, good. Try it. And if it goes wrong, don't worry, we'll look at it afterwards".'

Cruyff gave Barcelona a new identity and a new discourse: a footballing one. It did not replace the socio-political discourse but it did complement it, deepen it and offer up an alternative – one actually grounded in the game, a kind of footballing puritanism. Laudrup explains some of the shifts: 'the defensive midfielder was always just another defender before but Cruyff changed that: it was Milla or Guillermo Amor or Pep – and now today we have Xavi. He played 3-4-3 because it made the angles better.' Laudrup lifts his hand to his chest. 'Chapi Ferrer was about this high', he says, 'Sergi was like this. Amor, Milla, Bakero, Beguiristain. I'm not good in the air, Stoichkov's not. It was a different idea, another way of looking at the game. It doesn't matter if you're 1.65 metres or 2.02 metres. Cruyff is the only coach who would say tactical things you had never heard before and you would think "oh, of course". *Oh, of course*?! Yeah, well, it might be logical but 90 per cent of coaches wouldn't say the same thing. Cruyff marked us all. Barcelona teams before him were different.'

Cruyff propagated an idea that few believed in at the time, even if there were some parallels with the Quinta del Buitre. As Beguiristain says: 'We thought that style was fine for Holland but that it couldn't be applied to Spain. And as for Europe, when you face Germans or Italians, forget it. How could you play with three at the back? But he was convinced. When there are doubts, people tend to seek safety in numbers, to go with the herd. Not Cruyff. He wasn't scared of *anything*. His first solution was always to be more attacking, more expansive. Three at the back and the centre-back is Koeman? Instead of full-backs, midfielders? Every time he wanted a solution, he attacked more. When he told us what he was doing, we thought: "is he mad or what?"'

How, then, did he persuade you?

Beguiristain laughs. 'Because he's Johan Cruyff!'

Cruyff insisted constantly on the importance of position and the speed at which the ball circulated. *Rondos*, piggy-in-the-middle exercises, became the central drill. Laudrup describes a typical week's training: 'Play Sunday. Monday relax. Tuesday off. Wednesday, forty-five minutes' running then a small passing and positioning game. Seven versus four, six versus five, three teams rotating. Friday, the same or maybe three versus three in a thirty-metre space. Saturday, forty-five minutes. Never a corner, never a free kick. It all required a certain level of intelligence and with every day that passed you could see the players get more comfortable in possession.'

Stoichkov tells a similar story about the Cruyffist indoctrination: 'The first week we played possession of the ball. I was always running. We played six versus two. I was running, running, running, always chasing the ball. Johan was saying: "Stop. You stay here, receive the ball, pass. Pass and move. One touch, two touch." But I was always chasing after the ball. He made me stop. I didn't understand anything. Luckily, I am a clever player and I learnt.'

He continues: 'The first two years of Cruyff in 1988 and 1989 prepared the team and changed the mentality of the players. The exact movement of the strikers and midfielders and defenders – everything is together. In one game I changed my position five times. Not because I wanted to but because it was necessary: sometimes I go on the right, Goiko on the left, or the other way round. Or I play number nine and Txiki goes on the left. If you do not have discipline it is impossible to play. When you lose possession, even the strikers come behind the ball, everyone pressures very quickly to get the ball back. No space. That was Cruyff's concept.

'We had some of the best players in history. Koeman, Michael. I never spoke on the field with Laudrup. I just had to look at him.

'*This*,' says Stoichkov theatrically doing a look, 'is long ball.'

'*This*,' he adds, doing another one, 'is short ball. It was very easy.'

But it is mention of Romário, the man Cruyff describes as the most talented he ever coached, that really makes Stoichkov's eyes light up. 'Romário is the best number nine in the world, that's the truth. And now he's going into politics!' he laughs with a kind of giddy admiration, disbelief.

'He was the best striker at the 1994 World Cup,' the Bulgarian adds, pausing for comic effect '. . . after me! I never tell him I got one more than him in 1994 but he stayed at my house, I put a DVD on. "Hey, look, my goal is better than yours." Romário was extraordinary, a superstar. In the box, with no space, he's better than anybody. Romário in the training sessions was like Messi is now.' In the training sessions he attended, that is. Early in 2013, Romário's son was starting to carve out a career for himself. 'I'll go to his matches,' Romário said, 'but I don't think I'll go to his training sessions. I mean, I didn't even go to my own . . .' His game was so natural, his talent so effortless, that it mattered little: with his wide hips, big, low-slung backside and powerful thighs, he was unique and deadly. Electric, precise, unpredictable, technically impeccable, no one had seen anything like him.

Romário's greatest moment came in January 1994 when Barcelona destroyed Real Madrid 5-0. For many, it was *the* emblematic Dream Team performance: a game of art and guile, a destruction of their greatest rivals in which Romário scored a hat-trick. One of the goals came after turning Rafael Alkorta so comprehensively it was a wonder the Basque centre-back didn't end up with his legs in a cartoon knot, twisted round each other, knees pointing out the back, hips snapped in two. Travelling almost full circle, Romário dragged the ball with him, his foot never losing contact with it, pulling it across the floor, gliding like a bowling ball on a varnished lane, before finishing with the outside of the boot. It became known as the *cola de vaca* – the cow's tail, s*wish, swish* – and it was forever associated with the Brazilian, forever associated with the destruction of Madrid. A piece of skill that could almost be the defining footballing image of the Dream Team but for the fact that there was another one too: at the end of the game, Toni Bruins Slot, Cruyff's assistant, raised his hand to the crowd. A *manita*, or little hand, one finger for every goal. 'That gesture,' *Marca* later wrote, 'stung more than the 5-0 itself.'

That season Romário and Stoichkov were a force of nature, blowing everything and everyone to bits. Yet there is something contradictory about their status in the club's history, particularly when it comes to the Brazilian. His emotional impact outstrips his empirical importance, his partnership with Stoichkov proving as brief as it was brilliant. Ask fans to name the best ten *blaugranas* in history, and many, perhaps even most, will include Stoichkov and Romário even though the Brazilian was not part of the Barcelona team that finally won the European Cup in 1992, didn't arrive until 1993 and was gone by January 1995. So intense is the reverence with which they are remembered that it seems somehow wrong to recall that Stoichkov and Romário actually only played together for just over a year.

But what a year. Fights. A kidnapping. A proud father. An even prouder godfather. A scandal. Paparazzi. Betrayal. Red cards. And some of the most fantastic football anyone can remember. A league title, won in the final minute of the final day. A historic thrashing of the eternal enemy. A European Cup final. And goals. Loads of them. More than fifty between them, Romário finishing the 1993–4 league season with thirty in thirty-three games, having scored a stunning five hat-tricks – one on the opening day, another against Real Madrid and another against Atlético Madrid, despite having two goals disallowed – and finishing his Barcelona career with fifty-three in eighty-two games.

When Barcelona signed Romário from PSV in 1993, league rules meant that only three foreigners could play and Barça already had Stoichkov, Koeman and Laudrup. 'Signing a fourth foreigner is plain stupid,' the Bulgarian snapped. It was classic Stoichkov: blustering, outspoken, emotional. 'When Hristo was on the bench,' one team-mate recalls, 'he could start a fight with his own shadow and when Hristo's angry, he's dangerous.' Cruyff adopted a rotation policy that satisfied no one – and neither Brazilian nor Bulgarian could take being omitted. 'I remember one time that Romário was left out and I couldn't even talk to him, he was in such a funk,' Stoichkov later said.

Yet if that threatened to cause problems, Romário and Stoichkov became best friends. 'Romário basically never spoke to anyone in the squad: he did his own thing on his own terms all the time,' remembers one team-mate. The only person he did speak to was Stoichkov. 'It seems bizarre and I ask myself even now how it was possible,' Stoichkov wrote in his autobiography. 'He was introverted and I was the reverse. He likes to sleep, I like to live. We were night and day. But we became good friends right from the start. We were inseparable.' Their kids attended the same school and their wives, Monica and Mariana, became best friends. They protected each other. When Romário got a red card for punching Diego Simeone, Stoichkov admiringly remarked: 'it was worthy of Mike Tyson.' And Stoichkov knew a thing or two about punching people: he had given a *paparazzo* a right hook when he invaded Romário's privacy following the birth of his baby boy, Romarinho. When Romário found out his father had been kidnapped, it was Stoichkov who offered support; when he found out that his father had been freed, it was Stoichkov he smothered in relieved kisses; and when it came to choosing a godfather for his son, Stoichkov was the obvious choice.

Even now, despite admitting that the relationship turned sour and that he did not like the crowd Romário fell in with, despite the lurid tales and tawdry accusations, Stoichkov is defensive of his team-mate. 'There was a lot of newspaper talk about Romário. Newspapers would write: "yesterday, I saw Romário at five o'clock in the morning." Bullshit. It's lying, man. I can tell you. People said Romário too much drink – Romário never drink, ever. In 1994 we won the league and after that we go to the Princesa Sofia [Hotel]. Twenty millilitres of champagne and he goes to hospital. And he says: "What happened? No more, no more!" He drinks, he doesn't sleep? *Please!*'

Together, Stoichkov and Romário were a devastating partnership. 'Hristo enjoyed that year with Romário more than any other,' says Josep María Minguella, Stoichkov's agent. The goals are a testament to that. From the day of the 5-0 onwards, Barcelona were unstoppable. They collected twenty-eight of their final thirty points to win the league on the final day, Barça's fourth consecutive title. Four days later, they would play their second European Cup final, just two years after Wembley.

'The Dream Team?' Stoichkov smiles. 'Those five years are the best I have ever experienced. For me, that was the best team ever.'

The best? The luckiest, more like. That's the Real Madrid counter-argument, anyway. 'The Dream Team is a myth,' snapped Madrid's president Ramón Mendoza, 'they should thank Tenerife.' Of the Dream Team's four league titles, three in a row were won on the final day and thanks to their challengers blowing it. Each time, Barcelona's destiny was not in their own hands; each time, they were gifted the league and often in unbelievable circumstances. Laudrup says he can think of two 'lucky' coaches: Fabio Capello was one, Cruyff was the other. 'By the third title won on the final day,' Andoni Zubizarreta smiles, 'we were convinced that Cruyff had something. Some magical power. There was no other explanation.'

Two years in a row, Madrid travelled to Tenerife on the final day of the season, knowing that victory would win them the league. Two years in a row, Madrid travelled to Tenerife and lost. Two years in a row, Madrid blew the league. Two years in a row, Barcelona were the beneficiaries. And two years in a row the man who handed it to Barcelona, the Tenerife coach who took the title from Madrid, was Jorge Valdano: *their* former player, a league and UEFA Cup winner with Madrid and a member of the Quinta del Buitre. After the first Tenerife victory denied Madrid the league, Valdano left the pitch and took refuge in the dressing room: 'I didn't want to be in that confusion; I didn't know what face to wear.' Valdano's assistant coach, Ángel Cappa, talks of a 'thousand-year coincidence'.

Madrid travelled to the Canary Islands on 7 June 1992. 'The drama,' says Valdano, 'was almost surreal.' After eleven minutes, Madrid 'knew' they would be champions and Barcelona 'knew' they would not: a Fernando Hierro header had made it 1-0 and eight minutes later Gheorghe Hagi scored Madrid's second from a thirty-yard free kick that flew in off the bar. They were 2-0 up and cruising to the title. It was all so clear that, as Beguiristain tells it: 'we had accepted the title was theirs. Then, it was 1-2. Then, suddenly, 2-2, then 3-2.'

'The first game was incredible,' admits Laudrup. 'I wouldn't say the Dream Team was the luckiest team ever but there is an element of truth in that. Even at 1-2, when Tenerife had got one back, Buitre had two one-on-ones to have won it for Madrid.' He didn't take them. Then it all changed. Ricardo Rocha scored an own goal and Madrid conceded possibly the most ridiculous goal in their history: Manolo Sanchís hit a back pass from just inside his own half, looping it high towards goalkeeper Paco Buyo, fifty yards away. The 'pass' was going wide but in his attempt to reach it, Buyo pushed it back on target, the ball running across the goal-line, and Pierluigi Querubino ran it in. 3-2.

When the final whistle went, Madrid's players broke down, sobbing. Tenerife's players were celebrating. A little too much, say some Madrid fans: two Tenerife players later claimed to have been given a special bonus to beat Madrid – the infamous *maletines*, or briefcases, the third-party payments that invariably do the rounds in the final weeks of the season in Spain. The bonus, twenty-one million pesetas, was allegedly paid by Barcelona.

Being paid to win is one thing; being paid to lose, another. Madrid midfielder Luis Milla later claimed to have received a call from someone at his former club Barcelona asking him to throw the game in return for forty million pesetas but Madrid never pressed charges, insisting that there was no point as they couldn't prove anything, and never revealed who made the call either.

When the fixtures came out for the following season, Madrid and Tenerife were again paired on the final day. Again, Madrid went into the match ahead of Barcelona, knowing victory would clinch the title. Cruyff had already publicly given up on the league and a few weeks earlier Laudrup had conceded the title following Barça's defeat against Tenerife. Yes, Tenerife. 'That's the thing people forget,' Cappa insists, 'we took the league off Madrid? No, we took the league off both of them. We beat Madrid *and* Barcelona that season and we were heading to Europe for the first time in the club's history.'

The previous season played on Madrid's mind. It was a stiflingly hot day in July and they'd travelled across to the Canaries squeezed into two tiny planes. They were, as one player puts it, 'crapping themselves'. Their results had been awful in the second half of the season and there was a fatalism about them. Madrid appealed for three penalties but without much conviction. They were defeated before they had even started, crushed by the symmetry of it all. Tenerife won 2-0. 'They could never win that game,' Beguiristain says. Somehow everyone *knew* that Madrid's second visit to what became known as the cursed island was bound to end in defeat. Afterwards, the president of the Generalitat announced: 'Tenerife deserve to be awarded the Cross of

Saint Jordi', while Guardiola promised to make them honorary *socis* of Barcelona. Tenerife were invited to the Camp Nou as opponents in the pre-season Trofeo Gamper, where they were given a colossal reception.

After that second defeat, Valdano promised: 'One day I will give back what I have taken away.' The following season, he had the chance when Madrid approached him and assistant Ángel Cappa to become coaches. Valdano admits that they felt 'obliged' to join, 'indebted' to Madrid and when they arrived they caught a glimpse from the inside of just how much damage those defeats had inflicted. 'The club was depressed as an institution: there was an organisational vacuum, a melancholy,' Valdano recalls. 'The Tenerife games were *brutal*,' adds Cappa. 'We had to encourage them to play football a bit, to tell them that they were actually good enough.'

'Sometimes great changes in humanity are provoked by a single loose bullet, a stroke of fortune,' Valdano says. And yet Madrid winger Míchel does not see it as a stroke of fortune; for all that his tears were among the bitterest, he sees logic in that lost league. 'The miracle was not Tenerife, it was that Madrid even got to Tenerife,' says Cappa, words that have Míchel nodding his head in sad recognition when they are repeated to him. 'That was always catalogued as a failure but we could already see that we were a car running out of petrol,' he says. 'I think we only won one game away from home in the whole of the second half of the season. I don't remember the date of the game. And we didn't use the referee as an excuse, even though his decisions were . . .'

Míchel puffs out his cheeks. *Bad*.

'It was not a one-off, a fluke; it was a trajectory,' he continues. 'That second title seems more dramatic than it was because it was Barcelona. But we were running on empty already. People say "Tenerife this, Tenerife that", but no one took anything off us that we weren't perfectly capable of taking off ourselves. In fact, it speaks well of us that the Dream Team had to win two leagues in the final minutes, because their team was absolutely superior to ours. That's the definition of Madrid: we took them to the line. And we won five titles, they won four. Maybe they didn't have a heart as big as ours. But they were a great team, an *equipazo*.'

Still a lucky one, though. Just when it looked as If it couldn't get any more ridiculous, it got more ridiculous. On the final day of the 1993–4 season, it happened again. This time, it was Deportivo de La Coruña who were Barcelona's competitors for the title. Barcelona were at home to Sevilla; Deportivo were at home to Valencia. Deportivo, who conceded just eighteen goals all season, looked set for a first ever league title. Universally popular, Depor had been top since December and although Barcelona had roared back at them, winning eleven and drawing two of their final thirteen games, including the 5-0 demolition of Madrid, the Galicians only needed to win or to match Barcelona's result.

Their opponents Valencia had nothing to play for. Only, they did. This was a game that created one of Spain's other rivalries: Deportivo and Valencia. When the two sides faced each other at Riazor the following season, fake bank notes rained down from the stands and in 2008 Depor's fans had their suspicions confirmed. Fernando Giner, Valencia's centre-back, admitted that his players had been offered a 'sizeable bonus' to win the match and hand the Catalans the title; it was, he conceded, 'bitter cash'. Four years after that, *El País* journalist Cayetano Ros tracked down three more members of that Valencia team who anonymously confirmed that they had been on a bonus, collecting fifty million pesetas in a motorwayside meeting the following week.

At half-time, Deportivo hadn't scored. Amazingly, Barcelona were losing 2-1. It didn't last long: soon Barcelona were 5-2 up and waiting, champions as long as Deportivo didn't get a goal. It was still 0-0 in La Coruña. The clock was ticking down. Agonisingly slowly in Catalonia; terrifyingly fast in Galicia. And then . . .

Andoni Zubizarreta sits in a small, modern office at Barcelona's

Sant Joan Despí training ground and dramatically throws his arms out, cutting through the air, halting everything.

Silence.

Barcelona's goalkeeper can still see the crowd, can still hear the air being drawn in, hearts in mouths. Zubizarreta looks around, recreating the moment. That silent search for news. Something is happening, but what? The league had banned clubs from relaying scores from other stadiums on their electronic scoreboards while the games were still in play. But up in the stands, thousands of fans had radios. Down on the Barcelona bench they were also listening. The impact on Zubizarreta was profound; the impact on his team-mates too.

'The stadium was roaring,' recalls Laudrup. 'And suddenly, in the eighty-ninth minute: *shhhh*. A hundred thousand people and not a sound. Everyone. We stopped! The players stopped! One of the Sevilla players had the ball and he stopped as well. *What the . . . ?!* We were running, then we sensed it and we stopped. What happened? A penalty? *Bloody hell, in the last minute . . .*'

Up at Riazor, Nando had been brought down. It was the last minute of the last day. Donato would normally have the responsibility but he had been taken off, Bebeto didn't want to take it and the Serbian international Miroslav Djukic didn't really want to either but said he would. He looked absolutely terrified. Deportivo's first ever title depended on him. It was a dismal penalty, weak and fearful, easily saved by José Luis González Vázquez. That the goalkeeper seemed to take such joy in saving it, leaping to his feet and clenching his fists, earned him the enmity of Galicia forever and the gratitude of Catalans. Down the wires it came, from the radio to the stands and from the stands to the pitch. Deportivo had missed their penalty, Barcelona would win the league. 'The noise!' remembers Laudrup. 'Bloody hell, they missed!'

Zubizarreta sits in suspended animation, then drops his arms: news of the title delivered to the players by the fans. He's laughing now, still incredulous. 'Roar! We couldn't believe it.'

'I was a sub that day,' recalls Beguiristain. 'The entire bench had gone down to the dressing room where there was a telly. We weren't even watching our game any more. When they got the penalty, *madre mía*. Three years in a row was just implausible, too much. *That's it, it's over*. And then when he missed . . . we threw ourselves to the floor in celebration. Some sprinted out, down the tunnel and up towards the pitch. It all hung on Djukic's penalty: the difference between being nothing and being everything. And then he missed it. Our style counted for something but we also know that without titles it does not have the impact. And three years in a row we won like that.'

He continues: 'There is something strange about Madrid embracing *remontadas* and last-gasp victories when you think about what happened in the 1990s. And yet while people say we were fortunate, which we were, we got into that position three years in a row and when the knife was up against our throats, we won. We won, they didn't. Djukic's penalty changed the mentality of everyone at the club: *that's it, we've done it. Four leagues in a row. Now we can do anything.* And it was just handed to us; it felt like everything would be handed to us. We didn't have to worry about anything. We got to Athens for the European Cup final and we thought: "it's done". We'll win this for sure. The truth is that we were knackered. Completely *fundido*, melted. But we felt invincible . . .

. . . too invincible.'

Four days later, Barcelona faced AC Milan in the European Cup final in Athens. Their second final in two years, 18 May 1994 was supposed to be the night the Dream Team became immortal but became the night the Dream Team died. Cruyff promised to end AC Milan's hegemony; AC Milan ended theirs. Four league titles and a European Cup, over. Just like that. After Athens, Barcelona didn't win another trophy under Cruyff.

Cruyff later insisted that there was 'no way' Barcelona could have won that final: they were too tired, emotionally and physically. Rexach makes much the same point now. And in the pre-match press conference Cruyff detected 'too much euphoria' surrounding the team. But he too had contributed to that. 'Barcelona are favourites,' he said. 'We're more complete, competitive and experienced than at Wembley. Milan are nothing out of this world. They base their game on defence, we base ours on attack.' If the intention was to infuse his squad with belief, it was Milan's players who claimed to take strength from what he said. 'Cruyff's words were inappropriate and really struck the team,' defender Alessandro Costacurta recalled. 'Had they not been, things might have been different.'

On the morning of the match, *El Mundo Deportivo* claimed that Barcelona were at their 'sweetest moment', against 'the poorest Milan of the Berlusconi era: Cruyff is a winner. [Fabio] Capello, by contrast, has not been up to the task internationally.' Gullit, Van Basten and Rijkaard had gone. Milan were without two of their back four: Costacurta and Franco Baresi. 'We weren't favourites,' Paolo Maldini recalled. Barcelona knew that. *Salid y disfrutad* became 'you're better than them and you're going to win'. The comedy show *Crakòvia* does a satirical sketch in which Cruyff's tactics board has no tactics, just a message: 'Barcelona, champions.' 'They had two of the back four out and Cruyff talked like we were favourites,' recalls Laudrup. Rexach is explicit: 'We didn't prepare properly for the game and we went there with no concentration. Athens was the beginning of the end.'

In every game, Cruyff had to choose one of his four foreigners – Romário, Koeman, Stoichkov or Laudrup – to leave out. Increasingly, he had chosen Laudrup, especially since the turn of the year when rumours had begun over the Dane's future. Working with Cruyff was hard. Laudrup believed that the Dutchman played the media and fans, seeking always to come out on top: 'he's right, he's right, he's right . . . but sometimes he is not right!' He also felt that Cruyff was never satisfied with his performances; too often Laudrup sensed the finger of accusation pointing his way. And twenty years later, he wonders if he might have come to understand the reasons.

'I play a good game: nothing. I play one bad game: *Michael! Michael! Michael!* I remember we played in Burgos once and I was sick. He said I had to play so I played but I was not myself. At half-time we were winning 1-0 and he took off me and Stoichkov. Afterwards I was shivering, ill, sitting there and someone came up to me and said: "hey, have you heard what Cruyff said?" What Cruyff had said was: "it's great that we won playing with nine men." I said: "oh, thank you!" Arsehole. Hristo was throwing up at half-time. I would play five good games and it would just be normal. I play two bad games and I'd read about it in the papers. He used to give me some great compliments: "even when Michael's only at 90 per cent he's the best but I want 100 per cent". That's very nice but it was always about the 10 per cent.'

Laudrup continues: 'Looking at it retrospectively, I'm not annoyed about what he said when I did things wrong; what I missed was him telling me when I did something good. For me, that was one of his biggest mistakes and I think I know why he did it because once he talked to me about the 1974 World Cup. I remember watching that World Cup: Holland were my favourite team and he was my favourite player. They had the ball but Germany won. He was marked all over the pitch by Berti Vogts and afterwards in Holland they said he had not played well and that was the reason they lost the final, even though he had been fantastic throughout the whole tournament. I think that message was still in his mind [as a coach]. He thought: "I don't have to tell great players when they are doing things well because they know, I have to tell them what they are doing badly." I have been thinking about it and I think he treated players like that because that's how he was treated. He was the best and no one said so. But when he wasn't they told him. And he transmitted that as a manager.'

In Athens, Laudrup was left out again. It was the final straw for him, a relief to Capello. Milan smothered the Barcelona midfield. Marcel Desailly dominated. Guardiola could not settle and Barcelona could not bring the ball out. Romário never saw it, nor did Stoichkov.

'It was not that we played badly,' Cruyff said afterwards, 'it was that we did not play at all.' Milan scored twice in the first half, Daniele Massaro getting them both. Two minutes into the second half Dejan Savicévić scored a glorious lob. 'When the third went in we knew it was over,' says Zubizarreta. 'That was the worst night of my career.' Eventually, it finished 4-0: the biggest ever winning margin in the final. So much for boring, defensive Milan. Massaro went up to collect his medal in Stoichkov's shirt – the Bulgarian was his hero. It was AC Milan's fifth European Cup; Barcelona still had one.

'It was dead in the dressing room' recalls Mur, 'dead, dead, dead. And just then, when the team needed support, they didn't get it.' Cruyff paced in silence, then left the room. Eventually, Zubizarreta spoke, reminding them that they had won the league – and that they could fight for it again the next season.

At about the same time, Madrid's president, Ramón Mendoza was changing his answer phone message. It now ran: '4-0, hello?'

Zubizarreta's optimism was misplaced. Barcelona did not fight for the title the following season and he didn't even get the chance to. Without him, they finished fourth, nine points behind Madrid. Tensions that had built before the final were brought to the surface, exacerbated by defeat. Asked why Barça collapsed so quickly in the wake of the loss, Rexach responds: 'We didn't manage to plan for the future carefully. We didn't succeed in regenerating the team bit by bit. We rested on our laurels and then when we tried to act there was a vacuum.' Hurt by the 4-0, Cruyff reacted badly; the renewal process was accelerated. Too quick.

For much of the season Zubizarreta had been assured that his future was secure but he hadn't yet signed a new deal. 'I kept asking Joan Gaspart: "Joan, is there news?"' he recalls. 'Three or four times I asked him. "Joan, have you got anything to tell me?" At breakfast: "Joan?" As we prepared to leave: "Joan?" He kept avoiding it but by the final I feared the worst.' Zubizarreta had been Barcelona's captain but, eventually, Gaspart admitted that Cruyff did not want him to continue. Zubizarreta was told as the bus crossed the runway towards Barcelona's plane home from Athens, a decision that had Guardiola in tears. The goalkeeper now had to tell his family. 'I got on the plane and said to my wife, who was already sitting there, "we're going".'

Zubizarreta was not alone. 'Three days before we were all *fenómenos*,' says Beguiristain. 'Salinas, Goiko, Zubi . . . now, they were all out on the street. You need to be better prepared to take those kind of decisions and Barcelona weren't.' Laudrup then admitted that he couldn't work with Cruyff any more. A few days after the final he announced that he was going to Real Madrid. He left behind a club that had started to collapse. Romário returned late from the 1994 World Cup, barely talked to his team-mates, fell out with Stoichkov, performed abysmally – 'some joked that the man in Barcelona was a lookalike,' the Bulgarian recalled – and was gone within five months. He was not the only one whose performances dipped after the 1994 World Cup, just as Laudrup and others had foreseen.

Meanwhile, the friction between Cruyff and Nuñez grew and the Dutchman found himself accused of nepotism, playing his son-in-law Jesús Mariano Angoy in goal and his son Jordi up front. Never mind that he'd turned down offers from Ajax, Liverpool, Atlético and even Real Madrid, or that he was kept on a youth-team contract, Jordi Cruyff found himself in the line of fire: 'people attacked my dad through me,' he remembers.

Barcelona finished the 1994–5 season empty-handed and were closing in on a second campaign without silverware when, on 18 May 1996, Gaspart went to the dressing room to look for the manager, amidst reports that Bobby Robson would be taking over at the start of the following season. Cruyff was waiting for him. Through the walls, the voices grew louder and the accusations more bitter. Soon everyone could hear the shouting. 'The players listened aghast,' recalled Rexach, 'the insults went back and forth, the tension grew and Cruyff even picked up a chair and threw it.'

In the midst of the row, Gaspart snapped. He sacked Cruyff on the spot.

Rexach was asked to take the team for the remaining two matches of the season. He was in an impossible position, recalls Mur: 'Cruyff expected Charly to go with him, they were *íntimos amigos*, but he had been at Barcelona all his life – Barcelona was his friend too.' Cruyff never forgave him. When Rexach phoned the Cruyff home, he was told that Johan did not want to talk to him. The split destroyed a friendship and almost destroyed the club too. Trenches were dug, another civil war started; Nuñez versus Cruyff, a divide that still exists. On 12 June, Cruyff formally denounced Barcelona for breach of contract. He wanted a hundred million pesetas, they offered seventeen million. It ended in court, something that the new Madrid president Lorenzo Sanz wasted no time in publicly gloating about.

That weekend, Barcelona beat Celta 3-2. Rexach took Jordi off with five minutes to go – a symbolic decision that had been agreed beforehand and one that, in his words, 'left the directors wanting to string me up'. As Jordi departed, the Camp Nou gave him a huge ovation in the name of the father, chanting over and over: *Cruyff! Cruyff! Cruyff!*

16

NUNCA POSITIFO

The final whistle goes on the first *derbi* of the 1994–5 season and a huge roar travels round the Santiago Bernabéu. The home fans still can't quite believe it. The scoreboard says: Real Madrid CF 5 FC Barcelona 0. Madrid have returned the *manita*. Hands are raised, fingers outstretched. Down the tunnel, up the stairs, teams divided by a solid metal fence, a cage that keeps the beasts apart, and left into the Madrid dressing room there is shouting and cheering, celebrations. Players embrace. One man wears his satisfaction more discreetly. New signing Michael Laudrup, architect of the victory, turns to Madrid's assistant coach Ángel Cappa and smiles. Then, softly, he says it: 'I won 10-0.'

'Michael was a guy who spoke quietly, always prudent, reserved,' Cappa remembers. But there it was. *Ten*-nil. A shift in power had just been played out in front of a packed stadium and no one symbolised that quite like the Dane. Barcelona beat Madrid 5-0 on 8 January 1994. Almost exactly a year later, on 7 January 1995, they met again, this time with Laudrup on the other side. Now Madrid beat Barcelona 5-0. Two *derbis*, two 5-0s, a ten-goal swing and Laudrup on the winning side both times. 'Laudrup was good but not *that* good,' grins Cappa, but the association never went away. Laudrup tells the tale: 'a few years ago I was at Valencia airport and a father comes up with his son. He tells his son who I am and tells him: "this guy was a great player". The son, who can't even have been born in '95, looks at me and says: "*Cinco-cero, cinco-cero.* 5-0, 5-0". I was left open mouthed.'

Iván Zamorano scored a hat-trick before half-time that night, Luis Enrique, later to leave Madrid for Barcelona, scored the fourth and José Emilio Amavisca the fifth. Laudrup made two of them. Hristo Stoichkov, who spent much of his time trading insults with Madrid's *Ultra Sur*, was sent off, and so was Toni Bruins, the assistant coach who signalled the *manita* the year before. 'A wind of change is blowing through Spanish football,' one report in the capital giddily put it. 'That magic number, five, the number that once symbolised Madrid's opprobrium, took shape. This is the end of an era.'

They were right too. Barcelona were collapsing and by the time the rivals came face to face again four matches from the end of the season, Madrid knew that a win would clinch them the league title at last. And what better place to end a five-year wait than at the Camp Nou? It was the first time Laudrup had returned to the Camp Nou in Real Madrid's colours – and he did so as the architect of the 5-0. He was whistled and booed throughout, insults flying his way, missiles too. His former team-mates flew into tackles. He had become the incarnation of the power shift and of the rivalry, the devil himself. It did not matter that he had moved as a free agent or had felt forced out of Barcelona, nor that he had personified his problems in Cruyff. Every time he got the ball, the noise rose, and the venom.

'Michael suffered because he didn't expect it, even though we warned him that it was going to happen,' Cappa says. 'The fans couldn't bear seeing him in someone else's shirt, least of all ours. We told him what to expect but he still couldn't take it. He was surprised that his [former] team-mates went in so hard and he couldn't under-stand it. He suffered *muchísimo*.' Banners declared him a traitor. One offered simple advice: *die*.

Barcelona won 1-0 and Laudrup was awful, lost and bewildered. There's still a sense of bewilderment about him now: it remains hard for him to understand. 'That is the only game in my career when factors other than strictly football [ones] influenced my performance,' he says. 'It was the third game from the end of the season and if we had won we would have been champions at the Camp Nou – for fans of either side there's nothing worse. But I still didn't think it would be so massive. My move was different from Figo's, for example: his was about money and he gave his word whereas I had reached the end of my contract and wasn't playing.'

'I remember being in a restaurant with Nuñez and Gaspart [Barcelona's president and vice-president], talking about the future. We were sitting upstairs and the media were downstairs. I thought: "This is a little strange: we can talk but why call them?" By then I had decided almost 95 per cent for sure that I was going to leave anyway but not necessarily to Madrid. I knew it would be hard to change sides and I asked myself: "how will they react?" I thought: "wouldn't it be easier just to go to England?" But I knew Spain and Spanish football and I liked it. I thought: "well, it's a huge rivalry but I was at Barcelona for five years, I did a lot for the club, I won four leagues and the European Cup, this and that." In a naïve way I think I thought that they would recognise that. I knew it would be hard, but not *that* hard.'

On the flight home after the match, Madrid's manager Jorge Valdano approached Laudrup. 'I realised tonight just how much they loved you,' he said.

No one hates a man quite like his jilted ex-wife. By his second trip to Barcelona, Laudrup was ready, no longer so wide-eyed; at the same time, Barcelona's fans had softened. Over the years, they would be softened further, melted by his decency and vulnerability. Now, rather than hatred, there's a kind of battle over ownership: the question Laudrup is asked most often is which team he identifies with. He's always careful how he replies. *Both, of course.* Now, he is welcomed in Catalonia. 'And you know what you were saying about the ex?' he smiles. 'Well, I've got an ex-girlfriend – and with time, everything is fine.'

Defeat in Barcelona meant Madrid had to wait to take the 1994–5 league title but only for a week. It had been theirs almost from the start – 'journalists kept saying to me: "I bet you want to get it over with, to get that title in the bag",' Cappa recalls, 'but I always replied: "no, I want it to carry on. I'm enjoying this".' – and was reinforced by the 5-0, which came just before the halfway stage of the season. Five years on, Madrid were champions again and Barcelona's run had been ended. Madrid finished four points ahead of Deportivo de La Coruña, nine above Barcelona, and they did it in style: 'We didn't just take the league off Barça, we took the ball off them,' Valdano insists. His team had left a mark.

So, especially, had Laudrup. His first season had been wonderful, clinching his fifth consecutive La Liga title, and although his second had not, no one forgot him. Madrid might not yet have been able to build a dynasty but they did break one. *Cinco-cero, cinco-cero.*

One night soon after announcing that he would be leaving Madrid, Laudrup was eating at a restaurant in the capital. It was a private meal and he has never told the story. Until now. Now, he is confronted with it.

So about the time . . .

Laudrup has been waiting for this question.

'My wife asked me to ask how you knew that,' he says, smiling in disbelief.

It's true, then?

He grins. 'Well, yes, yes, it's true but . . . but, I'd never seen it anywhere before and I'd never told anyone either.'

Why not?

'I don't know. I guess it just didn't seem like the kind of story you tell . . .'

It was March, April time. At first, it seemed that there were only two tables taken in the restaurant: Laudrup's party on one table and a gay couple on another. Halfway through the meal, the Dane got up to go to the toilet. It was then that he noticed three guys with earpieces.

Odd, he thought, and returned to his table. Glancing up, he noticed another man with an earpiece. Then another, and another. *Weird*. Then, from the table across the room, half hidden from view, someone beckoned him to come over.

It was Juan Carlos I, the king. Laudrup checked it was really him the king was calling over. It had to be: there was hardly anyone else in the restaurant. He went over and, still a little unsure, sat down.

'So,' said Juan Carlos. 'I hear you're leaving us.'

'Yes.'

'That's good.'

'It is?'

'Yes,' said Juan Carlos. 'Now I can go back to being the only King of Spain.'

Laudrup was lost for words.

What did you say?

Laudrup smiles at the memory, his tongue-tied response.

'"Er, yes".'

About the time Laudrup was preparing to leave Madrid, Bobby Robson was preparing to arrive at Barcelona, their career paths marked by the same man. Robson had one season as coach at the Camp Nou – the 1996–7 campaign – and his team scored 102 league goals, the second highest total ever behind the Quinta del Buitre's 107 in 1990. Barcelona also won the Spanish Super Cup, the Cup Winners' Cup and the Copa del Rey, knocking Madrid out en route and winning the final 3-2 at the Santiago Bernabéu, an occasion their Catalan full-back Sergi Barjuan described as the *rehostia* – the absolute business. But Bobby Robson just wasn't Johan Cruyff, so Barcelona brought in the man who was.

That, at least, was the theory.

Louis Van Gaal touched down in Catalonia on 29 June 1997, the day Robson was standing on the balcony at the Plaça San Jaume with his players, trophy in hand. 'I feel like Gary Cooper in *High Noon*,'

Johan Cruyff was the revolution, changing Barcelona for ever. In 1973–74, he carried them back to the league title for the first time in fourteen years … and to a 5-0 win over Real Madrid.

February 1977: Cruyff is escorted from the field by police after getting sent off against Málaga. The photo became symbolic: for some in Catalonia, it reflected a struggle still going on in Spanish society.

'The sporting arm of the *transición* to democracy.' The Quinta del Buitre, Real Madrid's Vulture Squad: Butragueño, Pardeza, Míchel, Sanchís and Martín Vázquez. Spot the odd one out.

Barcelona vice-president Joan Gaspart celebrates the 1992 European Cup success with a late night swim in the Thames.

January 1994.
Barcelona 5-0 Real Madrid.
The ultimate expression
of the Dream Team,
led by Romário.

Hristo Stoichkov, the Bulgarian who joined Barcelona for a red sports car
and brought 'mala leche' (bad milk) to the Camp Nou, making Catalonia's battles his own.

The signing that tipped the balance of power. 'I won ten-nil.' Michael Laudrup (*left*) led Barcelona to a 5-0 win over Real Madrid ... and then, almost exactly a year later, led Real Madrid to a 5-0 win over Barcelona.

Luis Figo and *the* symbol of the Barcelona–Madrid rivalry in the twenty-first century: the pig's head.

The most glamorous, but ultimately flawed, team of them all.
Beckham, Figo, Ronaldo, Zidane, Raúl: the *galácticos*.

Zidane scores the goal that defined his first season in Spain and secured Madrid's ninth
European Cup at Hampden Park, scene of the club's greatest night, over forty years earlier.

Cruyff versus Louis Van Gaal: a battle that was destined to be played out off the pitch and particularly in the media many years later.

Too ugly to play for Real Madrid? Ronaldinho scores the goal that destroyed Real Madrid, 'retired' the *galácticos* and drew a rare standing ovation from the Santiago Bernabéu.

Barcelona come full circle: Wembley again, nineteen years on. Eric Abidal lifts the European Cup in 2011.

Barcelona reach the 1986 European Cup final on penalties and a ballboy runs onto the pitch to beg for Víctor Muñoz's shirt ... the ballboy's name is Pep Guardiola.

The way we were.
Pep Guardiola and Jose Mourinho,
together at Barcelona in better days.

The 2012 touchline brawl that famously ended with Jose Mourinho poking Barcelona's assistant coach Tito Vilanova in the eye.

More than a club.

Nine European Cups, one obsession. Cristiano Ronaldo is presented in front of the trophy that defines Real Madrid.

the Englishman told Jeff King. 'Sometimes I ask myself: "why has everyone got it in for me?" If I was coach of a team in England challenging for three trophies I'd be a bloody hero.' But something was missing. Or perhaps *someone* was missing. Robson's style was not their style, not Cruyff's way. Van Gaal's, on the other hand, was.

Van Gaal represented a return to Barcelona's Dutch connection, a chance to re-encounter continuity and re-establish an identity inspired by Total Football. Rinus Michels had become Barça coach in 1971 as a prelude to signing Johan Cruyff the player, winner of the European Cup with Ajax and the man who revolutionised Barcelona; Cruyff, in turn, had been coach of the Dream Team; and in 1995, the year after Cruyff lost the European Cup final in Athens against AC Milan, Van Gaal won it against the same team, avenging Barcelona's defeat and leading Ajax to a 1-0 victory in Vienna. Now he was becoming Barça's coach.

Those parallels feel especially prevalent now as Van Gaal recalls his experience in Catalonia one spring afternoon in 2012. He lives in Holland these days and much water has gone under the bridge, the coach going via Bayern Munich and Ajax to the Dutch national team, but Barcelona has marked him and he has marked Barcelona. Recently, there has been a rehabilitation of his image, a desire to see in him that continuity and identity of which Barcelona have become proud – Michels, Cruyff, Van Gaal, Rijkaard, Guardiola, Vilanova – and thus as part of an unshakable commitment to a kind of *Barça Way*, with Guardiola among those to have spoken of Van Gaal's influence on the philosophy and methods of the club.

'The reason they wanted me in 1997 was that they identified with the Ajax style,' Van Gaal recalls. 'We'd just been world champions and Nuñez liked our ideas. He wanted me to educate the kids, to be involved in youth development, bringing passing, attacking football back – the way that Barcelona used to play. That has been perfected by Guardiola but it's also the way that we played when I was coach. The team that played most like Barcelona was Ajax. The influence was there: Cruyff started it, I continued it, Rijkaard carried on and then Guardiola. Guardiola had been Johan's player and my player too.'

As if to reinforce the point, when he took over Van Gaal brought Ronald Koeman with him as assistant coach, scorer of *that* goal and the decision as to who to employ was particularly important because of the timing: Van Gaal was the coach during Barcelona's centenary celebrations – celebrations which opened with the Orfeó Catalá and with Joan Manuel Serrat singing the club's anthem.

'For the Barcelona directors, it was logical to turn to me. I was selected because of the style and because that Ajax team had an average age of nineteen or twenty,' he continues. He was in charge from 1997 to 2000 and he talks of his Barcelona side as a team with 'a Catalan character', a 'brave', 'attacking' team that 'played good football', 4-3-3. He imposed a blueprint for youth development at La Masia – he does not know if his 'vision' is still used but he sees his hand in the work that's done – and even helped to design the new accommodation built for youth team talents. He also gave debuts to Xavi Hernández, Carles Puyol and Gabri and later, when he returned for a brief second spell in charge in 2002, to Víctor Valdés and Andrés Iniesta, as well as Pepe Reina and Thiago Motta.

'Víctor, Xavi, *Puyi*, me . . . our generation is very grateful to him,' Iniesta says. 'I can't go on about that but the facts are that those players are playing now, ten years later,' Van Gaal adds. 'It's not normal to bring so many through. Those players are the backbone of Barcelona and a model for football in Europe. That's my contribution. They are polite and educated, modest, they think about the team, and they can influence the others. Xavi and Iniesta are as important as Messi. And who is a better captain in Europe than Puyol?'

Listening to Van Gaal present his case, it is easy to understand why he is proud of his time in Catalonia. Looking at the statistics, it is easy too. He turned up just as Ronaldo, the winner of the Ballon d'Or, departed but it didn't matter: under his management, Rivaldo won the Ballon d'Or in 1999 and Luis Figo won it in 2000. And, as the Dutchman puts it: 'Real Madrid was never the champion when I was coach; the year before they had been. We were always ten or fifteen points ahead of them.' In his first two seasons, Barcelona's record against their rivals read: played four, won three, drawn one, scored eleven.

In Van Gaal's first season, Barcelona won the league and the Copa del Rey, taking the title back from Madrid who finished eleven points behind, making him the first Barça coach to win the double since Helenio Herrera in 1958–9. Then, in his second season, he became the first Barça coach to win the title in both his first two seasons since Herrera. It also meant that, in almost half a century, only he and Cruyff had won more than one league title. And in his third season, Barcelona finished runners-up and reached a Champions League semi-final. In total, between 1997 and 2000 Van Gaal won three trophies, two of them league titles – a quarter of *all* those the club had won in twenty-five years.

List what Van Gaal achieved at Barcelona and it is impressive. Like the Dutchman himself, it brooks little argument. Yet the arguments have often been intense and although, given the evidence, it appears impossible not to love him, by the end some felt it was impossible not to loathe him. His spell is not regarded with particular fondness; rather, it is often forgotten. Van Gaal could be forgiven for feeling that ultimately everything he did was held against him. He was attacked for his constant use of a little notebook – as if writing things down was a crime. The question is: *why?* His is a case study in internal politics, player power, image and reality, in how *mès que un club* can sometimes work against you. 'People maybe have not valued what I did for Barcelona but *I* know,' he says.

Critics had accused Robson of being too soft; now they accused Van Gaal of being too hard. He certainly was tough and the day he walked away he admitted, 'yes, I am arrogant' – something he considered a positive quality. Discipline was intense and on his terms; for those who suffered it, it could feel authoritarian. A member of staff recalls that strict rules governed everything from tactics to *trajes*, what suits they wore; one training ground evisceration of Rivaldo still has eyewitnesses shuddering. Van Gaal saw it as a question of manners and respect: he made players apologise to the cleaning lady after they trampled over her newly mopped floor. One player insists that the work they did – tactics, technique, ideas – was exceptional, different from anything he had ever seen before, but that some players struggled with the manner in which it was delivered. 'When he left,' a member of the Barcelona team recalls, 'we practically threw a party.'

Sitting at the Polo Club in Barcelona, just minutes up the road from the Camp Nou, Hristo Stoichkov's response is sharp: 'I don't understand why we changed Robson and brought in Van Gaal. Robson's work and ideas were good, very good. I'm not speaking to this guy [Van Gaal], he's the past. Robson leaving wasn't fair. I don't want to waste my time talking about Van Gaal because my tie is very expensive!' And with that he bursts out laughing.

Stoichkov would say that: he is notoriously hot-headed and hardly played under Van Gaal, with whom he clashed often. One season, eight appearances and a solitary goal tell their own story. Van Gaal accepts that 'not every player can like you' and is aware that the ever-volatile Stoichkov could not stand him – the feeling is clearly mutual. 'I'm sure that Stoichkov and Rivaldo were not happy,' he admits, 'but I have a feeling that the players liked me as a coach but also as a human being.' When the Dutchman's words are conveyed to a member of the Barça squad, the text reply says simply: 'haha'. Another text arrives a moment later, a hint of guilt. 'If he feels like that, I'm pleased. And he was a brilliant coach on the training pitch,' it says. 'But in truth he was hard to get on with.'

Not for everyone. Both Xavi and Iniesta are swift to defend him, offering up a different portrayal. Iniesta invited Van Gaal to his wedding and says: 'He always treated me well. In good times and bad, he was always straight and honest with the players: he was very up front.' Xavi insists: 'People see him as arrogant or aloof but he's really not.' And yet the sense of confrontation never really went away, certainly when it came to the popular portrayal and that image filtered into the public sphere. Stoichkov and Rivaldo may not have been representative of the whole dressing room, but they were the most outspoken and they came to dominate the agenda. Rivaldo, in particular was a problem and he was also Barcelona's best player. His relationship with Van Gaal would become fraught. Increasingly public, too.

'He doesn't want to think for the team, he wants to think for himself,' Van Gaal says. 'For the first two years he was not a big problem. I invested a lot of time in him, but he thinks he is bigger than the coach. He won the World Player of the Year award when he was playing on the left wing, which was where he was of most benefit for the team. But he wasn't interested. He wanted to be a number ten. I like talented players and individual skill is vital but the team has to come first. Messi is a star but doesn't behave like one; Figo was a star but he didn't either. Rivaldo did.'

Van Gaal's tough exterior didn't sit well with the media, who are often protective of the players who confide in journalists. The complaints of players like Rivaldo and Stoichkov also made for great copy. The Dutchman believed that they had been indulged for too long and that kid gloves were counterproductive, an argument that would find echo in Jose Mourinho's experience of Madrid. A journalist in Barcelona recalls the coach pulling him aside one day to tell him that by always taking the players' sides, projecting them as the injured party bullied by their coach, he did them more harm than good. 'The media put the players on a pedestal,' Van Gaal says now. 'They adore the players far too much and most players cannot handle that because it's another world; everything is too easy for them.'

As the battle was often played out through the media, the attitudes of the judges could matter as much as the attitude of the judged. Van Gaal's size, his powerful jaw and boxer's nose, his sometimes blunt manner, made it too easy to portray him in an almost demonic light. In the hands of critics, he literally became a caricature. In Spain's version of *Spitting Image*, the *Guiñoles*, instead of a face, his character was a stack of bricks with a mop of hair on top, barking aggressively in mangled Spanish, repeating a catchphrase, forever transliterated from the correct *positivo* to the incorrect *positifo* in order to capture his accent. The catchphrase was: '*siempre negatifo, nunca positifo.*' Always negative, never positive. And even though he had first delivered the phrase in a press conference to bemoan the fact that the *media* was always negative, it came to refer to *him. Always negative.*

Van Gaal's initial intention had been to stay in Barcelona for a year before taking the job, improving his Spanish and Catalan. Perhaps if he had the judgements would not have been so *negatifo*. His Spanish sounded guttural. What he said was held against him at least in part because of the way he said it. His delivery meant that even if he said 'I love you', it could sound as if he was announcing plans to axe-murder your children. He was direct too, not afraid to take people on. Press conferences became battles and it was the conflict that made the headlines. *Tu eres malo, muy malo* – you're bad, very bad – Van Gaal told one journalist. That too became a kind of catchphrase, forever used against him.

Besides, success alone did not always convince, especially as some judged victories as being the least they could expect, given the squad Barça had and the opposition they faced. Critics saw flaws. In the first season, Van Gaal's title-winning Barcelona picked up fewer points than Robson's runners-up and lost ten times. Madrid, who had lost Fabio Capello after just one season, were no longer true opponents and with the quality of players at Barcelona's disposal supporters felt entitled to expect trophies. Rivaldo had cost 4,000 million pesetas (£16.7m), Sonny Anderson 3,500 million, Michael Reizeger 800 million, Christophe Dugarry 750 million and Winston Bogarde 700 million, while the Madrid coach Juup Heynckes insisted that in Rivaldo, Figo and Guardiola, Barcelona already had the best three players in the world. Besides, winning was not everything; it mattered how they won and who they won with, what it *meant.*

Barcelona had sought to embrace the Dutch–Barça model but some did not see a reincarnation of the Dream Team in the side that won the league in 1998, still less the reincarnation of Johan Cruyff in Louis

Van Gaal. He was, says one former player, *theoretically* a continuation of Cruyff's methods; another adds that he was, in fact, more method-ical, more meticulous than his predecessor, a better coach and certainly a more dedicated one, but without the charisma or stardust. Cruyff was locked into Barcelona's identity now, his presence permanent, part of the *entorno*, a word Cruyff himself had used to decry the whirlwind of pressure and interests that encircled the club, sometimes sucking it in. Stoichkov sees Van Gaal as a man in the shadow of Cruyff and not just at Barcelona. He seems to enjoy saying so too, offering up his theory as to why, in his words, Van Gaal 'couldn't handle the stars'.

'Maybe it's because he never played good football,' Stoichkov says. There's something taunting in his tone.

'I asked him once: "did you ever play for Ajax".

"No."

"Why?"

"Johan Cruyff."

The truth.'

But were they trying to get another Cruyff by signing Van Gaal?

'No. He never came close to Johan,' Stoichkov replies. 'Well, maybe they were thinking that. Maybe. Maybe one day I'm going to the moon!'

Another key factor was of course the 'national' discourse, Barcelona's idiosyncrasy. 'Barcelona is more than a club,' Van Gaal explains. 'I could feel it: you read it in the papers, it comes up in conversation. Whenever I saw things, I would ask the team manager and the assistant coach, who was Catalan, and they would try to explain it. Every coach has to prepare himself for the culture of the country but even more so at Barcelona. You have to know that Sevilla is another culture, another type of human being. The Moorish influence in the south, the French influence in Catalonia. You go to the shops and they speak to you only in Catalan. You have to know that.'

It is clear from what he says and how he says it that Van Gaal had a curiosity for his surroundings, a desire to understand his place. But one of the problems he faced, according to those who attacked him, was that he did not understand the Catalan issue well enough. Van Gaal had announced that his dream was to win the European Cup with a team of Catalans. Given that much of his focus was youth development and that Xavi and Puyol made their debuts with him, he would be entitled to argue that was necessarily always going to be a long-term project and one he was working towards; in the short term, though, he stood accused of undermining Barcelona's Catalan identity and its *Cruyffist* identity too. By his final season, Figo was the only Cruyff-era signing left. Barcelona had made sixteen foreign signings. The fact that the trend was not a new phenomenon was conveniently overlooked: when Dani García Lara arrived in 1999, he was the first Spaniard in twenty-three signings, going back before Van Gaal's arrival.

Dani joined a dressing room that included eight Dutch players. A nineteen-year-old Patrik Kluivert scored the winning goal in the 1995 European Cup final, joining Barcelona soon after. By 1999, none of Ajax's European Cup-winning team were still in Holland and six of them were at Barcelona: five Dutchmen – Frank and Ronald De Boer, Michael Reizeger, Bogarde, Kluivert – and the Finn Jari Litmanen. At first, their arrival was celebrated but soon it caused concern. When the De Boer brothers joined in January 1999, Kluivert admitted: 'So many Dutch players is dangerous. It is going to be too easy to blame us if things go wrong.' In the meantime, Guillermo Amor, Chapi Ferrer, Iván de la Peña, Óscar García, Roger García, Albert Celades and Carlos Busquets had departed. Cruyff asked: 'Is it really so hard to have a dozen local players in the squad?' Van Gaal is quick to respond: 'they called them "the Cruyff five" or something, but can any of them really compare to my products, Xavi, Puyol, Motta, Fernando, Iniesta, Valdés, Reina?'

This had become a contentious and live issue. When Jordi Pujol, the president of the Catalan parliament, complained of the lack of

Catalans, Van Gaal responded: 'what has he got to do with the club?' The facetious answer might have been: *rather a lot, actually.* Then, when José María Aznar, the president of the Spanish government and a Real Madrid fan, expressed his concerns at the lack of national players – Spanish national players – Van Gaal responded: 'I've told Pujol and I'll tell Aznar: you know nothing about football. Stick to your own business. I don't talk politics.'

Dutch dominance became a kind of running joke but for many Catalans it was no laughing matter. A banner at Valencia read: 'Welcome to Mestalla, Ajax'. Another banner, this time at the Camp Nou, demanded: '*Más catalanes, menos tulipanes*'. More Catalans, fewer tulips. One Catalan politician lost all sense of perspective to denounce melodramatically 'the most savage dismantling of Barça's traditions since Franco'. That was absurd but a poll showed that 63 per cent felt the club was losing its identity, Ferrer departed bemoaning the lack of Catalans at the club and Sergi said: 'I would prefer a dressing room where they speak Catalan or where I could at least make myself understood in Spanish without gesturing with my hands.'

'The *blaugrana* is sacred,' Sergi continued. 'I was brought up dreaming of playing for Barcelona; it is part of my family, my education. My parents passed that on to me and I will pass it on to my children. The foreign players gradually learn about Barcelona or Catalonia but let's not kid ourselves that they will ever feel the way I do. It is hard to keep on losing friends, people who have been brought up with the club . . . in the end, it is us who will seem to be the foreigners.'

The Catalan question tapped into a political battle that was brewing. The *entorno* reared its head once more. As the journalist Enric Bañeres put it: if Bobby Robson had been sitting on a hornet's nest, his successor touched down in Vietnam. The conflict in the media and in the boardroom between Cruyff and Nuñez had escalated and would soon be virtually an open war as a growing number of *culés* came to believe that Nuñez, despite being president for twenty-two years, did not represent the 'true' Barcelona.

In 1999, a young, dynamic lawyer called Joan Laporta announced the foundation of a pressure group in opposition to Nuñez called the Elefant Blau, the blue elephant. The Elefant Blau accused the president of running up a 7,600-million-peseta debt and attacked the board's 'obvious distaste for the democratic principles of the club'. The group started to collect signatures in order to force a vote of censorship. Among those who signed it was Cruyff and the movement cohered around him. 'Nuñez thinks he still lives in a different era and he acts like people used to act here,' Cruyff said. Armand Carabén, the man who brought Cruyff to the club in the first place as a player, was more direct: he called the president a 'fascist'. In the eyes of many fans, sacking Cruyff and turning some of the media against him was evidence of that.

Laporta explains the development of the Elefant Blau as a culmin-ation of factors from finance to football, from politics to identity, from the failure to properly acknowledge Sunyol to Nuñez's open conflict with Cruyff – the man who became a kind of guru to *culés* and to whom many felt an eternal gratitude. *The* embodiment of Barcelona's reawakening, both as a player and a coach, Cruyff lies at the heart of Laporta's discourse: the Dutchman was his idol and his inspiration. He was also Nuñez's sworn enemy. During Barcelona's centenary Vázquez Montalbán, whom Laporta cites more than once, argued: 'Barcelona only has its identity in the colour of its shirts and the convic-tion of its fans.' As for Nuñez, his response was to attack the opposition as *Madridista* stooges. There could be no greater accusation.

The denouncements went back and forth and in the middle of it all, like Robson before him, was Van Gaal. This was the final, decisive step in the rejection of the coach: far from *being* Cruyff, he was now projected as the *opposite* of Cruyff. If Cruyff was God in Pichi Alonso's sarcastic words, Van Gaal was the anti-Cruyff. The close association between coach and president was played upon: Cruyff was proud of the fact that he had always kept Nuñez at arm's length unlike Van Gaal, and when public pressure meant the Dream Team finally got their belated homage game on 10 March 1999, Cruyff and Van Gaal did not shake hands.

'There was a fight between Nuñez and the future president Laporta and that was in the media constantly,' Van Gaal recalls. 'Cruyff supported Laporta, Nuñez was not Catalan and he didn't like the media. I liked the way Nuñez treated the media; I saw things the same way. I had the media against me. Laporta, being Catalan, managed the media better.' That was only partly true – the *La Vanguardia* and *El Mundo Deportivo* group was critical, then and now, of Laporta and *Cruyffismo* – but the battle was brutal. Van Gaal continues: 'I was loyal to the president and that was why people turned against me. The battle was not me, it was Nuñez and the Elefant Blau but I was the victim. I never change. I'm sixty now and I will always be like this. I do not want to deny my own identity. Lots of coaches play a role, but I don't. Maybe I wasn't political enough.'

Just how much of a victim Van Gaal felt was revealed when in the third season the thing that mattered most deserted him – results. In an atmosphere that was already charged, white handkerchiefs came out in protest, calls for him to resign. When he did eventually depart he did so with the message: 'Barcelona is nowhere near as important a club as everybody here thinks it is. You have not won much. I won more in six years at Ajax than Barcelona have won in one hundred.' He thought those words summed up Barcelona's inflated sense of self-worth, the unrealistic expectations; critics thought that it summed up *his* inflated sense of self-worth, *his* failure to 'get' Barcelona.

In 1999–2000, Barcelona finished second in the league, behind Deportivo, who had finally landed their first title. They did reach the semi-final of the Champions League, after two seasons in a row when they had failed to get out of the group stage – finishing bottom to Dynamo Kiev, PSV Eindhoven and Newcastle in 1997–8 and below the finalists Bayern Munich and Manchester United in 1999, the year the final was played at Camp Nou on Barcelona's centenary. But having got there, they were defeated by Valencia. Héctor Cúper's side then lost the final to Real Madrid.

And there's the rub; here come those scales again, where both sides can never be up at the same time. There is another reason why 1997–2000 are years that some Barcelona fans would rather wipe from their memory, another reason why that era is largely forgotten, Barça's success somehow diminished: because it was on Van Gaal's watch that Madrid won the European Cup at last. Not once, but twice.

Eventually, Nuñez was pushed out. He resigned and called elections for July 2000. Van Gaal went with him: 'I rescinded my contract and I left without taking a single penny. My loyalty cost me.' When the Dutchman departed Barcelona for the second time at the end of a brief spell in 2002 under Nuñez's vice-presidency and successor Joan Gaspart, he cried, his chance to make amends gone, full of regret and sadness. The first time, in 2000, had been different; then there had been anger. Louis Van Gaal announced his departure in another famous press conference in which he sat before the media and delivered an opening line that became legendary: 'Friends of the media,' he said, 'I am leaving. Congratulations.'

17

THIRTY-TWO YEARS LATER

Pedja Mijatović eases into a wicker chair on a terrace just north of Madrid and pulls off his sunglasses, laying them down on the table in front of him. '*Siempre la séptima*,' he smiles. Always the *séptima*. Not a day goes by without someone reminding him about it, coming over to shake his hand, asking for an autograph or a photo, or just wanting to say thank you. 'That goal changed my life,' he says. It changed Real Madrid's life too. The captain Manolo Sanchís describes that night as the most important in the club's history, while his centre-back partner Fernando Hierro calls it an awakening. At last the time had come: Mijatović's moment.

On 20 May 1998, Madrid won the European Cup with a 1-0 victory over Juventus at the Amsterdam Arena. They finally had the *séptima*, the club's seventh. The Montenegrin scored the game's only goal, collecting Roberto Carlos's shot as it deflected off Mark Iuliano, stepping round Angelo Peruzzi and clipping the ball into an open net, just as Paolo Montero moved in to close the angle. Mijatović had been waiting eight months for that goal; Madrid had been waiting thirty-two years. For the club that was defined by the European Cup, it had been too long: three decades in the wilderness. In the meantime, *even* Barcelona had won it.

For Mijatović there was something mystical about that moment.

There's a kind of wonder in his voice as he explains: 'It was the sixty-sixth minute when I scored. Real Madrid won the European Cup for the first time since 1966. We played Juventus: black and white stripes, like Partizan Belgrade, the team Madrid beat in '66. *My* team. The team where I played. Destiny.'

Madrid had an impressive squad; president Lorenzo Sanz had come to power in 1995 and spent big. Manolo Sanchís and Fernando Hierro were the centre-backs, they had Roberto Carlos flying up the wing, Clarence Seedorf and Fernando Redondo in midfield, Mijatović and the Croatian Davor Šuker up front: the basis of the team that had won the 1996–7 league title under Fabio Capello, plus the striker Fernando Morientes, signed from Zaragoza and Christian Karembeu, the twenty-six-year-old French midfielder. Karembeu had been presented as a modern-day Alfredo Di Stéfano after a battle with Barcelona for his signature in which Madrid negotiated directly with the player, Barcelona went to Sampdoria, Karembeu announced 'footballers are not slaves' and newspaper front covers depicted him in photomontage half-and-half shirts and denounced each other's dirty tricks, while in the middle of it all FIFA president João Havelange, asked what he thought, replied: 'Karembeu? Who's he?'

Then there was Raúl González Blanco, the most important legacy of Jorge Valdano's brief spell in charge, the small, unremarkable looking kid who would come to represent Madrid like no other, despite having been at Atlético Madrid until their president Jesús Gil decided there was no point in paying to have a youth team. When Valdano joined from Tenerife in 1994 Raúl was playing for Real Madrid C. Promoted very briefly to the B team, the Argentinian coach had thought about giving him a chance in the first team but admitted that he was concerned about the young striker freezing. Raúl's response said it all: 'If you want to win, play me. If not, put someone else in.'

Raúl made his debut on 29 October 1994. It was week nine of the season and he was just seventeen. The game was only ten seconds old when he scuffed a one-on-one. He then went round the goalkeeper and put his shot over. Sent clean through, with his next chance he shot straight at the keeper. Another effort went miles over from inside the six-yard box. And he hit the bar with a header. He could have scored five; he scored none and Madrid lost 3-2. Valdano, though, was impressed. 'Some players are veterans even when they are kids,' he says. The following week, Raúl was again in the side, this time against Atlético Madrid. He provided one, won the penalty for another and scored a third in a 4-2 win, one report claiming that he had 'massacred his former club'. He scored nine league goals that season; the next season it was nineteen and the one after that he scored twenty-one. It was the start of an extraordinary story.

Raúl was skilful – his first touch was impeccable and the sheer number of goals he scored scooping the ball up and over the keeper suggested feet shaped like a court jester's – but his success was not about natural talent. It was about being astute, intelligent; about recognising his limitations and minimising them. He was bandy-legged, hunched, not especially fast. In Fernando Hierro's words, 'he was not a ten out of ten in anything but he was an eight and a half in everything'. Real Madrid's assistant coach Cappa explains: 'Raúl was a surprise to us, but not to himself. Raúl carries the ball badly, he dribbles badly, he can't head the ball, he strikes it badly.'

Cappa pauses for effect: '. . . and then the game starts.'

'When the game starts, he carries the ball well, he dribbles phenomenally well, he can head it, he scores a thousand different types of goal. He is suddenly perfect. Raúl is a born competitor. He's unique. If you analyse his discernible qualities to understand what he is, if you put together a checklist, there's little there. But he had such will that it transformed him into a player much better than he was in training sessions. I never saw a seventeen year old like it. He was completely sure that he would make it. If you're Leo Messi and you can get the ball and turn it into a white dove, of course you've got no doubts. But if you are a player who is limited technically, it's just not normal to have the confidence that Raúl had.

'I remember Hierro and Míchel practising free kicks. Raúl comes over. Hierro says: "You? Free kicks? Ha!" A few days later there was a Spain U21 game and he goes to take a free kick. I'm thinking: *éste pibe está loco*. This kid's mad. But he takes it and it's brilliant. Suddenly, he's Maradona. There were those spoon goals – how?! And when he scored his first against Atlético, I was thinking: "how did he do that?" We ended up convinced too. And relieved, because the man we had put on the bench was Butragueño.' Raúl was so grateful he named his first son Jorge after the coach who gave him his debut.

Raúl's preparation was intense, later even going so far as to sleep in an oxygen tent. He loves football, reeling off statistics and stories beyond many players. Likeable one on one, quiet and respectful – he rarely went for referees, is often lauded by opponents and has never been sent off – he also demonstrated the personality, will, dedication, strength of character, political awareness and sheer stubbornness that other, more talented players lacked. Especially within his own dressing room. He was a survivor: some team-mates admit to having found him hard work and one former manager suggests that some of his more ostentatious running was more populist than practical. Presidents, managers and coaches came and went; Raúl outlived them all. He took the game seriously and the captaincy *extremely* seriously. In the end, that weighed him down – to visit him in Gelsenkirchen, Germany, in April 2011 after he had joined Schalke was to witness a man liberated; 'I'd reached the point,' he said, 'where I needed to escape' – but it was also what made him so successful.

Perhaps his most emblematic goals are the winner in the Intercontinental Cup against Vasco de Gama in 1998 and his eighty-sixth-minute equaliser against Barcelona at the Camp Nou the following year. Not so much for the goal but the celebration. Raúl lifted his finger to his lips and hushed the Barcelona fans – an image that adorns the wall of countless bars in the capital. 'Raúl is synonymous with Real Madrid,' Valdano says. 'He has been the face of the club for the last twenty-five years. Quantity above quality, absolute commitment and endeavour above all else. Utter professionalism. Every. Single. Day. Of. His. Life. If you wrote a list of Raúl's qualities, it would be a list of the values of Real Madrid. He is the Di Stéfano of our time. He is the people, the incarnation of *Madridismo*.'

When Raúl finally left Madrid for Schalke in the summer of 2010 he had played 741 games and scored 323 goals for Madrid, more than anyone else in the club's history. Hierro referred to him as the Ferrari and he won six league titles and three European Cups, scoring in two of the finals. Yet it is the one he didn't score in that most marks him. Raúl describes the first of those finals, Madrid's *séptima*, as: 'the moment that the club returned to its place. The reaction to us winning the seventh European Cup was unforgettable. The fans had waited so long for it and it had become an obsession. I felt like the moment might never arrive.'

Raúl was not the only one and few expected Madrid to emerge from the wilderness that season. Capello had led Madrid to the league title in 1996–7 but he had gone, his relationship with Sanz having broken down so completely that the only surprise was that the pair of them succeeded in keeping a lid on it long enough to win the league. 'It was obvious that the relationship was not the best. With every passing day, Capello seemed a bit more distant from the board, from the president,' says José Emilio Amavisca, a regular starter during that season and on the bench in Amsterdam. 'For some players, it would have been a relief to discover that he was going. The mental and physical demands were extraordinary: you had to be thinking about football twenty-four hours a day, just as he did. But it was a shame for me: I would have liked him to stay another year at least. He would have done great things. It was practically his team that won the European Cup. In fact, he said: "hey, I built that team." And he was right.'

Capello's departure might have been a relief for some players but it resolved nothing. In fact, things got worse. Boardroom battles were bad enough but they were nothing compared to what was happening in the dressing room. Capello had been replaced as coach by the former Tenerife manager Juup Heynckes. Sanz later described Heynckes as 'too nice' for Madrid and his agent, Quique Reyes, insisted: 'he never got the backing of the club'. The players, Reyes said, 'got away with everything'. When Raúl suggested that Heynckes deserved to continue, Sanz responded, 'I'd ask Raúl what the dressing room has done to support him.'

Before the European Cup final, Christian Pannucci said publicly: 'Heynckes is a good coach but he has given us too much respect.' They had mostly given him none. He did not do himself many favours: one player describes the German as being out of his depth, lacking the kind of personality, charisma or authority needed to manage that Madrid. 'The players took no notice of him at all,' he says. Not least because, left isolated by the club, his authority undermined, they knew that they did not need to.

After the final, when Heynckes left, he admitted: 'this is the right decision, I couldn't go on working in those conditions.' He had changed training times and schedules to suit the squad but it did not help him win them over. 'The dressing room,' recalls Lorenzo Sanz 'ate him alive . . . ultimately, he couldn't continue because he couldn't control the squad. He recognised that himself. It was a tough dressing room that had just won the league and was packed with stars. He couldn't impose the necessary discipline.' Liberated by the departure of Capello, this was the beginning of an era in which that squad came to be known as the Ferrari Boys, big names and big personalities on bigger wages, surrounded by constant rumours of late nights and lax discipline. John Toshack would take over the same players in 1999, describing going into the Bernabéu dressing room as 'like going into Baghdad'.

Things were going wrong. Madrid were knocked out of the Copa del Rey in the first round by Second Division Alavés and in the league they were even more disastrous: Louis Van Gaal's Barcelona were running away with the title. Madrid won only five of nineteen home games that season, stumbling from one abysmal performance to the next against a backdrop of whistles and boos. Their top scorer was Fernando Morientes – on just twelve – and they finished fourth, not high enough to qualify for the following season's Champions League. 'It was as if we pressed the "off" button in the league, without even realising it,' Raúl recalls.

But in the Champions League it was a completely different story. By the end of the tournament Madrid had conceded just five goals in eleven matches. They came through a group with Rosenberg, Porto and Panathinaikos, losing only once – away in Norway – and then defeated Bayer Leverkusen in the quarter-finals. In the semi-final, their home leg against Borussia Dortmund was delayed after fans at the south end of the stadium pulled the goal down. It took seventy-five minutes for a replacement goal to be brought to the stadium from the Ciudad Deportiva, three kilometres up the Castellana, and the Germans wanted the game replayed entirely but UEFA upheld Madrid's victory. The Spanish football authorities then brought forward the final round of league games to the Friday night to enable Madrid an extra day's preparation for Amsterdam.

Still, few expected a victory. A week before the final, Sanz called Heynckes and asked how he was. The response? *Hundido*. Sunk. When he called him again on the evening of the game, the outlook was not much more positive. Raúl remembers seeing the Juventus team bus arrive at the stadium the next day – Zidane, Deschamps, Del Piero, runners-up the year before, winners the year before that – and thinking, 'they're winning 1-0 already'. The Madrid bus was different: 'it was like a funeral parlour,' one player says. 'No one said a word, the silence was absolute. We were *acojonados*, crapping ourselves.'

'*Acojonados*?' smiles Mijatović, before adding the superlative. 'No. *Acojonadísimos*.'

Centre-back Fernando Sanz, who was the son of the president, explains: 'Our entire season was in that game; we had long since blown the league. And we were playing a team that was infinitely better than us. We were very well aware of the task that lay before us. Then there was the historic thing. There was a sense of responsibility that was suffocating. It's very hard to withdraw from all of that. It was a huge moment. Tensions. Nerves. Your stomach is churning.' Ignacio Zoco was Real Madrid's delegate in Amsterdam. 'We weren't favourites,' he says. '*Joder*, you should have seen their faces every day. Nervous is not the half of it. Juve had a great team.'

Real Madrid were staying at the Dutch Football Federation's head-quarters, where Mijatović shared room five with Davor Šuker. On the night before the final no one could sleep. Bit by bit, the players gathered in room five to talk. Sanchís, whose father had been in the 1966 European Cup-winning team, and who had suffered the agony of the Quinta's semi-final exits, told them, 'you cannot possibly imagine how big this is'.

For all the tension, the weight of responsibility, there was something cathartic about the conversation, about the whole experience, especially for Mijatović. 'It's hard to explain why there was such a massive differ-ence between the league and Europe,' he says. 'We were just awful in the league. The fans were constantly on our backs and we performed desperately. Honestly, we were terrible. *Nada, nada*, just dire. We went to Holland three or four days early and stayed outside Amsterdam in the woods somewhere, cut off from it all. That was a good decision: it took us away from everything, away from the negativity and away from our season at home. It cleared our minds.'

'I had played well in Europe but I still hadn't scored. It had become a bit of an obsession,' he adds. Fernando Sanz was Mijatović's confidant. 'Pedja had chewed over it so much in the build-up to the final. We were very, very good friends – brothers. We still are. He was playing well but the goals were not going in. I remember sitting down for dinner in the hotel: Davor, Pedja, Guti, me. And I remember telling him not to worry, that he was going to score; he was going to go down in the history of the club – probably the biggest club in the world. That night, I woke up in the middle of the night and I was just convinced of it: Pedja was going to score.'

Legend has it that when Sanz awoke he ran down the corridor and into Mijatović's room to tell him. Sanz laughs. It's a nice story but it's not true. What is true is that, unable to sleep, Mijatović was having a similar revelation. His friend's words had touched him. He woke up and walked into the bathroom. Facing the mirror, looking at himself, he says it is as if some other part of him took over: *it's going to be 1-0 and you're going to get the goal.* He splashed water on his face, walked back into the room, climbed back into bed and said to Šuker: 'Davor, we're going to win 1-0 tomorrow.'

But Juventus were confident. Midfielder Angelo Di Livio had '1.0' written on his hand. Mijatović assumed that too was a scoreline, a prediction or a target. In fact, he discovered many years later, it was the bonus the Juventus players were on. One million lira.

They never got it.

'For a quarter of an hour they rolled over us,' says Sanchís. But after about twenty minutes two things happened, one that had an emotional impact and one that had a tactical impact: Raúl nutmegged Moreno Torricelli and Christian Karembeu was told to track Zinedine Zidane. Something else happened, too, but for now only Mijatović knew what. Bit by bit, Madrid grew more confident. Juventus were better controlled, their chances few, Madrid's fears fewer. And midway through the second half, Mijatović got his goal. When the ball hit the net, he turned and ran, finger pointing, to the bench to embrace the man who had told him he would score. The most long-awaited moment in the club's history and Sanz was at the heart of it.

'Only,' he laughs, 'the TV directors cut away just as Pedja reached the bench. If you watch it on television, you never see me.'

Madrid still had over twenty minutes to hang on, an eternity for the fans and for Lorenzo Sanz, who admits he had to take refuge in a hidden corner of the stadium, away from the dignataries. But Sanchís says he was now convinced Madrid were going to win. What had essentially been a defensive performance, intense and focused, was about to get its reward. When the final whistle went, Šuker booted the ball away in delight. Fernando Hierro could never understand why he hadn't kept it as a souvenir. The suffering was over: Sanchís and Hierro, so resilient, so resolute, became heroes.

None became heroes like Mijatović, though. 'They were all coming up to me and saying *"golazo, golazo"*. I told them to stop being such a bunch of crawlers. Sure, we had won the European Cup and it was a massive goal but, come on, I had an open net,' he laughs. 'But then I watched it back and I realised what I hadn't properly appreciated at the time. I saw that they were right. When I controlled the ball, Montero was coming across and I had to lift it to make sure that he didn't stop it. That kind of decision happens so fast that you're not even really aware that you are taking it in, computing the possibilities. But when I watched it again, I realised that the gap the ball went into was tiny. The shot was *milimétrico*. I suppose it was a *golazo*.'

It was also, Barcelona fans insist, offside.

Mijatović is ready for that one. There isn't even time to ask the question. 'And,' he adds quickly, a huge grin stretching across his face, 'it was onside.' Watching it again, and again, and again, it is impossible to tell with absolute certainty, there is no definitive angle, but Mijatović's insistence that the last defender played him onside at the moment the ball dropped from the rebound looks right. There is certainly no scandal screaming you in the face.

What even Sanz didn't know was that Mijatović should never even have played that night. A few days before he had felt a sharp pain in his calf. He had suffered a small tear, the kind of injury that would normally keep a player out for eight to ten days. 'But,' says Mijatović, 'there was no way I was missing the biggest game of my life.' So he sought treatment from the physios and swore them to secrecy. Behind everyone's backs, they silently worked on him, trying to get him as ready as they could. On the last session before the final at the Amsterdam Arena, Mijatović was wearing his socks up to his knees instead of round his ankles as normal to hide the huge bandage underneath. No one clicked. When he reached the end of the session,

Mijatović's overriding sensation was relief: he had not broken down and he had not been rumbled either. He had avoided sprints and leaps, tried to pass by unnoticed. But he could still feel it; it wasn't right.

That was when Heynckes announced that it was time to practise penalties.

'And that was when I panicked,' Mijatović says conspiratorially, leaning in, a glint in his eye.

'I had to think of something. I was convinced that if I started taking shots it would tear, something would go wrong. I also knew that if I told the manager my fears, if I told him my calf didn't feel right, he wouldn't play me. I had to come up with a plan, some lie as to why I couldn't take penalties. Some reason other than the real one. Then it occurred to me: "Relax, *mister*," I said, "it's not going to go to penalties tomorrow – we're going to win in normal time."'

Mijatović laughs. 'Well, better to look arrogant than injured.'

He's back at the Amsterdam Arena the night before the final, picturing the scene. 'The manager half said something but I started to walk off the pitch saying everything was fine: "there's no point, we're going to win." I could feel him looking at me, his eyes following me away. I was sure he was thinking: "who does that *gilipollas*, that tosser, think he is?" But I didn't care. The most important thing was that I got away with it. For the time being.'

There were tougher tests ahead, though. Mijatović picks up the story again the following night: 'I could still feel it during the warm-up. I knew it wasn't right and I feared that I might only last twenty minutes, or maybe not even that. I decided to try to ease my way into the game slowly. Bit by bit it went out of my mind; bit by bit I warmed up, loosened. And then I remember doing a sprint and it being fine; that was a kind of release. I never felt it again. And then . . . the goal.'

Down in the dressing room after the game, Madrid prepared to crack open the champagne. There was just one problem: no one thought they would win and they hadn't brought any with them. Their opponents had and didn't much feel like drinking it so they gave their bottles to the victors, leaving Madrid to celebrate with Juventus's title and Juventus's bubbly. Back in Spain, crowds gathered at the statue of Cibeles, goddess of fertility, thousands and thousands of people. For Sanchís, it was especially sweet: he was the last remaining member of the Quinta del Buitre and it was Míchel, Pardeza, Butragueño and Martín Vázquez who came to his mind as he celebrated. Them and his father: justice had been done. He could finally stand up for himself in arguments at home. The cover of *Marca* showed Sanchís wrapped in the Spanish flag, kissing the trophy. 'I've wanted you for thirty-two years, now you're mine' the headline ran.

Lorenzo Sanz framed the cover of the other national sports daily, *AS*, and hung it in his toilet. 'How could I ever forget? Every morning, when I wake up and go to do what I have to do, I see it.'

'We had never seen so many people in Madrid,' recalls Fernando Sanz. 'At the celebration we became conscious of just what we had done. It was absolutely immense. The *séptima* is the one where people really, really lived it. The *auténtica*. The seventh European Cup brought about a change in the mentality of Real Madrid. It removed a huge weight from the club, a millstone from our shoulders. We had waited so long. We went from black and white to colour; modern Madrid was written that day in Amsterdam. We'd been laughed at by Barcelona – thirty-two years and all that – and then suddenly it ended. What we thought was that it would start our cycle.'

'Heynckes put the clock back to zero, after thirty-two years,' Sanchís says. A week later, Heynckes was sacked. Few cared.

'There was also something about that victory that said: "we're here again, watch out",' says Mijatović. 'That moment was just over-whelming: it changed my whole life, and it never goes away. It's always there.' He calls the waiter over and pays for the coffee, picks up his phone, puts his sunglasses back on and gets up to go, pushing the chair in behind him. A woman hurries over holding a piece of paper and a pen. She's been waiting for her chance. Could I have an auto-graph for my husband? We were there that night in Amsterdam. It was just unbelievable, the greatest night ever. Pedja Mijatović smiles and signs. He flashes a knowing look that says 'see?' *Siempre la séptima*.

The floodgates had been opened. 'We're here again.' Real Madrid reached the final of the 2000 European Cup just two years later: the *octava* followed the *séptima* and quickly, while two years after that came the *novena*. But as Fernando Sanz admits, the belief that the same players who had ended the thirty-two-year wait were about to begin a new cycle proved to be wrong. Of the starting eleven that faced Valencia in Paris on 24 May 2000, only four had played in 1998: Roberto Carlos, Redondo, Morientes and Raúl. Hierro and Sanchís were returning from injury and on the bench; Bodo Ilgner had slipped out of the side, replaced by a kid called Iker Casillas, and, like Karembeu, was on the bench. They would be gone that summer. Pannucci, Seedorf and Mijatović had already left, as had Šuker. It was another European Cup and it felt like another era even though it was only two years later.

These were tumultuous times. In Heynckes's farewell press confer-ence he declared: 'there is too much press and too many directors who like to talk. I still think you don't have to be a dictator but Madrid need to reflect on how many coaches they have had in recent years.' Things did not exactly slow down. José Antonio Camacho, his successor, lasted twenty-two days and did not coach Madrid for a single match. Guus Hiddink followed him but was in charge for just seven months, smilingly describing getting sacked at Madrid as part of the game. He was replaced by John Toshack, returning for his second spell in charge having led Madrid's Quinta del Buitre in that record-breaking 1989–90 campaign.

According to *El País*, it was Toshack's job to be the *látigo* of the Madrid dressing room – the whip. He was the one who began to force the Ferrari Boys out and in the summer of 1999 Madrid made nine signings: Geremi Nitjap, Elvir Baljic, Julio César, Rodrigo, Edwin

Congo, Míchel Salgado, Iván Helguera and Nicolas Anelka. The Frenchman cost 5,540 million pesetas (£23.5m) from Arsenal. Sanz called it a 'beautiful madness'. Others dropped the 'beautiful'. Madrid's debt was mounting but it didn't stop them splashing out over 9,000 million pesetas.

Then there was Steve McManaman, joining on a free transfer from Liverpool, moving into Pannucci's old house – 'he had taken everything with him, even the lightbulbs!' – and getting an early taste of the way things worked. His signing was announced the day after Madrid had been knocked out of Europe, towards the end of the 1998–9 season, and he quickly grasped the significance: 'It was all PR: "that's the bad news, now here's the good news".'

The good news did not last long. Tensions remained and Anelka found that adapting to Madrid's dressing room was far from easy, especially when you don't particularly try. He would later be summoned to the club to explain his behaviour and suspended without pay for forty-five days. Before that, in November 1999, Toshack had publicly called out goalkeeper Albano Bizarri after another mistake. President Lorenzo Sanz demanded that the coach take back the remark but Toshack refused. 'There will be pigs flying over the Bernabéu before I take it back,' he responded.

John Benjamin – the Spanish invariably used Toshack's middle name as the first and therefore most important of his two surnames – regularly had Spaniards scratching their heads with his references to *bread and butter*, *water off a duck's back* and *hot potatoes* and this was just another in a long line of English idioms translated literally into Spanish. Many of them became popular and some even entered the Spanish lexicon. 'After the game, you think you won't play any of them next week. By mid-week, it's four, by Friday it's seven and by the time the game comes round, you play with the same eleven *cabrones* [bastards] as the week before' was another of his phrases that became the stuff of legend. Mostly they were indulged as funny, charming even. But this time the flying pig caused a huge stir and cost him his job.

The following morning, the cover of *Marca* showed a picture of the Bernabéu with a cartoon pig, pink and winged, flying over the top of it. Sanz took offence, as if somewhere along the line he suspected that the pig in question was him. 'If it is true that he said that I will sack him right now,' he told the media. When he called the Welshman into the office and asked if he really had said it Toshack replied simply 'yes' and Sanz followed through on his threat. Beneath the comedy there was a serious point: one board member accused Toshack of forcing a sacking because he knew that the dressing room had already turned its back on him; Toshack, meanwhile, pointed out there was no way that he could continue if he was not backed by the club. 'Without that authority,' he said, 'there's nothing.' For coaches at the Bernabéu it was a depressingly familiar feeling: Toshack was the eighth manager in three years.

Madrid's board put Vicente del Bosque in temporary charge. The plan was to replace him at the end of the season while also hiring a new director of youth football and director-general. Del Bosque was the ultimate club man, an elegant midfielder who played for Madrid for almost twenty years from his debut in 1966 to his retirement in 1984. He had then formed part of the youth set-up, coaching Real Madrid C and becoming involved in the scouting and development of young talent before briefly managing Real Madrid Castilla, the club's B team. That was where his future lay. 'I was convinced that my path was the formation of youth players. I had been given the chance to go and manage Logroñés but I had decided that I didn't want to be a coach.' The media began referring to him as Vicente the Brief but he remained in the job for four years. No one had been in the seat for so long since Miguel Muñoz's retirement in 1974 and del Bosque went four consecutive years – four years in which Barcelona won nothing – winning major trophies. Thirteen years later, a Marqués now, the man who didn't want to be coach has also won the World Cup.

'We had good players,' he says.

It was the third time Madrid had made Del Bosque the first-team manager. He had taken over for two months after the sacking of Benito Floro in 1994, bringing his assistant Rafa Benítez with him, and he had also been in charge for two matches in 1996 following the sacking of Jorge Valdano. 'The third time was like the other two,' he admits, 'we all thought it would be temporary. But this time I asked the club for just one thing: that they support us properly. I didn't want to be just a *parche*, a patch-up solution.

Things improved with Del Bosque. He had probably benefited from Toshack's work in laying the foundations and rooting out some of the more problematic elements within the dressing room – the Welshman has expressed the opinion that Del Bosque has been lucky to turn up to find the hard work done by his predecessors both with Madrid and Spain – but the man from Salamanca connected better with the squad. Quiet, undemonstrative, respectful, he gave players a certain latitude, one noting: 'in truth, we did not see much of him.' He listened and silently made changes. He had what the Spanish refer to as 'left hand', the ability to calm things down, a softly-softly approach. Loyal and defensive of his players, he was very likeable. Meet Del Bosque and one word leaps out at you: *decent*. He projects warmth and kindness. There was little in the way of pressure or imposition. He says there was no need, insisting that he did not encounter a dressing room of great egos. 'The *mediático* thing came later,' he says. 'People talked about the *galácticos* but in that year there could be nothing further from the truth – we had people like Raúl, Redondo, Hierro.'

'Toshack was more temperamental. He has his way of seeing football and we didn't really share it,' admits the central defender Iván Campo. 'Del Bosque brought tranquillity, relaxation, confidence. His discourse was: "gentlemen, we're Real Madrid: we're here to enjoy our football." There were already good players; he made us a team. We would go and have a beer, play basketball, everyone got on.'

As in 1998, the truth is that for much of the 1999–2000 season Madrid were not very good. For a third season in a row they finished behind Van Gaal's Barcelona. The stand-out game of their domestic campaign was when they were defeated 5-1 at home by Real Zaragoza, prompting a stadium-wide *pañolada*, white handkerchiefs waved in disgust. They travelled to Brazil for the World Club Championships in the winter and when they returned found themselves seventeenth. The fixture backlog meant that they had to play eleven games in twenty-five days and, although their league results improved, they finished fifth, seven points behind Deportivo. Just as in 1998, Madrid would not have qualified for the Champions League the following season had they not won it.

In Europe, they were on edge too, scraping through against Rosenberg in Norway – 'if we hadn't won that they would have shot us,' McManaman remembers. And yet things were starting to fall into place.

On the day they travelled to Old Trafford in the quarter-final, the cover of *Marca* had written out lines, an attempt to psyche up themselves and the players, to convince them that the impossible was possible: 'Manchester do not scare us, Manchester do not scare us, Manchester do not scare us, Manchester do not scare us, Manchester do not scare us, Manchester do not scare us' it ran over and over again. 'The truth is we were pretty scared,' the centre-back Iván Helguera admits; 'and yet,' adds striker Fernando Morientes, 'we also knew that we had nothing to lose.' Madrid's 3-2 victory, with Del Bosque switching to five at the back, giving McManaman the chance to run at his former rivals, and man-marking Paul Scholes – 'the milk-boy' as Madrid's coaching staff called him – was easily their most outstanding performance of the season.

It was marked, of course, by Fernando Redondo's implausibly good backheel to set up Raúl. 'That backheel killed Henning Berg,' jokes United's goalkeeper that night, Raymond Van Der Gouw. 'If he had done it to me, I'd have kept running to Buenos Aires,' laughs Campo, 'that was the play of the year. It didn't surprise me that Fernando tried it but it did surprise me that it came off so, so, so cleanly. Fernando took it all in his stride. He was cool as anything. But we were so happy afterwards. United were a terrifying team and Old Trafford . . .' Campo's words slow into a kind of reverential quiet. 'One of the things that we most talked about after the game was: "imagine if the Bernabéu was like this".'

The next morning, *Marca*'s cover declared them 'Eleven Di Stéfanos'.

In the semi-final, Bayern Munich. The Germans, Madrid's *other* great European rivals, had hammered them 4-2 and 4-1 in the second group phase and they were difficult opponents but Nicolas Anelka's goals, one in each leg, took Madrid to the final. Maybe that madness was beautiful after all. The Frenchman was sold in the summer of 2000 but his contribution, largely forgotten now, in those two vital games was colossal. Madrid were off to Paris; Valencia had denied them the chance to face Barcelona in a first ever *clásico* final by beating Louis Van Gaal's side, but from Madrid's point of view it was probably better this way

The *séptima* was a release like no other but Raúl draws one important distinction between the 1998 and 2000 European Cup finals that goes in favour of the *octava*: in Paris he was actually able to enjoy the occasion. The tension had been lifted. Although Madrid's opponents were Valencia, finalists the previous year and a side that had beaten them 3-2 at the Bernabéu earlier in the season, there were few nerves. Players still can't believe just how laid back the build-up was and the final itself was surprisingly comfortable: with Helguera protecting the back four, and the full-backs Míchel Salgado and Roberto Carlos pushing up, McManaman and Redondo controlled the game. Morientes scored the first with a header, McManaman volleyed in the second and, with Valencia pushing forward, Raúl was sent running through from inside his own half, no one anywhere near him.

It was as if time stopped; it seemed to take an age for him to reach the other end. 'Most of our lot just stood watching, but I started chasing: I don't really know why,' McManaman remembers. Raúl explains the thoughts racing through his mind as he approached the goal: go round him? Put the ball over him? Shoot early? The doubts were greater because the man confronting him was Santiago Cañizares, the former Madrid goalkeeper and a friend, someone who knew what Raúl liked to do. Eventually, the striker went round Cañizares to his right: 3-0. Madrid had done it again. Del Bosque took the opportunity to send on Hierro and Sanchís, a gesture to an entire generation. 'I don't envy my dad any more,' Sanchís said. 'I've got two now.'

'When Real Madrid play in the European Cup, their cup, anything is possible,' beamed Del Bosque. It hadn't exactly gone as planned but it was indeed their cup once more. They had equalled Barcelona's European Cups in colour in 1998 and pulled out in front again two years later. Barcelona had just lost the league title too, Van Gaal resigning, and just when the Catalan club thought things could not get any worse, they did get worse. 'All these directors were squeezing me to death in great bear hugs and I didn't know their names,' McManaman recalls of the celebrations after the final, 'and the next thing we knew, the president and directors who had been patting us on the back were gone.' 'We've entered into footballing mythology,' declared president Lorenzo Sanz but even the *octava* couldn't save him and his board. On 16 June, less than a month after winning the European Cup, Florentino Pérez was elected president of Real Madrid, voted in on the promise to sign the world's best player. Barcelona's Luis Figo.

18

AND PIGS DID FLY

'By the second or third corner I turned to Luis Figo and said: "Forget it, mate. You're on your own".' Míchel Salgado starts laughing. Real Madrid's former right-back won't forget that night at the Camp Nou in a hurry and nor will anyone else: 23 November 2002 produced arguably *the* defining image of the Barça–Madrid rivalry. 'I used to offer Luis the chance to take the short corner, drawing up close to him near the touchline, but not this time,' Salgado explains. 'Missiles were raining down from the stands: coins, a knife, a glass whisky bottle. Johnnie Walker, I think. Or J&B. Best to keep away. Short corners? No thanks.'

'And then,' Salgado says, 'I saw it.'

There it was, staring up from the Camp Nou turf: a *cochinillo*, the severed head of a suckling pig, secreted into the stadium and sent sailing Figo's way. 'In the dressing room afterwards, we were laughing about it,' Salgado remembers. '*A pig's head!* How the hell did someone bring a pig's head in? What was going through his mind? It was probably the weirdest thing I've ever seen, but then that's the *clásico*. I remember telling David Beckham: "You've never seen anything like it." And he hadn't. It's hostile and bitter, political, territorial. Much, much more than a football match.'

Especially when Luis Figo was around.

After the game, Barcelona director Gabriel Masfurrol accused the Madrid media of making the whole thing up with the help of a cunningly concealed *cochinillo* in the camera bag, while presidential adviser José María Minguella argued: 'We don't even eat *cochinillo* in Catalonia.' *Marca* and *AS* reacted fast, publishing additional pictures and stories from behind the cameras. *AS*'s photographer was 'disgusted', *Marca*'s found it 'pretty funny' and a week later they interviewed the King of the *Cochinillo*, a chef from Segovia who described it as 'an insult . . . to the pig.'

He explained: '*Cochinillo* is an exquisite dish and a symbol of Segovia. It doesn't deserve to be treated this way. You need to be seriously twisted to bring that into the ground; the head would have made a terrible mess because of the liquid leaking out and it must have smelt repugnant.'

That was Luis Figo's third season at Madrid since leaving Barcelona and there was no sign of the hatred or the hurt subsiding. When he had turned up at the Camp Nou the first time, the noise was deafening. Banners were hung round the stadium. Traitor. Judas. Scum. Mercenary. Figo came out and reached for his ears, twisting them inwards. It was *loud*. Thousands of fake 10,000 peseta notes had been printed, emblazoned with his image. Even real money was thrown about: a Catalan businessman had provided over a hundred bank notes, stamped with Figo's face.

'I must be one of the very few sportsmen to have had to perform with 120,000 people against me – and focused on me, not the team,' Figo says. There's a kind of wistfulness as he says so, a sadness too. Every time he got the ball, the noise rose, insults and missiles flying. Oranges, sandwiches in tin foil, bottles, cigarette lighters, even a couple of mobile phones. Figo was awful, Barcelona victorious, the match finishing 2-0. 'The atmosphere,' admitted Madrid's president Florentino Pérez, 'got to us all.'

'That night when Figo first went back was incredible,' says Iván Campo, 'I've never heard anything like it. Luis didn't deserve that.

He'd given his all for Barcelona. It was built up before: "a traitor's coming," the media said. No, Luis Figo is coming, one of the greats for you. That night hurt him, you could see. His head was bowed and he was thinking: "bloody hell, I was here last season . . ." But my lasting emotion was admiration: *you've got balls.*'

When Figo returned two months later to face Barcelona's city rivals Espanyol there were more missiles but this time was different; this time carnations tumbled gratefully from the stands. A banner declared: 'Not all Catalans are animals'.

In that first season, Figo hadn't taken the corners at the Camp Nou and in the second he didn't play because of an injury some thought a little too convenient but his absence didn't prevent more missiles, including a cockerel's head. In the third, they were waiting for him. Every time he came within range, beer cans, lighters and bottles flew, golf balls too. 'I was worried that some madman might lose his head,' Figo says. Some madman did. And so did a pig.

Midway through the second half Madrid won a corner. Amid a shower of flying objects, it took Figo two minutes to take it – and then he nearly scored, goalkeeper Roberto Bonano tipping away an inswinger. Another corner, over on the other side. As Figo strolled across he slowed to pick up the missiles and as he prepared to take the corner he swept the turf of debris, at one point reaching for a bottle of Cola, giving an ironic thumbs-up and smiling. Every time he began his run-up, something else landed and the ritual was repeated over and over – stop, pick it up, start again – until referee Luis Medina Cantalejo suspended the game.

It was held up for sixteen minutes and, in the midst of it all, someone spotted the pig's head. 'I didn't see it. If I had I would have eaten a bit: an *aperitivo!*' Figo jokes. 'It never even enters your head that someone could go into the stadium with a *cochinillo*. Or a whisky bottle. That's not sport; I understand rivalry and that goes beyond it. I've played Juve–Inter, Inter–Milan, and the world doesn't come to an end.' The Spanish Football Federation imposed a two-game ban although

Barcelona never served it, president Ángel María Villar eventually granting them a pardon.

'Figo provoked the fans,' moaned Barcelona coach Louis Van Gaal. 'He walked over to the corner slowly, picked up the bottle slowly, went back to the corner slowly . . . and all this consciously and deliberately, without the referee doing anything.' A Barcelona director snapped: 'Figo lives off lies, he's been provoking our fans for two years.' And Barcelona's president Joan Gaspart added: 'I'm not trying to justify events but Figo's provocation was out of place and totally unnecessary. I won't accept people coming to my house to provoke.'

Provoke? By taking corners? Gaspart's emotional reaction showed how hurt he'd been and how hurt he still is: few suffered as he did. The Portuguese's departure was Gaspart's destruction and a decade on he still insists: 'Figo walked all the way round the back of the goal. When does a player ever do that? And they weren't trying to hit him. If they had tried, they would have.'

Luis Figo became the new focus of the Barça–Madrid rivalry, its physical incarnation, a cartoon baddie in Barcelona's world. He was a Di Stéfano, Franco or Guruceta for the twenty-first century. His move to Madrid was huge because Figo was huge. The winner of the Ballon d'Or in November 2000, his transfer to Madrid and performances since arriving may well have earned him some extra votes but he'd basically won the award for what he did for Barcelona; it was there that he became the best in the world. When he returned to the Camp Nou for the first time, Barça's physio Ángel Mur asked Figo for a photograph of him with the trophy to go alongside the other Ballon d'Or winners in the mini museum he'd set up in the dressing room – a picture to accompany those of Johan Cruyff, Hristo Stoichkov, Ronaldo and Rivaldo. The next time Figo visited he found that someone had coloured his white shirt *blaugrana*.

Barcelona had lost a brilliant player but it was not just that Figo had been the best, it was that he had been so reliable, so committed. He had seemed to embrace Barcelona completely. A famous photo shows him in full Barça kit, posing inside the emblematic Palau de la Música; he'd been introduced to the city by Pep Guardiola, and he had celebrated his last success by dying his hair blue and claret and chanting: 'White cry babies, salute the Champions!' Fans sang: 'Don't stop, Figo, Figo, keep going, keep going!' and he did exactly that. As one player puts it: 'our plan was simple: give the ball to Luis. He never, ever hid.'

While he was at Barcelona, a biography of Figo was published by the Catalan newspaper *Sport*. It was called *Born to Triumph* and Guardiola wrote the prologue, which reads almost like a love letter. Guardiola opens by placing himself on a flight to Prague in the Champions League. Figo is suspended, 'staying behind in your adopted city, the one you love so much', and in his absence Guardiola pens an ode. 'We know you're always there [for the team],' he writes before comparing Figo to Diego Maradona, a player team-mates admired as much for his commitment as his quality: 'he was there when everyone else had left, every last one of them. He lifted his head and shouted when others were silent. He was being Maradona. He was loved. Venerated. Maradona did what Figo does. Figo does what Maradona did.'

The biography was published in April 2000. Within three months, Figo had joined Madrid. One former Barcelona player dismisses the complaints of supporters who, he says, can never see football the way players do, insisting 'of course Figo went: for that kind of money any player would go'. But Michael Laudrup, who made the same journey six years earlier, is quick to differentiate the two cases and one of Figo's team-mates at the Camp Nou is equally adamant that this was different: 'the lie,' he says, 'hurts more than the fact.'

Ask Figo and the uneasiness is still there, even now. The hint at something beyond his control. Why did you leave Barcelona and join Real Madrid? He sits on a sofa in a hotel in north-eastern Madrid and thinks. 'I felt that I was giving my all and I didn't feel that the directors gave me the recognition I felt I deserved,' he says. 'I told them that, I was clear about it, and they took no notice. They thought I was bluffing. And then things started taking the direction they took. It was uncomfortable because there were doubts and difficult moments. Maybe it wasn't very, very, very clear because it didn't depend only on me. And that made it hard.'

Did you want to go to Madrid really?

Figo doesn't say yes; what he does say is: 'It started with a *calentón* and it ended up being real.'

A *calentón* is a moment's hot-headedness, a spark of anger.

'But in the end it was the right decision,' he continues. 'I go back to Barcelona and there's no problem. I have nothing against Barcelona and *barcelonismo*. If they are against me, that's their problem, not mine.'

Real Madrid were immersed in presidential elections, called by the incumbent Lorenzo Sanz. His challenger, Florentino Pérez, was one of the richest and most powerful men in Spain. The owner of the construction company ACS, he boasted a fortune estimated at €600 million and was an ex-Madrid councillor for the now defunct centre-right Unión de Centro Democrático, a personal friend of the country's Madrid-supporting prime minister José María Aznar and part of a group of constructors close to power who stood at the heart of a spectacular and ultimately unsustainable building boom. But few gave him a chance of winning the presidency: Sanz had, after all, delivered two European Cups in three years after a thirty-two-year wait.

Pérez, though, had an ace up his sleeve. The news broke on 6 July while Sanz was at the wedding of his daughter, Malula, to Míchel Salgado. Pérez had struck a deal that would take Figo to Madrid if he won the election. He'd carried out a survey that showed that the player Madrid fans most wanted to sign was Figo and he thought he knew how he could do just that. In Spain, every player has a *cláusula de rescisión* – an official price at which his club is obliged to sell. The money is deposited with the league and the 'selling' club can do nothing to prevent a departure. The *cláusulas* are set prohibitively high – Leo Messi's currently stands at €250 million while Cristiano Ronaldo's is €1,000 million – are largely symbolic and never apply when a sale is agreed. But while Barcelona would never agree to sell Figo to Madrid, Pérez had spotted an opening: negotiations over his new contract with Barcelona had stalled and his buy-out clause, set when he had signed his previous deal, remained 10,000 million pesetas, around £38 million. That meant a new world record but it was just within reach.

Pérez offered Figo a guaranteed 400 million pesetas (c. £1.6 million) just to sign an agreement legally binding him to Madrid in the seemingly impossible event of his election victory. If Figo broke the deal, he would have to pay Pérez 5,000 million pesetas in compensation. If Pérez lost, Figo kept the cash and stayed where he was. To Figo's agent, José Veiga, and to Paulo Futre, the former Atlético Madrid player who acted as an intermediary, it looked like money for nothing. It might also help twist Barcelona's arm when it came to the new contract. What's not clear is whether Figo explicitly authorised Veiga to deal with Pérez. Read his words again: *it didn't depend only on me.*

When Veiga confirmed the deal, the impact was nuclear. Figo denied everything, insisting: 'I'll stay at Barcelona whether Pérez wins or loses'. He accused the presidential candidate of 'lying' and 'fantasising'. He told Luis Enrique and Guardiola he was not going and, relieved, they conveyed the message to the Barcelona squad: *relax, Luis is staying.* Maybe he hoped he was: Futre has claimed that Figo was furious with him and the way Figo spoke in the media suggested a man trying to torpedo Pérez's chances, just in case. On 9 July, *Sport* ran an interview in which he said: 'I want to send a message of calm to Barcelona's fans, for whom I always have and always will feel great affection. I want to assure [them] that Luis Figo will, with absolute certainty, be at the Camp Nou on the 24th to start the new season.' He added categorically: 'I've not signed a pre-contract with a presidential candidate at Real Madrid. No. I'm not so mad as to do a thing like that.'

Lorenzo Sanz was delighted, joking: 'maybe Florentino will

announce that he's signed Claudia Schiffer next.' But on 16 July Pérez, who had carefully been rounding up postal votes too, was named Madrid's new president with a three-thousand-vote margin.

Barcelona were also going through elections, former vice-president Joan Gaspart emerging as the winner a week later. His first task was to manage the crisis. He claims that Figo pleaded with him to block the move to Madrid: the winger did not want to leave but the clause was watertight. Veiga had been outmanoeuvred and was now cornered, pressuring Figo into leaving and even going so far as to turn on the tears. Gaspart says Figo told him his agent was 'suicidal' with worry. The only way Barcelona could rescue Figo from Madrid's clutches was to pay the penalty clause: 5,000 million pesetas, just under £19 million. That would have effectively meant paying the fifth highest transfer fee in history to sign their own player.

Raising the money was one issue but there was another problem too, according to Gaspart: 'To convince the *socios* that the Figo deal was real, Florentino had promised them they would go free for a year if he didn't sign. How? By financing that with the 5,000 million pesetas [penalty] we would have to pay on Figo's behalf. I couldn't do it. I'm the new president of Barcelona and I pay for *Real Madrid's* fans to watch them every week? I would die . . . die!' There was no way out. After final conversations between Gaspart and Figo had resolved nothing, Barcelona's new president called the media and told them: 'Today, Figo gave me the impression that he wanted to do two things: get richer and stay at Barça.'

Only one of them happened. The following day, 24 July, Figo was presented in Madrid, handed his new shirt by Alfredo Di Stéfano. His *cláusula* was set at 30,000 million pesetas. 'I hope to be as happy here as I was at Barcelona,' he said, barely smiling. 'Figo was born to play for Madrid,' Florentino Pérez later insisted. Gaspart vowed: 'I won't forget this. Whoever's responsible will pay.'

By the end of the 2000–2001 season, stung by the Camp Nou experience, Figo's conversion to the *Madridista* cause was complete.

He had led Madrid to their first league title in four years, Spain's outstanding performer as they finished seven points clear of Deportivo de La Coruña and seventeen above Barcelona. 'Because of the pressure, I felt relieved and satisfied at the decision,' he says. 'I felt like I was in the press every day. You have to justify your performances after you've been the most expensive player in the world. You go on to the pitch and you're not thinking if you cost fifty or seventy or if you earn one thousand or two thousand . . . but subconsciously it's there.'

On the other side of the divide the pressure was even greater. Losing Figo was a decisive blow for Barcelona, which had of course been part of the plan. Gaspart found himself staring into the void and never recovered from the trauma. 'Figo and I have spoken since but that deal was carried out with *nocturnidad y alevosidad*, traitorously and under cover of darkness,' he says. 'He left because of a deal his agent, whom he later ditched, signed with Pérez.' The impact was devastating. 'Gaspart entered a state of shock that affected his ability to think rationally,' Minguella says. 'He was ruined by Madrid, obsessed. He wouldn't listen to anyone. He had €70 million and he just wasted it, falling victim of Madrid.'

'Figo's move destroyed us,' Gaspart admits. He explains: 'Two things happen. One, the day you get elected, Figo tells you he's going to Madrid. Your best player gone. Two, they give you loads of money. *Loads* of it. And instead of saying what I should have said: "gentlemen, this season whatever will be will be", I tried to rescue the situation, so I went on to the street to sign. That was a disaster: everyone knows you've just lost Figo, they know you've got money, they know you're obliged to sign. You can't do what I did, you just can't. You're dead.'

Gaspart wasted every cent. He signed Marc Overmars for €39.6 million, Gerard López for €21.6 million, Alfonso Pérez for €15 million and Emmanuel Petit for €9 million. The following season Javier Saviola came for €30 million, Giovanni for €20.6 million, Philippe Christanval for €16.8 million, Fabio Rochemback for €14.6

million and Francesco Coco for €2.4 million. Not one of them had a lasting impact. Meanwhile, Patrik Kluivert was given the biggest salary in Spain, a millstone round the club's neck. 'Gaspart was desperate,' recalls one player. 'He threw money at us. There's no doubt he loved Barcelona with all his heart but he was the worst president imaginable. There were bonuses for everything and he gave us whatever we asked for, so naturally we kept asking for more. It got so ridiculous that we actually ended up feeling guilty.'

Barcelona were in apparently permanent crisis; opposition groups mobilised and results were awful. Barcelona finished the 2000–1 and 2001–2 seasons fourth, seventeen points behind Madrid and eleven points behind Valencia respectively. In 2002–3, they were sixth, twenty-two points behind Madrid. Gaspart tried new players and new coaches; the continuity of which Barcelona are now proud was conspicuous by its absence. He had Lorenç Serra Ferrer, Charly Rexach and even Louis Van Gaal for a second spell. 'I should have known that sequels are never any good,' Gaspart says; 'it was like the devil himself was returning,' one player adds. In 2003, he briefly turned to Antonio de la Cruz then hired the former Real Madrid and Atlético Madrid manager Radi Antić before resigning and calling elections. 'Those six months at Barcelona were like six years,' Antić says.

For Gaspart, the pressure had become unbearable. The image that defined him came in December 2002 when Barcelona lost 3-0 to Sevilla. It was their fourth loss in five, confirming the club's worst ever start to a season – one that left them two points off relegation – and at full-time supporters turned to the directors' box and chanted: 'Resign! Resign!' Gaspart faced his fate live on television, cameras zooming right in as he stood motionless and alone, 50,000 *culés* abusing him, a broken man close to tears. One by one Barça's directors encouraged him to leave, but he pushed them away and insisted on accepting his punishment. He stood there for seven minutes before heading back inside where a TV reporter asked if he was going to resign. Polls showed that 90 per cent wanted Gaspart to go and the morning's papers all led on *¡Dimisión!*, Resign!, while one match report declared: 'Barcelona attended their own funeral.'

'People didn't understand my reaction that night,' Gaspart says, sitting in his office, a refurbished Catalan-style farmhouse just up the road from the Camp Nou. There's a crucifix on one wall and pictures all over the others, going back decades. A life dedicated to his club. 'Lots of people thought it was an act of arrogance, of *chulería*, for me to stand there,' he continues. 'It wasn't. It was an act of responsibility; I was responsible for the disaster so I gave supporters the chance to say what they had to say – and to my face. People said to me: "don't stand there" but the supporters were right to be angry. I'd got it wrong from the very beginning. And it all started with Figo. You lose your best player and you lose him to your biggest rival. It was a double blow – you lose, they win.'

Figo was just the start. Real Madrid celebrated their centenary in 2002, a year in which they opened a theme park, the Vuelta a España cycling finished at the Bernabéu and Magic Johnson played with Madrid's basketball team. The celebrations were all-encompassing, quasi-religious, and *everywhere*. 'The club had organised some event *every single day*,' remembers Steve McManaman. Atlético's president Jesús Gil remarked sarcastically: 'Madrid are celestial, more important than the Holy Spirit. Florentino will appear before us and say "Spaniards, we are the glory of the earth and we have a place in heaven." Then he'll pass down the new tablets of Moses. Us infidels had better watch out!'

The headline event was a game against the rest of the world. A full orchestra was arranged on the pitch and Plácido Domingo boomed out the club's new anthem. As he did so, two teams lined up: one in blue, the other in white. The blues were a world XI but the whites had the more glamorous side and more famous faces: Ronaldo, Zinedine Zidane, Figo, Roberto Carlos, Raúl, Fernando Hierro, Casillas . . . There may never have been a team like it, not since the

Alfredo Di Stéfano era. It was as if they had cheated at the computer game *Championship Manager*. When Madrid's captain Hierro said 'of the ten best players in the world, we have five' it was hardly an exaggeration. Ronaldo had collected the FIFA World Player award the night before, meaning that of the previous six winners Madrid boasted five; Ronaldo and Zidane having won it twice. They came, of course, to be known as the *galácticos*.

Figo had been the first to arrive, next Pérez targeted Zinedine Zidane, secretly signed on a napkin at the Champions League gala in Monte Carlo and joining for a new world record fee of €75.1 million, then came Ronaldo. Madrid's interest leaked out in August 2002 but Internazionale president Massimo Moratti resisted their advances; the price was going to be huge. Gaspart at last saw a chance to take revenge. Pérez had been trying to raise the money to twist Moratti's arm when Gaspart made a €15 million bid for Madrid's unwanted striker Fernando Morientes, providing much-needed funds. Barcelona were helping Madrid buy a Camp Nou icon? It seemed too good to be true.

It was. At 10 p.m. on deadline day, Gaspart reneged, *accidentally* leaving Madrid cashless and, therefore, Ronaldo-less. That was the plan, anyway. The reality was that all Gaspart achieved was to save Madrid €10 million. Moratti had already bought Ronaldo's replacement, Hernán Crespo, and feared getting lumbered with both strikers. With the clock ticking, the price tumbled: €35 million plus an additional €10 million or McManaman or Santi Solari in December. When Solari turned down Inter's contract offer, the Italians demanded the €10 million. It was never paid.

How Madrid managed to pay was another bone of contention. The almost €200 million spent on Figo, Zidane and Ronaldo was a lot of money for a club with debts of €278 million. Pérez had announced in September 2000 that the club was 'seriously ill'. The cure was to sell the Ciudad Deportiva, Madrid's training ground, a sale made possible by Pérez's *enchufes*, or contacts: a deal was closed with the

Partido Popular-led council and the project was then seen through the *recalificación* process, in which the land, previously protected as green space for sporting use, was reclassified as fit for construction. Four gigantic skyscrapers were built, towering over Madrid's skyline and visible for miles, a monument to the lightning growth of the city. With the money raised, €446.7 million, Madrid built a new, 1,200,000 square metre training ground at Valdebebas, near Barajas airport, and cleared their debt at a stroke, enabling them to sign again. The four towers were nicknamed Figo, Zidane, Ronaldo and Beckham.

The team was defined by them too: stars were central to Pérez's vision. Madrid's policy became known as *Zidanes and Pavones*; they aspired to a team made up of superstars like Zidane and youth-teamers like centre-back Paco Pavón, whose commitment to and understanding of the club could be counted upon. It was presented as a philosophy but it was also an economic imperative. The only way to pay players like Zidane on wages of €6 million a year was by promoting youth-teamers who were paid far, far less – 'a pittance', as one team-mate puts it. In turn, the *Zidanes* carried Madrid's image around the world.

If anything defined Pérez's first presidency it was his obsession with marketing. He was a pioneer. Along with former marketing manager José Ángel Sánchez, now the club's general manager, he launched Madrid on an image crusade of evangelical zeal. In 1999–2000, not one Madrid league match at the Bernabéu had sold out – not even the *derbi* against Barcelona. In 2000–2001, eighteen out of nineteen matches had. Pérez claimed that the arrival of Figo and Zidane saw the 'value' of Madrid's badge rise almost fourfold and after landing Ronaldo added: 'Nothing is more profitable than signing a superstar: there are many players who score twenty-five a season, but Ronaldo's the only one who can pay for himself.' Whether or not he actually could was a different matter entirely but this was a central plank of the policy – a policy that, as midfielder Santi Solari astutely warned, tended to the extinction of the middle class. It was also one that meant the *galácticos* had to play.

Pérez's obsession was 'universalism'. The representative of Spain now aspired to be the representative of the world, a kind of hugely profitable imperial power, with pre-season tours not so much preparation as market breakers. When Madrid and the Spanish Post Office released centenary stamps, the blurb ran: 'We're sending the image of the twentieth century's greatest club to millions all over the world, over five continents, across languages and cultures, as is only right for Real Madrid, a club that defies frontiers, race and language.' And when David Beckham later signed, Inocencio Arias, Spain's ambassador to the UN and a Madrid fan, declared: 'What Philip II couldn't achieve because of the English, to establish an empire where the sun never sets, Real Madrid will achieve – paradoxically, thanks to an Englishman.'

The excitement, the glamour, that surrounded Real Madrid was astonishing. There was something outrageous in the ambition that delighted supporters and disgusted rivals. 'People enjoy just hearing our starting XI,' Salgado commented. Media interest rocketed and if their football was not always as sparkling as expected, the promise was there. So too flashes of brilliance. 'I enjoyed it so much,' Zidane says. 'If you were two down these days you'd say: "we're going to lose". We didn't. They scored two? *No pasa nada*. We'll score three. It was fun.' Few embodied that fun more than Ronaldo, a player of whom Figo says admiringly: 'he didn't need to train, the bugger!' Zidane recalls: 'Ronaldo was such a good player that no one minded. I remember a game when the president came along with some politician. "Ronnie, could you run a bit more?" "*Presi*, you pay me to score goals not to run." And Ronnie goes out there and scores two. That was one of the things that helped make Madrid so great.'

It was also, ultimately, one of the things that brought about their downfall. The fact that Madrid revelled in their status, humility absent, made winning an obligation, but the system was not set up for sustainable success. Each new *galáctico* was for ever associated with his debut season. The year 2000–1 was Luis Figo's and it ended with a league championship that Madrid had dominated from the start. Zidane's year, 2001–2, proved less easy. Madrid lost the Copa del Rey final in their own stadium on their 100th birthday, opponents Deportivo de La Coruña instantly becoming the rest of Spain's other team as blue-and white-shirted Galicians packed into the north stand singing *Happy Birthday to You*. They finished third in the league, nine points behind Rafa Benítez's Valencia and two behind Deportivo. And captain Hierro admitted that they were under more pressure than ever. No one suffered like Zidane. Criticised by the media and questioned by supporters in his first months, one team-mate reveals that Zidane even contemplated throwing in the towel.

'It's true,' Zidane confirms. 'Not quite saying that [I was going to ditch it all] but saying: "*a lo mejor me voy, eh*", maybe I'll go. But people said "it'll pass" and they were right. In the end, everything passes.'

It passed in the best possible way. Redemption came in Europe, where Madrid faced Barcelona in the semi-final – the first time they had been drawn together in the European Cup since 1960, one headline declaring it 'beyond words' and Vicente del Bosque calling it 'a civil war I could do without'. Salgado recalls: 'the reaction was: *me cago en la puta*. Bloody hell, couldn't we have been kept apart? This is going to be historic, for the rest of our bloody lives. The pressure was unbelievable. We knew it wasn't a normal *derbi*. If you lose, you don't just lose; you lose to your rivals in a game that will never, ever, be forgotten. We'd never played them in a game as big before. There's a European Cup final on the other side. But if you don't get there . . .'

The Madrid team bus arrived in Barcelona for the first leg on Saint Jordi's day. 'We could see people carrying flowers as they abused us and threw missiles,' Salgado continues, 'it was a surreal sight.' A few minutes from the Camp Nou, the shout went up. 'It's time.' Time for a familiar routine. Madrid's players left their seats and huddled together in the aisle, lying down as far from the windows as possible. The curtains were drawn and arms were placed on heads. And then it started: the stones and bottles hit the bus as it turned the corner, on to Travessera de Les Corts and into the tunnel below the stadium. Once they were safely inside, heads were raised and so were the first shouts: 'Come on!'

'It's part of the rivalry and we didn't see it as such a bad thing,' Zidane says. 'It maybe even helps you get into the zone.' Salgado agrees: 'We'd lift our heads, survey the damage, and then it would start: "let's do this!" It was extra motivation. I sometimes wondered if Barcelona fans would have been better ignoring us, greeting us with silence. It would have felt weird, disconcerting.'

Barcelona were the better side for an hour but Zidane and McManaman chipped a goal apiece to give Madrid a 2-0 win. 'I was just thinking: "we've just won by two goals, we're as good as in the Champions League final,"' McManaman later wrote, 'but to the Spanish lads it was an immeasurably bigger deal. The Barça factor, how can an outsider truly understand it? It meant so much to them. A hell of a lot.' Zidane's memories centre on the trip home: 'There were maybe five thousand people at the airport, people coming up and saying "*gracias* for the goal!" I saw there what the rivalry was. People wanted to eat me.'

A 1-1 draw in the second leg saw Madrid safely through to the final, which took place on 15 May – the day of San Isidro, the patron saint of Madrid. Their opponents were Bayer Leverkusen, the team who, if there was a competition for coming second, would still finish second. Runners-up in the league and runners-up in the German Cup, they were about to finish runners-up in the European Cup as well. Raúl scored the first, Lucio equalised and Zidane put Madrid back in the lead just before half-time. With Iker Casillas coming on as a late sub for the injured César Sánchez and making a string of vital saves, Zidane's goal proved to be the winner – an image that has been silhouetted and used over and over again, instantly recognisable. It could not have been more perfect: Madrid's ninth European Cup, won at Hampden Park, the scene of the 1960 final, with Zidane, that year's *galáctico*, redeemed by perhaps the most emblematic goal of all, left boot up near his ear to volley in.

Zidane looks up at the ceiling, turning his shoulder, remembering, going through the motions. The hotel's ornate chandelier plays the part of the ball, Roberto Carlos's 'assist' dropping from the sky. 'I shift sideways and I think: "I'm going to shoot". I looked across to see where the goal was. I had time. I know I'm going to hit it first time and . . . *whoosh!* When it went in, I felt so much happiness. I ran off shouting and in Spanish too. *¡Toma, toma, toma!* Take that!

'That was what I needed. The trophy I didn't have was the Champions League. I'd lost two finals with Juventus, one of them against Madrid, and when a club pays €78 million, you have to do something very big. The first three months were difficult: the media chased me absolutely everywhere and I thought "what is this?" Now people say: "well, he cost a lot but he won the Champions League". The king was in the dressing room afterwards, as if he was one of us. The king! You're there and you think: *¡Qué bonito!*'

Zidane's year ended with the European Cup. The following year, Ronaldo's year, ended with the league title, the Brazilian finishing top scorer. That season's *galáctico* had again decisively marked the campaign. But something was shifting; the flaws in Madrid's model coming to the fore, tensions too. Solari's concerns about the eclipse of the 'middle class' appeared ever more prophetic and would soon be confirmed in brutal fashion. Important players sensed that their faces didn't fit. In the weeks building up to the final game, which Madrid needed to win against Athletic Bilbao to clinch the title, a car pulled up outside the Bernabéu. The side of the stadium was draped in a huge tarpaulin banner depicting Madrid's stars. At the wheel, a Madrid player looked up at the banner and sighed: 'you'd think they were the only people at the club.' He was not alone in thinking that. 'However much you say so-and-so is an excellent player, if he doesn't sell lots of shirts, he's not a star,' Iván Helguera noted, while McManaman says that the *galácticos* couldn't be dropped, writing:

'Del Bosque didn't think it was fair – at one point he effectively told me his hands were tied. They were the rules set from above . . . the hierarchy of Perez's Real Madrid.'

Del Bosque always referred to himself as an 'employee' but his obedience made little difference. He didn't fit either and nor did Hierro. Men from a different mould to the president, in Pérez's mind they represented a challenge; an obstacle to his vision. Pérez had already forced out Fernando Redondo and had tried to sell Morientes, prompting Hierro to reprimand him for treating players like 'stock'. Slowly, Pérez chipped away at a dressing-room nucleus he distrusted, while he had taken such a disliking to Del Bosque that, unbeknownst to supporters, he had refused to travel on the same flight as his coach for over a year. As the final game approached, Hierro and Del Bosque's contracts had not been renewed. With two minutes to go on the final day, Del Bosque took Hierro off. The club captain, Hierro had been at Madrid for fourteen years, winning five league titles and three European Cups. Now, he was given a huge ovation that felt like a goodbye, a final homage.

If that was an indication that something was not right in Madrid, more followed. The lap of honour was cut short and the players planned to boycott the official reception at the cathedral and town hall the following day, claiming unequal treatment. It was not until late into the night that it was decided that they would go after all, Raúl hurriedly making calls and trying to get round the various restaurants, bars and nightspots to tell the squad. Two of them never got the message: when the team turned up at the cathedral the following day, McManaman and Ronaldo were only just waking up. Tensions had come to a head at the Txistu, a restaurant north of the Bernabéu where the team, directors and staff were supposed to be celebrating. There, Hierro learnt that he was not continuing. The following day, Del Bosque learnt the same.

Pérez said he wanted a coach with a 'modern' approach: Del Bosque, left-wing, mustachioed, old-fashioned, quietly dignified, didn't fit his vision. He had been in charge for four years, winning two league titles and two European Cups. It is almost ten years ago now and since then he has become a World Cup winner but there has been continued coldness in the relationship between the former coach and club president, and the departure still hurts. 'Of course, *hombre*,' Del Bosque says. 'Madrid were practically my family. People say: "bah, what's Del Bosque complaining about? He should be grateful." I am! But no one should be giving me lessons in *Madridismo*. I have thought about that so much and I am grateful, *very* grateful, but the pain . . .'

He falls quiet for a moment. 'The pain will not be cured in my lifetime.'

Madrid did not win another trophy for three years. Del Bosque's release at the end of the 2002–3 season is often presented as the turning point, and with some justification. But equally important were the other men departing the club and the sheer number, leaving the squad threadbare. Over a dozen players went, including Hierro, Morientes and the defensive midfielder Claude Makelele. 'We had eleven players plus Solari, nothing else,' says one director. 'Del Bosque went, Hierro, Morientes, Makelele, a man in every line. That's a lot when the normal rule is: *never change a winning team*,' admits Zidane. 'We had a very offensive team, even Roberto Carlos attacked. Makelele was the only one who always, always kept his position. He was the reference point and when he left we missed him.'

The symbolism of Makelele's departure – the undermining of the unsung hero – was made all the greater for the identity of the sole arrival, the man who ultimately replaced him. David Beckham was the most recognisable and marketable footballer on the planet. The fact that that perception is unfair on Beckham – 'people said "Beckham, image", but he was very, very professional,' Zidane insists – doesn't make it untrue. 'It wasn't Beckham's fault and his attitude and commitment were beyond reproach, but that was a turning point because of what he represented,' concedes one director. 'His arrival was the scientific proof that the spectacle was more important to us than the game itself. He represented the inversion of sporting values.' Madrid immediately set off on a tour of the Far East. As one player puts it: 'There were moments on that tour that I was thinking: "I'm always travelling, there are no training sessions, no rest".'

'If the most important thing is to put on a circus, then you have less chance of winning things,' Figo once said. His opinion hasn't changed much. 'One thing is the rules of a football team, another is marketing. There was a moment in which that balance didn't exist. We reached a point where we left the path a football team should take and we paid for that. External interests entered into the dressing room. We even had an actor on the team bench [from the film *Goal!*] and cameras filming us in the dressing room . . .' Seeing which way it was going, the sporting director tried to resign at the end of the 2002–3 season, only to be talked round. The new coach, Carlos Queiroz, also quickly feared the worst, even though Madrid won the first *clásico* of the 2003–4 season, beating Barcelona in the league at the Camp Nou for the first time in twenty years with Beckham declaring it 'as sweet as winning the European Cup'. In the spring Madrid were top and had also reached the final of the Copa del Rey.

On 11 March 2004, three bombs ripped through commuter trains near Atocha station in Madrid, killing 191 people. That morning, Real Madrid's players stood silently in a circle at the club's Ciudad Deportiva training ground. They didn't train that day; they did though, play on the Saturday, drawing 1-1 with Zaragoza. In the stadium, candles occupied a handful of vacant seats where season-ticket holders killed in the attack had once watched games. At half-time, news filtered through that five men had been arrested, members of an Al-Qaeda cell.

That night spontaneous demonstrations broke out against the government. The Partido Popular had insisted that the Basque separatist group ETA were responsible from the start, even though there was no evidence and the attack did not fit ETA's normal pattern. With elections looming, though, it had suited the PP to point the finger at Basque separatists; the government's decision to join the war in Afghanistan was already unpopular and the subsequent emergence of Islamic terrorism could cost them votes. The state news channel TVE toed the line, attributing the attack to ETA, while the foreign minister Ana Palacios sent a telegram to Spain's ambassadors to order them to 'take every opportunity to assert that ETA are responsible' and the prime minister José María Aznar phoned foreign correspondents on British newspapers, and at dailies in Spain, to tell them it was definitely ETA. Spain even asked the United Nations to finger ETA as the guilty party.

The following day, with electoral turnout rocketing, the PP were voted out of power, punished for their handling of the crisis. Conspiracy stories continued to dominate some media, attempts to link the attack to ETA, and it remained a deeply emotive issue, presented by the right as if the incoming Socialist government were happy beneficiaries of the bombing. Aznar had gone; he was replaced as prime minister by José Luis Rodríguez Zapatero, a Barcelona fan from León. Some saw symbolism in the change in government or even an explanation for Madrid's subsequent collapse; others explained that collapse as partly a product of the trauma of the bombings and its impact on the city.

There was something a little grubby in those attempts and, besides, the people on the inside at the Bernabéu could already see that Madrid's superb early season form was unsustainable. Queiroz was swiftly aware that his authority was as non-existent as his squad. When rumours circulated that Michael Owen would be Madrid's next *galáctico*, he privately joked: 'we're going to have to lobby FIFA to let us play in half the pitch.' He had already insisted publicly: 'A Ferrari can't run without tyres', and while he likened trying to win the league and Champions League without Makelele to climbing Everest without oxygen. He contemplated walking out at Christmas, but held on in the hope that his team could do likewise – in the hope that even if they limped over the line they would cross it first. After all, they had a substantial lead.

But, exhausted and divided, Madrid lost their final four games, a new club record. Valencia won the league and just before Madrid reached the line their recovering rivals Barcelona came flying past them, preparing to build a new dynasty of their own. Barcelona finished ahead of Madrid for the first time in four season and, after six years without a trophy, then claimed two league titles and the European Cup in the following two years. And it had all started with a promise of their own to sign David Beckham.

Madrid's empire was collapsing. They went three successive seasons without winning a major trophy. Not since 1953, before Alfredo Di Stéfano arrived, had Madrid endured such a drought. The most expensive, most glamorous team ever had been humiliated and Pérez resigned in February 2006, the emperor finally aware of his nakedness. He had created a culture destined for failure, provoking division and inequality, consigning sporting directors to irrelevance and stripping coaches of authority. When Pérez fell on his sword, coach Juan Ramón López Caro was liberated. 'From now on, I will play with players not names,' he said.

In 2009, during Cristiano Ronaldo's first few weeks as a Real Madrid player, a TV programme was discussing whether he could be dropped: would the coach, Manuel Pellegrini, have the nerve to bench a star? 'Well,' said Jaime Collazos, the presenter, 'why don't we ask a coach who has had the nerve to do just that?' He turned to Mariano García Remón, one of the panellists that day, and said: 'Mariano, you left [Brazilian] Ronaldo out once . . .'

The response was eloquent. 'Yeah,' García Remón replied, 'and it cost me my job.'

Pérez employed five coaches after releasing Del Bosque but none won anything. Del Bosque had been pushed out having just won the league; the following year, they finished empty handed and Queiroz was sacked; he was replaced by José Antonio Camacho, who was replaced by García Remón, who was replaced by Vanderlei Luxemburgo, who was replaced by López Caro. All in the space of just two years.

In total, there had been four sporting directors, six coaches and over €440 million spent on players in three years, nineteen players in and thirty-one out. But nothing had changed. Madrid had failed despite the *galácticos*.

Despite? Because of. Even the very word damaged them, what it represented. 'There was a negative tone to the word *galáctico*, a term we never chose to describe ourselves,' Ronaldo insists. 'We knew that there was already pressure at Real Madrid but over time that label heaped even more pressure on to us.' It was no coincidence that when Casillas headed up an advertising campaign designed to show him as down-to-earth, a true sportsman, its slogan ran: 'I'm not a *galáctico*, I'm from Móstoles.' 'That word did so much damage to the dressing room,' says Iván Campo: 'It ended up suffocating the team. I didn't see Zizou as a *galáctico*; I saw him as a person. But even though we all made up that group, not everyone was treated the same way.' Valdano makes a similar point: 'the term *galáctico* created a distortion; other players felt as if they were secondary in their company and when you put together characters as strong as Raúl and Ronaldo it can be hard to run a dressing room – they're both leaders of great influence, stature and symbolic power. A clash is perhaps inevitable.'

The rules of sporting success had been subverted, meritocracy going out of the window in the name of brand recognition. The structure was undermined in order to sign the stars. The *galácticos* were less a football team, more a collection of famous footballers, the embodiment of style over substance, entitlement over effort. A Real Madrid manager from that era sits in a private room at the back of a restaurant and waves in the direction of the door. 'Everyone,' he says, 'wanted to be the maître d', no one wanted to wash the plates.' A youth-teamer recalls going into a dressing room where 'the coach was irrelevant: the players did whatever they wanted and at the weekend the stars played no matter what.' 'We didn't abide by the traditional rules of football and football cornered us and stabbed us for it,' Valdano admits.

November the nineteenth 2005, the fifty-eighth minute of the first

Madrid–Barça of the season and Barcelona are already 2-0 up and cruising. Madrid have not had a shot. Samuel Eto'o has scored the first and Ronaldinho the second, dashing in from the left, putting Sergio Ramos on his backside, gliding past Iván Helguera and slotting beyond Casillas. A quarter of an hour later, the Brazilian does it again. As he runs to the corner flag, does a little dance, waggles his fingers and points to the sky, Madrid's fans, jaws on the floor, do something strange: they begin to applaud, the camera zooming in on a man with a moustache and a cigarette hanging loosely from his bottom lip.

His name is Juan Sánchez Gómez. He has since shaved off his moustache, for the first time in thirty years, and he's now barely recognisable as the man whose photograph was splashed across the papers, leading the first ovation of a Barça player for twenty-two years, since Diego Maradona scored a goal so good team-mate Lobo Carrasco burst out laughing. 'If I'd known all the fuss it would cause I wouldn't have done it,' he tells Sergio Fernández in *Marca*. He regrets it now, not least because some fellow fans criticised him for it. 'I would have loved to have done the same for one of our players but it was Ronaldinho who scored the goal and that's that,' he continues. 'Besides, we *were* at the Santiago Bernabéu, not the Camp Nou. We don't throw bottles or pigs' heads or anything.' Still, this was an astonishing, almost unique moment. *Marca*'s front cover said it all: '19 November 2005: The Day Barcelona Left the Bernabéu to Applause'.

Ten days later Ronaldinho picked up the Ballon d'Or. He also won the 2005 FIFA World Player award, his second in a row. After Figo, Zidane and Ronaldo, the world's best player was now at Barcelona, tipping the balance back towards Catalonia and doing things people had never seen before. 'Ronaldinho has the dribbling skills of Rivelinho, the vision of Gerson, the irreverence of Garrincha, the speed of Jairzinho, the technique of Zico and the creativity of Romário,' declared Tostao, a World Cup winner with Brazil in 1970. 'Ronaldinho,' says Barcelona team-mate Xavi, 'changed our history.'

It wasn't supposed to be this way. Originally, it wasn't Ronaldinho that Barcelona really wanted; it was David Beckham. In June 2003, Joan Laporta invited the media into his candidacy office on Paseig de Gràcia to drop the bombshell he hoped would see him emerge victorious in Barcelona's presidential elections: he had struck a deal with Manchester United to sign Beckham. He and his vice-presidential candidate, Sandro Rosell, ran through a PowerPoint presentation showing how the arrival of the Englishman would benefit the club economically; Beckham was a player they couldn't afford *not* to sign.

Laporta won the elections but Beckham didn't join; instead he signed for Madrid, just as Laporta and Rosell had always known he would. The choice was an obvious one: Barcelona were a club in crisis while Madrid were the league champions and it was there that Beckham could play with Zidane, Ronaldo, Figo, Raúl and Roberto Carlos. 'I never spoke to anyone from Barcelona,' Beckham insisted. 'I had always said that if I ever had to leave United, which I never thought I would do, then I would be going to Real Madrid. And *I* would decide my future.'

Barcelona turned their attention to Paris Saint-Germain's Ronaldinho instead. Madrid were also interested but wanted the Brazilian to wait twelve months – that year's *galáctico* was Beckham – and one Madrid director later gloated that the world had fallen in love with the Englishman while Ronaldinho was 'too ugly' to sign for them. He would have sunk Madrid as a brand.

So he signed for Barcelona and sunk Madrid anyway; second prize in this beauty contest turned out to be the first. Laporta's election victory represented *Cruyffism*'s triumphant return; he had, after all, been Cruyff's greatest fan, his lawyer and his friend, and he had first wanted Guus Hiddink as coach, then Ronald Koeman before finally settling on Frank Rijkaard. But another more recent tradition had also been re-established: Ronaldinho followed Romário, Ronaldo and Rivaldo as a Brazilian crowned the world's best player while in Catalonia, and it was his goofy smile that became the symbol of the new Barcelona, head tennis in the president's office projecting an image of the new era, young and dynamic. From the tricks and flicks; from the surfer's thumb and little finger waggle, fashioned from foam and sold in the club shop; from the Soul-Glow hair to the sheer fun of it all, Ronaldinho brought a different atmosphere to the club, releasing the tension. He was a cartoon footballer, the lead character in the *Barça Toons*, and his *Spitting Image* puppet summed it up with his catchphrase: *¡fiesta!*

The following summer Ronaldinho was joined by Deco from Porto and Samuel Eto'o from Mallorca. Eto'o was the perfect signing for Barcelona; not quite a Figo but symbolic nonetheless. He too had crossed the divide. He had first arrived in Spain from Cameroon aged thirteen, walking into the arrivals hall at Barajas, penniless and alone having been scouted by Madrid. He developed through the youth system but first-team opportunities had been few and he joined Mallorca where, driven by a burning sense of injustice and a permanent desire for vindication, he scored goal after goal – especially against Madrid. He celebrated one strike at the Bernabéu by pointing at the spot on which he stood and mouthing: 'I was here, I was here.' He explained: 'I was at Madrid for five years. I wanted to make a statement on behalf of all the kids from the youth system, to say that you have to give them opportunities. There are kids there that play well, better than some of the famous names.' That Eto'o included himself in that list hardly needed saying.

It was Eto'o who forced through the €24 million move himself. Even though Madrid still owned half of his registration and were reluctant to see him join their rivals, he refused to go anywhere else and was not prepared to listen to empty promises, nor play second fiddle to Ronaldo, Figo, Beckham or Zidane. 'If the bench isn't good enough for the *galácticos*, it's not good enough for me,' he announced. He got twenty-five league goals in his first season at the Camp Nou, including strikes in both *clásicos*, and his tenacity and talent drove Barcelona on, leaving Madrid trailing in their wake. He celebrated the title in 2005 by chanting: 'Madrid, you bastards, salute the champions!', but apologised the following day, conceding: 'I have spat on the plate that fed me.'

Eto'o and Ronaldinho eventually fell out spectacularly, but on the pitch they were unstoppable for two years, deepening Madrid's crisis. When Barcelona won the first *clásico* in 2004–5, *El País*'s Santiago Segurola wrote: 'some games hide the secrets of an end of an era: in the inflamed atmosphere of the Camp Nou, this felt like one of them.' And so it proved, *clásico* after *clásico*. Barça were superb, Madrid were shambolic. If *Marca*'s *clásico* headline in 2004 had been 'the beginning of the end'; by November 2005 it was no longer the beginning but a third successive Catalan victory in the capital. Ronaldinho's ovation consummated Madrid's collapse and *Marca*'s subhead read: 'A stratospheric Ronaldinho "retires" the *galácticos*'. Commentating on the game for American television, Paul Giblin announced: 'Ladies and gentleman, you've been watching a great football team tonight . . . you've also seen Real Madrid.'

When Madrid's supporters gave Ronaldinho an ovation, much was made of it being a gesture that had never been, and would never be, reciprocated: Madrid were a *club señor*, Barça were not. That ignored two things: first, a Madrid player *had* been given an ovation at the Camp Nou before, when Englishman Laurie Cunningham tore them apart in February 1980; and, second, the reaction of Madrid's fans in 2005 wasn't just about good sportsmanship. 'That was my worst *clásico* experience: unthinkable and painful,' Salgado says. 'Most took that as a gentlemanly gesture but it wasn't. Applauding Ronaldinho was a way of punishing us.' In the players' lounge after the game, a Madrid first-team veteran sighed: 'this club has lost its soul.'

The balance had tilted. Barcelona were league champions in 2005 and 2006 and Champions League winners the same year. On the morning of the European Cup final *El Mundo Deportivo*'s cover led on '¡Salid y ganad!' Go out there and win it. The reference to Cruyff's *Salid y disfrutad* from 1992 was inescapable. It brought memories of the Dream Team, who gathered to watch from the stands: Andoni

Zubizarreta, José Ramón Alexanco, Michael Laudrup, Miguel Ángel Nadal, Albert Ferrer, Guillermo Amor, Julio Salinas, Pep Guardiola, Txiki Beguiristain and Eusebio Sacristán were all there. Of the players who started at Wembley fourteen years before, only Ronald Koeman, José María Bakero and Hristo Stoichkov were not at the Stade de France for the match against Arsenal in May 2006.

Few doubted that Barcelona could emulate those men. This was arguably the finest side they'd had. In an article in *El País*, Pep Guardiola had excitedly likened them to the dream team, calling them a 'manifesto' as much as a team: they were 'recognisably Barça'. Iniesta had told Guardiola's brother: 'the dream team is back'. They had rediscovered their Dutch style, led by coach Frank Rijkaard, they had a Catalan core with Víctor Valdés, Oleguer Presas and Carles Puyol (Xavi Hernández was injured), they had Samuel Eto'o's voracity, Deco's guile and Ronaldinho's magic. Eto'o, inevitably, scored. What they did not expect was for their heroes to be full-back Juliano Belletti and substitute Henrik Larsson. Despite going down to ten men, after goalkeeper Jens Lehmann was sent off, Arsenal took the lead through Sol Campbell's header. Víctor Valdés saved Barcelona from conceding a second before two goals from Eto'o in the seventy-sixth minute and Belletti in the eighty-first, completed the comeback. Both goals had been made by Larsson, who had been studying the game intently from the bench. Barcelona were European champions for the second time.

A party in a Bois de Boulogne nightclub was followed by a flight to Barcelona, a helicopter ride across the bay past the statue of Columbus at the foot of the Ramblas, and a trip back into the city by boat, where an open-topped bus was waiting. Cameras zoomed in on a girl holding a banner: 'Ronaldinho, I want to make love to you,' it said. 'This is not a dream; it's a reality the size of the Eiffel tower,' cheered *El Mundo Deportivo*. Its cover led on one word printed three times: *¡¡¡Sí, sí, sí!!!* The lead editorial insisted: 'This team have put Barcelona back in their rightful place. It shouldn't take another fourteen years to be back. This is a new era.' Andrés Iniesta recalled:

'Saint Denis was the proof that more could come, that we didn't need to live solely off Koeman's goal.'

'The reaction after we won the league was amazing and I was thinking: "nothing could ever be bigger than this",' Larsson says. 'But after Paris it was *unbelievable*. Barcelona is a big club but it hadn't won the trophy for many years and had only won it once before. To be a genuinely big club, you need to win the European Cup every now and then.'

The man who had been taken off for Belletti was Oleguer Presas, the right-back. Oleguer is not your average footballer. He turned down the chance to play for Spain, judging it inconsistent with his Catalan nationalism, contributed articles on politics and economics to magazines and journals and drove a blue van while his team-mates drove Porsches. He publicly questioned the Spanish state and the independence of the judiciary with an article on the treatment of the suspected ETA terrorist De Juana Chaos and lost a boot deal with Kelme as a result, prompting the striker Salva Ballesta, a man of right-wing convictions proud to call himself a Spanish patriot, to spit: 'Oleguer deserves all the respect of a dog turd.'

'Barcelona is special,' Oleguer says. 'It represents the diffusion of Catalan identity and culture, a culture that's rich and fascinating. You have to understand the history of the club; it really was a conduit for a feeling in an age when people could not express themselves in the streets as they wished.' For him those titles had particular significance. 'When Barcelona win the league,' he wrote, 'we become the army of joy travelling up the Diagonal in the other direction [to the Francoist troops in 1939], finally able to front up to that blow. We imagine ourselves halting that pack of tanks, responding to their bullets with our anthems and song, laughing in the face of the fascist ire of those military men.'

19

THE BALLBOY AND THE TRANSLATOR

At the top of the steps stood a troupe of actors in Barcelona kits and football boots, socks pulled up to their knees. Eleven of them lined up in formation and handed Real Madrid's supporters a guard of honour as they emerged from Santiago Bernabéu metro station and into the evening air. The final *clásico* of the season was on a Wednesday night in May 2008, but it was not so much the game everyone was talking about as what was due to take place just before it, a humiliation so great that Samuel Eto'o and Deco had sought out convenient suspensions and taken up shelter six hundred kilometres away. It was all about the *pasillo*: the guard of honour Barça had to hand newly crowned champions Real Madrid.

In Madrid they'd been talking about it for months, first as an act of wishful thinking, then with a growing realisation that it could actually happen. If Madrid could clinch the league in week thirty-six the next team to visit them would have to applaud them on to the field and the next team would be Barcelona. On the morning of the game, *Marca*'s front page gleefully depicted the Bernabéu pitch with red dots showing the visitors where to stand beneath the headline: 'Barça, it's just here'. Some Madrid fans wore t-shirts declaring: 'I saw the *pasillo*' and there were even supporters who turned up, watched the guard of honour and left. The following day *Marca* gave away posters of Barcelona's humiliation.

Barcelona took up position with coach Frank Rijkaard at the head, applauded Madrid on, shook hands and proceeded to get hammered 4-1, *El Mundo Deportivo* describing it as 'the final stab in the supporters' back'. *Sport*'s front cover was completely black: 'You have dishonoured the Barcelona shirt' the headline said. For the second successive season, Barcelona had won nothing. Florentino Pérez's resignation had seen Ramón Calderón win presidential elections at Real Madrid and win two championships in a row. Fabio Capello's team claimed a barely plausible title on head-to-head goal difference in 2007, despite the Italian trying to resign in February, having given up and told the president he had a 'mid-table' team; now, under Bernd Schuster, they cruised to a final position eighteen points ahead of their rivals, who came third.

Barcelona had self-destructed. Discipline had gone, division took its place. Ronaldinho was out of shape, missing training sessions constantly – 'Ronaldinho's in the gym' became a running joke – Edmílson talked about 'black sheep', and Samuel Eto'o eventually exploded at an event in Vilafranca de Penedés, jabbing his finger at TV cameras and ranting about an internal civil war and 'bad people'. Rijkaard appeared powerless, especially after the departure of assistant coach Henk Ten Cate, 'the disciplinarian who made sure that everyone was on their toes', in the words of one player.

Up in the Bernabéu directors' box, Laporta and the Barcelona board watched the *pasillo* and then saw their side capitulate. They had long since decided to act. It was months since Txiki Beguiristain, the sporting director, had begun the search for a new manager. Candidates included Laurent Blanc and Michael Laudrup, plus Jose Mourinho, but Beguiristain quickly reached the conclusion that the solution was under his nose.

Laporta explains: 'We'd told Frank he wasn't going to continue. We'd decided to make Pep Guardiola the first team coach. Pep knew the club perfectly, he'd learnt with Johan Cruyff and he was doing a brilliant job with Barcelona B, who were on course to win their league. The only question was his lack of experience but I wasn't worried about that. So I had a meeting with him and told him I wanted him to be manager of the first team.'

Laporta grins. There is a twinkle in his eye.

'And do you know what he said to me?'

What did he say?

Barcelona's former president leans back on the sofa and starts to laugh.

'He said: "You haven't got the balls".'

Ballboy, youth-teamer, Catalan and captain, Guardiola enjoyed enormous goodwill but he was only thirty-seven and hadn't coached a top-flight side. He was about to win the league with Barcelona B in his first season as a coach, but it was Barcelona B. The first team needed authority, guarantees. Many thought this wasn't the time for half-measures; this was the time for Mourinho, not for a novice. Laporta admits that employing the Portuguese would have been the 'safe' option while, after his interview for the job, Guardiola asked the director Marc Ingla: 'Why don't you hire Mourinho? It would be easier for you.' Graham Hunter explains that Mourinho's agent, Jorge Mendes, had badgered Beguiristain to interview him and that Mourinho had then given a hugely impressive presentation explaining how he would turn the team around while also promising to play the Barça way.

Mourinho had worked at Barcelona before, as assistant manager to both Bobby Robson and Louis Van Gaal, and he had friends at the club. When he left in 2000, he promised to come back whenever he could and publicly declared himself a *culé*; this was the chance to prove it, to return to the place where it had all begun for him. Beguiristain and fellow directors Ingla and Ferrán Sorriano, who travelled to Lisbon to meet Mourinho, were convinced that he would be a success. But there had been a certain reluctance to interview him in the first place and, when they did, they found him abrasive and feared him becoming a fire-starter. The conviction grew that Guardiola was the right man, the embodiment of everything they felt Barcelona stood for. Laporta insists: 'we chose a philosophy, not a brand.'

If Mourinho was a *culé*, Guardiola was *the culé*. When Andrés Iniesta was a kid, he plastered posters over the walls by his bunk at La Masia. He had pictures of Laudrup and Catherine Zeta-Jones but most of all he had posters of Pep Guardiola, the man who won six league titles, four cups and a European Cup over eleven years and 475 appearances, the man who, when he offered the European Cup to fans, invoked Josep Taradellas. More than a player, Guardiola was a legend, a kind of ideologue: the metronome that kept the Dream Team ticking over, Atlético Madrid striker Kiko describing his game in a single word, repeated to recreate the rhythm of his passing: *pam. Pam, pam, pam, pam, pam, pam, pam.* Fernando Hierro, the Real Madrid captain, remembers him as a leader: 'He didn't so much talk during games as commentate.'

Born in Santpedor, a town of three thousand inhabitants, Guardiola went to school a hundred metres from the Camp Nou. Like Iniesta, he had been a resident of La Masia, he had championed Catalan literacy crusades and became an eloquent defender of an identity that's consciously Cruyffist and Catalan. In 2012 he gave his support for a vote on independence and during a *clásico* as a player he confronted the referee, berating him for 'playing with the feelings of an entire country'. He wasn't talking about Spain. During one press conference as Barcelona coach he described Barcelona's powerlessness in the face of Madrid's media muscle, noting: 'we're from a small country up there.' He was handed the Catalan parliament's Medal of Honour in September 2011, club president Sandro Rosell calling him 'the embodiment of the essence of Barça', and his acceptance speech drew a standing ovation as he talked about sitting in the dark watching videos until that Eureka! moment when you know you're going to win. It was, he insisted, a model for Catalonia, 'a cultured, civic and open society': 'if we all work hard and get up early, we're an unstoppable country,' he said.

By then, Guardiola was well on his way to becoming the club's most successful ever manager, winner of three league titles, two European Cups, two Copa del Reys, two Club World Cups, three Spanish Super Cups and two European Super Cups in just four seasons. No one could ever have imagined it when Barcelona turned to him in the summer of 2008. There were people who believed in him, though. Charly Rexach recalled: 'even at La Masia he was known as The Wise One', while Iniesta remembers putting his money where his mouth was in an argument with a friend who doubted Guardiola's capacity and Xavi insists: 'When they signed Pep I said: "*Madre mía*, we're going to be flying." He's a perfectionist. If Pep decided to be a musician, he'd be a good musician. If he wanted to be a psychologist, he'd be a good psychologist. He is obsessive; he'd keep going until he got it right. He demands so much from himself. And that pressure that he puts on himself, those demands, are contagious. He wants everything to be perfect. He is a *pesado*.'

On the day of his presentation, Guardiola announced that he had no place for Ronaldinho, Deco or Eto'o. Unable to find a club, Eto'o stayed for another season but Ronaldinho and Deco were swiftly moved on. Privately, Guardiola told friends the season before that, such was the talent, all it would take was seriousness and organisation to get Barça back on track. Ronaldinho's presence in the dressing room had made that harder. 'He had made Barcelona great again; seeing him as a shadow of what he was hurt players,' says one member of staff. As for Deco, he was a man with the charisma not only to go off the rails, but to take others with him. 'No one set a limit last year,' admitted the Mexican defender Rafa Márquez. 'There is order and discipline now,' added Xavi. Iniesta recalls: 'I immediately realised that Guardiola was very different from Rijkaard . . . Guardiola is more methodical.'

Discipline was imposed via a system of fines and incentives. Leo

Messi's diet was changed, Guardiola telling him that he could be the best player in he world – if he did the right things. The chat became a warning: *don't throw this away*. Videos became standard, the detail was striking and its application sharp and to the point. When Xavi, Iniesta and Carles Puyol joined the rest of the squad after Euro 2008, they could hardly believe their eyes. Barcelona were training at St Andrews in Scotland and something had changed dramatically; the intensity, the seriousness, was new. Pressure was a particular obsession. Guardiola demanded that his team play high up, asphyxiating the opposition. His other great obsession was positioning. 'His success was making us believe in his ideas – more than training us, he taught us,' says Iniesta.

Guardiola often repeated that Barcelona would 'respect our philosophy'. 'Pep suckled from the teat of Cruyff,' says one of his closest collaborators. Few sides have had a footballing identity so clear, one that runs through the club. Barça became almost like a sect in their commitment to playing 'good football' – a moralistic term that irritates Madrid fans. Even the fact that they called it a philosophy marked Barcelona out as different and the rivalry became not just a question of clubs, but also a question of concepts, an ideological war. Many Madrid fans could not agree more with Zlatan Ibrahimović when he dismissively, almost sneeringly referred to Guardiola as the Philosopher.

During one press conference Guardiola was asked to define Barcelona's model. His response, in English, was simple, a mantra: 'I get the ball, I pass the ball, I get the ball, I pass the ball, I get the ball, I pass the ball . . .' Few embody that better than Xavi, the Guardiola in Guardiola's team – a product of the youth system with a single-minded commitment to Barcelona's style. 'I'm a romantic,' Xavi says, stretching out on a sofa at Barcelona's training ground. It is spring 2010. 'Some teams can't or don't pass the ball. What are you playing for? What's the point? That's not football. Combine, pass, play. That's football – for me, at least.'

Xavi explains the system at youth level: 'Education is the key. Players have had ten or twelve years here. When you arrive at Barça the first thing they teach you is: "think . . . lift your head up, move, see, think. Look *before* you get the ball. If you're getting *this* pass, look to see if *that* guy is free. *Tac*. First time, one touch."'

He smiles and adds: 'In fact, Charly [Rexach] always used to say: *a mig toc*.' Half a touch. Rexach claims that he could shut his eyes and spot a good player by the sound the ball makes when they hit a pass. *Tac, tac*.

'You see a kid who lifts his head up, who plays the pass first time, *tac*, and you think: "he'll do",' Xavi continues. 'Bring him in, coach him. Our model was imposed by [Johan] Cruyff; it's an Ajax model. It's all about *rondos*, piggy-in-the-middle games. *Rondo, rondo, rondo*. Every. Single. Day. You learn responsibility and not to lose the ball. If you lose the ball, you go in the middle. If you go in the middle, it's humiliating, the rest applaud and laugh at you.'

Because the model is shared throughout the club, it makes taking the step up to the first team easier; because Guardiola had been through the system and coached Barcelona B, it made the step up easier still. Even Zidane, returning to Madrid with Florentino Pérez when he became president again in 2009, admitted: 'Barcelona's culture is the same at U12 and U14 level; the guy who looks after the U16s plays the same way as the first team. The style of Cruyff, of Guardiola, gives identity to Barcelona, which is something Madrid still need to find.' When Barcelona defeated Manchester United in the 2009 Champions League final at the end of Guardiola's first season, seven of the starting eleven had been through La Masia.

A traditional Catalan farmhouse, pretty enough, it's the fact that there's something incongruous about La Masia that really draws you in. Dwarfed by the city and the stadium that has engulfed it, La Masia was built in 1702. A peasant farmer's home, 610 square metres spread over two floors, during the 1950s it was used as a kind of works HQ – what would these days be a prefab Portakabin occupied by dusty shoes and luminous yellow vests – for architects and builders as they constructed the Camp Nou and when work finished it was abandoned. In 1966, it became Barcelona's social centre and then, in 1979, the club bought it and turned it into a residence for young hopefuls. From the windows, kids could see the pitch where the first team trained and, behind that, the Camp Nou: aspirations in concrete and grass.

Almost five hundred footballers had lived at La Masia until Barcelona's recent move to San Joan Despí, among them Cesc Fàbregas, Guillermo Amor, Mikel Arteta, Guardiola and Tito Vilanova. With room for sixty kids in bunk beds, there was a library, dining room, kitchen and school, and it became a kind of indoctrination centre in all things Barcelona. The official line calls La Masia 'the cradle of Barcelona's youth system' and it became shorthand for the entire *cantera*, even encompassing those kids who never actually lived there; it has become shorthand for a style too, which is why indoctrination is the word. There's a zealous, almost puritanical protection of their identity.

Michael Robinson, the former Liverpool player and now Spain's leading football pundit, insists: 'show me twenty kids in a park and I can pick out the two who are at Barça.' As one director puts it: 'Almost twenty years ago, Cruyff arrived and said we were going to play in a certain way and his vision was always about the technique of the kids, the speed of the pass, the speed of the mind.' Iniesta calls graduates 'sons of the system'. Stability, continuity, financial reward and ideological tranquillity, a kind of moral 'superiority', are the result. As Hristo Stoichkov says, with typical hyperbole: 'If Barcelona tried to buy the players they have created, it would cost them a billion dollars!' 'If we need a new player we will always look at the youth team first,' says the director of football, Andoni Zubizarreta.

Guardiola did. Few had heard of Pedro Rodríguez or Sergio Busquets when Guardiola gave them first-team debuts. A year later, they were world champions and they were not alone. When Spain won the 2010 World Cup, Laporta insisted: 'Barcelona won the World Cup, only they were wearing the wrong shirts.' Laporta is a Catalan nationalist who aspires to independence and who early in his presidency removed the Spain flag from La Masia, so he would say that. Spain's captain and coach were Madrileños and *Madridistas*, the right-back, Sergio Ramos, is from Seville and a Madrid player, and one of their central midfielders, Xabi Alonso, is Basque and a Madrid player. And yet Laporta had a point: when *la selección* took to the field against Holland in Johannesburg, six of Spain's starting eleven were Barcelona players, four of them Catalans: Gerard Piqué, Carles Puyol, Sergio Busquets and Xavi Hernández, plus Pedro Rodríguez and Andrés Iniesta. All of them were La Masia graduates and Spain's approach owed much to Barça's model too. In fact, that Spain's success has been driven by a Barcelona model and Barcelona players, and co-opted as Barcelona's accomplishment, has provoked a shift in allegiances; it is now the more radical *Madrid* fans as much as the Catalan nationalists who disown *la selección*.

One La Masia graduate not among them was the Argentinian Leo Messi, who joined Barcelona as a thirteen-year-old in 2000 when, after much boardroom debate and a desperate letter from his father Jorge, Barcelona finally committed to covering the cost of the hormone treatment he needed to grow normally. 'Don't write about him, don't try to describe him: watch him,' Guardiola has said and he has a point: there's not much you can say about Messi that hasn't been said before, little point in outlining his stats because every week he seems to break another record; he has made the ridiculous so routine that it no longer seems so remarkable. He has taken the debate on to a new plane: it is no longer absurd to ask if he is the best player ever. Barcelona's all-time top scorer at the age of twenty-five, he has won it all and is the man whose hat-trick against Real Zaragoza prompted Ander Herrera, playing for the other team, to remark: 'I'm not sure he's human.' During that game, a fan behind the Barcelona bench let out a *fuck me*. Guardiola turned round and said to him: 'If it wasn't for Messi, I'd be a Second Division B coach.'

Messi has won the Ballon d'Or four times in a row. Most years, his closest challenger is Cristiano Ronaldo, bringing the *clásico* to the heart of the individual awards too. The comparisons are inevitable and club-coloured; they are relentless and often angry, framed in a way that does not seem to allow for there being *two*, or more, brilliant players around. As the former Athletic Bilbao coach Marcelo Bielsa put it: 'the problem with choosing the best is that, rather than being a eulogy for the man you choose, it can appear a rejection of the man you didn't.' Xavi insists: 'I don't want to compare him to anyone else – because it would be unfair on them.'

And yet when Messi won the award in 2010, he was not up against Ronaldo. Instead, he shared the podium with Xavi and Iniesta. This was the ultimate satisfaction for Barcelona – *smugness*, they said in Madrid. It was only the third time the top three had come from the same club – the previous two were both from Arrigo Sacchi's Milan – and the first time they had all come through the same youth system.

'We create Ballon d'Ors,' Laporta bristled. 'Others buy them.' No prizes for guessing who the *others* are.

Youth development and team building has become one of the key battlegrounds in the rivalry, a question that also has a moral dimension. It is often summed up in the phrase: *cantera versus cartera*. Youth team versus wallet. Good versus bad in a different guise.

During the *galáctico* era, Madrid broke the world record transfer for Figo and Zidane and when Pérez returned he broke the world record to sign Kaká and then broke it again a few days later when he executed the deal to buy Cristiano Ronaldo, set up by outgoing president Ramón Calderón. Ronaldo cost £80 million, €93 million, and the Bishop of Barcelona declared the fee immoral. When Madrid faced Barcelona in 2010, their line-up cost almost €200 million more than their opponents' and their spending continues to rocket: Pérez has spent almost €800 million on players. Barcelona are bringing footballers through; Madrid are not. Plenty of good players have played for Madrid prior to first-team level – Juan Mata, Álvaro Negredo and Borja Valero among them – and Madrid have produced more First

Division players then anyone else but since Iker Casillas made his debut in 1999 no Madrid youth-teamer has become a first-team regular, with the exception of the returning Álvaro Arbeloa. By contrast, in November 2012 Barcelona played Levante with a team made up entirely of home-grown players.

But the *cantera* versus *cartera* dichotomy is simplistic, not least when applied as if it was timeless. Figo, Rivaldo, Ronaldo, Ronaldinho and Stoichkov, to list some of Barcelona's Ballon d'Or winners alone, hardly came to Catalonia on the cheap; Messi is the first Ballon d'Or they didn't sign. It is not as if Barcelona have spent nothing in recent years, either: on average, Barcelona pay the highest wages in Europe and Eto'o cost €24 million, Dani Alves €35 million, David Villa €40 million, Zlatan Ibrahimovic €65 million, and Alexis Sánchez €35 million. Neymar arrived in June 2013, joining Barcelona for €58 million. Chygrinsky, Keirrison and Henrique cost €60 million between them and failed. Barcelona also had to pay €40 million to get Cesc Fàbregas and Piqué back, La Masia 'graduates' who graduated elsewhere. The difference, though, remains significant. According to *AS*, since the turn of the century Madrid have spent €1,275.3 million on players compared to Barcelona's €837.8 million.

Pep Guardiola was under no illusions. Talk of philosophy was not empty posturing; it was a means to an end as well as an end in itself. He too was a pragmatist. The former Spain coach Luis Aragonés famously once claimed: 'finals are not for playing well, they're for winning.' Guardiola's response was telling: 'if you play well, you have more chance of winning.' As the new manager put it shortly after taking over: 'it will mean nothing if we win nothing.'

After two games, Barcelona had one point. Beaten in Soria by Numancia, the winning goal scored by a player who earned less in a year than Thierry Henry in a week, they were then held at home by Racing Santander. The pressure was on; not choosing Mourinho looked more questionable than ever. But in their third game, Barcelona smashed six past Sporting Gijón and never looked back. In week ten they climbed to the top of the table for the first time in eighteen months and didn't relinquish that position. In the days before the *clásico*, Madrid sacked coach Bernd Schuster after he announced that winning at the Camp Nou was impossible.

Schuster was right but under his successor, Juande Ramos, Madrid began a comeback. Between one *clásico* and the next, they won sixteen of seventeen and Barcelona arrived in the capital in May 2009 knowing that there was still a chance of their rivals closing the gap, maybe even of winning the league. The pursuit had been relentless, Madrid's breath on Barça's neck, and the talk was of the *cagómetro* – the crappingyourselfometer. Historically, the Madrid media insisted, Barcelona could not take the pressure. 'I don't know what it is that Madrid have got,' Xavi admitted, 'but they never know they're beaten.' That was a quality of which Barcelona did not traditionally boast.

And yet Barcelona did not waver. As the sun finally dipped below the stand just in time for kick-off, a banner engulfed the south end of the Bernabéu: 'to the very end' it read. They meant 31 May, the final day of the season, but the end was nigh. It finished Madrid 2 Barcelona 6. It was only the second time Madrid had ever conceded six at home – the first had been against Athletic Bilbao in 1931 – and it could have been more: Iker Casillas made seven saves in the first half alone. Thierry Henry and Samuel Eto'o tore them apart. Messi, playing in the false no. 9 role he would eventually make his own, left them dazed and confused. 'They had talked about having a *plan anti-Messi*,' recalls Iniesta, 'but they didn't expect him to play as a centre-forward with Samu on the wing.' 'We didn't know what to do,' Madrid central defender Christoph Metzelder admitted.

There was a smooth simplicity about Barcelona's goals and they almost scored one of the all-time greats too, only for Messi somehow to miss from seven yards. They were practically walking the ball in, so good it looked easy, *El Mundo Deportivo* judging it the 'best performance Barcelona had ever produced'. 'Football has a God,' added *Sport*. Leo Messi was described as 'Maradona, Cruyff and Best all rolled into one', Iniesta and Xavi as 'those gigantic dwarves', and Henry in just three words: 'Oh', 'là' and 'là'. 'This side are better than the Dream Team,' one radio pundit insisted. 'Barcelona are the best team I have ever seen,' said Canal Plus's commentator. And even *AS*'s editorial claimed: 'only in paradise can you see football like this.'

Iniesta recalls going off to a smattering of applause. 'Sometimes all that [Real Madrid] *señorío* thing is exaggerated but you have to admit that they always have a good taste for football . . . they were applauding a team that had scored six against their beloved side. And not just any team, but the team they most hate. That image has always stayed with me,' he later wrote. 'Afterwards we hugged each other more than we had done in all the other games put together. We were like Teletubbies.' Carles Puyol said: 'We only needed a game of that quality to complete a spectacular season. Losing here last year and giving them the *pasillo* was one of the worst moments of my career; this is one of the best.' The league title was Barcelona's again, a month later they won the Copa del Rey and then they added the European Cup, defeating Manchester United in Rome. It was a unique treble, never before achieved by a Spanish club.

En route to the final, Barcelona beat Chelsea. The Norwegian referee Tom Henning Øvrebo turned down two handball claims, against Piqué and Yaya Touré, sent off Eric Abidal and ruled that Touré hadn't fouled Didier Drogba or Nicolas Anelka. In the last minute Iniesta scored the goal that sent Barcelona through and sent Guardiola sprinting down the touchline. 'Every time I close my eyes and I try to sum up that season I see Stamford Bridge,' Iniesta says. In a hospital back in Spain, Iniesta's grandmother was shouting: 'My grandson! My grandson!' Nine months later it was maternity wards that were full: in Catalonia, Iniesta's goal provoked a 40 per cent increase in the birth rate, a spokeswoman said.

At the final whistle, Didier Drogba ran on in flip-flops and leant into the TV camera to call it a 'fucking disgrace'. In their fury, Chelsea found allies in Madrid: a match they never played in became one Madrid returned to again and again.

There was no such controversy in the final against Manchester United, Eto'o scoring the first, Messi leaping to head the second. 'When you see how they move you can't help but be amazed,' Ryan Giggs admitted. Iniesta had picked up a muscle tear seventeen days before but played anyway. Club doctors told him not to shoot. 'When you win you think of the pain, the suffering, the tears and you think how that all makes sense now,' he says. When the team came back to Barcelona the next day, one fan held a banner demanding another Iniesta-inspired baby boom, asking him to 'inseminate my girlfriend'. Queen's 'We Will Rock You' was adapted by the fans: *Coooo-pa, Liiii-ga i Champ-ions!*

The Super Cup followed, then the European Super Cup, then the World Club Championship at the start of the next season. By the end of that season, they had another league title. 'If you win this,' Guardiola had told his players before the World Club Championship final in Abu Dhabi, 'you'll be legends.' Not bad for a thirty-eight-year-old with no experience. Barcelona's *Cinc Copes* had been surpassed and Madrid had been obliterated, eclipsed. Six trophies out of six in 2010, although Laporta insisted that it was seven: the 6-2 at the Bernabéu was another. It was even better than a trophy, according to Iniesta: 'Titles can be won again, cups can be lifted again. But I don't think we'll ever see six goals scored in the Bernabéu again. I'll be able to tell my grandchildren that I experienced the best *clásico* in the history of football.'

A life-sized cardboard cutout stood in Jose Mourinho's office at Valdebebas, Real Madrid's training ground north-east of the city. It was him sprinting across the Camp Nou turf, finger in the air, celebrating at the end of the 2010 Champions League semi-final. That was the moment that Internazionale reached their first European Cup final in almost forty years, knocking Barcelona out and ending their dream of reaching a second successive Champions League final. It was also the moment that Mourinho became Real Madrid's hero . . . and their coach. His audition could not have gone better.

All year, a terrible threat hung over Real Madrid. Former president Ramón Calderón had requested that the Santiago Bernabéu host the European Cup final but the incoming board were furious. Far from something to celebrate, an opportunity to win the *décima* at home, they saw it as something to fear: Barcelona winning the European Cup at the Bernabéu was a horrible thought and, as the year progressed, the nightmare looked more and more likely: when Barcelona reached the semi-final, Mourinho was Madrid's only hope. He was about to become their knight in shining armour. Inter won the first game at San Siro 3-1 and lost the second 1-0, reaching the final after a last-minute goal from Bojan Krkić was disallowed, *Sport* whining: 'Inter didn't come to play football, they came to destroy. Mourinho is the embodiment of anti-football, unscrupulous and a born provocateur.'

At the final whistle Mourinho ran on, finger in the air. Someone at Barcelona turned the sprinkler system on. It is the image he was confronted by every day in his Madrid office. Leaning against an exercise bike, as big as he is, a memento of the moment he became Madrid manager. When Mourinho won the Champions League final at the Santiago Bernabéu, he already knew: his team travelled back to Italy to celebrate but he stayed behind in the Spanish capital to sign. Mourinho had done for Madrid what they could not do for themselves: defeat Barcelona and win the European Cup. The job he was entrusted with was to do it all over again. Mourinho had emulated Helenio Herrera, winning the European Cup with Inter for the first time in forty-six years; now he would emulate him again but at Spain's *other* club. He arrived in Madrid on a mission: *to knock Barcelona off their perch*.

It was perfect. Club and coach already shared an enemy, an obsession with defeating Barça. Mourinho had first joined Barcelona alongside Bobby Robson in 1996. Theoretically, he was a translator – a job description that Barcelona fans used to insult him – but in reality he was so much more. He scouted teams, assisted in training and drew up complex technical reports that Robson said were always 'first class'. He continued to work at the club under Louis Van Gaal and had appeared committed to the Catalan cause, accusing Madrid of buying opponents, complaining that no one protected his players like they did in the capital, and famously celebrating one title by grabbing the mic to proclaim: 'Today and forever, Barça in my heart!' When he departed in 2004, he insisted that his son was a Barcelona fan and announced that he would 'only ever coach Real Madrid to destroy them: I would never stop being a *culé*.'

But his relationship with Barcelona had grown fractious. As manager of Chelsea he had clashed with Barcelona during their meeting in 2006. He accused Frank Rijkaard of going into the referee's dressing room and Leo Messi of diving after Asier del Horno was sent off for clattering into him. 'Catalonia is a country of culture and you know what theatre is,' he told reporters, 'and what Messi did was good theatre.' His provocative style and taste for winding up opponents was already starting to make him a hate figure for Barcelona fans – the 'translator' chanted at to 'go to the theatre' – and Barcelona's rejection of him in 2008 in favour of Guardiola stung, an ambition denied, love unrequited. There had been further confrontations during the semi-final with Inter in 2010, cemented by that dash across the Camp Nou pitch, Víctor Valdés intervening to tell him not to wind up the home fans. Now, his signing for Madrid sent the rivalry rocketing; Madrid–Barcelona became personified on the pitch and on the bench, concentrated in pairs of protagonists, polar opposites who were the incarnation of their clubs. Ronaldo versus Messi and Mourinho versus Guardiola.

The task before Mourinho was gigantic and conflict increased. His arrival was a revolution. He decided that the best way to defeat Barcelona was to get under their skin, and under the skin of Guardiola in particular, to wage a war of attrition, all weapons allowed. Meanwhile, his arrival also changed Madrid, challenging some of the assumptions the club had embraced and threatening some of those on the inside: here at last was a coach given authority, his leadership theoretically unquestioned, his reputation and personality big enough to take on and beat those who stood in his way. Barcelona had long been a club defined by their coaches but until now Madrid had not. Power was ceded on one condition: that he won. Madrid had become desperate. This was a Faustian pact: Pérez had his concerns and was far from convinced that this was a good idea but he had gone four successive seasons without winning anything and the run could not continue, so he signed the only man who would definitely bring silverware – one season guidebook describing Mourinho as *toda una garantía de éxito*, a veritable guarantee of success. The club magazine, distributed to members monthly, said, 'now, the world's best coach is at Madrid'. *Now.* They never said that about Vicente del Bosque, Carlos Queiroz or Manuel Pellegrini. 'This year's *galáctico* is Jose Mourinho,' Pérez announced.

There had never been a coach like this at the Bernabéu. Witness the reaction when pages from his notebook were found following Madrid's win at Hércules. You would think they had discovered the Dead Sea Scrolls, documents that would unlock the secret. Four tiny pieces of paper with Mourinho's notes scrawled upon them, analysed over and over and lauded like a scene from Monty Python's *Life of Brian*. Notes! It is a sign! As the finding descended into farce, the papers were sent to a handwriting expert and a psychologist for further analysis – apparently, Mourinho's long Ts, round numbers and 'vibrant' style proved he was a 'good man' with an 'astonishing capacity for leadership', 'a strong, decisive character', 'noble' with 'incredible intelligence'.

Over time the fascination turned sour; much of the media turned against him and some of the dressing room did too, a conflict that had at its root the battle with Barcelona. By the end he was forgiven nothing, but at the start he was forgiven everything. *Marca* could hardly contain itself: Mourinho, one cover ran, 'provokes an *orgasmou*' and given the courting of him you wondered if in the editor's office he really did. Mourinho began to chip away at Barcelona, although he rarely named them, usually referring to 'other clubs': *other clubs* were always indulged, unlike Madrid. He pointed the finger at supposedly benevolent referees, favourable fixture lists and teams who didn't even try. After a match against Sporting Gijón, Albert Rivera, a former Madrid youth-teamer, insisted: 'these are not the values I learnt at Madrid' and Spain's competition committee decided to investigate a confrontation between Mourinho and Sporting's manager, Manolo Preciado. *Marca* responded by superimposing Mourinho's head on to Goya's most famous painting, *3 May 1808*, which depicts a humble, defenceless Spaniard facing a French firing squad.

Some were already uncomfortable and others were already critical but when it came to the Madrid mainstream there was no doubt whose side they were on – until Mourinho chose the wrong side, threatening the Spanish national team and its iconic captain Iker Casillas. *El País* called him the 'Michael Jackson of coaches'; within a couple of years, on the pages of the same newspaper he was called a 'psychopath' and a 'nazi', prompting Mourhino to sue and Arbeloa to defend his coach by tweeting: If you're not careful, the press will make you love the oppressor and hate the oppressed.' When Barcelona president Sandro Rosell said Mourinho would get the 'reception he deserves' at the Camp Nou, most didn't read it as a platitude but a dark promise. 'Those who attack him are just jealous because he is successful,' said Alfredo Di Stéfano, Madrid's honorary president. 'We didn't sign him to make friends,' said Emilio Butragueño, cutting to the core of a question that would come back to haunt them. 'We signed him to win.'

The problem was, he didn't. Not at first, and not at the last.

When the final whistle went on Mourinho's first *clásico* in charge of Real Madrid, Barcelona defender Eric Abidal raised his hand, Gerard Piqué raised his and the crowd that engulfed Jeffren Suárez raised theirs. Víctor Valdés raised his hand, latex glistening in the light. All round the Camp Nou, people raised their hands. So did the fans who gathered down the Ramblas. Not far away in a warehouse somewhere, they were already rushing off a batch of t-shirts. Blue and yellow and yours for just €9.95, on the back they read 'Great Theatre' and on the front they carried the date, place and score: Camp Nou, 29/11/2010. Barcelona 5-0 Madrid. Above that was a yellow hand.

Xavi, Pedro and then Villa, twice, scored Barcelona's goals as they took a 4-0 lead. Mourinho, already suffering his worst ever defeat as a coach, barely moved as fans chanted for him to 'Come out of the dugout! Jose, come out of the dugout!' Jeffren Suárez's late goal made little difference and yet it made *all* the difference: the fifth goal turned victory into something more historic, more emblematic: a *manita*, a goal for every finger. Perhaps Iniesta had been wrong about the 6-2; perhaps it could be bettered. Watching at home on television, Wayne Rooney got to his feet and started clapping.

'That game was wonderful, the best I've played,' Xavi recalls. 'Of course there are more important games, like at the World Cup, the European Championships, the final of the Champions League, but the feeling of superiority over Real Madrid was incredible . . . Against another team, fine, but Madrid?! They didn't even touch the ball. It was fantastic. Our feeling was one of leaving the pitch and thinking 'madre mía, *madre mía*, what a match!' In the dressing room we were jumping and cheering, it was spectacular. We gave ourselves a standing ovation a minute long.'

That must have been hard for Madrid's players to listen to . . .

'Luckily,' Xavi says, 'the two dressing rooms are some way apart. I don't think they heard it. And it was about our happiness, that's all.'

It was about more than that. If Abidal didn't know exactly what the gesture meant, Gerard Piqué, the son of a Barça director and a *soci* from birth, certainly did. That *clásico* was the game that, more than any other, would come to define Pep Guardiola's team and one of the reasons was that the result was one that defines Barcelona historically. It was the fifth time Barcelona had defeated Real Madrid

5-0. Beyond 1934–5 and 1944–5, two linger in the memory: victories for the 1974 team led by Johan Cruyff the player and for the 1994–5 Dream Team led by Cruyff the coach. No one could watch Guardiola's side defeat Madrid in November 2010 and not recall Cruyff or Romário. Just in case, television programmes drew on the archives.

Florentino Pérez called the 5-0 Madrid's worst ever result; it might have been Barça's best, another exhibit to present to the jury in the case of Guardiola's Barça versus All The Others, as if there was a checklist of things Guardiola's Barcelona side had to do to emulate their predecessors and beating Madrid 5-0 was one of them. Guardiola appeared in the press room and dedicated the win to Charly Rexach and Johan Cruyff, 'the men who started us off like this; laying down the approach we consider non-negotiable'. It was not just that Barcelona beat Madrid, that they defeated Mourinho – although they loved that – or even that Guardiola completed a *manita* of his own, racking up his fifth *clásico* win in five as a coach, boasting a barely plausible aggregate score of 17-2; it was that they did it their way, the second goal, for example, coming after more than twenty passes and a minute of uninterrupted possession to a soundtrack of *olés*.

Sport and *El Mundo Deportivo* leapt from the Dream Team to the Wet Dream Team. Barcelona, they declared, are the 'Orgasm Team'. For those coaches like Robson and Van Gaal who followed Cruyff, the Dream Team was the Sword of Damocles, a mythological image of perfection that subsequent sides could not live up to. But under Guardiola Barça did not just emulate the Dream Team, according to Josep Lluís Nuñez, president between 1978 and 2000; they bettered it. The 5-0 was the game that cemented that sensation. Since Guardiola's first season in charge, since his side won the European Cup in Rome, a question kept being asked: which Barcelona team is the best in the club's history? Against Madrid in November 2010, Guardiola's team raised their hand.

The chance for revenge came in the spring, the perfect expression of the dominance of the big two and the eclipse of the rest of Spanish football. For a while, it felt almost like the eclipse of everyone else in Europe. There would be four *clásicos* in eighteen days; all three major competitions being fought over by the same two sides, the planet's biggest clubs and bitterest rivals in a kind of World Series, a footballing end of days. Four games in little over a fortnight, each more important than the last, a crescendo of matches – Real Madrid versus Barcelona in the league, the Copa del Rey final and two legs of the Champions League semi-final.

On the eve of the final chapter, the Champions League semi-final second leg, one comment hit home more than any other: 'it is nearly over.' Guardiola was saying what many were thinking. As it turned out, he was wrong – the debris of those games is still picked over, even now – but the promise of liberation hung in the air: *one more night and we're free.* Guardiola had talked about 'eighteen tremendously hard days' and the text message from one Madrid player declared: 'sick of the fucking *clásico.*' A league, the Copa del Rey and a Champions League were decided – although the final was still to be played – but what stuck in the mind was something else. As one journalist wrote: 'when my grandchildren ask me what I remember about this historic run of games, I'll say: "erm, fights".' Fights, faking, arguments, accusations, paranoia and whining, cheating and assaults, propaganda and politics. And somewhere in the midst of it, largely hidden, some football.

The run started with a league game, a 1-1 draw at the Bernabéu which virtually guaranteed Barcelona the title. Madrid appeared to have decided that the title was already beyond them and rarely sought the victory, leading Di Stéfano to complain: 'Barcelona played like lions, Madrid like mice.' Then there was the Copa del Rey final at Mestalla, a tough, aggressive game won 1-0 in extra time by a towering Cristiano Ronaldo header. This was a first step for Mourinho and a first victory at last: Barcelona *could* be beaten. It was a trophy Sergio Ramos dropped under the wheels of the open-topped bus and one that can still be seen, mangled, at the Federation's museum; it was also a trophy Madrid then formally paraded three long weeks later.

The timing was odd but it was no coincidence. Madrid had apparently chosen May the thirteenth because it was the same day FC Barcelona mathematically wrapped up the league title, meaning that the following morning's papers were full of Madrid's celebrations, not Barcelona's: *culés* spilled down the Ramblas, but it was the Puerta del Sol spread across the photos. It would have been an act of genius had it not been so tragically transparent, Madrid striker Gonzalo Higuaín describing it with a sad, irritable sigh as a *paripé* – a hollow show, a smokescreen. Far from eclipsing Barcelona's success, it ended up taking the gloss off Madrid's. The Copa del Rey, Madrid's first in almost twenty years, mattered; but pitched directly against Barcelona's league title and their forthcoming Champions League final, it felt largely irrelevant. After all, in eighteen days that became the reference point of the contemporary *clásico*, Barcelona won the league, Madrid the cup, and Barcelona reached the European Cup final, emerging victorious from the biggest pair of *clásicos* in history.

Those two games will be remembered for what happened off the pitch as well as what happened on it. Real Madrid versus Barcelona for a place in the European Cup final produced another one of those moments that will come to define the rivalry, part Guruceta, part *lady, let's not piss about* – paranoia, conspiracy and victimism, only this time with the boot on the other foot. On the pitch, it unfolded over two legs; off the pitch, it unfolded in four acts.

Act one, the day before the semi-final first leg. Lunchtime.

The scene: the press room at Valdebebas.

Enter Jose Mourinho, stage left.

Following the Copa del Rey final, Guardiola had noted that Barcelona had been close to winning: had a Pedro goal not been ruled out for a very close but correct offside, described by the coach as 'the linesman's good eyesight', Barça might have taken the trophy. Mourinho seized upon the chance. 'A new era has begun,' he shot. 'Until now there were two groups of coaches. One very, very small group of coaches who don't speak about refs and then a big group of coaches, of which I am part, who criticise the refs when they make mistakes – people like me who don't control their frustration but also people who are happy to value a great job from a ref. Now there is a third group, which is only Pep, that criticises referees when they get decisions right! In his first season [Guardiola] lived the scandal of Stamford Bridge, last year he played against a ten-man Inter. Now he is not happy with refs getting it right. I'm not asking the referee to help my team. If the referee is good, everyone will be happy – except Guardiola. He wants them to get it wrong.'

Act two, the day before the semi-final first leg. Evening.

The scene: the pine-panelled press room of the Santiago Bernabéu. Enter Javier Mascherano, stage right.

'It's very clear what Guardiola wanted to say – and that's totally different from what some people want to understand him to have said. It is very easy to take things out of context. Our coach didn't criticise anyone: the goal was rightly ruled out, he was just saying that we'd been a hair's width away from maybe winning the cup. I can't talk about someone [Mourinho] I don't know. It wouldn't be ethical of me and I don't want to send anyone a message. If I wanted to talk about anyone directly, I'd name them. It's Barcelona versus Real Madrid. I would rather talk about football. What annoys me is that every day we talk less about football. This should be a great game, one for Spanish football to be proud of, but the attention is always diverted to other things.'

Act three, the day before the semi-final first leg. Evening.

Exit Javier Mascherano, stage right. Enter Pep Guardiola, stage right.

This time it's personal. Guardiola released a year of pent-up anger and frustration. The days of silence, of studied decorum and turning the other cheek ended. This was more like the weigh-in before a prizefight, complete with an air of 'you and me outside'. After a year in which Mourinho had waged a constant war, raising the stakes continuously, Guardiola was finally drawn into battle. 'He called me

Pep, so I answered,' Guardiola explained at the end of a breathtaking forty-five minutes, when it was finally all over. 'Normally, he talks in general terms about a team, a club or a manager, but this time he named me. If he says "Pep," I say "Hey, Jose".'

He had said more than 'hey'. Guardiola had walked into the press room and said good evening. 'As Mr Mourinho has spoken about me by name, and using *tú* [the informal form of you], then I will do the same,' he announced. He then asked which of the gathered cameras was 'Mourinho's camera', noting 'I suppose they must all be', and began:

'Tomorrow at 8.45 we will play a match here out on the pitch. Off the pitch, he is the winner. He has won all year, the entire season, and in the future. He can have his personal Champions [League] off the pitch. I'll give him that. He can take that home and enjoy it along with all the other awards. But this is a game of football. We will play and sometimes we will win, sometimes we will lose. Normally, he wins, that's what his career shows. We're happy with smaller victories, trying to get the world to admire us and we are very, very proud of this.

'I too could give you an immense list of things to complain about, but we'd never finish here. We could remember Stamford Bridge and twenty-five thousand things, I could bring out a list but I don't have secretaries and referees or a director-general who writes those things down for me. So tomorrow at 8.45 p.m. we will take to the field and we will try to play football as best we can.

'In this [press] room, he is the *puto jefe*, the *puto amo* – the fucking boss, the fucking master. I don't want to compete with him for a moment [for that title]. I just want to recall that we were together for four years. I know him and he knows me. And that's what I hold on to. If he wants to hold on to the comments made after the Copa del Rey final, if he would rather listen to his friends in the media, the friends of Don Florentino Pérez, then he has every right to do so. He can keep reading them and listening to them, to the *central lechera* you all know well in Madrid. If he wants to do that, fine. I'm not even going to justify my words. After their victory I congratulated Real Madrid for winning the Copa, which is what we do in our house, a cup that they deservedly won against a very good team, which is the team that I represent very proudly . . .'

Guardiola paused, looked up and said: 'Jose, I don't know which is your camera. But there you go.'

And with that the press conference started.

Joan Laporta had called it the *Caverna mediática*: the Madrid media cave. Guardiola called it the *central lechera*, the milk board, a phrase created by the Catalan journalist Carles Torras. Both essentially referred to the same thing, something which has its counterpart in Catalonia of course: journalists they accused of being at the behest of Pérez, running stories designed to discredit Barcelona and benefit Madrid, the club's dirty work carried out slyly and in silence, allowing the institution to maintain a respectable façade and keep its hands clean; those, in short, who take their editorial lead from the Santiago Bernabéu offices.

Now, speech over, journalists asked questions and Guardiola responded. 'If Barcelona want someone who competes with Mourinho, then they should look for another manager,' he said. 'We as an institution and I as a person don't talk about referees. I could talk about [Olegario] Bequerença [the referee from the previous season's Barcelona–Inter Milan semi-final first leg], about the offside goal from Diego Milito or the penalty on [Dani] Alves, but I don't. Well, I didn't until tonight! . . . If you think after three years that I always moan, always make excuses and always complain, then there is nothing I can do about that . . . I always thought that when people didn't understand me, it was because I had explained myself badly but now I don't think that. I said the referee [in the cup final] had been smart and very attentive. I said it was right. I pointed out simply that the result can be down to small things, that's all.'

The atmosphere was electric. All round the press room, fingers whirred, racing over keys. Phones were drawn from pockets like guns from holsters. On the Barcelona team bus, players reveal, mobiles started beeping: *the mister has come out swinging!* Back in the press room, others sat open-mouthed, shocked, waggling their hands as if they'd just trapped their fingers in a door. Incredulous glances shot round the room, journalists mouthing: *joder.* Did that really just happen? Immediately, the analyses began; what did it mean and how would it affect the match? Who would have the advantage when they stepped into the ring?

After almost three years of impeccable, almost exaggerated politeness, Mourinho had got under Guardiola's skin, provoking a breakdown. Guardiola was no longer in control. Or so they said. In fact, Guardiola had planned the response carefully and his discourse was deliberate. He'd decided that it was the message his players needed to hear after the Copa del Rey defeat and he had felt good delivering it too – liberated, infused with renewed energy. Asked during the remainder of the press conference if this was just a tactic, Guardiola replied: 'What? You think my players will run around more because I looked for Mourinho's camera? It's a semi-final!' Yet when he arrived at the team hotel, those players gave him a standing ovation, and the following night they defeated Real Madrid 2-0 at the Bernabéu.

Barcelona dominated possession and Messi scored both goals – the second was one of the finest goals the European Cup had ever seen – but not until after Pepe had been sent off for a challenge on Dani Alves, studs up, leg straight, aimed high at Alves's shin, sending the Brazilian spinning backwards and on to the ground. He became the fourth Madrid player sent off in four *clásicos* under Mourinho. What was not clear was how much contact there was, the image slowed down and sped up, stopped and started, over and over again on TV, arguments still raging weeks, months, years later. At the European Championships in Poland in the summer of 2012, Pierluigi Collina used the challenge as part of the typical briefing with players to explain what they could expect from referees. This, he told the Spain squad at their HQ in Gniewino, is red. The debate started again, Madrid and Barcelona players once again arguing the case.

Act four, immediately after the first leg.

The scene: the press room at the Bernabéu. Enter Mourinho, stage right.

After the game, Mourinho gave up on a place in the Champions League final, declaring it 'mission: impossible'. Not because Barcelona were too good but because of the dark forces lined up against Madrid. After a night in which he and Pepe were sent off he bemoaned the power that his rivals wielded in European football, effectively accusing UEFA of fixing it for Barcelona to reach the final. 'One day,' he said, pointedly using the Barcelona coach's full name, 'I would like Josep Guardiola to win this competition properly.' Mourinho said he felt 'disgusted' to be working in football, asking over and over again the same question: ¿*por qué*? Why?

It was an extraordinarily bitter, almost comical rant; one that, while it highlighted some truly questionable decisions, conveniently ignored evidence that pointed to different conclusions. The way *por qué* was delivered, a kind of high-pitched whiny *per qué*, made it even more striking, at once funnier and feebler. 'If I tell UEFA what I really think and feel, my career would end now,' Mourinho said. 'Instead, I will just ask a question to which I hope one day to get a response: Why? Why? Why Øvrebo? Why Busacca? Why Debleeckere? Why Stark? Why? Because every semi-final the same things happen. We are talking about an absolutely fantastic football team, so why do they need that? Why? Why does a team as good as they are need something [extra] that is so obvious that everyone sees it? Why Øvrebo three years ago [against Chelsea]? Why couldn't Chelsea go to the final? Last year it was a miracle that Inter got there playing with ten men for so long. A miracle. Why weren't there four penalties against Chelsea [in 2009]? Why send off [Robin] Van Persie [in the previous round]? Where does their power come from?

'It could have been 0-0 tonight, but then suddenly we are down to ten men and they have a free path to find solutions that they could not find before then: we could have played for three hours and they would not have scored. But today we have seen that it is not difficult, it is impossible.

'The question is *why?* I don't know if it is the UNICEF sponsorship or if it is because they're "nice guys". I don't understand. Congratulations to Barcelona on being a great team and congratulations for all the other stuff you have which must be very hard to achieve. They have power and we have no chance. Chelsea had bans for Drogba and Bosingwa; Wenger and Nasri were banned for Arsenal; me today. I don't know why. All I can do is leave that question here in the air and hope that one day I will get the response. They have to get to the final, and they'll get there, full stop.'

'Josep Guardiola is a fantastic coach,' Mourinho said, 'but I have won two Champions Leagues. He has won [only] one Champions League and that is one that would embarrass me. I would be ashamed to have won it with the scandal of Stamford Bridge and if he wins it this year it will be with the scandal of the Bernabéu. I hope that one day he can win a proper Champions League. Deep down, if they are good people, it cannot taste right for them. I hope one day Guardiola has the chance of winning a brilliant, clean championship with no scandal.'

Asked if Madrid, trailing 2-0, were now out, Mourinho replied: 'Yes, yes.'

'We will go there,' he added, 'with pride and respect for football. It is a world that sometimes disgusts me to live in and earn a living from, but it is my world. We have to go there without Pepe, who didn't do anything, without [the suspended] Ramos, who did nothing, without a coach who can't be on the bench. It is impossible. And if we score a goal and open up the tie a little, they will just kill it again. Tonight we have seen that we do not have any chance.'

A 1-1 draw in the second leg at the Camp Nou, with Madrid having a goal disallowed for an extremely questionable decision, sent the home side through to the final. Madrid's suspended manager watched it from the Rey Juan Carlos hotel. 'Mourinho was right,' assistant manager Aitor Karanka said, 'it *was* impossible for us to go through.'

Barcelona completed the circle on 28 May 2011. Wembley again, back where it all began. The perfect expression of a team that some considered the finest there has been and at the perfect location too. When Barcelona defeated Manchester United 3-1 in London to win their second European Cup in three years under Guardiola, their third in six, Alex Ferguson called the Catalans the best team he had faced: 'no one has ever given us a hiding like that,' he admitted. But it was about more than just the performance; it was about the symmetry and significance too. At the end of the match, Gerard Piqué fulfilled a now familiar ritual borrowed from basketball and took a pair of scissors to the goal, carrying off the net with him. Another Wembley souvenir to take back, another religious relic from their spiritual home. When Barcelona prepared for the 2010 semi-final, fans relished the prospect of winning the trophy at Madrid's ground but Xavi Hernández was more seduced by the following season in London. Aged twelve, he had cried because his parents wouldn't let him travel to the 1992 final.

'Everything starts with the Dream Team . . . we're all trying to emulate them,' Guardiola had said. But with that second European Cup, his team surpassed that of his mentor, in style as well as substance. Ferguson had warned before the 2009 final of the risk that 'Xavi and Iniesta get you on that carousel'. Warning was one thing, stopping them was another. Two years later, after the 2011 final, he said: 'they mesmerise you with their passing.' Iniesta, Xavi, Busquets and Messi wouldn't give the ball up, enjoying over 70 per cent of possession, a ridiculous amount in a final. As if it was not perfect enough already, at the end, captain Carles Puyol sent Eric Abidal, back after a liver tumour, to go and get the trophy.

It made for uncomfortable watching in Madrid. 'If we had got there we would have won it too,' sniped Iker Casillas. Madrid had not been forgotten, nor had Mourinho. During the celebrations, a two-part chant stood out: First, the question: *¿Por qué, por qué, por qué, por qué?* Why, why, why, why?, delivered in a mock Mourinho accent, replacing the normal *¡olé, olé, olé, olé!* And then the answer: *Porque somos los mejores, jodéte.* Because we're the best, fuck you.

No, fuck *you*. Mourinho's side was closing in and the rivalry was getting ever more bitter. Not least because it was becoming even more frequent, no longer a game that occurs twice a year. There had been five *clásicos* in 2010–11, four of them in eighteen days; there were six in 2011–12 and six in 2012–13; *seventeen clásicos* in three years. The following season opened with Barcelona winning the Spanish Super Cup against Madrid, but the second leg at the Camp Nou was remembered less for Messi's late goal to make it 3-2 than for confrontations that would ultimately sow the seeds of Mourinho's destruction and of Guardiola's departure. It would be remembered for Marcelo's scything challenge on Cesc, for Casillas then accusing Cesc of diving, for the touchline melee that ensued and above all for Mourinho tiptoeing round the back of Barcelona assistant coach Tito Vilanova, surreptitiously reaching round and poking him in the eye before backing away with a smirk on his face.

When Mourinho was asked about the incident after the game, he claimed not to know 'this Pito Vilanova or whatever his name is'. He knew very well, of course; just as he knew that *Pito* is Spanish for cock. He had quite literally added insult to injury. Far from censoring what he had done, a few days later a banner appeared at the Bernabéu, running along the front of the second tier, that declared: 'Mou, your finger points the way.' It remained there for months. The next time the sides met at the Camp Nou in the Copa del Rey, Casillas approached referee Fernando Texeira Vitienes and spat: 'I suppose you'll be going out to party with Barcelona's players now', while Mourinho waited for the official in the car park, where he accused him of 'enjoying screwing over professionals.'

Barcelona knocked Madrid out of the cup, just as they had won 3-1 at the Bernabéu in La Liga. But it was Madrid who were leading the league and they came to Barcelona in the spring and won 2-1 to clinch the title, the first Camp Nou *clásico* lost by Guardiola's side.

Ronaldo's goal, stepping past Víctor Valdés and finishing in style, brought the league back to the Bernabéu for the first time in four years. By the time the season finished Madrid had broken the all-time points and goals records, 100 points seeing them go past Barcelona's 99 in 2009–10, 121 goals taking them past the Quinta del Buitre's 107 in 1989–90.

As Ronaldo ran to the touchline after scoring he performed a gesture whose message was clear, arms out, palms down: 'relax, *I'm* here.' It made some sense, too. It was his forty-second goal of the season and for the third game in a row he had scored at the Camp Nou. It was his fourth goal in five *clásicos*. Often accused of going missing in the big games, *unlike Messi*, he was starting a run in which he would prove more decisive than the Argentinian when they came head to head. 'The league is his' ran one newspaper. When the final whistle went, Messi turned and disappeared down the tunnel without a word. Madrid's players turned to the few hundred fans high in the stand and punched the air; Pepe made a point of kissing the badge; Casillas sought out Barcelona's Spaniards and embraced them. The stadium emptied and Xabi Alonso, showered and changed, sat alone in the vacated stands, listening to Belle and Sebastian while TV technicians packed up around him. They had actually done it.

It was more than just a league success; it was a kind of release. Madrid would in all probability have won the league if they had drawn or even lost at the Camp Nou but there might have been something missing, something not quite right. Instead, this felt like they had really taken it from Guardiola's team, like their time had come. Mourinho won at the Camp Nou for the first time, Cristiano Ronaldo won at the Camp Nou for the first time and Madrid won at the Camp Nou for the first time in four years. Madrid had lost their fear, that inferiority complex was washed away and in overcoming it the trauma induced by Barcelona's success was revealed, the memory of the 5-0. '*¿Dónde está? No se ve, la manita de Piqué*' chanted Madrid fans waiting for the team at Barajas airport. 'Where is it? We can't see Piqué's hand.'

A few weeks later, Guardiola made public his decision that the time had come to resign – a decision greeted in Madrid like a personal triumph for Mourinho. He had won, his adversary had been beaten. Guardiola was his victim, a defeated man who no longer wanted to fight on. He departed as the most successful coach in Barcelona's history and he still had a Copa del Rey final to come but there was a weariness about him. The smile when he had noted that he was losing his hair disguised a serious message and when Mourinho had previously said that Guardiola should be given a contract at Barcelona for 'fifty years' the Catalan had joked: 'I thought Jose loved me more than that!' Barcelona is a club where the pressure is intense, the fatigue overwhelming; the change in president, Sandro Rosell now the man in power, had not helped. The relationship between Rosell and Guardiola lacked the warmth of that between Laporta and Guardiola and would dramatically explode in July 2013. The *entorno* reared its head once more. Throw in Mourinho, Madrid and the media, and it became too much.

The game, which was everything but the game, had become relentless, twisted and nasty. Even the things Guardiola did well could be held against him: 'Maybe it's true,' he had said, 'maybe I do piss perfume.' Some said his decorum was a façade, others that it was easy to maintain when he was winning: and now, at last he had a proper challenger. Mourinho insisted that he and Guardiola were the same beneath the masks, that at least the Portuguese was honest about it. Told what the Madrid manager had said, Guardiola responded: 'I'll have to revise my behaviour then.' It sounded as if he probably meant it too, as if he didn't like where this was heading. In early 2012, it was privately suggested to him that Madrid and Barcelona might not face each other in the Copa del Rey; they had drawn opponents capable of knocking them out. When Guardiola replied that, on the contrary, another *clásico* was inevitable, he said so with resignation: there was no joy, no enthusiasm. Publicly, meanwhile, he turned increasingly to sarcasm and at times it carried a bitter sting.

Guardiola took a year off to rest and rediscover his enthusiasm for football, to escape the stress. His next stop, Bayern Munich, will be a very different environment. Under Guardiola, Barcelona won fourteen trophies out of a possible eighteen. Seven of them – three league titles, two Copa del Reys, a Spanish Super Cup and one Champions League – had been won in confrontations with Madrid, Barcelona beating their rivals into second place or knocking them out en route. Yet of the four trophies that Barcelona had not won under Guardiola, three had been ceded to Mourinho: a European Cup against Inter, plus a Copa del Rey and now the league title against Madrid. That was why Mourinho was brought to the Bernabéu: to beat Barcelona. His side had succeeded in competing against the team many considered the best ever, even if that equation can be turned on its head: Barcelona had competed against one of the most powerful teams ever assembled too. Together they had taken Spanish football to another plane, consuming the rest of the country's clubs. Or, if you prefer, they had plunged it to new depths.

When Guardiola resigned to be replaced by his assistant Tito Vilanova, he was asked about his memories of the meetings between Real Madrid and Barcelona. He had overseen the 6-2 and the 5-0, reached the Champions League final and claimed the Spanish Super Cup. He'd witnessed arguably the greatest performances in Barcelona's history and seen Messi stake a claim to be the best player ever, scoring one of the great European Cup goals, but he responded: 'I don't have good memories of them.' He departed sadly; in Madrid they celebrated. Mourinho had won. Guardiola bowed out with a Copa del Rey success against Athletic Bilbao, stopping on the confetti-strewn Vicente Calderón turf, past one in the morning on a warm night in May, to pose with the cup. Another one. Then he picked it up and disappeared through the tunnel at the south end of the stadium.

A year later Mourinho had gone too. In truth, he had left the building well before he actually departed, his mind elsewhere. His exit was lamented by many but not by all and in the final weeks, as the inevitable drew near, everything unravelled. Even some of his most virulent defenders deserted him. On the last day of the season, the press room at the Santiago Bernabéu, scene of *that* moment, stood empty. He refused to talk to the media and he bade farewell to only part of the stadium, pointedly waving to the *Ultra Sur* at the south end and no one else. They had supported him throughout but not everyone had followed suit, his name periodically whistled when read out over the PA system. For many, it was a relief to see him go; for others, it was a victory.

When Mourinho was presented as manager of Chelsea soon after, he described himself as 'the happy one'. It was a telling choice of words. He had rarely enjoyed Spain as he had England: there, players, press and presidents were different and so were fans. His time had been marked by controversy and confrontation, both with other clubs and with his own. During the presentation at Stamford Bridge, a journalist brought up a recent interview with Andrés Iniesta in which the Barça playmaker said: 'Mourinho did more harm than good. He damaged Spanish football.' There was no refuge from the rivalry. 'I "damaged" football because I ended Barcelona's hegemony,' Mourinho replied. That was what he came to do.

Cristiano Ronaldo's header defeated Barcelona in the final of the Copa del Rey in 2011, his winning goal in the *clásico* late in the following season virtually secured the league title, and at the start of the 2012–13 season he scored again when Madrid defeated Barcelona in the Spanish Super Cup, a 2-1 second-leg victory overturning a 3-2 defeat in the first. Madrid then drew 2-2 at the Camp Nou in the league, won 2-1 at home and knocked Barcelona out of the Copa del Rey, 4-2 on aggregate. Ronaldo's goal in 2011 had begun a sequence of *clásicos* that from Madrid's point of view read: four wins, two draws and only one defeat in seven. Mourinho had come to knock them off their perch. Mission accomplished, then?

Not exactly. And for all the other ingredients, it was the lack of success that mattered most. Mourinho's final season had started with the Spanish Super Cup but ended without a major trophy. By his own definition, it had been a 'failure'. Madrid's last chance of silverware came in the Copa del Rey final against Atlético Madrid. Atlético had become crushed by fatalism having not beaten their neighbours this century, their run going back fourteen years and twenty-five matches, and the final was being played at the Bernabéu. Yet still Atlético won 2-1. In the second half, Mourinho got sent off. It appeared deliberate and afterwards he didn't go up to the royal box to get his medal, something that didn't go down well with the Madrid board. As King Juan Carlos saw assistant manager Aitor Karanka approach up the stairs, he turned to the president of the Spanish Football Federation, Ángel María Villar, and said: 'What, do I give it to this guy?'

Mourinho had been proud of winning the cup for the first time in nineteen years when his side beat Barcelona in 2011; now he'd lost to Atlético for the first time in almost as long. He had been proud too of taking the league off Barcelona in 2012 and doing so by racking up one hundred points – a record, he said, that could never be taken away. But Barcelona had won the league back and done it by reaching one hundred points too, finishing fifteen points ahead of Madrid, the biggest ever gap between first and second. Bernd Schuster had been sacked in 2008 for publicly saying that his team could not win the following week at the Camp Nou; in 2012, Mourinho had publicly said that his team could not win the league title before they had even reached Christmas. At the end of the season Tito Vilanova and Eric Abidal, two men who had overcome cancer, paraded Barcelona's sixth league title in ten years. It was an emotive moment and a significant one too. Never have Barcelona enjoyed a decade as dominant – not exactly the end of their hegemony. In Mourinho's three years in charge, Madrid had won two major trophies, Barcelona had won four, including the European Cup, the trophy that defines Madrid.

The period between 2010 and 2013 made a huge mark on the rivalry and had a profound and divisive effect on Real Madrid. It is difficult to predict how lasting it will be but the emergence of supporters who define themselves as *Mourinhistas*, fiercely critical of the media and others within the club, from fans to players and directors, could continue to have an impact, opening up fault lines that find tentative parallels with the Cruyff–Nuñez splits that persevere on the other side of the divide. Some felt that Mourinho never fully understood Madrid, others that he understood it better than Madrid itself; the club needed to change, not the coach. Certainly one of the things critics overlooked was that much of what he said was right. He sought to overcome the *galáctico* model, for instance, but was partly undermined by the very system he'd come to overturn. He fell out with Sergio Ramos and, particularly, captain and icon Iker Casillas, who he dropped for the second half of the season. Ultimately, that confrontation proved decisive. In turn, he dismissed critics as *pseudo-Madridistas*, by which he essentially meant *anyone who doesn't agree with me*, even if their claim on *Madridismo* was far stronger than his own. It was not lost on anyone that he talked as often about trying to win his third European Cup as about trying to win Madrid's tenth.

Mourinho challenged the structure of Madrid, fighting to be granted greater authority than any coach they had ever had. The battle was symbolised by his successful bid to force Jorge Valdano out of the club and fires were started at every turn: with Valdano, with the Castilla manager Alberto Toril, with club doctors and with players. He also launched an assault on the club's very identity and by extension forced Pérez, who had bet so heavily on this hand that he had little choice but to keep raising the stakes, to do the same. The concept of *señorío* was publicly redefined and so was *Madridismo*, largely as a way of justifying Mourinho's behaviour.

Madrid's anthem lauds the club as an 'honourable gentleman' who 'when he loses gives his hand without jealousy or rancour', while the book Pérez handed to all the players during the centenary, complete with **bold text** and CAPITAL LETTERS on particularly important passages, beseeched them to be 'elegant of spirit', and always turn the other cheek. 'We are,' it insisted, 'a winning team, but we must always WIN WELL. When Real Madrid loses, its players shake hands with their opponents. Protesting to referees or confronting opponents leads nowhere, deteriorates our image as a *club señor* and is a clear sign of weakness. **Real Madrid does not complain**. No comments are made regarding the referee. This is never done.' Now, though, Pérez declared: '*señorío* is also defending what we think is right; it's also denouncing injustice. What Mourinho says is *Madridismo* too.'

It didn't wash but for some Mourinho supporters the issue was simpler than that: *señorío* was obsolete and unnecessary; what mattered was competing, winning. *That* was the true essence of Madrid. It is also true that no matter how bad his behaviour, the idea that Mourinho alone had trampled upon an otherwise proudly upheld tradition of *señorío*, single-handedly sullying a history entirely free from conflict, controversy or complaint was evidently nonsense. Just like the idea that with him now gone everyone would live happily ever after.

Mourinho encountered issues at the Santiago Bernabéu that his predecessors will be familiar with. But the greatest source of his problems may just have resided at the Camp Nou. He had been hired to bring about Barcelona's downfall but it is tempting to conclude that Barcelona brought about his. Constant conflict with Barcelona contributed decisively to increasing pressure on players and deteriorating relationships in the dressing room. Some Madrid players simply didn't see the need for such a confrontational approach and when the tension surrounding the *clásico* threatened to derail the Spanish national team, Casillas and Xavi reapplied an unwritten code of fraternity that had always existed within *la selección* and came together to bring an end to the war. Mourinho was furious; when Casillas, captain of Madrid and Spain, made the peacekeeping call to his Barcelona team-mates it was the beginning of the end as far as his relationship with the coach was concerned.

As Mourinho's spell at Madrid drew to a close, he described Barcelona as 'the best team of the last twenty or thirty years'. Of all the things he had said, this was perhaps the line that irritated Madrid fans most but it revealed something about the way in which the Catalans lay at the heart of his experience, an obsession for him and his club on both an emotional and a footballing level. He had come to defeat them and win the European Cup but it was almost as if the two things became mutually exclusive. The focus was solely Barcelona, as if other teams did not exist. Madrid were set up to beat the Catalans but were found wanting when it came to facing other sides against whom the perfect style for picking off Barcelona was not so easily applied. Besides, when Guardiola departed, it felt like Mourinho had been left orphaned; his adversary overturned, victory achieved for now, he no longer had a nemesis, a target, someone with whom to wage war. So he waged war with his own club.

On the day that Pérez announced Mourinho's departure he insisted that the Portuguese had taken Madrid 'back to their rightful place'. Rightful place? Empty-handed and fifteen points behind Barcelona? His point was that, as the coach had insisted, for three consecutive years Madrid had reached the Champions League semi-final after six seasons in which they had failed to overcome a single knockout tie. But however much they sold the idea of success, everyone knew that this was not it. Mourinho was supposed to be a guarantee and the investment had been gigantic: he had the most expensive team ever. The promise, the obsession, was the *décima* ten years on. They had progressed but a semi-final does not satisfy, still less a semi-final lost to Barça. The European Cup final still eluded them, never mind a tenth victory.

For two years, it eluded them both. When Madrid and Barcelona were kept apart in the semi-final draw in 2012 and again in 2013, it had felt inevitable that they would meet in the European Cup final for the first time ever. But the definitive showdown, the ultimate *clásico*, was postponed two years running and even in defeat they could not be kept apart, as if it was wrong somehow for one to go through and not the other. Neither made it. Parity was restored, parallel lives. Leo Messi missed a penalty, Cristiano Ronaldo missed a penalty and Bayern Munich and Chelsea reached the final in 2012. A year later, the two clubs went to Germany within twenty-four hours of each other and both let in four goals – victims, some said, of their own domestic dominance, their greedy destruction of the rest of the league. First Barcelona lost 4-0 in Munich, then Madrid lost 4-1 in Dortmund. 'Madrid conceded four as well!', cheered the front of *Sport*, saying it all.

An advert occupied billboards across London and expressed the difference between expectation and reality; it called the final *Der Klassicher*. Bayern Munich won at Wembley, a new superpower to challenge Spain's giants. Fate had been capricious. Their victory set up a European Super Cup final that immediately captured Spanish imaginations: Bayern Munich versus Chelsea. Pep Guardiola versus Jose Mourinho. It is a game to be contemplated with a little sadness, like a love lost. *That was our game, the biggest there is.*

They need not worry; Guardiola and Mourinho will be missed but the *clásico* will resist. It always has, always will. No other match will ever have its meaning: the biggest and richest clubs on earth facing each other, two cities, some would say two countries; two identities yet much that is shared, including an obsession with each other and the need to be the best on the planet. Mourinho and Guardiola have gone just as others went before them but Ronaldo and Messi remain, true greats capable of making a match a homage, of simultaneously eclipsing and enhancing conflicts centuries old.

After them will come others just as they came after Zidane and Ronaldinho, Stoichkov and Butragueño, Cruyff and Amancio, Di Stéfano and Kubala, Samitier, Zamora, Bernabéu and Alcántara. No sooner had the season ended than Barcelona signed Neymar and no sooner had Barcelona signed Neymar than Madrid began preparing their response, the arms race accelerating. Their first signing was Spain's most outstanding creative talent Isco, a man who has a pet dog called Messi, and then came their multi-million Euro pursuit of Gareth Bale.

Real Madrid and FC Barcelona will meet again and when they do the cast will be the most impressive in the game, tickets will sell out in hours and millions will gather in front of television screens across the world, more than for any other club match anywhere. And on the morning of the game they will still be there, clutching flowers, pleading for a victory. Once more into the fray. Life in ninety minutes.

ACKNOWLEDGEMENTS

This is supposed to be the nice bit but it's a nightmare too. It's two years since I started researching and preparing this book and so many people have generously helped that I'm bound to miss someone out. This, then, is a thank you . . . and in all probability an apology too.

I'd like to thank the Madrid and Barcelona players, coaches, directors and presidents named at the start of the book who gave so much of their time, from Alfredo Di Stéfano to Zinedine Zidane. Others who shared experiences that contributed to this story include Alan Kennedy, Raymond Van der Gouw, Zoltan Czibor, Toni Strubell, Isidro, Mariano García Remón, Gonzalo Suárez, Quim Molins, Jordi Molina, Javier Igual, Juanma Lillo and Carles Santacana. It was a real honour to meet Sergio Cunningham and Sylvia, Brendan Batson and Cyril Regis. Laurie's story awaits.

I'm grateful to Fernando Macua and everyone at Real Madrid's veterans' association, to everyone at Barcelona's veterans' association, and to Chemi Terés, Sergi Nogeres and the rest of the staff in the Barcelona communications department. My thanks to Paloma Antaraz and everyone in the communications department at the Spanish Football Federation. Friends and colleagues have helped to set up interviews and reach protagonists when doors appeared shut. They include Félix Díaz, Santi Segurola, Rodrigo Errasti, Sergio Fernández,

Javier Tamames, Johanna Gara, Diego Torres, Dani García, María Bretones, Alberto Pereiro and Graham Hunter. Particular thanks to Marta Santisteban, Gina González, Jordi Finestres, Roser Vilardaga; very special thanks to Santi Giménez and Lu Martín, two true superstars. *FourFourTwo*'s recent feature enabled me to revisit the *galáctico* era with Luis Figo and Zinedine Zidane; I first spoke to Xavi for the *Guardian* and *World Soccer*'s fiftieth anniversary was the excuse to spend time with Emilio Butragueño.

Staff at the Archivo Histórico Nacional, the Archivo General de la Administración, the Archivo Municipal de Madrid, the Biblioteca Nacional, and the Hemeroteca Municipal have been unfailingly helpful. Jordi Finestres kindly provided unpublished archival material. Others have done so anonymously. Juan Castro facilitated access to the complete collection of *Marca*. Bernardo Salazar has been generous with material and expertise: no one knows Spanish football history like he does. So too Carles Santacana at the University of Barcelona, whose knowledge of Barça's history is second to none. Steve Lynam re-found and photographed *Ya*. Carlos Marañon provided a copy of *Los Ases Buscan la Paz* and explained aspects of the film. Quim Molins was enthusiastic and extremely generous, providing a constant supply of DVDs, cuttings and information.

As well as those already mentioned, all of whom did far more than just provide access, countless people have helped guide me through the stories covered in the book and the history not just of Madrid and Barcelona but of Spain. Among those offering information, material, clarification and advice during the last two years and beyond are Felippo Ricci, Martin Ainstein and the X-Men, Gemma Herrero, Rafa Macía, Jeff King, Quique Ortego, Fred Hermel, Paul Preston, Mary Vincent, Alison Bender, Andy Mitten, Cayetano Ros, Javier Tamames, Luis Villarejo, Michael Robinson, Guillem Balague, Rob Palmer, Paul Giblin, Ian Hawkey, David Gladwell, Tim Stannard, Dan Thomas, Duncan McMath, Joel Richards, Kay Murray, Eduardo González Calleja, Paco Villacorta and Sandra Souto, plus Colin, Bas and Eric.

Special thanks to Pete Jenson and Graham Hunter, always an inspiration. Ángel Iturriaga was the first port of call for any doubts on Barcelona and my guide round the cemetery of Les Corts. Antonio Esteva got the last word. Michu got the first – and kindly let me use it. Thanks to everyone at La Sexta, GolT, Héctor Fernández and everyone at Al Primer Toque and Phil Kitromilides and Martin Egan and everyone at the international version of Real Madrid TV. The *Guardian* and *Sports Illustrated* were accommodating when I most needed them to be. I'll never be able to properly repay Sean Ingle for getting me into this fine mess in the first place.

My editor Matt Philips first proposed this book two years ago and has seen it through to the end. David Luxton had to make sure that I did the same. Both have shown skill, enthusiasm and patience, whilst probably putting down the phone and quite rightly calling me rude names. Frances Jessop saw it through the final, decisive weeks.

Ian Hawkey, Sally Taylor, Pete Jenson, Graham Hunter, Toni Strubell, Richard Lowe, Felippo Ricci, Santi Segurola, Santi Giménez, Sean Ingle, Charlie Cumming and especially Simon Baskett dedicated attention to part or all of the manuscript at one point or another. It's a miracle there are still mistakes, but I'm sure there are. Don't worry, I'll think of someone to blame. Claire Venables helped to bring together the bibliography, ploughing through a pile of books. Estela didn't eat my homework. Derek and Judy won't be going on *that* holiday again. Thanks, always, to Tom, Fran, Ben and Andoni; Bean, Sean and Sally, and to my mum and dad. And of course to Claire and Charlie, to whom this book is dedicated. For everything.

Thanks. Gracias. Gràcies.

BIBLIOGRAPHY

ABC, *Historia viva del Real Madrid 1902–1987* (Madrid, 1988)

Aguirre, José Fernando, *Ricardo Zamora* (Barcelona, 1958)

Artells, Josep Joan, *Barça, Barça, Barça* (Barcelona, 1972)

Badia, Jordi, *El Barça al descobert* (Barcelona, 2009)

Bahamonde, Ángel, *El Real Madrid en la historia de España* (Madrid, 2002)

Ball, Phil, *Morbo: The Story of Spanish Football* (London, 2011)

— *White Storm: 100 Years of Real Madrid* (Edinburgh, 2002)

Barend, Frits, and Van Dorp, Henk, *Ajax, Barcelona, Cruyff: The ABC of an Obstinate Maestro* (London, 1998)

Barnils, Ramón, and Finestres, Jordi, *Història crítica del Fútbol Club Barcelona 1899–1999* (Barcelona, 1999)

Bassas Onieva, Antoni, *Pequeña historia del Barça* (Barcelona, 2012)

Burns, Jimmy, *Barça: A People's Passion* (London, 1999)

— *When Beckham Went to Spain: Power, Stardom and Real Madrid* (London, 2004)

Caioli, Luca, *Messi: The Inside Story of the Boy who Became a Legend* (London, 2010)

— *Ronaldinho: el futbolista feliz* (Barcelona, 2006)

Calvet Mata, Rossend, *Historia del Fútbol Club Barcelona* (Barcelona, 1978)

411

Cañamero, Paco, *Vicente del Bosque: el valor de la dignidad* (Madrid, 2010)

Carabén, Armand, *¿Catalunya és més que un club?* (Barcelona, 1994)

Carrasco, Lobo, *Regate y propina* (Madrid, 2011)

Carreño, Fernando, *Guante blanco, manga ancha: la historia negra del Real Madrid* (Madrid, 2003)

Casanovas, Josep María, *Cruyff: una vida por el Barça* (Barcelona, 1973)

— (ed.), *Barça campeón: la liga volvió al Camp Nou* (Barcelona, 1985)

Casanovas, Josep Maria (ed.), *El Dream Team* (Barcelona, 1993)

Closa, Antoni, and Blanco, Jordi (eds), *Diccionari del Barça* (Barcelona, 1999)

Coromina, Xavier, *Ser del Barça* (Barcelona, 2010)

Cruyff, Johan, *Mis futbolistas y yo* (Barcelona, 1993)

— *Fútbol: mi filosofía* (Barcelona, 2012).

Cruz Ruíz, Juan, *Viaje al corazón del fútbol* (Barcelona, 2011)

Cubeiro, Juan Carlos, and Gallardo, Leanor, *Liderazgo Guardiola* (Madrid, 2010)

Dávila, Sancho, *De vuelta a casa* (Madrid, 1954)

De Echarri, José Luis, *Samitier: el mago del balón* (Madrid, 1958)

Diario *AS, Cien años del Real Madrid*, 12 vols (Madrid, 2001)

Di Stéfano, Alfredo, *Gracias, vieja* (Madrid, 2000)

Duran, Lluís, and Oranich, Magda, *Sunyol y el Barça de su tiempo* (Barcelona, 1998)

El Mundo Deportivo, *Barça vs. Madrid: clásicos que hacen historia* (Barcelona, 2011).

Ellis, Arthur E., *Refereeing Round the World* (London, 1954)

Fernández Santander, Carlos, *El Fútbol durante la guerra civil y el franquismo* (Madrid, 1990)

Franco Salgado-Araujo, Francisco, *Mis conversaciones privadas con Franco* (Madrid, 1976)

Frieros, Toni, *Figo: nacido para triunfar* (Barcelona, 2000)

Fundación Real Madrid, *100 Momentos involvidables en la vida del Real Madrid* (Madrid, 2002)

Galeano, Eduardo, *Football in Sun and Shadow* (London, 1997)

García Candau, Julián, *Madrid – Barça: historia de un desamor* (Madrid, 1996)

— *Bernabéu, el presidente* (Madrid, 2002)

— *El deporte en la Guerra Civil* (Madrid, 2007)

Gargallo, Santiago, *Romario, Rey del gol: pasado, presente y futuro del goleador del Barça* (Barcelona, 1994)

Gatius, Alfredo, and Huch, José María, *Barça–Real Madrid: compitiendo por liderar el negocio del fútbol* (Madrid, 2012)

Girard, Martín, *Los once y uno* (Barcelona, 1964)

Gómez Marco, Guillem, *Francesc Calvet: el pagés que va triomfar al Barça* (Barcelona, 2011)

González Castro, Andreu, *100 momentos estelares del Barça* (Barcelona, 2011)

— and Castañeda, Armando Luigi, *100 motivos para ser del Barça (y no ser del Madrid)* (Barcelona, 2012).

González Gil-García, Antonio, *100 motivos para ser del Madrid (y no del Barça)* (Barcelona, 2012)

González Ledesma, Francisco, *Zamora: mito y realidad del mejor guardameta del mundo* (Madrid, 1978)

González, Felipe, and Roca, Miguel, *¿Aún podemos entendernos?: con-versaciones sobre el encaje de Cataluña en España* (Barcelona, 2011)

González, Luis Miguel, *Butragueño: la fantasía hecha fútbol* (Madrid, 1997)

— *Cien años de leyenda 1902–2002* (Madrid, 2002)

— and Gallardo, Juan Ignacio, *Las mejores anécdotas del Real Madrid* (Madrid, 2011)

Guibernau, Montserrat, *Catalan Nationalism: Francoism, transition and democracy* (London, 2004)

Hernández Coronado, Pablo, *Las cosas del fútbol* (Madrid, 1955)

Hernández Petit, Juan, *Lo que tal vez no sepa de . . . 1968–1972: años del deporte español* (Madrid, 1972)

Herrera, Helenio, *Yo: memorias de Helenio Herrera* (Barcelona, 1962)

Hooper, John, *The New Spaniards*, (London, 1995)

Hunter, Graham, *Barça: The Making of the Greatest Team in the World.* (London, 2012)

Ibáñez Escofet, Manuel, *Kubala: un barceloní de Budapest* (Barcelona, 1962)

— *Parlem del Barça* (Barcelona, 1991)

Iniesta, Andrés, *Un año en el paraíso* (Badalona, 2009)

Irurozqui, Jose Antonio, *Bernabéu Campeón* (Madrid, 1976)

Iturriaga, Ángel, *Diccionario de técnicos y directivos del FC Barcelona* (Barcelona, 2011)

— *Diccionario de jugadores del FC Barcelona* (Barcelona, 2012)

King, Jeff, *High Noon: The Story of Bobby Robson's Year at Barcelona* (London, 1997)

— *FC Barcelona: Tales from the Nou Camp* (London, 2000)

Kuper, Simon, *Football Against the Enemy* (London, 1994)

Lainz, Lluís, *De puertas adentro: los 113 años del FC Barcelona contados en 113 historias* (Barcelona, 2012)

Laporta, Joan, *Un sueño para mis hijos* (Barcelona, 2010)

Linares, Miguel Ángel, *Barça–Madrid, la gran guerra* (Madrid, 2012)

López, Toni, *Josep Seguer: el primer comodí del Barça* (Parets de Valles, 2000)

Lorente, Rafael, *Di Stéfano cuenta su vida* (Madrid, 1954)

Luque, Xavier, and Finestres, Jordi, *El caso Di Stéfano* (Barcelona, 2006)

Maluquer, Alberto, *Historia del Club de Fútbol Barcelona* (Barcelona, 1949)

Marca, *Samitier: el mago del balón* (Madrid, 1963)

—*Ramallets: el sucesor de Zamora* (Madrid, 1963)

— *Luis Suárez: mister Fútbol* (Madrid, 1964)

Martialay, Félix, and Salazar, Bernardo, *Las grandes mentiras del fútbol español* (Madrid, 1997)

McManaman, Steve (with Sarah Edworthy), *El Macca: Four Years with Real Madrid* (London, 2004)

Melcon, Ramon, and Smith, Stratton, *The Real Madrid Book of Football* (London, 1961)

Mendoza, Ramón, *Dos pelotas y un balón* (Madrid, 1996)

Minguella, Josep María, *Casi toda la verdad* (Barcelona, 2008)

Mitten, Andy, *Mad For It: From Blackpool to Barcelona, Football's Greatest Rivalries* (London, 2008)

Munné, Antoni (ed.), *Cuando nunca perdíamos* (Barcelona, 2011)

Murillo, Enrique, and Murillo, Carles, *El nuevo Barça: contando por sus protagonistas* (Barcelona, 2005)

Narbona, Juan, *Selección Española, campeonato del Mundo 1950* (Barcelona, 1950)

Ortego, Enrique, and González, Luis Miguel, *Alfredo Di Stéfano: historias de una leyenda* (Madrid, 2010)

Pasamontes, Juan Carlos, *Todos los jefes de la casa blanca: de Julián Palacios a Florentino Pérez* (Madrid, 2003)

Peinado Moro, Enrique, *Futbolistas de izquierdas* (Madrid, 2013)

Perarnau, Martí, *Senda de campeones: de La Masia al Camp Nou* (Barcelona, 2011)

Piqué, Gerard, *Viaje de ida y vuelta* (Barcelona, 2010)

Pirri, *Mi Real Madrid: el campeón* (Madrid, 1976)

Prados de la Plaza, Luis, *Real Madrid: centenario* (Madrid, 2001)

Preston, Paul, *The Spanish Holocaust: Inquisition and Extermination in Twentieth-Century Spain* (London, 2012)

Radnedge, Keir, *50 Years of the European Cup and Champions League* (London, 2005)

Real Madrid Club de Fútbol (ed.), *Historia del Real Madrid, 1902–2002*, two vols (Madrid, 2002)

Real Madrid Club de Fútbol (ed.), *Libro de Oro del Real Madrid C. de F. 1902–1952* (Madrid, 1952)

Relaño, Alfredo, *Nacidos para incordiarse: un siglo de agravios entre el Madrid y el Barça* (Madrid, 2012)

Rexach, Carles, *Ahora hablo yo* (Barcelona, 2008)

— and Carol, Márius, *Dos maneras de vivir el Barça* (Barcelona, 2012)

Roncero, Tomás, *La Quinta del Buitre: historia de una leyenda* (Madrid, 2002)

Ruíz Arias, Heliodoro, *32 meses y 11 días con los rojos* (Madrid, 1939)

Sabartés, Jaume, *Barça cara i creu: el FC Barcelona sota el franquisme (1939–1975)* (Barcelona, 1982)

Sánchez Guerra, Rafael, *Mi convento* (Pamplona, 1960)

Sánchez Guerra, Rafael, *Mis prisiones* (Paris, 1947)

Sanchís, Alberto, *Nicolau Causas: el señor del Barça* (Barcelona, 2003)

Santacana Torres, Carles, *El Barça y el franquismo: crónica de unos años decisivos (1968–1978)* (Barcelona, 2005)

Semprún, Martin, *Santiago Bernabéu: la causa* (Barcelona, 1994)

Shaw, Duncan, *Fútbol y franquismo* (Madrid, 1987)

Solé i Sabaté, José M., Llorens, Carlos, and Strubell, Antoni, *Sunyol: l'altre president afusellat* (Lleida, 1996)

—and Finestres, Jordi, *El Barça en guerra (1936–1939)* (Barcelona, 2006)

Soler, Bernat, *El clàssic: Barça–Madrid, 1902–2012* (Barcelona, 2012)

Sport, *100 opinions Barça* (Barcelona, 1999)

Stoichkov, Hristo, *Ciento por ciento Stoichkov* (Barcelona, 1995)

Strubell, Toni, *What Catalans Want* (Barcelona, 2011)

Suárez, Gonzalo, *La suela de mis zapatos: pasos y andanzas de Martín Gerard* (Madrid, 2006)

Suárez, Orfeo, *Palabra de entrenador* (Barcelona, 2011)

Taylor, Rogan, and Jamrich, Klara, *Puskás on Puskás: The Life and Times of a Footballing Legend* (London, 1997)

Torras, Carles, *La historia ocuta del Real Madrid, contada por un culé* (Madrid, 2013)

Tremlett, Giles, *Ghosts of Spain* (London, 2006)

Valdano, Jorge (ed.), *El siglo blanco: once historias madridistas* (Madrid, 2002)

—*El miedo escénico y otras hierbas* (Madrid, 2013)

Valdillo, Fernando, *100 famosos del deporte* (Barcelona, 1964)

Vázquez Montalbán, Manuel, *Fútbol: una religíon en busca de un Dios* (Madrid, 2005)

Venables, Terry, *Venables: The Autobiography* (London, 1994)

Vincent, Mary, *Spain, 1833–2002: People and State* (Oxford, 2007)

Viñes, Carles, *Barcelona blaugrana: una història de la ciutat a través del Barça* (Barcelona, 2012)

Winkels, Edwin, *Escuchando a Cruyff: su vida y su fútbol en 150 frases* (Valls, 2010)

LIST OF ILLUSTRATIONS

1. Barcelona vs Real Madrid, 7 October 2012, Cristiano Ronaldo celebrates scoring the opening goal; Lionel Messi celebrates scoring; Barcelona fans display a Catalan flag prior to the start of the match; Barcelona fans wave flags calling for Catalonia's independence (all courtesy of Getty Images)
2. The cemetery at Les Corts (Claire Venables); Ricardo Zamora makes a save in the 1936 cup final (Antonio Campañá); Barcelona squad for their 1937 tour of America (Joan Bert i Vila/Archivo FCB)
3. Barcelona president Josep Sunyol (Archivo FCB); Sunyol's grave; the scene of Sunyol's assassination (both Claire Venables); Rafael Sánchez Guerra (Antonio Campañá); Santiago Bernabéu (Getty Images)
4. Fernando Argila (Massimiliano Minocri); Real Madrid players celebrate scoring during their 11-1 victory over Barcelona in 1943; the disconsolate Barcelona goalkeeper after conceding during the same match (both Ministerio de Educación, Cultura y Deporte, Archivo General de la Administración, IDD(03)084.001, F00951)
5. Government file on the transfer of Alfredo Di Stéfano; correspondence proving the intervention of the Franco regime in the Di Stéfano transfer (both Ministerio de Educación, Cultura y Deporte, Archivo General de la Administración, sec. gen. movimiento IDD09017002, 51/19035); Di Stéfano, László Kubala and Ferenç Puskás in Barcelona shirts (Antonio Campañá)
6. Di Stéfano scores the first goal during Madrid's 7-3 win over Eintracht Frankfurt to win the 1960 European Cup final; the Real Madrid

team for that game (both Getty Images); Evaristo de Macedo scores a diving header to knock Real Madrid out of Europe (Offside/Marca)

7. Puskás leans against his car (Getty Images); Di Stéfano with five European Cups (PA); Helenio Herrera (Getty Images)

8. Franco hands the Copa del Generalísimo to Barcelona captain José Antonio Zaldua, 1968 (Marca); 1970, Copa del Generalísimo quarter-final. Over 30,000 cushions were thrown onto the pitch in protest (Antonio Campañá)

9. Johan Cruyff (Antonio Campañá); Cruyff being escorted off the field by police during a game between Barcelona and Málaga, 1975 (Getty Images)

10. The Quinta del Buitre (Offside/Marca); Barcelona vice-president Joan Gaspart celebrates the 1992 European Cup success with a swim in the Thames (Antonio Campañá)

11. Romário celebrates scoring for Barcelona during their 5-0 victory over Real Madrid, 1994 (Offside/Marca) Hristo Stoichkov (PA)

12. Michael Laudrup playing for Real Madrid during their 5-0 win over Barcelona, 1995 (PA); the head of a pig lies on the pitch besides Luis Figo as he takes a corner kick inside the Camp Nou, 2002; the pig's head (both Offside/Marca)

13. The *galácticos* (PA); Real Madrid's Zinedine Zidane scores against Bayer Leverkusen as they win the European Cup for the ninth time, 2002 (PA)

14. Johan Cruyff and Louis Van Gaal during a match between Ajax and Sparta Rotterdam during the 1982/1983 season; Ronaldinho of Barcelona scores a goal against Real Madrid; Eric Abidal of Barcelona lifts the European Cup after the Champions League final match between Barcelona and Manchester United at Wembley Stadium, 2011 (all Getty Images)

15. Víctor Muñozs' and a young Pep Guardiola (Zoltan Czibor); Pep Guardiola and Jose Mourinho sit side by side at Barcelona (Offside/Marca); Real Madrid coach Jose Mourinho argues with Barcelona's assistant coach Tito Vilanova after poking him in the eye (TopFoto)

16. The Camp Nou (Getty Images); Cristiano Ronaldo with Real Madrid's nine European Cups (Action Images)

INDEX

INDEX